AIR CANADA

AIR CANADA
THE HISTORY

PETER PIGOTT

DUNDURN
TORONTO

Project Editor: Shannon Whibbs
Editor: Allister Thompson
Design: Courtney Horner
Photographs: Peter Pigott
Printer: Webcom

Library and Archives Canada Cataloguing in Publication

Pigott, Peter, author
          Air Canada : the history / Peter Pigott.

Includes bibliographical references and index.
Issued in print and electronic formats.

ISBN 978-1-4597-1952-1

          1. Air Canada--History. I. Title.

HE9815.A93P53 2014   387.706'571   C2013-907431-7
                                                 C2013-907432-5

1   2   3   4   5   18   17   16   15   14

We acknowledge the support of the **Canada Council for the Arts** and the **Ontario Arts Council** for our publishing program. We also acknowledge the financial support of the **Government of Canada** through the **Canada Book Fund** and **Livres Canada Books**, and the **Government of Ontario** through the **Ontario Book Publishing Tax Credit** and the **Ontario Media Development Corporation**.

Care has been taken to trace the ownership of copyright material used in this book. The author and the publisher welcome any information enabling them to rectify any references or credits in subsequent editions.

J. Kirk Howard, President

The publisher is not responsible for websites or their content unless they are owned by the publisher.

Printed and bound in Canada.

Visit us at
Dundurn.com | @dundurnpress
Facebook.com/dundurnpress | Pinterest.com/Dundurnpress

Dundurn	Gazelle Book Services Limited	Dundurn
3 Church Street, Suite 500	White Cross Mills	2250 Military Road
Toronto, Ontario, Canada	High Town, Lancaster, England	Tonawanda, NY
M5E 1M2	LA1 4XS	U.S.A. 14150

For Agnes Selwyn

CONTENTS

INTRODUCTION

The poet William Blake wrote: "Crooked roads ... are roads of genius." The road to this book was far from straight. From the moment I was born, I must have been hooked on aviation, for the place of my birth was the Battle Hospital in Reading, England. My parents returned to India soon after, where my father became a flight dispatcher for Trans World Airlines at Bombay's Santacruz airport. My earliest memories are of playing in the garden as DC-3s and Constellations clawed their way into the air over the house. Rattled windows, conversations on hold, and sooty trails overhead were accepted and appreciated — at least by me. My mother said that when I began to read, I would try to pronounce aircraft registrations. This familiarity with airports continued throughout my life since, when my father was posted to England, we lived near Heathrow, and on immigrating to Canada our backyard ended at the runway fence of Montreal's Dorval Airport.

When I joined the Department of Foreign Affairs in Ottawa, I assumed that I would put away childish things and from that point on it would be all cocktail parties and composing policy papers for the minister. But demonstrating that one cannot escape one's destiny, throughout my Foreign Affairs career, wherever in the world I was posted, it was my job almost daily to be at the local airport. There I met the Canadian diplomatic courier and exchanged the classified bags with him. Through the years, I got to know airports well, among them New York's LaGuardia and Kennedy airports, Vienna's Schwechat, Amsterdam's Schipol, and Hong Kong's Kai Tak. I spent so much time at the last, watching as Boeing 747s threaded their way through the Kowloon tenements, that my first book was a history of Kai Tak Airport for the Hong Kong government.

Back in Ottawa, I began churning out books on bush pilots and air aces in the Flying Canucks series on the history of commercial aviation in Canada and on Canadian airports and aircraft. Two major works followed these, both of which are the basis of this book. *Wingwalkers* celebrated the life and death of Canadian Airlines, and *National Treasure* detailed the same of Trans-Canada Air Lines (TCA). As for Air Canada, by 2003, with the merger and effects of 9/11, the national airline was confused and in financial turmoil, and writing its history would have to wait. In any case, I was soon embedded in wars in Afghanistan and Sudan for other books and much later in the North researching Canada's Arctic sovereignty.

But in 2012, with the seventy-fifth anniversary of Air Canada's birth, a book detailing its history could be put off no longer. From the outset, I wanted to write what would be of interest to the general public — a non-aviation audience. I kept technical details to a minimum and inserted poems, anecdotes, and personal insights to support what I hoped was a "conversationalist" text. As with my other airline histories, I chose a narrative style, using archival materials at the Canada Aviation and Space Museum, Ottawa, and publicly accessible documents. I focused on the major milestones in Air Canada's history: TCA's creation as a means of joining the country closer together, the name change to Air Canada, privatization,

deregulation, the Airbus order, the hostile near-takeover, the merger with arch rival Canadian Airlines, in its evolution from state-owned social instrument to competitive business.

Airline investor Warren Buffett once said, "The worst sort of business is one that grows rapidly, requires significant capital to engender growth and then earns little or no money. Think airlines." The airline industry has been compared to a circus bear riding a tiny unicycle. No matter how clever or lucky the bear is, there is any number of factors (think harsh weather, fuel prices, unfavourable foreign exchange, labour problems, safety issues, shortsighted CEOs, terrorism, meddling politicians, icing delays) to bring it crashing down. And this for minuscule profit margins generated by a few unpredictable passengers? The book is also written within the broad historical backdrop of the airline's relationship with whichever party was in power in Ottawa and policies of the ministers of transport, from C.D. Howe to David Collenette. But if there is a recurring sentiment throughout this book, it is that for all the advances in technology and cabin comfort in seventy-five years, the kudos and complaints of passengers have changed little.

Canadians have a love/hate relationship with their national airline. All airlines overbook, have eliminated once-complementary amenities, and lose luggage. But when Air Canada does, Canadians feel personally betrayed, because for most it is the only airline they've ever known. If Canadian Pacific Air Lines and Wardair are forever enshrined as the spunky underdogs that took on the establishment, Air Canada is the Death Star, the lightning rod and everybody's favourite whipping boy. No matter that it was privatized in 1988, many Canadians still think of it as somehow being part of the federal government. And as former president and CEO Robert Milton noted, no one remembers the awards that Air Canada consistently wins, or the 99 percent of flights in which everything goes well.

Another of the airline's presidents, Claude Taylor, used to tell the anecdote of a traveller in medieval times who was walking along a road and came upon three men cutting building stones from a boulder. He asked them what they were doing. The first said, "I'm cutting a block of granite." The second said, "I'm making a cornerstone." But the third said, "I'm building a cathedral." The story of Air Canada is the vision that Gordon McGregor, Claude Taylor, and Robert Milton had for it, their influence, for better or worse, indelibly stamped upon its corporate image. I interviewed the gentle, affable Taylor twice and would have loved to have met McGregor. That Dorval Airport was renamed after Prime Minister Pierre Trudeau, who almost strangled it, and not McGregor, a three-time Webster Trophy winner, Battle of Britain air ace, and (in my opinion) the best president that Air Canada has ever had, is a travesty. As for Robert Milton and his love of airports, with my childhood memories I empathize completely. I remember taking my first date to the airport to look at the aircraft and couldn't figure out why she'd rather go dancing instead. And as my daughters

will attest, I have dragged them to countless aircraft museums and air shows. The presidents/CEOs apart, the Air Canada employees featured in this book should be regarded as representative of the thousands that are/were employed in similar positions.

Given the passage of years, the book is as historically accurate as I can make it. No doubt there are omissions, in people and planes. It would be impossible to record every last detail in the airline's seventy-five years and keep it interesting. There may also be errors, and I hope they are few, but they are mine alone. It is my hope that the book does justice to the story of one of the world's greatest airlines and that I have successfully integrated the disparate themes of technology, politics, and economics into a coherent text.

As I write this, Air Canada is in "debt talks," its shares closing at $2.62 as it faces hefty pension obligations and looks for financing of its Boeing 787 order. I can only surmise that when the playwright Eugene O'Neill said there is no present or future, only the past that happens over and over again, he must have meant the airline industry.

— Peter Pigott, Ottawa, April 2013

CHAPTER ONE

THE RAILWAY PRESIDENTS

The public first became aware on October 5, 1964. In all major Canadian cities, newspapers carried full-page advertisements in black and red: TAKE A NEW LOOK AT AIR CANADA. This was repeated in weekly and monthly magazines as well as roadside billboards across the country. Canada's national airline was changing its name from Trans-Canada Air Lines (TCA) to Air Canada.

Company president Gordon R. McGregor wrote to all employees "with the object of clarifying the situation with respect to the company's name." The company, he reminded them, had been incorporated in 1937 as part of the Canadian National Railway under the name of Trans-Canada Air Lines. An amendment to the TCA Act in 1953 authorized the company to use the words "Air Canada" as a trade name for any purpose connected with the business of the corporation. "As time went on," McGregor

wrote, "the relative prominence given to the name 'Air Canada,' particularly in Europe, increased but in no case was the name 'Trans-Canada Air Lines' or its initials, TCA, abandoned."

Bill C-2 had just been passed by both Houses in Parliament, the president explained, which had reversed the previous status of the two names, making Air Canada the primary and official corporate name with the company retaining the right to use Trans-Canada Air Lines as the trade name. The action had been taken to prevent the old name from being adopted by some other carrier. "I expect all of us will view the passing of the name Trans Canada [sic] with regret, and for those who feel strongly on this subject, it will be small consolation to realize that in a sense we brought it on ourselves. However descriptive the name Trans-Canada was in the early days, the rapid expansion in international operations made the old name poorly descriptive of the Company's recent activities." McGregor ended by commenting that domestically the new name had the advantage of having exactly the same meaning in both official languages.

The last point was intentional and clearly meant to emphasize that this time the change of name was going through. On May 14, 1953, an amendment to the Tran-Canada Airlines Act of 1937 had authorized the company to use the name "Air Canada" as a trade name, especially overseas. The name had been proposed for the whole airline in 1959, when the introduction of TCA's jet service presented a perfect opportunity to update the company image. The reason the idea never gained altitude was tied to TCA's origins and its unique relationship with Canadians. For from its inception, the company had always been much, much more than an airline....

Almost three decades old, TCA was a relative newcomer to commercial aviation. Unlike the United States and countries in Western Europe, until almost the Second World War Canada had no national airline — or any airline at all. Given the country's vastness, inhospitable climate, and dual railway systems, it was accepted that commercial aviation in Canada would never pay for itself, let alone be profitable — and this had been repeatedly proven.

Below the border, when President Calvin Coolidge signed the Kelly Act in 1925, taking airmail delivery away from the post office and giving it to private contractors, he unwittingly began the rise of the American aviation industry. In a relatively short time, by 1933, when the ten passenger, all-metal Boeing 247 entered service with United Air Lines, its pilots flew (in heated comfort) along nationwide four-course radio range systems, performing instrument approaches at specially equipped airports. The DC-3 and Lockheed Electra that followed the Boeing 247 allowed U.S. airlines to operate on a schedule, at night, in poor weather, and, most importantly, at a profit.

Flying was still a fair weather exercise north of the border, restricted to whenever climate, visionary (or foolhardy) entrepreneurs, and available cash permitted. Commercial aviation in the Dominion was a precarious living for a passionate few, and not only because of the elements or the aged, open-cockpit, wood-and-wire aircraft they used. There were several air companies across the country that flew trappers, prospectors, missionaries, and Mounties to wherever the rivers or railways could not take them. But they were primarily freight haulers tied to the fortunes of the resource industries — mining and trapping — in the bush, and to stay aloft even marginally, the bush companies undercut each other to the point of bankruptcy. When Winnipeg grain financier James Richardson began Canadian Airways Ltd. (CAL) in 1927, he counted on the mining industry to keep it solvent. But even before the onset of the Depression, CAL was rarely out of deficit, and Richardson's only hope for his airline's survival was securing the airmail contracts for which he constantly lobbied the post office.

For in Canada it was all about airmail, the Internet of its day. The telegraph was not secure and was limited in scope as to what it could send. But without airfields, radio direction finders, or modern aircraft across the length of the country, all Canadian airmail, whether from Toronto to Vancouver or Halifax to Montreal, went south of the border and into the U.S. transcontinental mail system. Because Ottawa needed access to the U.S. mail system, it had to enlist American companies like Canadian Colonial Airways (which despite its name was owned by the Aviation Corporation of Delaware) to fly the mail between Montreal and Albany, New York, and United Air Lines to do the same between Vancouver and Seattle. Still coping with its overbuilt, ruinously duplicated railway system, with the exception of sponsoring a few flying clubs and building Saint-Hubert Airport, Montreal (for British airships), successive federal governments did little to encourage any aviation infrastructure. Civil aviation in Canada was controlled by the Department of National Defence, with the RCAF eager to fly the mail or perform any other civilian duties to give itself a *raison d'être*.

The federal government apart, the only institutions in Canada with pockets deep enough to bankroll the losing proposition that was commercial aviation were the two railways, the Canadian Pacific (CPR) and the Canadian National (CNR). These

THE WESTBOUND MAIL

The drizzling rain was falling,
A nearby clock tolled eight;
They watched the sky with an eager eye
For the Westbound Mail was late.
The rain beat down on the old tin roof;
The hangar chief stood by.
When the drumming tone of a motor's drone
Came from the misty sky.

The beacon sent its welcome beam
To the flyer of the night;
He brought her down to the soggy ground
Down to the guiding light.
They swap the mail and shout, Okay,
And she roars and lifts her tail!
She's up again in the rain and hail;
On with the Westbound Mail!

The crystals stick to the windshield
And form a silvery veil;
The icy struts, a man with guts
And a sack of westbound mail.
Over the peaks of the mountains now,
Clear of their treacherous rim;
Away up there in the cold night air,
Just God, the Mail and him.

His thoughts turn back to a summer night
And a girl, not so long ago
Who shook her head and firmly said,
"While you're flying, No!"
He tried to quit the blooming job
And stick to the concrete trail;
But his wish came back to the canvas sack
And the feel of the Westbound Mail.

— Author Unknown

last were much more than locomotives, rails, and parlour cars; each had grown into multi-industry conglomerates, with interests in shipping, communications, hotels, and real estate throughout the Dominion, and in the CPR's case around the world. Such a concentration of wealth and power in an industry was not unusual in Europe or the United States, but for a thinly populated country like Canada that could barely support one such railway, the intense rivalry between the CNR and CPR left little investment (or interest) in commercial aviation, thus keeping Canada firmly in the Railway Age.

In contrast, in Europe as the United States, commercial aviation had progressed far beyond the pioneering stage. In Britain, the Netherlands, Belgium, and France, an airline was not so much aircraft and pilots but a "chosen instrument" with which to fly the flag and bind distant colonies to the mother country. Completely state-owned or heavily subsidized, the fact that the "chosen instrument" ran at a loss and served only a fraction of the population was unimportant. It was a symbol of national prestige, much like the naval fleets of a previous era. What protected it from competitors both foreign and domestic were walls of regulations put in place by bureaucrats in London, Paris, Brussels — and later, Ottawa. Even in the United States, where the privately owned Pan American Airways was the country's de facto flag carrier, so vital was Pan American's survival to national prestige that the Civil Aeronautics Board (CAB), an

independent agency the members of which were appointed by the White House, kept all rival airlines in a regulatory straitjacket. Airfares, routes, personnel, aircraft, and even onboard meals had to be approved by the CAB, which kept all contenders to Pan American's international crown at bay.

Through the late 1920s, when these chosen instruments carried mail, colonial administrators, and tourists to distant parts of Asia and Africa, Canadians could only watch with envy. Britain's Imperial Airways had begun with a single faltering flight to Paris in 1924 and had reached India in 1929, Hong Kong the next year, and South Africa the year after. Sadly, when Canadian commercial air companies were contracted in the Maritimes and Prairie provinces to carry mail (on the basis of the post office warning "Letters First, People Perhaps"), it coincided with the onset of the Depression. In 1931, Prime Minister R.B. Bennett cancelled all airmail contracts, telling the House of Commons, "... there was very little gratification in seeing an aeroplane passing day by day, when the unfortunate owner of the soil could hardly see the aeroplane because his crop had gone up in dust." A former CPR corporate lawyer, Bennett held that taxpayers should not be paying for what benefited a few and which should be financed — as in the United States — by private enterprise.

What Bennett did encourage was an unemployment relief project called the Trans Canada Airway. Proposed by the Canadian Air Board as early as 1920, it was a cross-Canada network of airfields begun

The airline was named for the Trans Canada Airway that it was to operate on. Created as a relief project so that the RCAF could reinforce the Pacific coast, the airway made commercial aviation in Canada a reality.

in 1929 that were sometimes equipped with runway lighting, radio beams for night flying, and meteorological and navigation aids. The airway hadn't been planned for commercial aviation but as a defensive measure to allow the RCAF to move its squadrons across the country and reinforce either coast. By 1935, with aid of the thousands of able-bodied men, unemployed and homeless because of the Depression, this chain of airfields from Vancouver to Montreal (with a sideline from Lethbridge to Calgary and Edmonton) had almost been completed, and it was possible (in theory at least) for commercial aircraft to fly across the country.

Elected on October 14, 1935, the Liberal government of Prime Minister William Lyon Mackenzie King took full advantage of the airway's near completion. On November 22, at a commercial aviation conference with Britain, Ireland, and Newfoundland, the Liberals brashly committed Canada to starting a transcontinental airline to operate on that airway. It was to be part of an Anglo-Canadian scheme where airlines of the British Empire would encircle the globe before the Americans did so.

King appointed Clarence Decatur Howe czar of all railways, marine routes, and canals — in effect, the country's first minister of transport. A self-made millionaire, civil engineer, and aviation enthusiast (he was the only cabinet minister who had actually flown), Howe reorganized the transportation system with a ruthlessness that he would put to good use in the future war effort. Howe recognized that despite the Depression, commercial aircraft, like motor vehicles, had become competition to the railways. By creating a national airline, he sought to end the age of railway supremacy so that the CPR and the CNR were no longer the only means of transporting mail or passengers across the country.

With passage of the Department of Transport Act in 1936, the minister set about reforming Canada's transportation system by taking it away from the military and the Board of the Railway Commissioners. The new federal Department of Transport consolidated the functions of the three departments: Railways and Canals, Civil Aviation, and the Marine Department, putting them all under the jurisdiction of the Board of Transport Commissioners and the minister of transport. The new board was more limited in authority than the former Railway Board; in the aviation sector, for instance, it could only approve licensing of rates for air service. To whom those routes were given, what aircraft it could buy, and whom its president and directors were would all be firmly under the jurisdiction of the cabinet, i.e. the minister of transport, stipulations that would protect (and hamstring) Trans-Canada Airlines/Air Canada for decades to come. Transportation policy after the First World War, whatever the government in power, revolved around maintaining a delicate balance between the two railway

systems, one public and one private, and civil aviation (which in 1936 was viewed at best a minor supplement to the railways) fitted into that pattern.

Through his long political career, Mackenzie King committed himself to fighting what he saw as the stranglehold that the mighty Canadian Pacific, with its railway and shipping line, had on the national transportation system. From its inception in 1885, the CPR had been given a monopoly in most of Canada, and (in King's view) was amply rewarded by successive Conservative governments with land and resource grants. King hoped that the nascent commercial aviation industry would not follow in the ways of the railways, i.e. with rivalry and animosity. But despite the prime minister's efforts, the railway "curse" mutated into civil aviation, with Canada enduring two airlines, one public and one private, until the distant year 2000.

It would have been simple for the new Liberal government to buy up all of the bush air companies and rationalize them into a state airline. The British and French governments had done just that a decade before, taking over a number of faltering airlines in their countries to create Imperial Airways and Air France respectively. But having been burdened with ongoing problems when it merged several bankrupt railways from 1918 to 1923 to create the CNR (which it then had to prop up through continuous deficits), the federal government was loath to repeat the pattern with commercial aviation.

The only other potential contender was James Richardson, who, in anticipation that his airline would be chosen to operate on the airway, bought at great expense a pair of Lockheed 10A Electras, CF-AZY and CF-BAF, the first modern, fully enclosed, "wheels-up" metal airliners to be introduced in Canada. Richardson had heard that Howe favoured Lockheed aircraft over all others then available, and hoping to get the contract he enthusiastically proposed that a wholly new airline be set up using Electras exclusively. But the prime minister mistrusted Richardson, feeling he had been too close to the Bennett government, and Howe did not reply to his suggestion. If anything, the dismal record of CAL's years in deficit proved that private enterprise did not have the political, financial, and technical clout to run an airline in Canada.

In order to defray the expected financial losses of an airline, the Liberal government initially encouraged both the CNR and CPR to buy an equal number of shares in the proposed venture, as they had done with Canadian Airways Ltd., in which each owned a 10 percent share. But for covering the operating losses of the new enterprise, the Department of Transport required absolute representation on the airline's board, and of the nine directors, four were to be elected by the CNR's shareholders and the remaining five appointed by the governor-in-council.

CPR President Sir Edward Beatty rejected this arrangement outright on the grounds that the CNR and cabinet board members represented the same interests, and

if able to appoint five of the nine directors to the board, the government would dominate decision-making.

On November 26, 1936, Howe announced that a wholly new airline would be given the monopoly to fly the airway. A subsidiary of the CNR, it would be mandated to provide air transport services both domestic and international for mail, passengers, and cargo (in that order) throughout the country. Whether it made a profit was less important. It was to be a social instrument — an essential service like the provincially owned electricity companies or the Canadian Broadcasting Corporation, designed to bind the country together and withstand the encroachments of American and British interests. The purpose of the state-owned airline was to pursue social objectives, like joining the country "from sea to sea" and providing Canadians with a safe national and international air service. While the airline was to be run as a business, since it was a public utility it was not to make a profit. If it did so, it was obviously charging the passenger (who had already financed it through his taxes) too much.

The minister promised that as an instrument of national policy this company would guarantee a year-round daily air service, initially from Montreal to Vancouver, connecting all the population centres in between like Winnipeg, Calgary, and Edmonton. This was especially essential for the post office so that it could calculate its airmail revenues. The pilots would be trained to fly by radio beam and on gyro instruments, the aircraft would operate on a schedule, and only the latest metal all-weather airliners equipped with radio direction antennae would be used. Americans experienced in commercial aviation would be brought in to get it off the ground, and as with the airlines in the United States and Europe, personnel were to be trained in their professions, wear uniforms, and be paid regularly. A safety code for both employees and customers would be strictly enforced, and the passengers would be looked after by young women called "stewardesses" (as on the transatlantic liners) who were professional nurses (flight attendants being commonplace today but novelties then, at least in Canadian aviation). Howe had flown a number of airlines in the United States and ensured that the Canadian national airline would be created in their image — at least technically.

As for the monopoly it would have on the airway, in an era before the federal government financed public highways, the prevailing feeling was "Why should the shareholders of a private company profit from the massive government investment in the airway?" Only a public enterprise should have the exclusive right to fly mail, passengers, and freight. The monopoly would allow for cross-subsidization: the lucrative routes would subsidize the money-losing but politically necessary ones. There was nothing inherently wrong with monopolies, Howe frequently said. It wasn't competition that made a business flourish, he continued, but good management and relentless drive. If they wished, the "bush airlines" like CAL could feed off the airway at convenient points — but regulations would prevent them from ever competing with the government airline on its transcontinental network.

In the hope that the CPR would eventually agree to participate, in February 1937 the Liberal government introduced a bill in the House of Commons which established TCA as a subsidiary of CNR, but which would allow private interests to purchase up to 49 percent of the 50,000 shares from the government railway. In this version each railway was assigned four directors, with one appointed by the minister of transport. On March 10, Howe had second thoughts and the composition was changed to three directors from each railway and three from the minister. Beatty realized that the CPR would always be in a minority position, and on March 17 he formally withdrew from the scheme. The CPR did not purchase the shares (nor did any other private investor), and TCA would be born a Crown corporation.

Bill 74, the act to establish Trans-Canada Air Lines as the national airline, was put before the House on March 4, 1937, and the only comment came from former Prime Minister R.B. Bennett, now leader of the opposition.[1] He advocated complete government ownership of the whole enterprise. Relieved that Bennett did not seize on the monopoly aspect, Howe replied that the experience of other countries hardly indicated that this would be wise. As a subsidiary of the CNR, he said the airline would be "... getting the best features of government ownership without the obligation of direct government operation." The only amendment to Bill 74 was to change the number of directors yet again from nine to seven, with an executive council of three. With the CPR out, the CNR subscribed to 51 percent of the stock with the remaining 49 percent held by the minister of transport. As a child of the government, the birth of Canada's national airline can be marked precisely at 9:00 p.m. on April 10, 1937, when the bill received Royal Assent. It would be July 30 before most of the radio ranges on the airway were working, and to publicize the project's near completion (at least as far as Montreal) on July 31, using his department's Lockheed 12A CF-CCT, Howe arranged for a "dawn to dusk" flight from Saint-Hubert Airport, Montreal, to Vancouver.

Named for its purpose on the airway, TCA was to be based in Montreal, where the CNR had its headquarters, and for operational reasons in Winnipeg, the geographical and (thanks to Richardson) also the aeronautical centre of the country. A decade later, it would be centralized in Montreal, the postwar aviation capital of the world, home of International Civil Aviation Organization (ICAO) and the International Air Transport Association (IATA).

Under the act, TCA was a proprietary corporation for the conduct of an air transport business on behalf of the Crown. Like Imperial Airways and Air France, it was a "chosen instrument" for the implementation of government policy with respect to air transport. Control was exercisable not only by Parliament but also in a substantial measure by the government in power through the minister of transport. In Europe, financial losses incurred by "chosen instruments" were written off as the price of national prestige (Imperial Airways received an annual subsidy of £750,000 to fly the flag) and King did not want to associate his government with what was going to be a money-losing venture for the foreseeable future. With the CPR out, the company called Trans-Canada Air Lines could be buried deep within the CNR empire, its losses covered by the CNR Financing and Guarantee Act, as those of the money-losing Canadian National Steamship Company had been since 1928.

Like the CNR's railway network and the rivers, lakes, and canals, the other transportation sinews that bound Canada together, TCA would be completely subject to the dictates of a triumvirate: the minister of transport, the postmaster general, and the governor-in-council. All rates charged, routes flown, aircraft, buildings and equipment bought, and personnel hired, would be strictly regulated by the government of the day. Through the CNR it would be government ownership, Howe said, but without the direct government operation that in other ventures had proved so troublesome. "The device of using a crown corporation to run a government-owned enterprise," explained Yves Pratte, a later company president, "was intended to free management from political pressure and interference with technical matters, while retaining Parliament's right to question and discuss overall policy."

"The problem," commented Claude Taylor, who succeeded Pratte, "was that everyone seemed to believe that like Santa Claus, TCA/Air Canada was to provide transportation at no cost."

But unlike the rival CPR with its hotels, ships, and travel agencies, TCA was not allowed to compete with its parent by attempting to run its own such ventures. Nor was it allowed, if surplus capital ever appeared, to float a bond issue. It was indentured servitude to the railway, giving TCA an inflexible capital structure from its birth. But in 1937, no one could foresee a day when the airline would overtake the railway in passengers carried.

To furnish TCA with "start-up" capital, the CNR borrowed $5 million from the Treasury in debentures. This was divided into 50,000 shares at a par value of $100 per share, all of which were held by the CNR, and the airline was responsible for paying an annual 5 percent interest on this. The railway's commissioners were astute enough to ensure that the government rather than the CNR would make good any deficits that the fledgling company was sure to encounter. TCA's auditors (like the CNR's) would report annually to Parliament through the minister of transport.

Since the carriage of mail accounted for 75 percent of the airline's initial revenue, one of the board members had to be the postmaster general. Airmail was paid for on the miles flown, not the poundage — something that helped the airline when it flew comparatively few miles and was assured of the revenue from the mail — unlike the little it would get from passengers, especially in the airline's early days. Used to dictating terms to the poor bush airlines, the postmaster general knew his worth, and initially TCA was careful to keep on his good side. This changed when wartime transatlantic services began and the rate per mile halved while the load per mile doubled. The postmaster could then be counted on to veto any change in rates, and TCA staff felt their company unfairly used.

Several of the CNR's directors were also put on the TCA board, and S.J. Hungerford, the CNR's president (who had begun his career as a machinist's apprentice for the Canadian Northern Railway at age fourteen), would be the first president of TCA from 1937–41. An example of the close relationship between railway and airline was the office of the secretary. From 1937 to 1974, the same person held the offices of the secretary of TCA (Air Canada after 1964) and the secretary of the CNR. Responsible for maintaining the minutes of the board of directors meetings and all records requiring the corporate seal, as an executive officer the secretary worked closely with the presidents of both companies in the areas of research and economic control, personnel and organization, accountancy, legal, medical, and insurance matters.

The CNR paternalism was also a practical arrangement in that its network and bureaucracy were already in place nationwide to handle the airline's management, legal, sales, and logistical requirements. All CNR station agents were authorized to sell airline tickets, and TCA's own offices were

Lucille Garner Grant, TCA's earliest stewardess, with the airline's first board of directors. Second from the left is S.J. Hungerford, who as president of the Canadian National Railway would also be TCA's first president from 1937–41. Fourth from the left is Winnipeg lawyer Herbert Symington, TCA's second president.

located downtown in the railway's eminent hotels like the Royal York in Toronto or the Macdonald Hotel in Edmonton. In many places across the country, the CNR line actually paralleled the Trans Canada Airway, and the railway station, the airport, and the airline worked hand in glove.

So dangerous was flying over the Rockies that TCA pilots were paid an extra $50 monthly for doing so. As for finding experienced pilots at short notice, "Canadian Airways was the cradle of our pilotage," remembered Don MacLaren, TCA's very first employee. "That's where we got the best of the lot that formed the strength of TCA."

For the airline's first seventy-one employees, this was more than a job during the hungry days of the Depression. Conscious that they were the pioneers of a new way of travel (there had never been such an airline in Canada before), they were imbued with that sense of mission that comes with great enterprises. From the very first day, working for TCA was a way of life where family, vacations, and even personal advancement took second place. Impossible as it may seem today, their mindset in launching the airline was that it was a great patriotic adventure. "I wanted to do something for Canada," one of the original seventy-one staff would give as a reason, "so I joined TCA." The "family atmosphere" where everyone (although strung out along the airway) knew each other remained until after the war.

Typical was Stan Knight, who joined on October 4, 1937, and was soon manager of the TCA station at Regina airfield. For incoming night flights, the staff was responsible for putting flares along the sides of the runway to guide the pilots in. "We used to run contests to see how fast we could leave the terminal with flare pots in an old cab, place them, light them, and get back to the terminal," he recalled. "One night we were in a bit too much of a rush to get back after dousing and loading the flares into the car. It seems that one of them was not out. The whole cab went up in flames."

Part of the daily routine for TCA's radio operators was "going remote." This meant keeping the pilot on final approach informed of local weather, runway conditions, and other traffic in the vicinity. To do this the operator dashed out of his radio room and climbed to the roof of the building for a quick visual check to ensure that everything was all right, then scrambled back to position, earphone and microphone in hand, in time for the final approach and landing. Al Took, one of TCA's first radio operators, recalled, "We had to move pretty fast when we 'went remote.' And often went up top in shirt sleeves with the winter wind biting through us."

One anecdote I remember was a flight I took from Winnipeg to Montreal. The Lockheed 14s were notorious for their poor heating systems. California designers didn't appreciate the weather conditions in Canada! This particular night it was 40 degrees Fahrenheit below zero in Winnipeg and the passengers were loaded aboard the aircraft in the hangar, which was the custom in those days so they would at least get a warm start. It really was cold in the air and we all kept on our overcoats as well as all the blankets the stewardess could find. When we landed at Kapuskasing, the ground crew opened the cabin door. A passenger called out, "What's the temperature here?" The crew man answered, "Ten below, sir." The passenger yelled back, "Leave the bloody door open and let some heat in here!" The heating system was eventually improved.

— Dudley Taylor, October 1, 1999

A labour-intensive industry, commercial aviation was unionized from its birth. Much of TCA's maintenance personnel in Winnipeg had worked for the CNR and were already members of the International Association of Machinists, a powerful American–Canadian railway (and now airline) labour union. The professions that aviation had recently created — the pilots, flight dispatchers, and stewardesses — organized themselves into associations, thus attempting to distance themselves from the working class connotation that the label "unions" had.

The pilots formed the Canadian Air Line Pilots Association (CALPA) as early as

Conception: Vancouver Airport on September 1, 1937, with United Air Lines Boeing 247 in the foreground and the former Canadian Airways Lockheed Electra CF-AZY that TCA had just bought.

April 1938, and seeking wage parity with their American counterparts, almost went on strike that same year. The TCA flight dispatchers organized themselves as the Canadian Airline Dispatchers Association (CALDA) during the war. But given the social prejudice of the time, it was more difficult for the professions that contained females — the stewardesses and passenger agents — to organize and bargain collectively.

The young airline equipped itself with the most modern aircraft in Canada, namely Richardson's two Lockheed Electra 10As, which were purchased initially for radio calibration and training flights on the air-

way. The decision to use Lockheed aircraft exclusively in TCA was Howe's.[2] Before the impact of the Douglas DC-3 on commercial aviation, the Lockheed Electra in its 10A and 10E versions was the best-known airliner then available. Of the 101 Electras built, one (NR16020) had been chosen (with maximum publicity) by the aviatrix Amelia Earhart for her globe-girdling flight in March 1937, and another (British Airways G-AEPR) would also feature in the newsreels in an equally doomed mission when it flew British Prime Minister Neville Chamberlain to meet with Adolf Hitler in September 1938 in an effort to avoid war.

It was also faster than either the Boeing 247 or DC-2, and when MacLaren and Herbert Hollick-Kenyon went to pick up CF-AZY from the Lockheed plant at Burbank, California, they would set a speed record on August 4, flying from there to Vancouver in 6 hours, 23 minutes. TCA's second president, H.J. Symington, a prominent Winnipeg lawyer, would tell the story that when Howe called him to serve as director of the airline, his answer was "Yes, provided you don't buy any airplanes before I get there." Mr. Howe, he would chuckle, didn't quite take him at his word. In July 1937 both men braved the famous cross-Canada "Dawn to Dusk" flight in the Department of Transport's Lockheed 12.

To keep the airmail system going, TCA also bought a Stearman biplane CF-ASF from Canadian Airways for mail duties, only disposing of it to Northern Airways in 1939. Using CF-AZY, TCA's first scheduled flight occurred on Wednesday, September 1, 1937, from Sea Island Airport, Vancouver to Boeing Field, Seattle, but not before the words "Canadian Airways" were removed from above the door and "Trans-Canada Air Lines" hastily painted in its place. The Electra left Vancouver at 5:00 p.m. and arrived at Seattle at 5:50 p.m. At its controls were Billy Wells and Maurice McGregor. The passengers were D.R. MacLaren, assistant to the vice-president, and Percy Baldwin, the CNR's auditor. The schedule was governed by the post office regarding mail deliveries in both countries. A daily service on the same route with paying passengers began on October 17, the fare $7.90 one-way and return $14.20. This was the first revenue that the airline would bring in, and its first international route. Pat Eccleston was one of the stewardesses who flew the Vancouver–Seattle route in 1938 and remembered: "The flight was beautiful on a clear day. We flew only 2,000 feet above the water and you could see schools of fish. I would point out certain houses to the passengers and tell them who lived there." Unusually for TCA, it did not have a monopoly on this route — the competition was United Air Lines Transport's Boeing 247.

Three other 10As were bought soon after, with the airline's first brand new aircraft, CF-TCA, CF-TCB, and CF-TCC, all becoming the "Five Sisters" of the fleet. When war began they were all sold, four going to the RCAF and one to the Department of Transport. The airline's first colour scheme was all silver with the red cheat line extending the length of the fuselage, the TCA symbol on the tail and near the forward door, and "Trans-Canada Air Lines" in red on the upper fuselage. TCA was also the first airline in North America to equip its Lockheeds with smoke detectors in the cargo compartment and to put oxygen masks in the cockpit and cabin long before government regulations required them.

By April 1, 1939, the first simultaneous transcontinental flights left Vancouver and Montreal, each bound for the other city. It was all such a daring undertaking

The first TCA flight took off from Vancouver Airport for Seattle at 5:00 p.m. on September 1, 1937. The weather was brilliantly clear — a good omen for the airline.

in a country that had been joined by rail only forty-three years before. TCA's fourth stewardess, Lela Finlay-McKay, remembered one of her passengers telling her how he had first come out to Winnipeg with the Governor General's Foot Guards to fight Louis Riel. Another passenger talked about how he had come out west as a young man fifty-four years earlier to survey the rail line at Kicking Horse Pass.

Even then there were those at the airline who could see the potential in air travel and marketed its package tours to cater to tourists, one of which began: "Leave Toronto by early morning Trans-Canada airliner to North Bay, then by motor to Callander for an opportunity to view the Dionne Quintuplets."

———

Despite the country's focus on the Second World War, TCA kept extending its route so that by April 16, 1941, when the TCA Lodestar touched down in Halifax,

C.D. Howe, Canada's first minister of transport (third from the left) ensured that he would be on TCA's first revenue flight. The well-dressed ladies are buyers for Eaton's, Hudson's Bay, and Simpson's department stores. Unlike the media jaunt that preceded it, everyone on this flight appears to be sober.

the airline had fulfilled its purpose, that of providing Canadians with commercial air transport from coast-to-coast. Coast-to-coast travel from Halifax to Vancouver was now nineteen hours flying time. The *Halifax Herald* noted in April 1942: "TCA becomes the more truly trans-Canada with the inauguration on May 1 of daily airmail services between Victoria, British Columbia and Sydney, Cape Breton with an additional run into the sister dominion of Newfoundland." Within five years Howe had built an airline operating from the Atlantic to the Pacific. Sadly, unlike the hammering of the last spike at Craigellachie on the CPR line in 1885, there were no photographers

to record the historic landings at Sydney, Halifax, or Gander, Newfoundland — that dominion still seven years away from joining Confederation.

As for CAL, when the Second World War began it was still the largest air carrier in the country, and in 1940–41, flush with money from its wartime industries, the railway moguls of the CPR bought it and as many of the bush airlines as they could at bargain basement prices, melding the rivals together into the Canadian Pacific Air Services (later Airlines). But with a total of eighty-four outdated aircraft of twenty-nine types, its operations stretched out over five provinces and banned from the trans-

APRIL 1, 1939: THE FIRST TRANSCONTINENTAL PASSENGER FLIGHT

I was the stewardess on the Montreal–Toronto leg of TCA's first cross-Canada trip. There were huge crowds at the airport, and the number of times we were introduced to the press covering that flight was unbelievable. There were many questions for us to answer. C.D. Howe was among the passengers; he was very nice to us and addressed us by our first names. The start of the trip was delayed due to weather. We were to have left Montreal early on Saturday, April 1, but it was 9:00 p.m. before we took off. We landed about half an hour later in Ottawa. We could not proceed because of bad weather in North Bay, and we were taken to an Ottawa hotel. We were invited to the home of a VIP for dinner around ten o'clock, and then we returned to our hotel. About four o'clock in the morning, we received word that we were leaving for North Bay, but again we were unable to land, and we were diverted to Kapuskasing. We then flew on to Toronto, arriving about 7:00 a.m. on Sunday, April 2, where the crew for the Toronto–Winnipeg leg of the inaugural flight took over from us.

We waited in Toronto for a while before flying back to Montreal; a few passengers came with us. We touched down in Montreal at nine o'clock on Monday morning, April 3. Our return flight was scheduled to arrive back around noon on Sunday, April 2, but we were delayed at every stop by weather. The trip was so exciting that we did not mind; being young, we did not require much sleep.

My family was very proud and excited, knowing that I was a crew member on TCA's first transcontinental flight.

— Annette Brunelle Donovan

continental Airway, CPA was hardly competition for TCA. That did not prevent Mackenzie King emphasizing on April 2, 1943, that TCA alone would continue to be the only transcontinental carrier as well as the only Canadian international carrier. And although CPA was not mentioned, under no circumstances would two air carriers be allowed to compete on the same domestic route. It was only after King's retirement in 1948 that the government's air policy would change.

———

Throughout the war, although Howe was minister of munitions, he somehow retained TCA in his ministerial portfolio, pleased that its transcontinental route extended to St. John's and in 1943 to Prestwick in Scotland. Best of all was that it was usually in the black, requiring no government subsidy. So vital did the minister consider the smooth operation of TCA during the war that unlike the Canadian Pacific Air Services (later Canadian Pacific Air Lines), its pilots were forbidden to take part in the ferrying of bombers to Britain or training Commonwealth aircrew.

Almost since the start of the war, because of Beatty's friendship with Lord Beaverbrook, the Canadian-born British minister of aircraft production, the Canadian Pacific Air Services had been flying bombers bought from the neutral United States to beleaguered Britain as part of the Atlantic Ferry Organization (ATFERO). Using the long-range Liberator bombers that the French government had ordered before their country fell to the Germans, the precious ATFERO pilots were flown back to Montreal by the British government in a Return Ferry Service. To avoid giving offence to American isolationists, London ensured that this was entirely a civilian operation run by British Overseas Airways Corporation (BOAC), with the familiar BOAC "speed bird" logo painted on the bomber's sides. King and Howe were not fooled. Laudable as their efforts were, Canadian Pacific and BOAC were gaining valuable transatlantic expertise. The American ally was worse; by 1942 Pan American Airways had been joined by American Export Airways and Trans World Airlines in flying the Atlantic. Unless TCA did the same, both men knew that it would lose out in the postwar aviation boom.

While this was taking place, Vincent Massey, the Canadian high commissioner in London, kept imploring Mackenzie King to do something with the volume of military mail, machine parts, and blueprints that threatened to bury "Canada House." It seemed that the British and Americans had other priorities than taking airmail to Canada. The problem for the Canadian government was that there were no suitable long-range aircraft available in Canada. Nothing demonstrated to the Canadians the commercial aviation rivalry to come when their erstwhile allies suddenly discovered that there were no Liberators (or DC-4s) available for a Canadian-run transatlantic service, especially one to be operated by a potential postwar rival.

Although TCA maintained them at Dorval Airport, the British refused to allow their BOAC Liberators to be piloted by TCA aircrew or to accommodate Canadian passengers and mail. The RCAF had no four-engined, long range transport aircraft at all. Run by a former TCA captain, Wing Commander Zebulon Lewis Leigh, its 164 Transport Squadron flew the same Lodestars that TCA did and were at that time occupied with supplying RCAF units along the Alaska Highway. As for Trans-Canada Air Lines itself, although it carried 50 percent of the airmail in Canada, it had only been in existence for six years and was still too limited in personnel and planes; it had only eighteen of the 214 commercial aircraft in the country. But none of this deterred Howe, who in November 1942 set up the Canadian Government Trans-Atlantic Air Service (CGTAS).

It was said of Mackenzie King that he always believed the worst of the British and the best of the Americans, but this time it was the British who came through. In August 1942 A.V. Roe sent over from Britain a pattern Lancaster R-5727 to speed up tooling of the Canada-built Lancasters at Victory Aircraft Ltd. in Toronto. Howe appropriated it and had it re-registered as CF-CMS, the country's first four-engined transoceanic airliner. The airline's pilots did have some experience in four-engined aircraft since its pilots, George Lothian and J.L. "Lindy" Rood, had been training the RCAF's 10 (BR) Squadron on their first Liberators.

——

The whole airline took pride in the CGTAS Lancastrians, especially on January 12, 1944, when Captain Jock Barclay broke the transatlantic record by flying Dorval–Prestwick in 11 hours, 14 minutes.

The summer of 1943 is forever enshrined as TCA's transatlantic summer. It all began on April 2 when the prime minister reminded the House of Commons that TCA, by its charter as the instrument of the Canadian government, had the exclusive right to operate transatlantic services. On July 19, 1943, under the authority of Order-in-Council P.C. 5742 the government provided the aircraft that TCA would fly, with the Department of Civil Aviation paying for operations out of its budget. Operated by TCA on behalf of the federal government, the Canadian Government Trans-Atlantic Air Service (CGTAS) was not part of TCA or a commercial service at all — or even permanent. No fare-paying passengers were to be carried nor mail other than the government's and armed forces'. Howe became the first passenger on CF-CMS when he flew to Britain on May 15, 1943. The flight was a lot quicker and safer than his previous trip across the Atlantic, when his ship had been torpedoed and the Ottawa newspapers published his obituary. Crammed with mail, the first eastbound CGTAS flight took off from Dorval Airport on July 22, 1943, touching down at Prestwick, Scotland, 12 hours, 26 minutes after takeoff and setting a speed record.

The aircraft that had begun it all, CF-CMS, would be joined by eight Victory Aircraft Lancasters that had been civilianized to carry ten passengers.[3] As Howe knew, the Americans and British could not protest what was blatantly a TCA operation. The former had refused to provide the aircraft, and when CF-CMS was replaced by the Canadian-built Lancastrians, as they were called, so had the latter. Through the remainder of the war the converted bombers called "Lanky the Lancaster" staggered into the air heavy with mail and fuel. With 543 TCA employees working for CGTAS by 1945, the airline did gain valuable transatlantic experience, especially in the maintenance of its Rolls-Royce Merlin engines, the same that the North Star would use.

Never designed for mundane airline flights or lengthy use, the Lanc was dangerous to operate; parts constantly fell off, there were no tail or wing de-icers, and the Merlin engines, not designed for low speeds, clogged with lead deposits and shut down — sometimes in mid-Atlantic. Even worse was that with fuel tanks filled to the brim, fuel escaped from the overflow pipes and ran along the length of the fuselage, making the aircraft a potential firebomb.

Despite frequent engine failures, only one Lancastrian was lost when CF-CMU disappeared somewhere over the Atlantic on December 28, 1944. The prevailing wisdom was that it simply exploded as the aircraft filled with fumes when the pilot was transferring fuel from the bomb bay tanks to the wing tanks using a wobble pump while the wireless operator was sending a Morse code message using the key system, the sparks from the radio igniting the fumes.

———

Rules were relaxed at war's end, and CGTAS brought home war brides and minors. TCA pilots Lindy Rood and Jack Wright made an

I was seconded in 1943 to be a part of the Canadian Government Trans-Atlantic Air Service and started flying the Avro Lancastrian in 1944. The "Lanc" was a modified Lancaster bomber equipped to carry passengers and freight, it was unpressurized and cold and you could count on getting soaking wet in a rainstorm. Nevertheless, it was reliable and a good airplane to fly once you got the four engines synchronized, that was the trick. The outbound routes took us to Gander, Newfoundland, over Greenland and across the North Atlantic to Scotland with the return trips no less challenging, often flying further south stopping in the Azores. Flying the North Atlantic was tough and the weather made the journey long and unpredictable, and rarely was a trip routine. In 1946 I flew the first all-express trans-Atlantic cargo load in Canadian commercial aviation history using a Lancastrian.

—Captain Roger Lovell Smith

By 1945, three TCA crew members had each made more than 100 Atlantic crossings. They were Captain George B. Lothian (left), Flight Lieutenant Harold B. Thomae, navigator (centre), and Radio Officer Alan J. Blackwood (right).

unscheduled stopover at Sydney, Nova Scotia, in "Lanky 106" on January 22, 1946, bringing over seven British war brides. It was an overnight delay, so TCA staff took the women out to dinner at a local hotel. Steak was on the menu that night, and when the first steak arrived at the table one of the women began to cut it into six equal portions to share with the other six. Told that there was a steak that size for each, she broke into tears and explained that they hadn't seen anything like that for the last six years. In April 1946 the government abolished the passenger priority system, and commercial reservations began.[4] TCA was allowed to formally adopt CGTAS, and if there was a surplus in revenue, to keep half, returning the remainder to fund research and development expenses. There was little of that as the postmaster general vetoed any change in rates.

The government put CGTAS on a civil footing by establishing Trans-Canada Air Lines (Atlantic) Ltd. Financially separate from TCA, it was responsible for overocean routes only, a corporate distinction that remained on the books until 1952, when it was absorbed into the airline.

THE TRIALS OF A STEWARDESS OR ANYTHING FOR TCA

In civilian air circles a "short" is a non-priority passenger who must be removed from a flight if a priority passenger comes along. If possible what is known as "protection" is given him and arrangements are made to continue the journey by flight, by train, pony cart or whatever is available.

Recently a young stewardess, unfamiliar with flight vernacular, went to work for TCA. An hour out of Winnipeg, she received by radio the following instructions: "Prepare to remove shorts at Toronto. No protection." For a while she wondered how much she really wanted this job.

— From *Between Ourselves*

With a Commonwealth Conference on postwar commercial aviation to begin in May (when the other Dominions would be asking for a declaration of Canadian principles), on March 17, 1944, King had Howe table the country's post-war aviation policy in the House, the ramifications of which would guide (or straitjacket) civil aviation in Canada until 1967.

Howe's speech, the most important policy statement in Canadian aviation to date, stated:

- Canada proposed the creation of "an international air transport authority" to license and regulate air traffic between nations.
- The Canadian government was not about to change its policy that Trans-Canada Air Lines was the sole Canadian agency, which could operate international services.
- Within Canada, Trans-Canada Air Lines would continue to operate all transcontinental systems.
- Competition between air services over the same route would not be permitted, whether between a publicly owned service and a privately owned service or between two privately owned services.
- The two national railways would remove themselves from the ownership and operation of airlines within a year of the war ending.
- An Air Transport Board (ATB) would be created to advise the government on the licensing, regulation, and control of all commercial air services in Canada. It would have the power to assess all route applications and to grant franchises from now on.

A second coast-to-coast service in Canada, Howe elaborated, would be wasteful and unjustifiable, and that "... the newly formed Canadian Pacific Air Lines had lost no time in challenging the non-competitive position of Trans-Canada Air Lines and reaching out for new franchises." As to the small carriers, he said that they could continue to develop the bush and that the new airports along the Northwest Staging Route would provide employment for returning servicemen to start their own air companies. Finally, on the recommendation of TCA, the federal government had acquired the rights to manufacture a ver-

The Montreal Traffic Office in 1938 was at 1465 Peel Street within the Sheraton Mount Royal Hotel. Note the teletype machine, telephones, and reservations staff.

sion of the Douglas DC-4, a four-engined transport aircraft suitable for domestic and international use.

The speech was written to appeal to all political parties since no one could argue when it promised to safeguard the government's investment in Trans-Canada Air Lines. All would agree that the duplication of routes in the two railways should not be repeated in the air. Best of all for the wartime workers, the Liberals pledged continued employment in the aircraft industry.

The Transport Act of 1936 was amended on September 11, 1944, to provide for "the removal of commercial air services from the jurisdiction of the Board of Transport

Commissioners." Simultaneously, the Aeronautics Act created the Air Transport Board (ATB) to provide licensing and regulatory functions. The ATB was to be an administrative body under ministerial control, with all of its actions subject to the approval of the Minister of Transport. That TCA's monopoly would continue was clearly underlined in the ATB's first annual report: "In accordance with laid down policy, direct competition is not permitted on scheduled air routes. The reason is that, at the present stage in the development of air transportation in Canada, the volume of traffic is such that there is not room for competing services and it is considered

TCA North Star Mk 1 appropriately over Ottawa in 1946. When the Americans and British refused to provide airliners for a Canadian transatlantic service, Howe ensured that Canada could build its own.

uneconomical to try to divide the small available business between two or more carriers. While at some later date a policy of competition might be justified, at the present time it would be disastrous and is considered against the public interest."

Although Mackenzie King and Howe wanted both the CPR and the CNR to jettison their airlines, they soon discovered that if orphaned, TCA and CPA could not sustain themselves financially. Now flying across the Atlantic Ocean and in the process of equipping itself with Canadair North Stars, TCA was more heavily dependent on its CNR subsidy than ever. Off the airway and servicing the bush and North, CPA's air services had become essential to the country's transportation system. The pre-war arrangement was thus continued, and in fact, with the war surplus aircraft and rising demand for air services in the 1950s, the federal government was forced to also allow regional airlines to proliferate — as long as they did not challenge the TCA monopoly.

CPA might have remained one of those regional carriers had it not been for its irrepressible president, Grant McConachie. He consolidated the airline in Vancouver far away from the CPR moguls in Montreal's Windsor Station, and then lobbied Ottawa for permission to fly the ocean that the CPA was named after. Getting to the Orient via Alaska on the Great Circle route had been a cherished dream of his, and for McConachie the timing was right. Only Pan American Airways flew from San Francisco via Honolulu to Sydney and Wellington, and the northern Pacific was covered by Northwest Airlines from Seattle through Alaska to Tokyo and Shanghai. To counter this American influence in the Pacific and to foster postwar Commonwealth relations, on June 11, 1946, Canada and Australia concluded bilateral air agreements for reciprocal landing rights.

That September, the Australian airline British Commonwealth Pacific Airlines (BCPA) lost no time in flying weekly from Sydney to Vancouver. Embarrassed, the Liberal government promised that a Canadian airline would soon be operating to Australia. Social activist Stanley Knowles was the member of Parliament for Winnipeg, home of TCA's maintenance base, and with jobs for returning veterans at stake, he badgered Howe and Lionel Chevrier, the minister of transport, in the House for TCA to begin flights across the Pacific. The Australians also engaged in some

INAUGURAL TCA NORTH STAR FLIGHT, LONDON–MONTREAL

I transferred to Montreal, the overseas base, and in April 1947 I flew to London on a Lancaster. On overseas flights I was the only female crew member. My return trip was the inaugural flight of the TCA North Star from London to Montreal. The overseas flights were fourteen hours to London and eighteen hours returning — and longer if there were headwinds. We had some passengers who became very nervous when they saw what appeared to be fire around the North Star engines. I would tell them, "As soon as you don't see that, there's trouble."

On another return flight from Prestwick, we stopped in Reykjavik, Iceland, and then at Goose Bay, Labrador. We were held up due to weather ("socked in" as the pilots called it), and we were put up in quarters very much like barracks. A VIP on board was annoyed by the delay. Our purser, Gordie Kay, had become somewhat impatient with the VIP's attitude; he borrowed a raincoat and hat, an umbrella, a flashlight and rubber boots. Carrying them all, he approached the man in the bar: "Sir? These are for you. Canada's that way." Nothing adverse happened, of course: Gordie had the charming ability to get away with anything. I loved flying with him; he was a hard worker, and the flights were always fun.

— Dorothy Gilmore Labelle

diplomatic arm-twisting, and as an incentive BCPA suddenly showed interest in buying Canadair North Stars. The United States too was more than pleased to allow a Canadian airline to refuel at Shemya in Alaska and at Honolulu, because it needed reciprocal commercial landing rights at Gander and Goose Bay airports in Newfoundland, the British colony soon to become Canada's tenth province.

Transatlantic service had been extended from Prestwick to the tent city of Heathrow Airport outside London, and on November 4, 1946, TCA carried its millionth passenger (a Mrs. L.D. Nelles). But after five years of profit, the airline was about to bring in its first deficit, a paltry $111,500 but a deficit nevertheless. It was obvious to all that whichever airline was chosen, it would require decades of subsidies, whether from Ottawa or Windsor Station. Howe must have taken all of this into consideration and bowed to the pressure in 1948 to designate TCA to fly the Pacific — had not the airline's new president, Gordon McGregor, strongly objected. With the North Star, the airline's first pressurized airliner, TCA was then expanding into Europe and coping with the airline's postwar deficit (caused by political interference), and McGregor refused to consider the Pacific. There would not be a market in the Far East for years to come; Tokyo was still smouldering from years of bombing, and it looked as if Shanghai and Hong Kong were about to fall to Mao Zedong's armies. And as a pilot himself who had flown in Alaska, McGregor had no intention of using the temperamental North Stars foisted on him by Ottawa to ply the lonely Pacific. Why not allow McConachie to lose his shirt on this venture?

The Department of External Affairs' Escott Reid and Lester B. Pearson vehemently opposed this, saying that the government was caving in to exactly the sort of pressure from commercial lobbies that the setting up of TCA in 1937 had been designed to prevent. But on May 11, 1948, in an unaccustomed role for the minister of transport, Lionel Chevrier convinced the cabinet that CPA should be given the monopoly on the Pacific; the Australians had been promised a Canadian airline (the treaty didn't specify that it would be the official airline), and TCA could only benefit from this since CPA's Sydney–Vancouver flights would feed into its transcontinental service. On July 13, 1948, to satisfy the Australian government and to throw a bone to private enterprise, Howe permitted CPA to fly to Australia and New Zealand, throwing in the Far East as well. This last was an easy giveaway — no Canadian would want to go the war-torn cities of Tokyo, Hong Kong, and Shanghai.

Reid and Pearson were right; the Australian government felt slighted, and its prime minister, Ben Chiffley, refused to meet with anyone other than H.J. Symington, the president of TCA. It took a personal telegram from Chevrier to his opposite number in the Australian ministry of transport to confirm that CPA was indeed Canada's "chosen instrument" in the Pacific. When BCPA bought DC-6s instead, the pound of flesh that Howe exacted from McConachie was that CPA buy four Canadair North Stars.[5]

Canadian Pacific's first North Star flight departed Vancouver on May 28, 1949, landing in Sydney, Australia, on June 3 to great fanfare. Although McGregor and Howe were proven right in that the Australian service would be a money loser for CPA, giving up the Pacific was a decision that the federal government and its airline would regret not only in later years, but almost immediately. On June 25, 1950, when North Korean tanks and troops struck across the 38th parallel, Ottawa awarded CPA the contract to airlift American soldiers from Tacoma, Washington, to Tokyo. For McConachie, it was a good deal all around. As part of Canada's contribution to the war effort, DND paid the entire cost of the airlift. After the troops were landed in Tokyo, the CPA airliner went on to Hong Kong, where it picked up Chinese immigrants and brought them to Vancouver. The aircraft was packed each way so that when the airlift contract ended in 1955, McConachie had made $16,839,790 on the route, more than enough to cover the almost empty Vancouver–Sydney flights. McGregor, who would never admit to regretting his decision to turn down the Pacific routes, summed it up nicely. "Jesus Christ!" he marvelled. "Only McConachie could be that lucky."

CHAPTER TWO

GORDON MCGREGOR AND THE ADOLESCENCE OF THE AIRLINE

It was commonly known that C.D. Howe would retire from politics in 1946 and succeed Symington to guide Trans-Canada Air Lines through its adolescence.[1] The minister had expressed this wish many times in public, but when Mackenzie King asked him to stay on in Louis St. Laurent's cabinet, the question of Symington's successor was unexpectedly raised.

Howe's reliance on Americans like P.G. Johnson to get the national airline running had been criticized in the press, so Symington was careful to vet candidates who were not only native-born heroes but had some administrative experience in aviation as well. In 1945 he hired three Group Captains directly from the RCAF, all highly decorated, all with organizational experience from having commanded wings in battle. They were Paul Davoud, Ernest Moncrieff, and Gordon McGregor. Davoud

had commanded 143 Fighter Bomber Wing of three squadrons, with their rocket-firing, tank-busting Hawker Typhoons. Early in the war, Ernest Moncrieff had been the commanding officer of RCAF recruiting centres and later commanded 39 Fighter Reconnaissance Wing in 83 Group, 2nd Tactical Air Force. Davoud would leave TCA in 1948 to run the air-sea rescue program for Canadian Breweries/Argus Corporation, and in 1959 the federal government appointed him the chairman of the Air Transport Board. Moncrieff would also resign from TCA soon after being hired to become president of Standard Aero Engine Ltd. of Winnipeg. Thankfully, Gordon McGregor would remain with TCA for the next twenty-three years.

Born in Montreal in 1901, the son of a dentist, as a boy Gordon McGregor had actually "helped out" at the Great Air Meet

C.D. Howe and Gordon McGregor. On assuming the presidency on February 2, 1948, McGregor asked the minister for terms of reference. Howe told him: "Run it safely, run it efficiently and keep out of the taxpayer's pocket."

that took place on Montreal's West Island in 1910. Three times winner of the Webster Trophy for the best Canadian amateur pilot (1935, 1936, 1938), McGregor worked at Bell Telephone and by 1938 was Montreal district manager. His straightforward manner and fearlessness was evident when one of his tasks was to collect a $4,000 bill from the city's infamous mayor, Camillien Houde. When TCA began, McGregor applied for a job, but though he was the three-time winner of the Webster Trophy, he got no more than an acknowledgement of his application.

Joining the RCAF Reserve, he was posted to England with No.1 Fighter Squadron when war began. The oldest fighter pilot in the Battle of Britain, he was awarded the Distinguished Flying Cross on October 25, 1940 with the citation: "This officer has destroyed at least three enemy aircraft and has damaged many others. He has led his flights and frequently the squadron with gallantry and dash." By the end of his tour, "Old Gordie," as the young pilots called him (he was thirty-nine years old then) had shot down six enemy aircraft with eight "probables."

41

Because of his managerial experience with Bell, he was then confined to a desk and it took all his powers of persuasion to get a posting to the Aleutian Islands to command 111 Squadron and meet the expected Japanese invasion of Alaska. In 1943, McGregor returned to Britain as the commanding officer of 126 Wing for the D-Day landings. Now Wing Commander, McGregor's skills with the logistics for moving the Wing through France into Germany were noted by TCA president Herbert Symington, who recruited him after the war as general traffic manager. On assuming the presidency on February 2, 1948, McGregor met with Howe and asked for terms of reference for the job. "You stay out of the taxpayer's pockets and I'll stay out of your hair," was the reply. Howe's advice to McGregor was: "Run it safely, run it efficiently and keep out of the taxpayer's pocket."

The prudent, assertive Scot would be an ideal president to get the government airline out of the red; his infatuation with TCA was equalled only by Howe's. He concurred with the minister's idea of TCA as a state-run monopoly: "Who would think of having a municipality with two sources of lighting supply, sewage disposal or garbage collection?" he would say. "It doesn't make good economic sense." No socialist, he did not oppose private enterprise and used to sum up his philosophy by saying that, "There isn't a reason in the world why a corporation financed by taxpayers shouldn't be as well managed as one financed by private capital."

When workers in the vital wartime industries rose up against wage restraints to keep them turning out armaments, the government quickly promised a better tomorrow. In 1944, egged on by the Co-operative Commonwealth Federation (CCF), the Liberals enacted Order-in-Council 1003 (which would become the basis of the Canada Labour Code in 1967), which recognized that organized labour had the right bargain collectively — but only when the war had ended.

During the war 35 percent of the TCA passenger agents working either at the airport or downtown were female, and they were being paid an average of less that $5 monthly than their male counterparts. The TCA airport agents formed the Canadian Air Line Passenger Agents Association (CALPAA) in 1946, a name that must have confused everyone since it was so close to CALPA, the pilots' association. When the downtown traffic agents joined, it became the Canadian Air Line Traffic Employees Association (TEA). Airline management was less than pleased to have to deal with still another union and was initially hostile. Bargaining was cap in hand, with both sides aware of the flood of returning veterans who would be pleased to take any job — and deserved to. Given the postwar depression, nor was there any thought of striking; these were exclusively grievance committees.

The association's executives were untrained in labour negotiations and unpaid

And they did it all without computers.... The early TCA reservations office used telephone lines and entirely manual recording.

(union fees of $1.25 monthly were still voluntary), and would remain so until 1955 when the company agreed to have them deducted from the employees' pay. The first TEA collective agreement, signed on November 8, 1946, provided for an increase in pay for all but still had the holdover that female agents made $5 less monthly than males. Hindering the early labour organizers was the fact that the wartime patriotism within TCA persisted, as did the "one happy family" atmosphere,

allowing management to treat employees with paternalism — and sexism.

No one experienced the latter more than TCA stewardesses. Knowing that she had a job (but not a career) more glamorous than either teaching or nursing, the only other middle-class professions open to her, it was an unwise young woman who complained of the long hours, being called out while on leave, or that she had to quit once she was engaged (let alone married) or arrived at the age of thirty years. The attitude that the airline industry (and society as a whole) took towards the stewardess "profession" was that it was what a woman did until getting married. Because of the temporary nature of their service and the war, the TCA stewardesses would not begin organizing until 1946, when Muriel Campbell was instrumental in forming an association that became the Canadian Air Line Flight Attendants' Association (CALFAA), and she remained an important force in its development throughout her career with TCA. Years later, she remembered how it all began: "We called the organization an association because nurses, as all professionals at that time, did not belong to unions. It wasn't the unregulated hours or length of employment that we were fighting. Our biggest concern then was transportation to and from Malton airport."

The uniforms worn by the stewardesses through the years revealed much about the airline's aspirations and society's current mores, to say nothing of the women's duties at the time. In July 1938, the first two stewardesses wore "off the rack" beige gabardine business suits with a two-button jacket, red blouse, brown tie, and comfortable shoes, all topped off with the wedge cap with silver TCA badge. The wedge was correctly worn on the right side, exactly one inch above the eyebrow. The uniforms had to be brushed daily, kept body odour-free and dry cleaned weekly. Once transcontinental flights began, Tip Top Tailors designed and manufactured navy serge suits (grey in the summer) with slash pockets, white

"Tooke" blouses in the summer, and white sweaters in the winter. During the war, TCA had their stewardesses wear the "military look" of grey suits (there were complaints that the navy blue showed dandruff) with three-button jackets, long sleeve "Tooke" blue blouses, blue-and-white "spectator" shoes, and navy handkerchief in breast pocket. The navy blue handbag and gloves were optional.

Designed by Morgan's department store and manufactured by T. Eaton Co., postwar uniforms were once more beige lightweight linen suits, patch pockets with buttoned flap, white blouses, brown-and-white shoes, beige gloves, and a stitched brim cap from Stetson Co. The male purser-steward (from September 1945 onward) wore the same uniform as the captain except for the stripes, which were one gold and one white.

From 1953 to 1964, Tip Top Tailors designed a light blue linen weave suit with four-button jacket with TCA badge on lapels, no pockets or lapels, complemented by a short sleeve, white sharkskin tuck-in blouse with roll collar. The hat from Mae Hanover of New York was the same material as the suit and white gloves, the whole outfit completed with navy blue shoes and an over-the-shoulder bag. In the winter, the "TCA blue" (which was lighter than navy but darker than royal) Venetian cloth suit was worn with navy blue gloves.

———

The postwar TCA and early Air Canada were very much McGregor's creation. Strict fare management and the cross-subsidizing

TCA stewardesses pose before the workhorse North Star, 1953. With the exception of four, TCA never named their aircraft as BOAC did with its Argonauts and CPA its Empresses. The four that TCA did christen were named *Cartier, Cornwallis, Champlain, and Selkirk*.

of the thinner (and thus more expensive) routes with the high-traffic, high-density ones meant that Canadians got a bargain in fares through the 1950s and sixties. But since TCA had a monopoly on the most lucrative routes, there had never been a need to market itself; it relied on the CNR to do that. Nor had it been necessary to rationalize aircraft, routes, or the number of maintenance bases. On July 1, 1948, on orders from the post office, TCA became the first airline in the world to accept carriage of all first class mail by air without surcharge. What was a bargain for Canadians hurt the airline's bottom line, but when McGregor fought to take TCA out from the tyranny of the post office and the CNR, he was bluntly told to forget any ideas of making a profit; TCA was a public institution and the railway did not want to lose potential customers or freight to it.

Gordon McGregor beside a Vickers Vanguard in 1959. President of TCA/Air Canada from 1948–68, "GRM" was already three times Webster Trophy winner and the oldest air ace in the Battle of Britain. A great Canadian.

But the tough former fighter pilot loved the airline dearly and spoke his mind to protect it. It was typical of McGregor that during a labour dispute he asked if he could talk to the rank-and-file personally, to appeal to their "better natures." Never one to hide his opinions of aircraft acquisition, McGregor blamed Ottawa for dumping the noisy Canadair North Stars on TCA, which was competing on the Atlantic run against airlines that operated quieter, more

reliable DC-4s. He adamantly refused to purchase the Toronto-built Avro C-102 jetliner in 1950 and the Canadair CL-44 airliner in 1966, despite pressure from the government to do so and keep both companies in business.[2] Criticized for being an Anglophile because of his preference for British aircraft, McGregor bought fifty-one British-built Vickers Viscounts, the nimble little airliner popular with passengers because of its silent turbines and large windows. It was said that the only mistake he made in aircraft acquisitions was acquiring the Vickers Vanguard from his friend at the company, Sir George Edwards. But given that CPA intended to put the turboprop Britannia on the transcontinental route and the only alternative turboprop airliner then on the market was the trouble-plagued Lockheed 188 Electra, history has justified even that purchase.

Just as he strove to drop all money-losing domestic routes, McGregor refused to take up the route to Australia, knowing it would keep TCA in the red for decades. He proved correct in his assessment — CPA lost millions of dollars on the Australian route, and it was only the U.S. troop-carrying contracts during the Korean War that made the Far East profitable for McConachie. At least McGregor could console himself that the subsidy CPA needed to sustain those ventures did not come from the taxpayer.

As president of a very visible Crown asset, once the airline's annual report had been tabled in the House, the TCA president endured an annual grilling before

Elegant and sleek after the North Star, the Vickers Viscount was quiet and free of vibration because of its Dart gas turbine engines.

the Commons Committee. The sessions usually lasted for three days, although in 1949 it went on for ten. Unlike the parent CNR, which had historically been allowed to respond to members' questions by letter, TCA had to answer verbally — and immediately. With his comptroller Bill Harvey and the company records, the president would appear before the committee, able to succinctly field replies about everything from the freshness of sandwiches onboard to lost luggage to why the airline did not fly to a certain city (usually in the MP's riding).

With the airline's North Stars and Lockheed Constellations now flying to the eastern United States, Europe, and the Caribbean, getting closer to those markets was one of the reasons why McGregor moved the airline's maintenance base to Montreal. Another was the cost savings that would ensue from the consolidation of facilities, and on October 29, 1957, he announced in Winnipeg the company's intention to build an overhaul base at Montreal. At the same time a commitment was made to continue the overhaul of Viscount aircraft and their engines at Winnipeg. In doing this McGregor knew he was taking on the two political giants of the day: John Diefenbaker and Lester Pearson. At the height of the Cold War, Diefenbaker described the monopolistic position of TCA "as evidence of creeping socialism," and Pearson proved quite willing to sacrifice the airline's bottom line for votes in Manitoba. But McGregor stuck to his guns, saying "The Wallace Clark Report had left no doubt that there would be substantial economies to be gained if all turbine powered aircraft overhaul was consolidated at Montreal immediately upon construction of the new facilities."

The company's decision to continue overhauling Viscounts at Winnipeg was to lighten as much as possible a blow to the Winnipeg economy and to its own staff. In 1966, when CAE Electronics offered $3 million for the TCA facility, a fraction of its value, the government was quick to accept. But McGregor made clear that when the maintenance base at Dorval Airport was built, approximately 100 technical specialists required to service the DC-8s and Vanguards would be transferred east. The purchases of additional Viscounts and their associated overhaul requirements would offset this group movement.

———

The "Trans-Canada" connotation obsolete, "Air Canada" was unofficially already being used in Europe and in some francophone communities at home. Changing the airline's

name officially fell within the jurisdiction of the board of directors, which at an upcoming meeting was about to approve a new colour scheme for the aircraft. Adding "Air Canada" while they were being repainted made economic sense. A proposal to do so was circulated in an internal memo to senior staff on June 24, 1959.

Proposal to Adopt Company Identification of "Air Canada."

The name Trans-Canada Airlines is no longer indicative of the nature of total Company service.

• With TCA's entry into the jet age, the time to make a name change is propitious.
• The present name is not bilingual. The use of both "Trans-Canada Air Lines" in the English market and "Air Canada" in the French is divisive, aggravating an already difficult national situation.
• The present name is unwieldy for advertising. The advantage of "Air Canada" is that it follows an established airline pattern like Air France and Air India.
• Finally, the name has brevity, is succinct, is easy to remember and avoids the mental limitations that work against the airline in Europe.

The disadvantages to the name change would be:

- That a large investment has already been made familiarizing the public with Trans-Canada Air Lines. The change would incur costs in all areas of activities.
- Canadian Pacific Airlines (CPA) has been allowed to trade on a name that has been identified with prestige around the world. "Air Canada" would not have that advantage.

We have studied other names like Canadian Air Lines, Canadian National Air Lines, Canadian International Airlines and all have been discarded for one reason or another.

Finally, we have the solid backing of the ad agencies would have promised that they could convert all of the Company's assets from Trans-Canada Air Lines to Air Canada by 1961.

The board adopted the proposal's recommendation on July 2, 1959, and set a target date of August 11 to make the decision public. The project was so far advanced that the September timetable booklets would show the names "Air Canada/Trans-Canada Air Lines" together and only the first in October.

Adverse reaction was not slow in coming. "Word is getting around within the company about the use of Air Canada as a trade name replacing Trans-Canada Airlines," warned Herb W. Seagrim,

vice-president of operations on July 7 in a memo to the president. "… this is causing considerable resentment, not so much because of the change itself, but because, in the minds of many people, 'Air Canada' is a French designation having little meaning in English." The employees feel, he wrote, that they "have been sold down the river."

"We are unanimously opposed to such change," members of the Vancouver Flight Dispatch wrote to the president on July 18. "Our Company has always been admired for the high calibre of its employer-employee relationship. This will certainly suffer if the proposed name change is carried out arbitrarily."

R.P.M. McConkey, the TCA station manager in Boston, thought that the proposed name change too closely resembled Air France. "We are endeavoring to copy the name of another airline to satisfy a certain minority group in Canada. If the principle of copying is to be applied, why not use a more Anglo-Saxon airline instead — we could become Canadian Overseas Airways Corporation."[3]

McGregor would personally reply to all who wrote, the last Air Canada president to do so, that the matter was only being discussed and that Public Relations was dealing with launching it. He was not opposed to the new name himself, and such was his stature with the rank-and-file that the employees might have put aside their anxieties out of loyalty to him. But since the change of name would require an amendment to the Trans-Canada Air Lines Act, the government had to approve it.

Parliament was then in recession, but Prime Minister Diefenbaker wasn't. Opposed to French Canadian nationalism, Diefenbaker, while no friend of the airline (they had lost his luggage on his first flight as prime minister), recognized political dynamite when he saw it. He summoned George Hees, his minister of transport. "Who does this fellow McGregor think he is?" the prime minister demanded. "And what is he up to?" Did he not know that this was a political matter and should have been submitted to the prime minister's office for approval in the first place?

McGregor knew that antagonizing a prime minister who had campaigned to end the TCA monopoly was hardly a wise thing to do, and Diefenbaker's refusal to even consider changing the name could not have come at a worse time for TCA.

The Conservatives had campaigned on the benefits of competition in commercial aviation, something that both CPA and Pacific Western Airlines were quick to remind them of. As a businessman representing Toronto's Spadina district, Hees mistrusted the Department of Transport bureaucrats, all of whom had served under C.D. Howe. In 1959, the minister wanted TCA to sell its securities held by the CNR to the public — and no doubt McGregor would have endorsed the move.

The airline's president watched as the ridiculous relationship of debt to equity capital grew more disproportionate as capitalization increased. Airmail that had represented 48 percent of the airline's revenue in 1942 by 1951 was down to 15 percent and less than 4 percent in 1968. Yet the postmaster general was still on the board and worked to rein in route expansion because for every mile flown, its payments to TCA increased proportionately. It was only in 1945 that the mail contract was renegotiated and the post office would pay TCA to fly the mail on a ton-per-mile basis. This meant that the airline had no incentive to extend its routes into the North, where the loads would be too light to pay the costs. The TCA Act of 1937 was clearly obsolete, and McGregor favoured a corporate divorce from both the CNR and the government. His long-cherished dream, he would write, was that one day the airline's employees would become its shareholders.

But Donald Gordon, the railway's president, opposed cutting TCA free, saying that the present situation was "simple and equitable" and TCA's finances continued to be covered by the CNR Financing and Guarantee Act. Gordon's reluctance might have been influenced by the rival CPR, which had its airline CPA under firm control. Hees' deputy minister, John Baldwin (a future president of Air Canada), also advised caution.

Hees tackled the question of TCA's monopoly by commissioning British economist Stephen Wheatcroft to study airline competition in Canada. Wheatcroft gave McGregor full marks for his prudent stewardship of TCA but concluded that there was now sufficient traffic to permit small carriers to take over regional routes from the government airline and that CPA should be allowed up to four daily transcontinental flights. Neither of these policy changes, he said, would cause TCA to go into deficit.

"It is not suggested that it is wrong to subsidize the low traffic routes," Wheatcroft would state. "On the contrary, there appears to be the strongest possible case for Government aid to local and regional air services in Canada. A policy of direct subsidy would make possible a new approach to local and regional operations. Small carriers can almost certainly perform these at a lower cost than a major trunk route airline. Hence TCA might be relieved of some of its unprofitable social services if the Government agreed to subsidize local carriers on these routes. An additional consideration is that the present financial difficulties of most of the small airlines appear to make some assistance essential for their survival. A review of the overall policy towards local and regional air services is required urgently." This was music to the ears of the Conservatives, all provincial governments, and the whole Canadian commercial aviation industry — everyone except Air Canada.

The minister met with McGregor in Montreal and instructed him to immediately drop the proposal to change the company's name. But by way of compensation, Hees promised to consider favourably TCA's request to fly to Tokyo and Hong Kong, the routes that it had lost to CPA in 1949. As the state airline, BOAC (which it was said stood for "Bring Over American Cash") only served Montreal. The British government was lobbying for landing rights to Toronto with its huge English Canadian market. London's trump card was the Crown Colony of Hong Kong that TCA

wanted, and Hees hinted that an exchange of rights might be effected. As for the change of name, at its subsequent meeting the TCA Board carefully approved only the new colour scheme for the aircraft: all white fuselages with the same red cheat lines.

———

In October 1959 TCA and CPA ordered their first jet aircraft, five DC-8-43s, each from Douglas Aircraft at a unit price of $6 million. Both McGregor and McConachie ensured that their purchases were fitted with Rolls-Royce Conway fulljet bypass engines instead of the troublesome Pratt & Whitney J-75s. Since the Conway was so untried, TCA had Rolls-Royce sign a "Never be Sorry" agreement, ensuring that the manufacturer would fix all problems without charge — something it would neglect to do with the RB211 engine for the L-1011.

"Jet indigestion" was a worldwide ailment among airlines in the 1960s, since to keep up with each other, they scrambled to buy and find financing for fleets of the earliest jet aircraft. CPA was already in financial trouble because of long, thin, unprofitable routes, its DC-8 purchase sinking it further, and McGregor warned Hees that because of the cash outlay, TCA would now also go into deficit. On January 22, 1960, McGregor suggested to Diefenbaker that since both airlines were losing money, they should be merged. TCA's domestic network could feed into CPA's Pacific one, and a single strong airline would present a unified stance for

What it took to get a TCA DC-8 into the air in 1962.

Canada in bilateral negotiations. But the Conservatives would have none of that and worked, it seemed, to the contrary. When the Olympic Games were held in Rome that summer and CPA obtained landing rights to that city, Ottawa inexplicably reciprocated by not only handing over landing rights to Toronto *and* Montreal to the Italian airline Alitalia, but also Fifth Freedom rights onward to Chicago, Los Angeles, and Mexico City, where no Canadian airline flew.

Rather than commiserating with McGregor, about to be promoted to minister of trade and commerce, the cabinet position that Hees had always wanted, Hees called McGregor in to blithely refuse TCA's request to serve Tokyo and Hong Kong because he said CPA was now in deficit and could not afford another Canadian airline's competition on its Asian routes. McGregor's observation that giving in to CPA was "like paying hush money to a blackmailer" has become one of the classic quotes in aviation history. Hees then dropped the other bombshell. On the advice of the Department of External Affairs, the minister was about to give BOAC landing rights to Toronto to promote Anglo-Canadian relations.

FLYING THE DC-8

Transitioning from the Lockheed Super Constellation to the McDonnell Douglas DC-8 was by far the most challenging and exciting time in my career. While I liked the "Connie," the DC-8 was big, powerful and fast and could ascend to heights we had never reached before and presented new challenges, which was the part I liked the best. The "stretch" version of the DC-8 carried more passengers and longer range which I preferred as most of my flying was to Europe and the Caribbean. In 1961, I logged a world speed record between Winnipeg and Prestwick by knocking one hour off the regularly scheduled time, taking advantage of strong tail winds at the higher altitudes. There was little doubt that moving from the prop age to the jet age changed commercial aviation as we knew it and we never looked back.

— Captain Roger Lovell Smith

The Wheatcroft findings were passed on to the Air Transport Board (ATB), which invited both airlines to make their case concerning the transcontinental monopoly. Broadcast over radio for the first time, the hearings were held at the Château Laurier hotel in Ottawa. On January 31, 1959, the board handed down its decision. Despite the brilliant defense of CPA's case by their legal counsel Ian Sinclair, the four transcontinental flights were whittled down to one, the board stipulating that CPA could use its DC-6B with eighty-nine-passenger capacity on a Vancouver–Winnipeg–Toronto–Montreal route. He knew that McConachie had no

intention of doing so, not when he had already taken delivery of six turboprop Bristol Britannias, which not only carried ninety-eight passengers but were faster than the TCA Constellations, and CPA's DC-8s with their 124-passenger capacity were not far behind. On May 4, 1959, two CPA Britannias flew the first east and westbound flights. TCA's monopoly had been breached. It never ceased to amaze the TCA president that having invested so much money in the national airline, the government of the day would actively attempt to put it into deficit. But worse was to come.

Hees was succeeded by Leon Balcer, the member of Parliament from Trois-Rivières, Quebec. While he was pleased with the construction of the airline's maintenance base at Dorval Airport in 1959, Balcer could not resist using his ministerial clout to force TCA to take on a money-losing route to his own Trois-Rivières riding. In 1957, the bush airline Boreal Airways renamed itself Nordair and moved to Montreal. Authorized to fly to Fort Chimo, Frobisher Bay, and Cape Dyer, to survive it wanted to enter the more populous and lucrative market in Southern Ontario. To compete with TCA, Balcer gave Nordair the Montreal–Kingston–Oshawa–Hamilton–Windsor route, and Quebecair Montreal–Chicoutimi.

But neither the minister nor the TCA president brought up the change of name again. It had been a salutary lesson that McGregor did not forget. Thus when the airline entered the jet age on January 5, 1960

The two giants of Canadian commercial aviation: G.R. McGregor, president of TCA/Air Canada, and G.W.G McConachie, president of Canadian Pacific Air Lines.

with the delivery of its first DC-8, it was with the name that it had in 1937 with the Lockheed Electra.[4]

———

By the late 1950s, airlines had outgrown their telephone and teletype reservation systems that only allowed customers to book flights a week in advance. American Airlines was the pioneer in considering the use of an automated reservation computer to book seats. It was nicknamed "Girlie" because it "told all." TCA customers purchased their tickets in person, either at a travel agent or the company's office, or reserved them by mail or phone, and when early in his tenure as traffic department manager McGregor discovered that the TCA sales office switchboard was only staffed from 9 to 5 p.m., the former Bell Telephone manager instituted a twenty-four-hour, seven-days-a-week reservation system. To keep track of what seats were sold, to whom and when, airlines still relied on tools their railway predecessors used: ledgers and blackboards, both of which multiplied as routes and passengers exponentially increased. Agents sold seats on flights while teletypists notified "Space Control" agents at the

The heart of ReserVec was the central processor made up of two UNIVAC 1108 multiprocessor computers, giving TCA/Air Canada a "Total Reservations and Passenger Traffic Computerized System."

TCA Central Payload office in Toronto, who gathered all flight load data manually, entering the names in books, tracking the sales, and ensuring that there was always a "cushion" of a certain number of unsold seats. This made every complementary flight for TCA employees travelling "standby" fraught with the chance of being offloaded along the route.

In 1957, to aid with the North American Cold War defensive system, the Defence Research Board in Ottawa encouraged the British firm Ferranti to set up in Canada. Ferranti did so and adapted the British-made Manchester Mark 1 computer for the post office to computerize mail sorting. McGregor saw the value of a computerized reservations system, and TCA provided Ferranti with $75,000 to design and build six prototype transactors, which were connected to telephone lines for an experimental booking program. Since this allowed for the booking, querying, and cancellation of seats in minimal time, in 1959 TCA bought Ferranti's deployment system for $2 million (a vast sum at the time), wherein all information could be stored in five magnetic drums of 32,768 25-bit words each. Using the earliest software, reservations were routed into two central processing units known as Castor and Pollux (from the Gemini star constellation), the computer as a whole thus becoming known as Gemini.

In 1961, a contest among TCA employees to name the system resulted in "ReserVec" for Reservations Electronically Controlled. The whole system was installed in the airline's Toronto booking office in August 1961 and connected with all other offices by the following summer. On January 4, 1963, TCA switched from manual reservations systems to ReserVec, allowing for the reduction of phone lines and telephone operators on staff. What passengers must have appreciated was that instead of the mandatory week's notice, the turnaround response time was in seconds, with ReserVec able to process ten transactions a second. The Canadian system was two years ahead of SABRE, which American Airlines had funded at five times the cost. Its only drawback was that unlike SABRE, ReserVec did not store passenger information. This had to be processed manually, and for that TCA developed "Pioneer," which linked its three-letter codes with passenger records on a former Burroughs military computer. This was only used at the Montreal and Toronto ticket offices, the remainder keeping paper records.

Unfortunately for Ferranti Canada, its British head office, perhaps jealous of the accomplishments, did little to encourage or market the technology in Europe. Although the company marketed ReserVec to Lufthansa, KLM, and QANTAS, when the airlines in the United States chose IBM's much more expensive SABRE system, ReserVec was destined to be a "one-off."

———

The 1960s were unhappy years for TCA, with few successes. The last DC-3 and North Star flights occurred in 1961, and when the Constellations left in 1963, TCA became the first large airline to operate an all-turbine fleet in the world. But heavy government oversight continued to bedevil the airline. The purchasing of aircraft built outside Canada and the absence of French Canadians in senior positions were two growing irritants between the airline and Ottawa. These, along with the breaching of the transcontinental monopoly, meant that its privileged status was fast eroding.

The company's godfather in Ottawa, C.D. Howe, died on New Year's Eve, 1960, never achieving his ambition to run the airline. As Canada's first minister of transport, Howe had fought off political interference of the airline his entire career. As if mourning his death, in 1960 TCA recorded its first deficit in ten years of $2,607,350, as McGregor had predicted. The president suffered a stroke in June 1961, hearing in his hospital bed that the Diefenbaker government was going to allow CPA to use its DC-8s to fly Vancouver–Calgary–Gander–London. Although this never took place (because the British government blocked it, claiming that the volume of traffic was insufficient to allow a second Canadian carrier to land at London) to compete on the transcontinental route, TCA lowered it fares, causing what would be the largest deficit in its history: $6,450,000.

President G.R. McGregor, Lucille Garner Grant, the first stewardess, and Lindy Rood, director of flight operations and senior pilot, before the Lockheed 10A used on the airline's twenty-fifth anniversary cross-Canada flight in 1962.

Jack Pickersgill replaced George McIlraith as minister of transport, and as a former history professor and having served both prime ministers Mackenzie King and St. Laurent, he was well aware of the ruinous competition between the CPR and the CNR. No one, it was said, knew the workings of Parliament and the bureaucracy better than "Jumping Jack," who could be counted on to jump up and argue every debate in the House. It was also no secret that Pickersgill wanted to rationalize the whole national transportation system with a merger of the two transportation giants that would include their airlines. Then there were the former "bush airlines," now rich with contracts made supplying the DEW Line, and the number of air carrier applications that arrived at his office, coupled with the challenges posed by provincial governments, which felt that air travel within their boundaries was above federal jurisdiction. This prompted Pickersgill to formulate a regional air policy in 1966. Equipping themselves first with turboprops and then jets, the regional airlines wanted scheduled routes connecting the main cities in Canada, which would put them in competition with TCA/Air Canada.

———

In history the month of October 1962 is remembered as the best of times and the worst of times. The Beatles had their first hit, "Love Me Do," and Ian Fleming's first James Bond book, *Dr. No*, had its movie premiere. But not far from where Ursula Andress was emerging bikini-clad from the water, the Russians were setting up missile launchers in Cuba, the Cold War was at its most dangerous, and the human species faced annihilation. There must have been many at TCA who wondered if the airline would survive another twenty-five years. For that summer they had celebrated the twenty-fifth anniversary of TCA's first scheduled passenger flight. The Lockheed 10A CF-TCC, one of the original "Five Sisters," was found for a journey through time. Then in service with Matane Airways in Quebec, it was chartered and (because there wasn't time to return it to its original metallic finish) painted white for a cross-Canada commemoration flight, the names of the cities it was to stop at listed on one side.

It would be flown by George Lothian, Lindy Rood (who did a couple of turns with it over the new offices at Place Ville Marie opposite the Queen Elizabeth Hotel and CNR station), Art Rankin, and Rene Giguere, with some of the original stewardesses on board. On the final leg from Vancouver to Seattle, Billy Wells, who had made that first flight in 1937, took over, the memories flooding back for many as he did so. The Electra was returned to Matane Airways after the commemoration and in 1965 was sold in the United States.

Retirement might have been far in the future for the original TCA flight attendants when they joined in 1938, but not so thirty years later. Many were now approaching fifty, having been forced to remain single to keep their jobs, and given the lack of a company pension, few were ready to leave. In some ways, TCA flight attendants discovered they were better off working for a Crown corporation. Years before the provinces did so, in 1953 the Canada Fair Employment Practices Act (later part of the Canada Labour Code) was enacted, and in 1956 the federal government passed the Act to Promote Equal Pay for Female Employees, applicable to employers and employees engaged in businesses under federal jurisdiction. It still took the airline (now Air Canada) twelve years to eliminate the age, marriage, and maternity restrictions, doing so in 1965.

Other contentious issues for female flight attendants were the compulsory retirement age and pensions. In 1964, the Air Canada pension plan was amended to provide retirement at age sixty with full pension for male flight attendants and at age fifty (with reduced pension) for female flight attendants hired prior to January 1, 1960. But the airline required that female flight attendants hired after January 1, 1960 resign at age thirty-two.

The name change to Air Canada flashed by yet again. On November 5, 1962, the Liberal

First class meal service on board a TCA DC-8, 1961–2.

member for Niagara Falls, Judy V. LaMarsh, introduced Bill C-2, Trans-Canada Air Lines Act: Amendment to Change English Name of Air Lines. But as with most back-bencher bills, it never got a second reading.

Company employees, especially those in Montreal, could not have been unaware of the Quiet Revolution taking place around them. Quebec was being transformed with appeals to government and industry for fairer treatment of the country's French-speaking minority. More disturbing were the declarations from the nationalist paramilitary group Front de Libération du Québec (FLQ), which called for a violent insurrection against all "Anglo-Saxon" imperialist oppressors — and TCA was a prime target. It was no wonder that when the Liberals were elected in April 1963, Prime Minister Lester B. Pearson speedily established The Royal Commission on Bilingualism and Biculturalism that would soon make English and French the official languages of the country.

In solitary splendour at the time: the Air Canada Maintenance base, Dorval Airport, 1964.

For TCA, 1963 was proving to be the worst year in its history. Although it emerged with a net profit of $527,875, a result of the boom in the national economy, the beginning of the phase-out of the TCA maintenance base at Winnipeg angered many on the Prairies. Prompted by the Liberals now in opposition, a commission of inquiry as to the airport's future was set up. Published in June 1964, its report stated the hope that the local Manitoba airline Transair would be given international routes that would compensate.

The base transfer might have alienated Westerners, but nothing was as controversial as the company's selection of the Douglas DC-9 over the French-built Caravelle for its short-to-medium range requirement. The reaction it provoked was unprecedented: University of Montreal students rioted outside the company's offices at Place Ville Marie, shouting "Hang McGregor!" and throwing eggs at the building's windows. This led English Canadians to commend McGregor for rising above local French Canadian demands and not opting for the Caravelle. In vain did the airline's public relations department respond that the decision to purchase the DC-9 had been made solely on technical and economic grounds. The Caravelle was not yet in airline service, while the DC-9 was — technical assessments of aircraft not in airline service, as McGregor pointed out, were risky — as the airlines that had made early purchases of the first series of Comets (like CPA) discovered. Given the emotions in Montreal, it was interesting that no one mentioned almost half of the DC-9 airframe would be built by de Havilland Aircraft at Malton, Ontario, providing employment for more than 2,000 presumably English Canadians.

THE DOUGLAS DC-9

When you mention the DC-9 to my generation of AC pilots I guarantee you will get a smile. It's like remembering your first love. For this was the aircraft that many of us learned our craft on. The '9 was the normal transition for beginnings, as it was traditionally the first aircraft a newly hired pilot would fly, and also the aircraft on which an experienced co-pilot would be promoted to the heady position of Captain. It was acknowledged by all that the job of DC-9 co-pilot was the busiest seat in the airline. Five takeoffs and landings a day was the norm with all the associated paperwork, planning and running from one gate to another was your way of life. It also flew where the weather was the worst — the Maritimes. The nickname we had for that region was "the swamp," which fit it to a "T." The constant decision making, demanding stick and rudder flying was an aphrodisiac to the young captains and co-pilots.

No matter what aircraft you went on to for the balance of your career, just a mention of the '9 would bring back instant memories and a smile.

— Captain Bruce Olson

Designed to operate on short- and medium-haul routes, the DC-9 entered service in 1965, and more than 976 were built. The airline became the first outside the United States to operate the model, receiving its first a DC-9-14, fin 702 CF-TLC (Tender Loving Care) on February 24, 1966. For Air Canada, the DC-9 was the aircraft of many "firsts." The first solely in Air Canada colours, the first equipped with air stairs, the first with liftable arm rests, the first with a galley large enough to accommodate larger meal carts that eliminated the need for stewardesses to go up and down during meal times, the first to have an Auxiliary Power Unit (APU), which gave it a self-sufficient ground, start, air conditioning, and electric power. But most importantly, it was the first aircraft that thousands of Canadians flew on.

The airline would buy a total of fifty DC-9s between November 1963 and February 1973 in the 14, 15F, 31, and 32 series. It was called "the pilot's plane," and many Air Canada pilots were trained on the aircraft, with Captain Carl Sandelin logging the most DC-9 flying time in the world. It was not until 2001 that removal of the DC-9s from the fleet would begin, to be replaced by Airbus 319s. On September 26, 2002, a retired DC-9 fin 711 that had been in service since July 7, 1967, logging 81,559 hours, more than any other Air Canada DC-9, was presented to the Canada Aviation Museum in Ottawa.

———

H.W. Seagrim (left), senior vice-president, operations, with a gold key presented by Donald Douglas Jr. at Long Beach prior to the departure of Air Canada's first DC-9 Fin 702, CF-TLC, June 7, 1966. Air Canada became the first airline outside the United States to operate the model.

The year 1963 ended on a sombre note. On November 6, one of the DC-8 freighters overshot the runway at London's Heathrow Airport and skidded through a cabbage field. There were no fatalities but it cost the company $2 million to rebuild it, and the aircraft did not return to service until July 1964. Even while the world was mourning the assassination of President John F. Kennedy on November 23, six days later TCA Flight 831, the DC-8 CF-TJN, plunged into the ground near Sainte-Thérèse, Quebec. All 111 pas-sengers and seven crew on the Montreal–Toronto flight were killed. In subzero weather on December 20, a common burial service was held adjacent to the old cem-etery at Sainte-Thérèse.[5] "Perhaps the best thing about 1963," McGregor would write, "is that we have reached the end of it."

The winter of 1963–64 saw the Pearson government in constant debate with the opposition and its own Quebec members. The issues, both contentious and inflammatory, ranged from a new national flag without the Union Jack in the upper corner to the use of French at the post office. The Liberals did not need more strife, and whenever questions in the House came up about making the name of the national airline bilingual, the outgoing minister of transport George McIlraith cited the expense involved, to which Conservative MP Louis-Joseph Pigeon rather facetiously replied that he and few other MPs were willing to "pool their pennies" to buy the paint and refurbish the entire TCA fleet themselves. The minister brushed the suggestion off in the same vein by replying that he "would not be put in the position of commenting on the artistic ability of members of parliament."

Pigeon's suggestion was noticed on Bay Street and taken up by the *Financial Post*, its editor demanding an end to the interminable debate. "Why not call our government airline 'Air Canada'? Why perpetuate a dualism that is clumsy, confusing and wholly unnecessary?" The Liberal member from Sainte-Maurice–Laflèche, Quebec, saw the article, and having just wrested that riding from the Social Credit party, the twenty-nine year old Jean Chrétien hoped to make a name for himself in the federal arena. He had read of the name change "in the great financial paper of Toronto" and seized on the issue.

Young Chrétien's first attempt to change the airline's name came on July 4, 1963, when he introduced Bill C-81, The Trans-Canada Air Lines Act: Amendment Respecting Name of Company. It garnered no interest and was, according to *Le Devoir*, "accorded a first class burial." When the House considered private members bills on March 3, 1964, the young man changed tactics and moved for a second reading of Judy LaMarsh's Bill C-2, respecting the Trans-Canada Air Lines Act. The life and death of a Private Member's Bill is governed by what occurs in the second reading, where the subject is to debate within an hour and if need be is referred to a committee for further study. Standing up at 5:00 p.m., Chrétien had to ensure that no other members talked out the proposal in the allotted time and prevented a vote by the hour's end.

"Mr. Speaker," he began, "I would like to summarize some of the main factors behind the introduction of Bill No. C-2. First, the name Air Canada is certainly bilingual. It has precisely the same connotation and meaning in English and in French, the two official languages of the country.

"The name Air Canada is a shorter appellation that does away with the cumbersome translation, as is the case with Trans-Canada Air Lines that in French is Les Lignes aériennes Trans-Canada. Originally the name Trans-Canada Air Lines served to designate an airline that served a domestic network of communications. This designation is no longer acceptable because the airline service routes go beyond the nation's geographical borders, indeed routes that touch many parts of the world." Chrétien then drew attention to Judy LaMarsh's bill and to the editorial in *La Presse* on October 12, 1963, which said that this was not confined to Quebec, that "… even Toronto wanted the designation Air Canada."

Several members offered Chrétien their congratulations, and one asked if Pickersgill intended to address the bill and also talk of rumours of a future merger between TCA and CPA. The minister replied that he was a politician and not a prophet. But he did not respond to Chrétien's suggestion one way or the other. It was obvious that Pickersgill and the prime minister wanted Chrétien's bill to succeed. Had this not been the case, a word from either would have shot down the unknown backbencher in his first few minutes. Perhaps they were testing the waters for the Great Flag Debate soon to begin.

The second reading of Bill C-2 was sped through with a chorus of approvals, ending with the MP Louis-Joseph Pigeon asking that it "not be referred to a committee ... since its coming into force is a matter of national urgency." Read a third time, it was approved unanimously and passed on to the Senate, to the relief of Chrétien and the government.

As surprised as anyone at the turn of events, by the time McGregor flew to Ottawa the bill was in the Senate. He appeared before a Senate committee to convince its members that the C-2 should be returned to the Commons to be amended so that the name Trans-Canada Air Lines and its abbreviation TCA could be protected from use by any other organization. In its amended form, the bill was approved by the Senate, and on March 30, 1964, received Royal Assent. Thus the name Trans-Canada Air Lines died, in the same room in Parliament where it was born

on another March day, twenty-seven years before. It was scheduled to become law on January 1, 1965, a date proclaimed by the governor-in-council.

And so that name passed into history. Contrary to popular belief, the last subsidies it (or Air Canada) would receive from the federal government were from 1960–62 to help inaugurate the first pure jet turbine fleet in North America. It had recorded a deficit in the years 1937–9, 1946–50, and 1960–61 — all major re-equipment stages in its development. Whatever TCA's losses, they were a small price to pay for giving Canadians safe, reliable air transport at bargain rates and fulfilling its mandate of joining the country by air.

As the name change catalyst, Chrétien was hailed by the Quebec press as "the champion of recognition for the rights of Quebec, of French and of bilingualism." When the Trois-Rivières newspaper Le Nouvelliste did a feature interview on him, he called the Air Canada bill "an example of nationalism that is positive without whining."

On the other side of the country, a British Columbian who signed himself as "One of the Majority" wrote to the Vancouver Province. "Why should the government spend the taxpayers' money on another pacifier for the Quebecois? I guess the next step the Liberals will take is to change it again, this time to 'Air French-Canada' and adopt the lily in place of the maple leaf as our national symbol."

A perceptive Mrs. Alice Dalziel pointed out in the Montreal Gazette that Chrétien's assertion of "... the words being the same in both languages" was inaccurate. "To be churlish, however," she wrote, "the words do not mean the same. In English, the word 'Air' so positioned is a verb. Its principal meaning is 'to ventilate,' with a secondary rather colloquial one 'to broadcast by radio or TV.'" Perhaps there was more symbolism in the meaning 'Ventilate Canada' than was realized.

"Never in the field of airline operation have so many old-timers been so upset," George Lothian would recall. "All the deep feelings came to the surface and it was not possible to walk through a hangar without being buttonholed by an angry old-timer. Personally I liked the new name but it was no place to venture such an opinion."

Responding to criticism from within and without the company, McGregor reminded everyone that TCA had nothing to do with the draft of the Private Members Bill, nor any foreknowledge that it was likely to be passed by the House. The company, he said, was quite prepared to resist "the demands of pressure group," but it could not disregard a federal law. He also reminded staff that as employees of a wholly owned affiliate of a Crown company, it was not their function to comment pro or con on government policy.

The advertising campaign for the change of name began in April, headed by W. Gordon Wood, the airline's senior vice-president of sales. Forms, ticket covers, claim checks, uniforms, silverware, the marking on buildings, vehicles and aircraft — wherever there was the TCA name and logo — all were to be graphically redesigned

to foster immediate public recognition.

There were still thirty of the original seventy-one employees who had been hired in 1937 and many more who joined during the war. As expected, they asked, "Why change the TCA style and trademark?" After all, it was the same company in personnel, tradition, and spirit. A corporate design committee of senior vice-presidents Herb Seagrim and F.T. Wood, Director of Public Relations R.C. MacInnes, and Director of Advertising J.A. McGee was set up to consider a change in the TCA maple leaf and the slanted lettering signature. They concluded that the old corporate signature hampered rapid identification with its ungainly length, and decided that "due to the faster tempo, to increased marketing spirit and ingenuity, the requirements for unique identification were more vital than ever." The simple "visual efficiency" of "Air Canada" with the stylized maple leaf, its roundel joining at the stem, was much more unique, legible, flexible, and appropriate for the Jet Era.

The contract for the redesign of the maple leaf corporate symbol was given to the firm of Stewart, Morrison, and Roberts, and since it was a government airline, John C. Parkin, the president of the National Design Council, approved of their campaign. Only three years old, the council was soon to be in the midst of dealing with such advanced designs as the logos of Expo 67 and the almost completed Montreal Metro. At a cost of approximately half a million dollars, painting the new company colours of red and black over silver was the largest and most expensive paint job in Canadian history. In retrospect, it was a prelude to what was soon to come: a new national flag and identity based on biculturalism, in effect the re-labelling of Canada.

It was also an opportune time to change the aircraft colour scheme from the pre-war all-silver to all-white with a red cheat line the length of the fuselage covering the windows, and the red tail with the new Air Canada maple leaf logo in white. The new name of "Air Canada" was in black forward on the upper fuselage with the aircraft's registration number at the base of the tail. Sloping down from the cockpit windshield was the black nose.

Employees were told that effective June 1, when answering the phone from outside sources and in conversation, they should use the name Air Canada and not Trans-Canada Air Lines. All company letterhead and business cards were to be revised by that date. "I believe the change in company name," wrote Gordon Wood to all employees on September 28, 1964, "and the consequent redesign program provide us with a marketing opportunity we will not have again in our lifetime. Make the most of it by injecting a new enthusiasm, a new aggressiveness into everything you undertake on behalf of the company."

Perhaps the best advertisement was what occurred less than a fortnight after the announcement, at Ottawa and Heathrow airports, when on October 13, 1964, the first DC-8 in Air Canada markings would carry Queen Elizabeth II from Ottawa to London. Millions on both sides of the Atlantic Ocean saw on television Her

Majesty and His Royal Highness Prince Philip descending from the door of the aircraft with "Air Canada" writ large. That Her Majesty had consented not to use a military or even a British commercial aircraft somehow bestowed the royal seal of approval on the change of name. This was not lost on company management as symbolically important in pro-monarchist English-speaking Canada.

By the end of that same month both IATA (International Air Transport Association) and ICAO (International Civil Aviation Organization) accepted the designator code "AC" for the airline. Getting the two letters had not been without problems since "AC" had long since been designated by IATA to the Colombian airline, Avianca. It took a personal letter from McGregor to Avianca's president to obtain its release. But the Colombians only agreed to do so if McGregor could convince IATA to give them the code "AV," which at that time belonged to a charter airline in Dakar, Senegal. Since Air Canada was not without some clout with the international organization, this was expediently done. For not only was IATA headquartered in Montreal, not too far from the airline's Place Ville Marie office, but both he and Symington had been its president.

AIR CANADA
(May 2, 1964)
Dear …
Re: Change of Name to Air Canada
For your information, under the provisions of an Act of Parliament

of Canada, being Chapter 2 of the Statutes of Canada, 1964, the name of the Corporation has been changed to AIR CANADA. This change of name becomes effective on the first day of January, 1965.

The change of the Corporation's name does not affect its legal status, that is to say, all property, rights, obligations and liabilities belonging to or incurred by Trans-Canada Air Lines are deemed to be the property, rights, obligations and liabilities of Air Canada.

Yours very truly,

Gordon McGregor

———

With attention focused on the name change, on April 20, 1964, Pickersgill took the opportunity to announce the Liberal government's civil aviation policy for the 1960s. There would not be competition in the international field by Canadian carriers, the status quo would continue wherein CPA served the Pacific, South and Central America, and Southern Europe (and Amsterdam), and Air Canada had Northern and Eastern Europe and the Caribbean. Domestically, any development in competition would not be allowed to compromise the viability of Air Canada, the nation's official carrier. Finally, the two main airlines would take responsibility for encouraging regional carriers to feed into their networks. Pickersgill also stated that the government intended to rehire aviation consultant Stephen Wheatcroft in 1965

to advise whether there should be further competition on domestic mainline services.

Aware that the two main criticisms levelled against Air Canada were that its monopoly on the best routes was anti-competitive and also that it was an Anglophile "old boys club" (or worse "Scottish mafia"), that September the airline did some soul-searching and launched a major market research project to discover the public's knowledge of (and attitude) towards it. Five hundred people across the country were polled by mail with questionnaires also handed out to customers at airports. The results, published on April 9, 1965, were indicative not only of the airline's insularity from the mainstream but also that commercial aviation in Canada was still very much a niche market.

"The Air Canada customer of 1964 is not an average Canadian." So began the corporate, product, and customer study. "He is male, professional, or managerial by occupation, earns above average income and makes 3 out of 5 trips annually by air."

What were his complaints? Forty percent of the sample thought baggage handling at the destination atrocious and 38 percent complained of the lack of help by airline staff in reclaiming baggage. Nonexistent or unintelligible in-flight and airport announcements, poor taxi service from the airport, unappetizing onboard meals, and slow check-in procedures made up the remainder.

McGregor would write that all too often the complaints were justified, but a sizeable proportion dealt with such matters as the airport terminal facilities, customs handling, and ground transport, with which Air Canada was concerned but over which it had no authority. "Then that was that amusing phenomenon encountered," he wrote, "the recognizable core of frivolous complaints voiced solely to imply an elite traveler's boredom — a form of one-upmanship: 'As I told the president of Air Canada…'"

But when asked why they went to the local airport, 70 percent of those interviewed said it was to "watch the planes land and take off." Only 17 percent were actually travelling somewhere. The prevalent view was that the airline was also responsible for the management of the airport, and it was blamed for everything from dirty public toilets to inadequate parking. One out of two Canadians did not know who owned Air Canada — 44 percent had an idea that the federal government did, 9 percent thought it was privately owned, and only 2 percent knew that it was part of the CNR. Two out five Canadians knew that it was based in Montreal, but 30 percent thought it was Toronto. Asked to name the president of Air Canada, only 26 percent answered correctly, and bizarrely, 20 percent (mainly in British Columbia) thought McGregor was of French origin. Proof that the railway was still a major national transportation mode was that 44 percent were able to name Donald Gordon as the president of the CNR.

The airline's new name received 80 percent public approval ("It's alright as long as it has 'Canada' in it.…" was a common response), but significantly, only 6 percent made any reference to it being a "French" name or it being in any way connected with current nationalistic developments in the province of Quebec. Asked about Air Canada's attitude to French Canadians, only 2 percent thought it actively discriminated against them, while 80 percent disagreed that it did. Even among French Canadians, the total agreeing was only 6 percent, while in Ontario and the Maritimes it was nil. But if there was little feeling awareness of discrimination, there was evidence that the status quo regarding the speaking of French by Air Canada employees left something to be desired.

What was the actual customers' impression of the airline? Before there was in-flight entertainment to distract them, passengers could while away the long hours by reading, smoking, chatting with the flight crew (who sauntered down the aisle with the air of sky gods), or playing cards. But invariably the first thing they did on claiming their seats was explore the folder in the seat pocket. This contained the airline route map, timetable, postcards, pens, stationary with the airline letterhead, luggage tags — and a questionnaire. Once completed, this last was to be sealed in the envelope provided and handed to the stewardess. Interestingly, the respondents of the survey thought that the Air Canada stewardess was close to the ideal, "… except she is too serious, a little arrogant and not as attractive as she should be." Her distinct differences from the ideal were: "… too much like a waitress, coldly efficient and a little younger than she should be."

Read in the year 2014, when food, drinks, and even pillows have to be purchased, when cabin crew are too few and too overworked to socialize with passengers, the comments are a mirror to another age (see sidebar).

———

As the world's ninth largest airline in 1964, Air Canada operated over 39,840 route miles, linking Canada, the United States, the British Isles, continental Europe, and the Caribbean. It accepted its fifteenth and sixteenth DC-8s that year, completing the order for that aircraft, the total fleet now thirty-nine Viscounts, twenty-three Vanguards, and sixteen DC-8s.

The Olympic Games held in Tokyo (then serviced only by CPA) that fall allowed the airline to take part in a complex communications venture. The games were relayed from Tokyo to California by satellite and by micro-wave to Montreal. Between October 10 and 24, the airline operated daily charter flights between Montreal and Hamburg carrying videotape of the games to Europe for viewing by nineteen nations. An Air Canada DC-8 was also chartered to fly the Canadian Olympic team to Japan. On its return it would make the return flight from Tokyo to Montreal in record time: twelve hours, twenty-four minutes, a distance of 7,100 miles.

The years of deficit for TCA were 1946–50, while the profitable ones were 1951–59 before the deficit returned once more in 1960–62, mirroring the state of the national economy. But by 1964–65, its last year as TCA, because of McGregor's careful husbanding the airline was solidly in the black. The Annual Report for 1965 records

Airline telephone service is awful.

Your stewardesses lack diplomacy and the courtesy of other airlines. On last flight, appear to resent being asked to provide legitimate services like coffee and papers.

Some of the Toronto office employees, I have found, are rather "fresh" or "aloof" in handling customers.

Mrs. McCabe would like to know who won the first prize in the Air Canada baggage-smashing contest this year.

The food is below par. Eggs taste like powdered eggs and serving coffee in paper cups with pre-mixed cream is like a third rate restaurant.

Airport Flight Information: Several agents at various airports promised to teletype a message to my wife who was waiting at my destination that I had missed my connection. But no message was put over the loudspeaker, as a consequence my wife, in more than one instance was kept waiting for 2 hours.

It is indeed a pleasure to fill out this survey. Gives me an opportunity to express my appreciation for an airline which is the best in the business.

Could the pilots point out the towns we are going over, informing as to their size and industries?

a net income of $3,989,960. Operating profit from 1964 to 1965 was $2,341,569. Passenger revenues had increased 19 percent with the average revenue per passenger mile at 5.93 cents. Operating expenses at $237,400,980 had increased to 17 percent, while production of available ton miles rose 21 percent. No federal or provincial taxes had been paid in 1965 since sufficient capital cost allowances were available from previous years.

———

The women's movement gained momentum in the Canadian aviation industry through the 1960s, mainly due to coverage of similar events in the U.S., and both Air Canada and CPA were prime targets. It was only in 1957 that Air Canada stewardesses were not required to be registered nurses or needed parental consent to fly. The enactment of the Civil Rights Act in the United States in 1964 allowed stewardesses there to challenge their employers. The newspapers enjoyed the whole issue with headlines like: BATTLE OF STEWARDESSES: GLAMOUR VS. EXPERIENCE (*Vancouver Sun*, August 4, 1965) and TEA, COFFEE OR LOLITA? (*Globe and Mail*, August 7, 1965). With the help of the Canadian Labour Congress and Harold Winch, the NDP member of Parliament for Vancouver East who brought Air Canada's discrimination against its stewardesses before the House, after negotiations with CALFAA (and three years before CPA did), on December 2, 1965, Air Canada dropped the requirement for compulsory retirement at age thirty-two,

allowing its stewardesses to continue working after marriage and providing maternity leave. But it kept the proviso that all stewardesses had to retire at age fifty. In exchange, CALFAA agreed to a ten-year contract for new female employees. Both Air Canada and CPA were also guilty of putting recently hired male flight attendants, or "pursers," in charge of the more experienced females. From the airline's point of view, males gave the profession some continuity since they did not have to leave for the same reasons as women. It took federal legislation in 1968 to end this blatant form of sex discrimination.

———

While five collective agreements were successfully negotiated in 1966, the first strike in the company's history occurred in November 1966, when 5,200 members of the International Association of Machinists and Aerospace Workers (IAMAW) went on strike. But the precedent to this (and all future Air Canada strikes) was the passenger agent "near-strike" that summer.

The Trans-Canada Air Line Sales Employees Association (SEA) officially changed its name to the Canadian Airline Employees Association (CALEA) on November 1, 1965. With the collective agreement up for negotiation, CALEA then began negotiating with the company in December. A majority of the membership rejected the "Proposed Revised Agreement" in January 1966 that had been accepted by the negotiators. This reoccurred in June, and negotiations broke off completely. This militancy was so alien to senior management that it really was at a loss how to defuse the situation. In the House of Commons, Tommy Douglas, the NDP leader, questioned Air Canada's policy concerning labour negotiations, and on June 11 Prime Minister Pearson asked Deputy Minister of Labour Bernard Wilson to mediate.

The situation deteriorated so much that Executive Vice-President Seagrim announced that in case of a strike by CALEA members, the airline would continue to operate with volunteers and "those employees who chose to work." Without the required six-week notice, he then said that the vacation leave of all CALEA members was to be cancelled. The airline promised the public that if the first strike in Air Canada's history took place it would keep flying by using management to issue tickets at the airport. A majority of CALEA members voted to walk out on June 15, and the other unions in Air Canada, IAMAW, CALDA, and CALPA, all pledged their support. There was speculation that their members would refuse to cross CALEA picket lines if they went up, especially at Malton. By now both the media and public were resigned to the inevitability that Air Canada would be shut down by midnight, June 15, and the lack of alternatives to the national airline was made glaringly obvious. Early the next day, the eastern stations began closing down as the picket lines went up. The knowledge that this was going to spread to Malton, Dorval, and the West was bad enough, but that the members of the other unions would not cross the picket lines frightened senior

management, and at 11:30 a.m. McGregor accepted the latest CALEA contract and the strike was called off. The transformation from association to union was formalized in 1967 by CALEA joining the Canadian Labour Congress for greater bargaining strength. It would continue to expand in the 1970s with the representation of traffic employees from other airlines: PWA in 1971 and EPA in 1975.

The first strike in Air Canada's history was significant not only because members organized nationwide against management, but it also heralded the end to what was seen as the company's paternalism toward organized labour. The days of the "one big happy family" of old had definitely ended.

———

A brass band, majorettes, beauty queens in bikinis (with coronets and scepters), and civic and company dignitaries greeted Air Canada's inaugural DC-9 jet flight at Miami on August 1, 1966. "As Capt. Ralph Leek wheeled the trim twin-engined jet into position precisely on schedule at 2:30 p.m., the band blasted, the baton twirlers twirled, the beauty queens smiled, dignitaries nervously adjusted their ties and the picketing strikers ogled...." Keys to the City of Miami were presented to Frank I. Young, regional sales manager for Air Canada, as the beauty queens "Miss Miami" and "Miss Shower of Stars" and the June Taylor Dancers from the Jackie Gleason show "... provided spectacular and provocative elegance to the inaugural ceremonies."

THE DC-8

The pilot's plane for me was the DC-8-63. Designed only a decade after WWII, it was one of the truly first high altitude 400+ MPH transports, born in the days when fuel was cheap. TCA/AIR CANADA operated close to 6 different variants of the type over a stretch of 20 years.

By the time I got to fly the '8 it was approaching the end of its operational life. Mostly there were DC-8-63s — the sexiest of the breed with smooth controls and those long, skinny engines. I was 28 years old and I can tell you that sitting in the right seat of that aircraft was the biggest thrill of my career to date.

She was long like a greyhound. When you rotated the nose for takeoff you could feel the cockpit pitching up nearly 12 feet to the lift off attitude. Controls were light and responsive. Years before "fly by wire" was invented, it was truly an aircraft that was flown on takeoffs and landings. She demanded ability to land correctly. Unlike the Boeing 727, which was already nose up while approaching to land, the '8 demanded experience to correctly judge the height to rotate the nose from a nose low approach attitude to the nose high touchdown. On some dark dirty nights when it was hard to judge, you could make a landing that would humble you for months.

— Captain Bud Olson

Economy class family fares had just been introduced on North American routes, with the head of the family travelling at full fare and all other adult family members at 75 percent of the regular fare. Economy seating increased capacity in some DC-8s from 117 to 123 seats. For the third consecutive year commodity traffic had expanded, increasing 29 percent to 41,197,000 ton miles. Two of the new DC-8s were reconfigured to carry an additional 5,000 pounds each and were put on a one-day cargo service between Vancouver and London, England.

———

That summer the interchange of major components for the first two Anglo-French Concordes took place between England and France. Two centre wing fuselage wing sections were completed and loaded onto flatbed trucks at Sud-Aviation's Toulouse plant to be taken to Cherbourg, where they were ferried to Southampton. There they were again put on trucks and transported to the BAC plant at Filton. The aircraft's Bristol/Snecma Olympus 593 test engines had already logged over 500 hours. The airline had been studying the purchase of supersonic transports since 1964 and was late in making a decision to buy either the Boeing-built SST or the Concorde. On September 27, 1966, Jack Dyment and Herb Seagrim recommended to McGregor that if the airline did not place an order soon, by 1977 when its competitors would have supersonic transports in service, it would be jeopardizing its long haul routes, Toronto–Los Angeles or Montreal/Toronto–London, and its pooling arrangements with BOAC. Consequently, line positions for four Concordes at $875,000 and six SSTs at $1,200,00 were held, the government permitting the funds to be committed from the 1967 capital budget.

Unlike other airline presidents, McGregor was less sure of the SSTs. He would write that there were just too many unknowns, and because of this Air Canada did not want to be an early operator of the aircraft. Speaking at the Canadian National Exhibition in September 1966, he referred to the deposits made by airlines to secure positions in the delivery queue as the first time in history. They had been asked to make deposits on an aircraft of unknown design, delivery date, purchase price, or performance. "To the people of Air Canada, this seems to be a very expensive pig in a very opaque poke and thus far we have refrained from lending anybody our money, interest free, for an unknown period of time." The supersonics, he said, would not have the same impact on the current aircraft industry as the current subsonic jets had when they had been introduced in the early 1960s — nor would they lower the price of air travel. Never before in history, McGregor noted, had so much money been spent on something that no one wanted. Although a lover of all things that Rolls-Royce engineered, McGregor resisted the pressure exerted by Sir George Edwards, now chairman of the British Aircraft Corporation, who said if Air Canada did not hold some line positions (fifty Concorde aircraft had been spoken for by other airlines), it would be left behind.

"Herb Seagrim, our Vice-President of Operations, laid down the party line to the rest of us," remembered vice-president of operational planning Clayton Glenn, "i.e. that we were not going to be rushed into a decision; however … the chances would

be that we would purchase the larger U.S. SST, as it had the potential of superior economics [it could carry twice as many passengers as a DC-8 and make two round trips daily across the Atlantic instead of one]." But its development appeared to be about three years behind that of the Concorde. Jack Dyment was made the chairman of the Supersonic/Jumbo Jet Coordinating Committee, to which the directors of Flight Operations, Passenger Service, Operations Planning, and Station Service belonged, and they recommended that Air Canada reserve positions on both aircraft. In December 1966 the company announced that it had reserved delivery positions on the production lines for four Anglo-French Concordes and three Boeing SSTs.

———

Using the findings of the MacPherson Royal Commission on streamlining the national transportation infrastructure, in January 1967 Pickersgill shepherded the National Transportation Act through the House. It created the Canadian Transport Commission (CTC), which absorbed most of the previous boards: the Board of Transport Commissioners, the Air Transport Board, and the Canadian Maritime Commission. The act allowed railways, trucking companies, and airlines (other than TCA) more freedom. The CTC's Air Transport Committee was mandated to allow restricted competition and to regulate air licensing and tariffs. It announced on March 27, 1967, that acting on Wheatcroft's recommendations, Canadian

73

Pacific Airlines would be allowed to double its transcontinental service to two return flights a day, and Calgary, Edmonton, and Ottawa were to be added to its Vancouver, Winnipeg, Toronto, and Montreal transcontinental route. Pickersgill felt that the privileged status of the publicly owned Air Canada could withstand that.

The country's centennial year of 1967 was also the company's thirtieth anniversary of operations, and there were still twenty-five of the original seventy-one staff employed on its first day of operations. It was also the first year that the number of seat miles operated by Air Canada's jet aircraft exceeded that of turbine propeller aircraft. The Canada–U.S. air bilateral talks gave Air Canada its first U.S. continental route: Vancouver–Seattle, the inaugural DC-8 flight taking place on January 30, 1967. This was followed by the Montreal–Toronto–Los Angeles route. The company had been flying to Paris (1951), Düsseldorf (1952), Zürich and Brussels (1958), and Vienna (1959), but in 1966, just four years after the Cuban missile crisis, it became the first North American airline to inaugurate service to Moscow via Copenhagen.

This last provoked U.S. President Lyndon B. Johnson to write personally to Prime Minister Lester Pearson as Washington applied diplomatic pressure to prevent the signing of the bilateral air agreement between Canada and the Soviet Union establishing a regular air service between Montreal and Moscow. The president put forth a number of arguments as to why such a service would

increase communications between Moscow and Havana. The United States had just successfully prevented the countries of Guinea, Senegal, and Algeria from allowing Aeroflot landing rights. But the Canadian government, which had recently earned Washington's displeasure for selling wheat to China, did not back down.

The Soviets were about to showcase their industrial prowess at Expo 67's "Man and His World," the Montreal World's Fair, and were keen for an airline connection with North America. Responsible for bilateral negotiations concerning the company's new routes, Claude Taylor was sent to Moscow to negotiate the four flights weekly while Stephen Anderson, Air Canada's area manager in London, met with Aeroflot's director Paul N. Chulkov to arrange the inaugural flights. President McGregor was attending the IATA meeting in Mexico City and could not accompany the Canadian delegation going to Moscow. The inaugural flight, Montreal–Copenhagen–Moscow Flight 876, left Montreal on November 1, 1966, and with a refuelling stop in Copenhagen, landed at Moscow's Sheremetyevo International Airport on November 2. The Canadian delegation was led by Minister for Public Works George McIlraith, the former minister of transport. The airline hoped to bring Maurice "Rocket" Richard, who was known to the Soviets, as part of the delegation and have a friendly hockey match, but it was not to be. The only hiccup in this was that the Soviets refused to allow their interpreters to accompany their delegation, considering them of

On September 13, 1967, the first of the company's seven DC-8-61s arrived from Douglas Aircraft, Long Beach, California.

"lower echelon," and Air Canada had to find Russian speakers among its staff.

On November 4, the distinctive sounds of Kuznetsov engines with contra-rotating propellers were heard at Dorval Airport as the Aeroflot Tu-114 arrived from its 4,550-mile flight from Moscow. All were well aware that the airliner was the civilianized version of the Tu-95 strategic bomber. Air Canada charged $600 for a first class ticket, and as the only North American carrier flying to the Soviet Union (and later to Czechoslovakia on May 1, 1970) it earned the respect of the incoming Prime Minister Pierre Trudeau, who enjoyed unilateral detente. But although diplomats

from Ottawa, Washington, and the United Nations in New York took advantage of the connection, the Montreal–Moscow flight was never a moneymaker for the airline.

"Our Man (and Woman) in Moscow" was how Air Canada thought of its District Manager Vlad Slivitzky and his wife Tanya. The airline had to acquire the first apartment in its history for them. Since all accommodation in Moscow was administered by the state, Vlad had been fortunate to be quickly assigned one in the "foreign" section of the city. On the eighth floor in a building without elevator service, it was, by Canadian standards, tiny. The airline had hoped to get two adjoining suites and put them together, but even with government influence this proved impossible. The conversion of the Slivitzkys' major Canadian appliances to local current took weeks, and the television set, because of transmission difficulties, had to be a Soviet model. Because of the airline's stopover in Copenhagen, cupboards and furniture — including the kitchen sink — could be shipped from Denmark. Four long months after the apartment was taken, it was almost habitable — only the drapes had not arrived.

———

The first of Air Canada's seven long-body DC-8-61s touched down at Dorval Airport on September 13, 1967. Boeing had traditionally been a military aircraft manufacturer; even its 707 had begun life as a refuelling tanker for Strategic Air Command. The airliner builder from the DC-2 in 1936 onward was Donald Douglas. In 1965 Douglas sought to recapture the market that the Boeing 707 had usurped by stretching the basic DC-8 into the "Super Sixty" series. To add thirty-seven more feet to the fuselage, and thus increase passenger numbers from 189 to 259, the engineers at Douglas took advantage of the DC-8's wing sweep and its location on the fuselage that allowed the same jigs and landing gear to be used. When Boeing tried to stretch the basic 707 design, it found that its tail would scrape the runway every time it took off. Douglas had won this round. But Boeing had its proposal for the large military freighter competition available. When that

was won by Lockheed and its C-5A, the company civilianized this as the 747. That it could carry some 490 passengers meant the wide-body era had begun.

———

In preparation for the Canadian Centennial Year of 1967, the Air Canada's aircraft sported the national centennial sign with the Expo 67 "Man and His World" insignia, carrying them to all seventeen countries they visited. The architecture of Air Canada's participation at Expo 67 was intended to evoke the spirit of flight. The focal point

THE CO-PILOT

I am the co-pilot, I sit on the right,
It's up to me to be quick and bright.
I never talk back, for I have regrets,
But I have to remember what the Captain forgets.

I make out the plans and study the weather,
Pull up the gear and standby to feather,
Check the tanks and do the reporting,
And fly the old crate while the captain is courting.

I call for my Captain and buy him Cokes,
I always laugh at his corny jokes;
And once in a while when his landings are rusty,
I always come through with "By gosh, it's gusty."

All in all, I'm a general stooge
As I sit on the right of the man I call "Scrooge".
I guess you think that is past understanding,
But maybe some day he will give me a landing.

— Ken Murray, CCA

of the pavilion's exterior was a helical roof with twenty-three blades that fanned out from a sixty-foot central column. The design was meant to represent the turbine of a modern jet engine. Beneath the roof, three cylindrical "pods" contained the exhibition areas. The circular windows of Pod 1, "The Dream," showed Man's subconscious desire to fly throughout history and depicted "… the envy of earthbound man as he endeavoured to emulate winged creatures."

Pod 2 was "The Achievement," the second stage of "… his eventual breakthrough to achieve crude forms of propulsion through elementary aerodynamics." Here were Bell's kites, a balloon basket, the "Silver Dart," and a cockpit of a modern jetliner.

In Pod 3, visitors leaned over a circular balcony to watch *New Worlds* below, a four minute movie illustrating "… the impact of aviation as the jet age broke barriers and changed Man's concept of living" — all in keeping with Expo's theme. The Air Canada pavilion was so popular that when Expo 67 opened its doors to the public at 9:30 Friday morning, April 28, by 10:30 792 persons had already filed through the company's pavilion.

———

Montreal designer Michel Robichaud designed an avant-garde stewardess uniform that corresponded with the change of name and the dawn of the jet age. Manufactured by D'Allaird's, his charcoal-green wool suit, three button boxy jacket, hat with high crown (straw hat in the summer), black eight-button kid gloves, black

Designer Michel Robichaud shown making a minor adjustment to the angle of stewardess Denise Cantin's lapel. Watching is Billie Houseman, supervisor of flight service training and measurement.

calf shoes, and handbag (black leather boots were optional), topped off by the "lighting" design Air Canada badge on hat and pocket, remains sixty years later the ultimate fashion statement it was meant to be. On overseas Flights 870 and 871, a maroon, double-breasted, collarless, three-quarter-sleeve wool jacket was worn, and during beverage and meal service from 1965–68 a black-and-white patterned and ruffled "fantasy." In Canada's centennial summer, Air Canada flight attendants wore an all-weather coat of turquoise antron and cotton, turtleneck collar with company badge on a low crown, small brim hat, and ID pin on blouse tie.

———

As with all other Canadians, Air Canada employees celebrated the centenary with parties, picnics, and parades, one of the largest held in Winnipeg where it was tied to the opening of the Pan American games in the city. Selected by the City of St. James for their experience with past parades in the area were Chairman of the Parade R.F. Kirby (Ticket Sales Control) and H.A. Moody (Assistant Foreman, Metal, Viscount Maintenance). There were bands, clowns, floats with a Manitoba Indian princess, the theme depicting travel in the city led by authentic oxcart, followed by a 1903 Cadillac, a Piper Colt, and ending with a Black Brant rocket from the space research station.

Centennial celebrations also provided the impetus for many historical projects across the nation, one of which was preservation of the company's records. In March 1966 McGregor announced a study was to be initiated for preserving the company's historical resources. This would culminate in the signing of two agreements a year later between Air Canada, the Public Archives of Canada, and the National Museum of Canada. The resting place of the company's records were to be in new Public Archives building on Wellington Street in Ottawa and the TCA artifacts in the Science and Technology Museum, the former Morrison Lamothe

bakery on St. Laurent Boulevard. At the formal opening of the latter on November 15 the Honourable Judy LaMarsh, secretary of state, and Herb Seagrim, wearing the garb of an early aviator, were photographed beside a 1910 McDowell Bleriot. Bill Sadler, vice-president administrative services, and dominion archivist Dr. W. Kaye Lamb signed the agreement with Public Archives in May.

The only tragedy that marred that historic year was an air crash on May 22. On a training flight from Montreal, CF-TJM, a DC-8-54F, was attempting a "touch and go" at Ottawa airport when it rolled to the right and crashed inverted. The flight crew was trying a two-engine approach with two engines shut down on one side. They got the aircraft below the minimum speed for that condition, and when they increased the thrust on the two operable engines, the DC-8 yawed violently and rolled over on its back. A similar accident had occurred with Delta and the manouevre had been removed from the Douglas-approved training schedule — but had not yet caught up with Air Canada. It was the same DC-8 that had ploughed into a Heathrow cabbage patch in 1963. There were no survivors among the crew of three.

———

Air Canada gave Boeing a letter of intent in July 1968 to purchase three 747-133s for delivery in 1971. When the first "jumbo jet" was rolled out of the Boeing assembly plant at Everett, Washington, on September 30, 1968, on hand were several thousand airline representatives, news media, and government officials. Representing Air Canada were Executive Vice-President Herb Seagrim, Regional Operations Manager Kelly Edmison, and Manager of Aircraft Contracts Ken Rutledge. But standing alongside the twenty-five other stewardesses representing the buyer airlines was Vancouver-based stewardess Judi Robertson. Women broke bottles of champagne along the aircraft's nose. The PR handout said that the 747 was expected to enter service with Pan American Airways in 1969, "the 368 passenger jet to feature five double-width boarding doors on each side of the fuselage and two wide aisles running the length of the cabin. Lavatories and galley complexes were going to divide the cabin into five separate sections. An upper-level compartment behind the flight deck, reached by a spiral staircase, will offer opportunity for a lounge. The four Pratt & Whitney JT9D turbofan engines each rated at 43,500 lbs of thrust will make it the fastest jetliner in the world, with a 625 mph cruise speed."

Seagrim summed it up: "Quite apart from sheer size, I can't help but be impressed with the airplane's functional qualities, all of which remain comfortably within the known state of the art but promise to provide safety, comfort and reliability beyond the fondest dreams of our passengers."

Lockheed and Douglas both announced in 1966 that they would build "mini-jumbos" or tri-jets, the wide-body DC-10 and the L-1011 respectively for the short/medium-haul market. The three-engine configuration

had been influenced by U.S. airlines that wanted optimum payload/range performance on the Chicago–Los Angeles route coupled with the ability to take off from short runways with full payload. In 1968, Dave Tennant took a team from Air Canada to Burbank and Long Beach to see both of the aircraft. The DC-10 would have an added advantage in that its wings would be built at Downsview, employing Canadians.

The L-1011-100 was superior to the DC-10-10 for several reasons but especially because of its Rolls-Royce RB211 engines — and Air Canada had a lot of experience with engines made by the British company. On November 28, 1968, Herb Seagrim, Norm MacMillan, the acting president of Air Canada, Clayton Glenn, and Yves Pratte, the new chairman and CEO, went to Ottawa to meet with the minister without portfolio, James Richardson, and inform him of the decision. It was explained that the L-1011 was a better choice and that Air Canada was going to buy ten (six for delivery in 1972, three in 1973, and one in 1974). Richardson thought that Air Canada should buy some of each aircraft.

———

Air Jamaica had been started up on a trial basis managed by that island's government in 1966. When Air Canada was approached for technical help in 1968, encouraged by Ottawa, the board of directors appointed a six-man management team from Air Canada that included Managing Director John McGill, A.E. (Ozzie) Candy, Doug

Clifford, Captain E. Ralph Leek, Guillermo G. Machado, Tom De Wolfe, and Michael Lazarus to run the new airline "Air Jamaica (1968)." Using DC-8s, Air Jamaica began scheduled services on April 1, 1969, to New York and Montreal. As the airline's debts grew, in 1975 Air Canada purchased 26 percent of its assets, relinquishing them to the Jamaican government in 1977. In 1968, the Department of External Affairs asked Air Canada to "make recommendations concerning the operation and administration" of Air Congo with the intent of providing support, and the following year the Canadian International Development Agency asked for a survey on Guyana Airways. The airline sent missions to both countries and made recommendations, but nothing further developed.

By 1968, Gordon McGregor was past retirement age and looking forward to leaving the company and travelling the world with his wife. Twice he had broached the subject of retirement with the board of directors but had been asked to remain on. Fearing that a political appointee would replace him, he had groomed Herb Seagrim, the airline's executive vice-president with thirty-five years experience in commercial aviation, for his job. But on meeting Seagrim, Pickersgill thought he was too close to McGregor in outlook and turned down the appointment. Clive Baxter of the *Financial Post* wrote that if Air Canada employees had their choice it would be Herb Seagrim, but the government thought there was a need for "adventurous management from an outsider." This meant

that it was going to be a political appointee, and expecting the worst, employee morale at the airline plummeted.

The Pearson government's indecisiveness in choosing McGregor's successor followed on the heels of its dithering over who would replace J. Alphonse Ouimet, the president of the Canadian Broadcasting Commission (CBC). By cancelling the controversial television program *This Hour Has Seven Days* (1964–66), Ouimet, who was revered in Quebec as the "Father of Television," had run afoul of the Toronto CBC producers responsible for the program and for English language media. A parliamentary enquiry ensued, and in 1967 Ouimet was retired to run Telesat Canada. The government did not want to repeat this with Air Canada.

Pearson himself retired from politics in April 1968 and Gordon McGregor followed on May 31, gallantly saying, "Change of identity in the chief executive in industry was healthy and desirable." CNR president Norman MacMillan was appointed the airline's interim president and the decision to choose McGregor's successor was left to the new government.

McGregor became chairman of Orenda Ltd. and a director of Hawker Siddeley Canada Ltd. Many of the "Class of '37" left with him. The Canada they had known where the government worked hand in glove with the official airline no longer existed. Sadly, his retirement was short-lived and he died on March 8, 1971. His rival, Grant McConachie, had suffered a heart attack and died on June 29, 1965, and at his funeral McGregor had been one of the pallbearers.

One by one, the aviation pioneers who had begun their airlines, Eddie Rickenbacker (Eastern Airlines), C.R. Smith (American Airlines), Juan Trippe (Pan American), Howard Hughes (Trans World Airlines), relinquished the cockpit, leaving the field to bankers, lawyers, and accountants.

Through the winter of 1968 charismatic Minister of Justice Pierre Elliott Trudeau emerged as a strong candidate for the leadership in the Liberal Party, winning unexpectedly at the convention and becoming prime minister on April 20. In the federal election held that summer, Trudeau toured the country in one of the new Air Canada DC-9s while the Progressive Conservative candidate, Robert Stanfield, was lumbered with a Maritime Central Airways DC-6 — a lesson not lost on future leadership races.

———

In response to complaints from residents on the west side of Montreal Island that the noisy Boeing 707s landing at Dorval International Airport were making life untenable, the Department of Transport was looking to relocate Montreal airport to what would be a "hub," long before the term became fashionable twenty years later. After the marvels seen at Expo (where the Concorde was featured in the British pavilion), it was only a matter of time before supersonic aircraft would dock at a "port" away from the city, enabling passengers to reach other cities by smaller "transporters." The Concorde and the SST were sure to be noisier (no one knew for sure) and

several cities like London (Maplin), Miami (Everglades), Los Angeles (Palmdale), and Copenhagen (Satholm) were also considering or building their own rural "hubs."

The new prime minister seemed incapable of doing wrong, and when on June 16, 1969, he leapt out of a helicopter onto a field north of Montreal, the local mayor of Sainte-Scholastique praised him as a magician who was going to rearrange the rural landscape into a "jetport" similar to that being built at Dallas–Fort Worth, Texas. Trudeau labelled the airport "a project for the 21st century" and no one could disagree. Montreal had just held Expo 67, built a subway, the Décarie Expressway, and skyscrapers. It was only fitting that the city have a $1 billion airport that was revolutionary in its design, with a railroad station in its basement and a road tunnel under the runways to take drivers right to its international terminal. Even as an Air Canada DC-9 flew over, Trudeau spoke to the cheering crowd from the top of an Air Canada loading platform of his vision of building a North American hub on this spot by 1974.

Pickersgill and his successor, Paul Hellyer, had worked on a regional airline policy, but it was Don Jamieson, later given the transport portfolio, who announced it. The government established its regional airline policy in 1969, allocating various parts of the country to Quebecair, Eastern Provincial Airlines (EPA), Transair, and Nordair. Designated the carrier for western Quebec, eastern, and southern Ontario and the eastern Arctic, Nordair continued attempts to break into the southern market and compete with Air Canada, even beginning negotiations to merge with Quebecair and EPA.

It was left to Paul Hellyer in the new government to select who would run Air Canada and perhaps take it out of the CN empire. Previously Pearson's defence minister, Hellyer had rammed through the unification of the Canadian armed forces, causing mass demoralization and early retirement of several members of senior staff. He had the Winnipeg mining financier R.L. McIsaac, already a director on the Air Canada board, in mind for the position. Others the media considered frontrunners were former Rhodes Scholar John Baldwin, the present deputy minister of transport, once considered for the presidency of new Canadian Transport Commission until Jack Pickersgill grabbed it instead. The trouble was that Pickersgill saw no difference between being minister of transport or president of the CTC — a cause of problems with future ministers of transport.

The young minister of national revenue, Edgar Benson, was another candidate, but the prime minister feared criticism of patronage if he moved Benson over. Appointing the president of Nordair, R.G. Lefrancois, would be a good political move; he was French Canadian and already based in Montreal, but James Tooley, the airline's new owner, was reluctant to see him leave. Tooley hoped to make Nordair the "flag carrier" for the province of Quebec, an ambition that many in Ottawa watched with interest with the emerging regional

airline policy. Lucien Saulnier, Montreal's executive committee chairman and the fiscal responsibility behind Mayor Jean Drapeau's grandiose schemes, was another promising candidate. English Canada was backing Air Vice-Marshal Frederick "Flat Top" Carpenter, who had run Air Transport Command, where the RCAF's logistics on UN missions had earned him high praise. Carpenter, now commandant of the National Defence College in Kingston, was one of Hellyer's unification campaign causalities — and hardly the minister's choice. There were even calls in the House that Judy LaMarsh, the former secretary of state who had presided over the Centennial Year celebrations and who had retired from politics in April 1968, be made the airline's president. It had been her suggestion that the airline's name be changed to Air Canada. Two dark horses were Quebec City lawyer Yves Pratte and Montreal businessman Gerard Plourde.

Trudeau then appointed the Winnipeg Member of Parliament James Richardson (whose father had founded Canadian Airways) as the minister without portfolio to preside over a Special Cabinet Study concerning Air Canada. Its mandate was to search for ways of making the airline independent of the CNR and rebuild corporate morale, but most importantly, to make it attractive to investors. All knew that the era of the "jumbo" jets, to say nothing of the supersonic airliners, was just over the horizon, and the Crown corporation would soon require millions of dollars in funding.

CHAPTER THREE

YVES PRATTE AND THE AUGEAN STABLES

The Empire Club of Canada had seen some of the country's most distinguished aviators address its luncheon meetings at the Royal York Hotel in Toronto. Alexander Graham Bell (1917), Air Marshal William "Billy" Bishop (1940), Gordon McGregor (1949), and Max Ward (1973), all had told of their endeavours and hopes for aviation.

At the luncheon on January 31, 1974, the club's president, Robert L. Armstrong, introduced the chief executive officer of Air Canada.

Today we are privileged to have as our guest of honour Yves Pratte, Q.C., the Senior Officer of Air Canada. Mr. Pratte is a native of Quebec City and at the age of nineteen received a Bachelor of Arts degree from College Garnier in that city. Three years later he was granted a law degree "summa cum laude" from Laval University, following which he attended the University of Toronto and took postgraduate studies in Taxation and Corporate Law. He was admitted to the Quebec Bar and became a member of the law firm of St. Laurent, Taschereau, Noel and Pratte in 1948. These are names of great significance in our Canadian history. From 1954 to 1968, Mr. Pratte was senior partner in the firm, Pratte, Cote, Tremblay, Beauvais, Bouchard, Garneau and Truchon, and if I may be pardoned this observation, a partnership unlikely to be accused of being overtly anglophile. In 1968, he was honoured by Laval University, being named

Professor Emeritus. Mr. Pratte served as special Legal Counsel for Quebec Premier Jean Lesage and the late Premier Daniel Johnson, and was a member of the Federal Royal Commission on Security from 1966 to 1968. Mr. Yves Pratte, one of Her Majesty's Counsel, learned in the law, was appointed Chairman and Chief Executive Officer of Air Canada in December, 1968. He will address us on the subject "Air Canada-Challenges and Outlook."

After six years with the airline, if anyone knew about challenges, it was Yves Pratte. But he could have had no idea that his days with Air Canada were already numbered. Probably the furthest from his mind as he stepped up to the podium was a casual remark by a board member who had just returned from Barbados and heard something about the airline owning villas there.

The choice of Yves Pratte for the position of chairman of the board and chief executive officer of Air Canada was Trudeau's alone. Before the appointment the two had never met, contrary to popular belief. As late as November 1968, even as the opposition hammered him in the House about naming McGregor's successor, the prime minister was considering Lucien Saulnier for the position. The pair met several times but it was rumoured couldn't agree on terms of reference. Then on November 22, 1968, the *Ottawa Citizen* reported that talks between Saulnier and Trudeau had

broken off and that the post would go to Yves Pratte. In November 1978, former minister of transport and Trudeau confidante Jean Marchand admitted, "We knew that he [Pratte] didn't know anything about airlines but we wanted a French Canadian involved." The Air Canada board officially announced on November 26 that the Quebec City lawyer had been chosen for the new position of chairman of the board and John Baldwin, the deputy minister of transport, as president.

This last was seen as a shrewd move on the prime minister's part. If anyone knew how to keep the balance between the public and private sectors, it was Baldwin. The Rhodes Scholar and former diplomat had been chairman of the Air Transport Board from 1949 to 1968. As deputy minister of transport he had advised Hees on the Canadian Pacific bid for transcontinental routes in 1958. The archetypal mandarin, Baldwin was a perfect mentor for the neophyte Pratte and was expected to handle the day-to-day running of the company. He told the story of meeting Howe sitting on the steps of Parliament's Centre Block after he had lost his seat, and Howe saying to him, "John, take care of TCA."

————

Pratte and Baldwin were at the controls of the world's fifth largest airline, with 16,656 men and women on the payroll and 107 aircraft (twenty-seven DC-8s, thirty DC-9s, seventeen Vickers Vanguards, and thirty-three Vickers Viscounts). Three Boeing 747s were expected between March and June

1971, and on order to be delivered between February 1972 and February 1974 were ten Lockheed L-1011s TriStars. As for the Supersonic Transports (SSTs), the airline was holding four line positions on the Anglo-French Concorde and six positions on the Boeing 2707. With the imminent arrival of these fleet additions, it should have been the best of times for Air Canada.

At the dawn of the 1970s, despite a sluggish economy, Air Canada was about to reap the productivity benefits of converting its remaining propeller fleet to an all-jet one. The decreased use of its Viscount and Vanguard turbo-prop aircraft, which in terms of maintenance were substantially more expensive to operate than the DC-9s replacing them, would result in cost savings and more convenient schedule changes. The Vanguards ended passenger service in October 1971, the freight version a year later. As popular as the Viscounts were with passengers, what was ending their usefulness with Air Canada was economics; by 1965 they were already too small for the high-density intercity routes and didn't have the range for the longer ones. Both turboprop airliners were replaced with eight DC-9-15s bought from Continental Airlines.

The nimble little aircraft also seemed to be approaching the end of its days. Viscount CF-THK had just taken off from Sept-Îles, Quebec on April 7, 1969, when a fire in the landing gear spread to the No. 1 engine nacelle and the pilot returned to the airport for an emergency landing. Of the seventeen passengers on board, one collapsed and died. It was the only fatality that TCA/ Air Canada had with the thirty Viscounts bought in 1954–55. When the last two Air Canada Viscount flights landed in Toronto and Montreal on April 27, 1974, it was as if the Gordon McGregor era closed forever. Two Viscounts were donated to the National Aviation Museum in Ottawa (CF-THI) and the Western Canada Aviation Museum in Winnipeg (CF-THS), while the remainder was stored at Winnipeg until gradually sold off, some crossing the Atlantic Ocean once more. In 1978, two British companies, Aldair and Field Services Aviation, which specialized in refurbishing Viscounts, bought eight and they were flown to East Midlands Airport. Here four were repainted in the red and white livery of Zaire Aero Services and flown to Kinshasa. That airline lasted three years, and as late as 1995 the hulks of the ex-Air Canada Viscounts could be seen at the edge of Kinshasa Airport.

Well underway by 1970 was construction on the engine test cell at Dorval Airport designed to meet the company's requirements until the 1980s. The two rectangular buildings on the north side of the base access road were being built to test the Pratt & Whitney JT9 for the expected Boeing 747s and the Rolls-Royce RB211 for the Lockheed L-1011s. There were also had provisions for future testing of the Rolls-Royce Olympus to be fitted to the Air Canada Concorde SST as well as the GE-4 of its Boeing 2717 SST. And in case the airline's future aircraft needed it, the cell also had the capability of testing supersonic engines equipped with afterburners, which provide extra power for

85

takeoff or acceleration from subsonic to supersonic speeds.

———

It was a coming-of-age ritual for baby boomers in the late 1960s. This was the first generation in history that did not have to go off to war as their parents and grandparents had. Yet many of the eighteen- to twenty-five-year-olds ended up in Europe anyway, taking a summer (or a year) off to hitchhike about. Flying across the Atlantic Ocean by the cheapest means possible became a priority. Previously confined to the military, sports teams, and ethnic and religious groups, the charter industry was still unregulated by the government, and as a consequence was booming. Aircraft filled with youth and highly suspect "clubs" were bound for Europe and the Caribbean. Besides being the country's largest scheduled carrier, Air Canada also found itself the second largest Canadian charter airline, in 1969 holding 12 percent of the market and with 71,270 passengers, mainly on the Toronto–London route. Upstart charter carrier Wardair was the largest with 95,671 passengers and 16.3 percent of the market. At charter prices, Max Ward's airline gave exemplary cabin service that compared with first class in Air Canada but at less than economy class prices. Canadians across the country were being seduced by ads that simply said: "Holidays by Wardair" while the Air Canada ad running at the same time, "We've Got a Lot Going for You," was seen as confusing. In September 1972, Air Canada tried to buy a 1/3

interest in Wardair to get their service and charter expertise, but the deal collapsed.

Handsome and meticulously dressed, Pratte reminded people of a young Orson Welles. He took command by first acquainting himself with Air Canada. His verdict of the first few months while he was feeling his way, he told the *Globe and Mail*, was "Rough, rough, rough. It was rough for the officers of the corporation. They had to get used to me. They were very kind." His initial impression of Air Canada was of a rank and file devoted to the airline and its sacred mission of joining the country together, but (he felt) this had led them into believing that they were "all virtuous."

"Large companies, like large people," he would write, "tend to develop cardiac conditions. They suffer a certain hardening of the arteries that restricts the flow of growth-producing blood." Accustomed to a cast-iron protected monopoly on the country's most lucrative routes, Air Canada had little interest in marketing itself effectively or fostering good customer relations. And Pratte took it upon himself to change that.

If anything demonstrated the shift in culture, it was the 1969 company Christmas party, when both Pratte and Baldwin blew out candles on a huge cake topped with icing that spelled "Going Places." The pair was then presented with epaulettes, while those employees who were bilingual sang: "*Ils ont gagné leurs épaulettes*" — literally translated as "They have won their spurs." When the Official Languages Act became law on September 9, 1969, the airline was made legally liable to provide service in both

YVES PRATTE AND THE AUGEAN STABLES

official languages. This was closely watched by Keith Spicer, the official languages commissioner, who focused on the airline as a "test bed," and the unions that ensured their unilingual members not be made surplus at various stations by the federal language act.

Pratte tackled the thorny question of bilingualism in 1970 by choosing the Ottawa Air Canada station to implement a fully bilingual policy, especially with the counter staff. Because it served Gatineau–Hull as well as Ottawa, Uplands Airport, where only fifty-six of 125 Air Canada staff were bilingual, had been at the centre of several complaints. The new president wanted it to be a fully bilingual showcase and moved to implement the language policy at the station, but when some of the agents wanted to take French language training, management refused to pay. And while CALEA was in favour of increasing bilingual staff at Ottawa, it did not want this to occur at the expense of the unilingual employees. A joint management/CALEA language committee was set up in 1971 to help in the implementation of language rights requirements. As for French use within the company, Air Canada agreed that French might be spoken but the technical language was to remain English — and it was the only language on the flight deck.

As the heady 1960s ended, the expansion of commercial aviation was slowing down, and not only in Canada. The major United States trunk carriers' growth in terms of passenger miles in 1970 was 5.5 percent compared with 9.7 percent in 1969 and 14.8 percent in 1968. And

although its traffic volume grew by 16 percent in 1970, when Air Canada had carried more passengers, freight, and mail than at any other point in its thirty-three-year history, it suffered a net loss of $1,072,000 (down from a net profit of $1,548,000 in 1969) when it had shut down for a month because of a strike by the machinists.

Much more serious for the airline were the strikes. Throughout 1969–70, there were strikes or impending strikes across the country: post office workers, longshoremen on the west coast, the entire Montreal police force, Inco steel workers in Sudbury, and airport personnel across Ontario, all of which kept Labour Minister Bryce Mackasey busy. In late April 1969, in the airline's second nationwide strike within two years, 6,350 Air Canada machinists and service employees, all members of International Association of Machinists & Aerospace Workers (IAMAW) District 148, went on strike. The issue was wage parity with U.S. airline employees and a paid lunch period, an additional paid holiday, fully paid group insurance, improved vacation benefits, and higher shift premiums. In 1969, an Air Canada machinist got seventeen cents per hour less than his counterpart on a U.S. airline. The union demanded a 20 percent increase in a one-year contract, and Pratte offered 23 percent over three years or 8 percent for the first year. This was rejected by 3,333 to 1,116 in a membership vote, and on April 20 when the machinists went on strike, the airline was shut down.

Prime Minister Trudeau, who had just brought in voluntary wage hike guidelines of 6 percent to 7 percent annually, termed the company offer "generous" and stated that he was opposed to wage parity for Canadian workers. IAMAW rank and file declared that Trudeau had placed himself clearly on the side of management and pointed out that Air Canada had similar fare structures and used the same type of aircraft as its U.S. counterparts, and that the airline had made an $8 million profit in 1968. It took thirty days of negotiations and grounded aircraft for the machinists to settle for 8 percent annually. By then the company had lost $40 million, and although CPA (CP Air) tried hard to pick up the slack, the absence of any alternative airline comparable to Air Canada, especially domestically, demonstrated to the public and the government the need for competition.

Having alienated the rank and file, Pratte tackled the sacred legacy of the McGregor era. In an increasingly competitive market, the old TCA philosophy of running a break-even operation, he said, was no longer valid and the Quebec City lawyer aimed to make the airline profitable.

He could not help but notice, he said, that there was a lot of confusion in the corporate structure at headquarters, where responsibilities were ill defined and little empires had proliferated. The chairman announced on February 5, 1970, that the major reorganization of Air Canada's corporate structure would begin. The news spread across the company on Friday, February 6, which Air Canada staff henceforth referred to as "Black Friday," just as Avro employees did when the Arrow was cancelled. Setting

out to clean up the Augean stables, he was quick to caution: "The fact that we are today embarking on a major reorganization in no way suggests a vote of non-confidence for past achievements. There will be more room than ever in Air Canada for all the virtues that have served us so well in the past."

In words that would return to haunt him, Pratte admitted, "I had no orders from the government on this, but as soon as I took over and talked to the senior executives of the airline I realized that changes had to be made ... we needed expertise. So I set out to find it." He contracted with the Chicago management consultant company McKinsey & Co. for that expertise. "I wanted a Canadian company but then I read how McKinsey had made over Shell, Alitalia, Air France, and KLM. They looked like they had what we needed."

The McKinsey consultants moved into the airline's Place Ville Marie offices and began by preparing a detailed comparison between Air Canada and eleven major U.S. airlines. Initial reports only demonstrated what customers had been saying for years: that when it came to technical expertise Air Canada was second to none, but when it came to public relations and dealing with passengers, it trailed last. In contrast to Wardair and CP Air, Air Canada's counter staff and cabin crew were seen to be surly, uncaring, and curmudgeonly, having adopted the worst traits of a government department.

A detailed questionnaire was prepared and sent to 2,000 of the top airline staff. It was made clear to them that only the over-

President J.R. Baldwin, chairman, CEO Yves Pratte, and Executive Vice-President Herb Seagrim shake hands, belying the tension between them. McGregor had groomed Seagrim for Pratte's job.

all results would be made public and the remainder would be confidential. "Frankly," said Pratte, "I was surprised how deep the concern over Air Canada's future was." The results of the questionnaire confirmed his deepest fears — marketing was bad but interdepartmental communication was worse. Senior staff was seen as "autocratic," headquarters was cut off from employees at the airport, and the personnel department was thought to be unconcerned.

Following McKinsey's recommendations, three task forces were set up for improving communication with the public, creating a customer oriented company, and determining best use of human resources. Each of the task forces were subdivided into project teams, and all reported to Pratte, Baldwin, and Dave Tennant, vice-president of operations. A "war room," a large, open space, was set up surrounded by conference rooms that were covered with wall charts to plot progress each team made. Meetings, presentations, consultations on the findings of those presentations, reams of paper and gallons of coffee characterized the months from February to the May 1 deadline. "In more than twenty years as a consultant, mainly in the reorganization of major corporations," admitted J.O. Tombs, the McKinsey managing director, "I have never seen the activation of a new organization more efficiently carried out than at Air Canada."

"It was an incredible period," Pratte later recalled, "those teams worked from 8:00 a.m. to midnight, weekends included. But bit by bit we put the new structure together — and we had it ready for the May 1 deadline I had set."

The shake-up of the reorganization made many in the airline reconsider their careers. Claude Taylor got an attractive offer from a company in California. "I didn't know whether I would survive or not — none of us did. So I took my family and went down to California. But it was right at the height of the Vietnam mess, my son Peter was sixteen at the time and it looked as if he'd be serving in the U.S. Army. If that hadn't been a factor I'm not too sure I wouldn't have gone." Taylor returned to be put in charge of government and industry affairs, becoming Air Canada's ambassador abroad, and in the increasingly alien world of Ottawa.

Those who did not remain to witness Pratte's master plan were the last of the "Class of '37," the original TCA members who had begun their careers when Herbert Symington was in Pratte's job. First Vice-President Herb Seagrim, who McGregor had groomed to succeed him, retired in March. At Seagrim's retirement dinner held at the Queen Elizabeth Hotel, Pratte paid tribute to the man who many in the room thought should have had his job. "We are very sorry that Mr. Seagrim is leaving the company," he said. "I am per-

sonally very grateful to him for his valuable counsel and guidance during my first year in office, which was indeed a difficult one." To great applause, former president Gordon McGregor took the microphone and delighted the audience in his inimitable manner when he spoke about Herb's contributions to TCA and Air Canada. Seagrim was known to be a pilot's pilot and up to his last day with the company that he had helped create, he was the only airline vice-president checked out to line pilot standing on large jet aircraft.

Through the summer others left. W.S. (Bill) Harvey, the vice-president of finance, who had joined in the accounting department in 1937, retired to work for IATA as director general, finance and administration. R.C. Baudru, assistant to the first vice-president, Montreal, retired in June. He had joined on December 1, 1937 as a clerk and in his spare time began typing and mimeographing the first company newsletter, *TCA News* (later *Between Ourselves*) filling it with "company and national news, local gossip, bad poetry with a few statistics thrown in." The company's senior executive in the Atlantic provinces, Walt Fowler, also retired in July. One of the pioneers of Canadian aviation, Fowler had begun his career with Canadian Airways in 1928, flying the first Montreal–Toronto airmails and the first Montreal–Moncton airmail. Rod MacInnes also left in September. He had been a reporter on the airline's first transcontinental flight and then joined its public relations department.

The Univac-based ReserVec II introduced at the end of 1970 allowed for individual computer terminals instead of the punched-card systems.

Even as the original members retired, a new generation with different skills entered the company workforce. The faithful Reser-Vec had been running all of Air Canada's reservations for a decade, with an average downtime of only 120 seconds a year. Once designed for a daily 60,000 transactions, by 1970 it was processing over 600,000. It was replaced at the end of 1970 by a new Univac-based system called ReserVec II, which allowed for individual computer terminals instead of the punched-card systems.

Vice-president, computer and systems services Pierre Jeanniot appointed E.G. Ashton, J.M. Grossman, Norm Stoddart, Jack Maloney, and Anne Bodnarchuk to the designing, programming, and mainte-nance of the ReserVec II computer equip-ment. Bodnarchuk had joined the airline in 1959 in the maintenance department and in 1968 was appointed mathematical statistician and senior operational research designer. As the director, computer plan-ning systems, she was now responsible for integrating all corporate requirements for computer and communications facilities, including evaluating all "hardware and software packages."

COMPLAINTS AND COMPLIMENTS

The other day I had the misfortune to fly on your Flight # 957 Montreal–Toronto. I selected this flight as I knew that I would not have time for lunch on my arrival in Toronto. Much to my amazement, once we were airborne the Purser announced that due to expected turbulence, they would be withholding service throughout the flight. We did not encounter any turbulence — or lunch in Economy. But from where I was sitting I was able to observe First Class passengers enjoying both lunch and alcoholic refreshments. If Air Canada has designed a plane that permits turbulence only in Economy, then you have created an economic breakthrough....

I would like to register a complaint on my flight from Regina to Vancouver — Flt No. 943. I expected to get considerable work done but was greeted by three of the most charming stewardesses I have ever seen on any flight with any airline. The girls were not only very pretty and possessed pleasing personalities but they were attentive to all passengers. I enjoyed myself so thoroughly watching them throughout the flight that little work was done.

I would like to tell you that I sit on my patio by the pool and watch for our Air Canada DC-8 to come into Kingston Jamaica Airport every day. I enjoy watching her make a grand entrance as she flies directly above us. It makes me proud to be a Canadian, to have such a wonderful airline.

Dear Air Canada,
I really liked that trip our class had yesterday. It was the best trip we had this year. It was the first time I ever went up in a plane. After that experience I want to go up a lot more times. Thank you very much for the gum and candy. It was very comfortable.

This letter has been hastened by a rather unhappy encounter between a male passenger and a stewardess on Flt. 871. He expected rather extraordinary service considering that it appeared to be a full flight as his rudeness to your employee could not have been in the worst taste.

My wife and I recently had reservations on Air Canada for Bermuda. The itinerary was Ottawa–Toronto to connect with Flt 682 to Bermuda. At Ottawa Airport we were informed that because of the hour's delay in the Toronto flight we would miss our Bermuda connection. An alternative Ottawa–Montreal–New York flight was offered and taken but there was no possible way that our baggage could accompany us. As it transpired, four weary, disgusted people arrived in Bermuda for a holiday in heavy clothing, without even a toothbrush.

Bodnarchuk was a pioneer of her sex, her profession, and in the airline, as the findings of the Royal Commission on the Status of Women in Canada attested, published in September 1970 (aviation pioneer Elsie McGill was one of the committee members). The commission had been set up by then-Prime Minister Lester Pearson in 1967 to ascertain the status of women in Canada and what the federal government could do to ensure them equal opportunities with men. The commission discovered that even in 1970 there were some banks in Quebec that still required women to produce their marriage contracts when taking out loans in their own names, while others, wary of the possibility of legal complications, made it their policy to require husbands to sign. Ironically, although the feminist movement had come to Canada by then, CALFAA discovered that not all of its members were enthused. There were many stewardesses who did not want the responsibility of being in charge — especially over men. There were others who did not want to work under a woman. And there were still many who saw this as a temporary job before leaving to get married.

The McKinsey study revealed that the airline was weak in four areas: finance, personnel, marketing, and planning. The solution was a breaking down of empires and social structures and cross-fertilization, appointing vice-presidents from divisions other than the ones they would head. "The company's reorganisational pattern ... and the end we have in view is the building of a bigger and better Air Canada," the CEO would write in the February 1970 issue of *Between Ourselves*. The new organizational structure was designed, he continued, to satisfy five major requirements for the next decade:

- Upgrading marketing to make it "the competitive cutting edge of business."
- Dramatically improve the quality of customer service if we are to achieve the required levels of excellence.
- Strengthen all phases of planning to ensure that management attention is properly focused on improving overall economic performance.
- Maintain our high level of technical excellence.
- Strive to develop a stimulating and challenging internal environment that will help every employee develop his full potential.

As a result of the changes being implemented, "Morale," Pratte told the media, "is sky high. But," he cautioned, "we clearly have to do better in the marketing field." For that he recruited from the United States. In early May 1970 he got a call from a friend in New York about "the best possible man." He was a former executive vice-president of marketing at Johnson & Johnson and before that was at the ad agency of Young & Rubicam, at that time the highest-billing agency in the United States. On May 23, Pratte announced that he had filled the position of vice-president of marketing with Yves Menard, who would report directly to him. Menard was at the time counsel for Herdt & Charton Limitée, agents in Quebec for wine, fine foods, and toiletries. They had provided him with a car and generously allowed him continued use of it in his new job with Air Canada, and in return Menard continued as director of the firm. Although Pratte had asked that all executives of Air Canada on joining the company disclose their directorships, he was unaware that Menard was still employed by Herdt & Charton.

Somehow the scuttlebutt around the base was that the boss wanted to load Air Canada's top jobs with French Canadians, despite the fact that Pratte simultaneously appointed to vice-president status company veterans like W. Gordon Wood (government and industry affairs), J. "Lindy" Rood (flight operations), Dave Tennant (personnel), and J.W. Bill Norberg (maintenance).

———

At 8:00 a.m. on a bright sunny July 5, 1970, Flight 621, an Air Canada DC-8-63 CF-TIW on the Montreal–Toronto–Los Angeles route, was about to land in Malton, as Toronto International Airport was then known. The aircraft was almost brand new, having been delivered to the airline in April. Because it was going to Hollywood, Air Canada had marketed this as the "California Galaxy" flight. There were 100 passengers on board (twenty-two were Air Canada employees) with nine crew members. It was to pick up 127 more passengers at Malton, and because there was only one terminal at the airport, all were waiting at the boarding

gate and would have an unobstructed view of what was about to occur.

Captain Peter Hamilton had been a bomber pilot in the Second World War with 3,000 hours on DC-8s. He had flown before with First Officer (F/O) Donald Rowland, who had 5,500 hours on the same type of aircraft. They had an arrangement as to when the DC-8's spoilers should be armed. The captain held that they should be armed once the aircraft had touched down, while his F/O thought they should be armed during the flare. It was agreed that when the captain was flying the aircraft the F/O would arm the spoilers when the aircraft had touched down, and when the F/O was flying the captain would arm them on the flare, as his F/O wanted.

But on this approach on Runway 32, although the captain was piloting the landing, he asked for them on the flare. Sixty feet from the runway, Hamilton reduced power in preparation for the flare and told Rowland to deploy the spoilers. The F/O did so, but as the aircraft began to fall heavily, Hamilton pulled back on the control column and applied full thrust to all four engines. While the aircraft's nose lifted, it continued to "sink," hitting the runway with enough force that the No. 4 engine and pylon broke off.

The DC-8 managed to lift off, but the torn engine had taken part of the lower wing plating with it, exposing open fuel lines that ignited. Rowland radioed permission for a second attempt on the same runway but was told it was closed because of debris — from his own aircraft — and was directed to another. By then it was too late. What was left of the right wing exploded, to be followed by another explosion at No. 3 engine, which also fell off in flames. The DC-8 then went into a nosedive, smashing into the ground at high speed, killing instantly all 100 passengers and the nine crew members on board.

The crash had occurred in what was then Woodbridge (now Brampton), the plane digging a furrow eight to ten feet deep through the field, ending less than 200 feet from a home where a family of ten had been sleeping. The immediate cause of the crash was said to be premature spoiler deployment, and other airlines, especially Alitalia, would encounter similar problems with their DC-8s. Ten years later, on July 5, 1980, the results of the inquiry into the crash were made known. It blamed the captain for deviating from the prescribed landing routine because he had an intense distrust of the spoiler system, McDonnell Douglas for not putting some sort of guard on the spoiler lever, and Air Canada and the Department of Transport for accepting the system without adequate testing.

In separate services, mourning relatives, company personnel, and Montrealers would fill both Mary, Queen of the World Cathedral and St. James United Anglican Church to mourn the crash victims. In Los Angeles, an interdenominational service was held in the Westminster Chapel of the Emmanuel Presbyterian Church on Wilshire Boulevard. For what pitifully few remains there were, a mass burial service was held at Mount Pleasant Cemetery in Toronto that July.

This wasn't the last time that Toronto's Pearson Airport would be the scene of an Air Canada incident. On June 21, 1973, Air Canada DC-8-53 CF-TIJ, which was being refuelled for a scheduled flight to Zurich, caught fire and burned beyond repair. Fortunately, there were no casualities.

————

"To Whom It May Concern: A bomb has been installed this morning at one of the following places, either in an Air Canada plane, the Air Canada hangar or in the airport itself." It was Pratte's misfortune that the end of the sixties featured bomb threats, hijackings, and strikes. Delivered to his office one September morning in 1970 was an envelope containing three sheets of foolscap with the words cut out from a French-language newspaper. The extortion attempt stated that if $200,000 was not delivered to the men's washroom of Da Giovanni Restaurant at the corner of St-Hubert and Sainte-Catherine Streets, a bomb would go off at 3:15 p.m. somewhere on Air Canada property. Although the suspects were apprehended by 3:30 p.m. when they came to collect the money, the cancelled flights and overtime cost the company $24,700.

————

Claude Taylor, who had negotiated the Moscow flights, succeeded Wood to the position of vice-president, government and industry affairs, on November 1, 1970. Born in Salisbury, New Brunswick on May 20, 1925, one of Taylor's first summer jobs during the Second World War was bringing water to the construction crew building the Commonwealth Air Training Plan airfield near Moncton. He would also cycle twenty miles from his home to the municipal airport to watch the TCA Lodestars take off. While working on his chartered accountant's certificate he joined a small retail company in 1947. When his landlady heard from a bridge-playing friend that TCA was hiring, Taylor immediately applied for a job and was hired as a reservations agent on the night shift in 1949.

When he was transferred to Montreal, his ultimate ambition was to one day be the airline's chief accountant, and to achieve that he took McGill University's extension courses from 1950–53 in finance. In 1957, when Taylor emphasized sales strategy over "flying the flag" on operations, he came to the attention of Dave Tennant, the director of operations. Taylor was promoted steadily up the ranks, becoming general manager of commercial planning in 1962 and general manager, marketing services, two years later. He got to know Gordon McGregor well; one of his jobs was to carry the president's briefcase and accompany him to the annual parliamentary hearings in Ottawa. Interviewed for television years later, Taylor would say of McGregor: "He was our leader. We would have followed him into battle anywhere." (In 1980, when Taylor was awarded the RCAF Gordon McGregor Memorial trophy, he was deeply touched.)

The future Air Canada president would give an idea of his corporate philosophy in a presentation to the Saskatoon Board of Trade on October 25, 1973: "You might well ask why Air Canada as a Crown corporation should be concerned with the economic side. There are three main reasons: the first we are a Crown corporation — if we do not operate on the basis of sound business economics, then the financial burden would fall on all Canadian taxpayers, whether they use our services or not. The second is we must continually spend large amounts of money for new equipment, and we have to be financially sound to be able to attract that money. The third is that Canadians as owners of Air Canada have a right to expect that their airline is operated efficiently — and no one has devised a better yardstick than profit to determine whether a company is being operated efficiently."

———

In May 1970, Don Jamieson, the minister of transport, reiterated government policy concerning regional airlines and Air Canada. "I have no intention whatsoever of ensuring the survival of regional airlines at the expense of Air Canada," he told the House. "In other words, I do not believe there's any rationale in simply taking things away from Air Canada purely for the sake of giving them to another airline." But he added that the government was aware that none of the regional airlines would survive unless they had access to some major metropolitan point into which to channel local passengers. After a company study about which regional routes it could give up, Air Canada's Edmonton–Calgary–Lethbridge route was transferred to PWA, and the

CTC gave Transair permission to fly its Avro 748 between Winnipeg–Regina–Saskatoon–Prince Albert and a daily Boeing 737 flight between Winnipeg–Thunder Bay–Toronto. In the Maritimes, Eastern Provincial Airlines' daily Boeing 737 service replaced Air Canada's Vanguard on the Halifax–Stephenville–Gander–St. John's route.

Although primarily a defense contractor, Lockheed had been building commercial airliners since 1927, naming them after the stars. Its Lockheed 10 Electra, chosen by Amelia Earhart and Howard Hughes for their pioneering flights, was Trans-Canada Air Lines' first aircraft. In the 1940s TCA also bought Lockheed 14 Lodestars and in the 1950s possibly the most beautiful piston-engined aircraft ever built, the Lockheed 1049 Constellations. The sorry experience of the L-188 Electra somewhat dampened Lockheed's enthusiasm for building commercial airliners, something that the L-1011 promised to rectify. It could be said that the L-1011 owed its birth to Lockheed's winning of two military contracts: the C-5 and the P-3 Orion. The California branch of Lockheed had a design for a twin jet anti-submarine aircraft it could no longer use, and the Georgia branch was experienced with high-bypass turbofan engines.

When American Airlines needed a 250-seat wide-bodied airliner that could use the restricted airports at New York (LaGuardia) and Chicago (O'Hare and Midway) and also fly over water, the three-engine design was born and on March 29, 1968, Lockheed was able to launch the aircraft with 144 firm orders. The name "TriStar" was chosen through a contest held by Lockheed employees and won by Mrs. Marg Stewart, a stenographer who was given a $250 savings bond for doing so. The airliner's three Rolls-Royce RB211 engines were touted as the "good neighbour engine" because they were the quietest high-bypass engines ever designed.

And that was the aircraft's Achilles heel. Rolls-Royce had produced some exceptional engines over the years: the Merlin, the Nene, the Avon, the Dart, and Conway, but the RB211 for the L-1011 was entirely different. Their first high-bypass ratio engine, it was also the largest they had ever designed. In 1968, the same year that Lockheed gave it the contract to provide engines for the L-1011, Rolls-Royce pioneered the use of Hyfil and a lightweight carbon reinforced epoxy for the RB211. Since it was unproven, it deterred potential customers that preferred the General Electric and Pratt & Whitney engines of the DC-10. Sales of the TriStar were so sluggish that the manufacturer resorted to bribing Japanese government officials to influence All Nippon Airways to buy the aircraft. Lockheed was already in financial trouble because of the C-5A, but undeterred, it rolled out the first L-1011 in September 1970 and its first flight took place in November with the launch customers TWA and Eastern Air Lines expecting to have their TriStars for crew training by 1972.

Introduced in 1973, the Air Canada TriStar accommodated 257 passengers (thirty-two First Class, 225 Economy) and was to be used on the Company's Toronto–Miami and transcontinental routes.

In January 1971, when the Hyfil engine blades showed a propensity to disintegrate, Rolls replaced them with stronger titanium. This meant a weight increase, not only because of the fan blades themselves but also the containment structure around the fan to prevent the blades (in the case of an engine failure) from being flung out through the casing. To re-engine the RB211, Rolls needed a massive injection of funds. The British aero engine company was also becoming worried about indemnity against claims for late delivery of engines to Lockheed, which itself was facing millions of dollars in fines for not delivering the aircraft on time.

"There is a rule of thumb," explained Air Canada's Clayton Glenn, "that if an engine manufacturer spends say $500 million in developing an engine to the point where it receives its certificate of airworthiness, it will spend another $500 million during the lifetime of that engine making it reliable and acceptable to the airlines, from the operating cost point of view." Grasping at straws, Lockheed then asked both GE and Pratt & Whitney if they would re-engine the L-1011— but the first was already heavily engaged with the DC-10 and the other with the Boeing 747.

When the news broke on February 4, 1971, that Rolls-Royce had gone into receivership and terminated production of the RB211, Air Canada's decision to purchase the L-1011 instead of the DC-10 was questioned in the media and House of Commons. The airline had already advanced $30 million of taxpayers' dollars to Lockheed and Rolls-Royce for its ten L-1011s, and although Pratte said he could see little justification in supporting Rolls-Royce, he wondered how he was going to explain that to Parliament? But since eleven Canadian companies, including two in Winnipeg, Bristol Aerospace Ltd. and Coldstream Products of Canada Ltd., built components for the L-1011s, it helped soften the announcement.

Since the L-1011s had been slated for the Florida and Caribbean routes, the company scrambled to find the equivalent passenger capacity for the winter of 1972. Maintenance was contacted to overhaul and release DC-8s in the summer months and to consider refurbishing the Vanguards that were about to retire.

But the highly respected British aero engine manufacturer was not alone its death spiral. Accompanying it was Lockheed, a major American defence institution taking

with it a number of U.S. defence subcontractors — to say nothing of L-1011 customers like TWA, Delta, and Eastern Air Lines, all of whom had powerful friends in Washington. Anxious to save what was after all the very symbol of British aero engineering, on February 15, 1971 Her Majesty's government agreed to provide financing for the RB211 and in last minute negotiations, the Nixon administration (1972 was an election year) agreed to bail Lockheed out with a loan guarantee of $250 million.

To defuse the selection of British-built engines over American ones to power the TriStar, Lockheed and Rolls-Royce organized Air Holdings, a company that bought fifty L-1011s to resell to carriers in the Commonwealth like British Airways, Cathay Pacific, BWIA, and Air Canada. Being powered by Rolls-Royce engines put the TriStar at an advantage in the Commonwealth since its power plants were tax exempt. At $18.1 million each, the Air Canada TriStar was designed to accommodate 257 passengers (thirty-two first class, 225 economy) and was to be used on the Company's Toronto–Miami and transcontinental routes. "As easy to fly as a Piper Cub," said Air Canada Captain J.D. Gallagher.

The airline approached Lockheed with a request that some of its TriStars be altered to provide extended range capability to allow nonstop service between Edmonton and Prestwick–London and Toronto–Frankfurt. The transatlantic routes required an additional 820 miles and this meant an additional 19,000 pounds of fuel. Lockheed modified the L-1011s by adding two new centre section fuel tanks forward of the galley. The longer trips meant double the meals for the passengers, and the standard galleys were no longer large enough to prepare them. A galley was built into the lower deck, where, unseen by the passengers, a stewardess prepared the extra meals.

————

When Pan American Airways inaugurated its Boeing 747 service on January 21, 1970, Pratte had cabled Najeeb Halaby, Pan American's president, "Air Canada offers its congratulations on this historic occasion and looks forward to the day when these magnificent aircraft painted in our colours share the skies with yours." Rather than being built to carry a privileged few across the Atlantic at horrendous expense like the SSTs, the Boeing 747 promised air transport for millions.

"It was obvious," wrote Clayton Glenn, "that we would be in trouble on our Atlantic routes if we were not operating the Boeing 747. The Boeing 747's direct operating costs per available seat mile were lower than the DC-8-63 and substantially lower than the Boeing 707-320. The 747 had the prospect of being a very cheap form of air transportation, even at $23 million each — that is if a reasonable passenger load factor could be maintained." Giving Boeing a letter of intent in 1968 to purchase the three 747s meant that Air Canada would lag behind the other airlines in getting their 747s. By now (1970), Pan American World Airways, Trans World Airlines, BOAC, and Air France already had theirs in service.

This was not thought a problem. McGregor's dictum had always been that a small airline could not afford to be the guinea pig for a new aircraft, and Pratt & Whitney was experiencing deficiencies with their JT-9D engine that the 747s used. By the time Air Canada got its three in 1971, this would be overcome. The airline also had to prepare for the volume of passengers that the 747 would bring. Across Canada, as in many of the main airports in the United States, Europe, and Japan, terminal facilities were being built to handle the 747s. Loading bridges, specially constructed gates, passenger holding rooms, more check-in counters, had to be completed by January 1971 for the jumbos' arrival.

The first Boeing 747 that Air Canada employees actually saw belonged to Trans World Airlines, and when it visited Montreal in December, 1969, the company's flight service instructresses, Francine Poitras, Anna Johnson, Shirley Cormier, and Kay McIntyre were on hand to inspect it. The 747s galleys had been designed by cabin crews so everything was where it should be; trolleys could be put on board fully preloaded with food trays, glasses, and ice cubes. They climbed the spiral staircase leading up to the first class lounge and marvelled at the 42-inch wide doors that would allow for the first time two people to walk through. The former flight attendants knew that all would take getting used to. "With the Company's Boeing 747s and Lockheed Tri-Star will come luxury in air travel undreamed of a few years ago," promised the company brochure. Passengers would be "provided with the comfort of an easy chair, the elegance of a swank salon, and the service of a luxury liner."

The airline was engaged in preparing for its own jumbo jets, and depending on the route, there would be a "mixed" cabin crew from eight to thirteen plus a senior officer-in-charge. For the two new aircraft, simulator training for the captains, first and second officers would for the first time be in Canada, the TriStar simulator in Montreal and the 747 simulator in Toronto.

Resplendent in their all-white colour scheme with the red cheat line across the length of the fuselage, the first Air Canada 747s were nicknamed "Fat Albert" by the employees, after comedian Bill Cosby's childhood friend. The first class up front had thirty-two seats, economy (seating 333) was separated into four compartments each with a different colour, blue, gold, green, and brown, and the boarding passes were colour coded for easy identification. The first compartment had smoking but no

THE 747: BIG BY ANY STANDARDS

- A pilot sits at the same level in the cockpit of a 747 as he would if he sat on top of the tail of a DC-9.
- The tail section of a 747 is 63 feet 5 inches high, compared to the present-day Boeing 707 jet's 42 feet, 5 inches.
- The tractor required to tow the aircraft weights more than a fully loaded Vanguard (155,000 lbs vs. 146,000 lbs).
- To clean the pilot's windshield, a man must climb the equivalent of a three-storey building.
- Engine power is 2.5 times greater than a standard DC-8.
- The diameter of the engine intake is 8 feet 5 inches, which is approximately the same diameter of a DC-3.
- One wheel, tire, and brake assembly weighs 610 lbs.
- One section of the windshield weighs 152 lbs.
- Accommodations are provided for 16 cabin attendants that are equivalent to a full load including passengers and crew of a Lockheed 18.

- A man of average height can walk upright inside the main fuel tanks, and the fuel capacity (47,000 U.S. gallons) is sufficient to run the average family car for about 80 years.
- Compared to the single galley on a DC-9, the 747 has three: one forward, one amidships, and one aft.
- Double aisles — also cross aisles — will make it easier to operate the carts.
- The First Class section will accommodate 32 passengers and have its own galley plus two washrooms on the main deck and one in the upstairs lounge.
- The lounge accessible by a spiral staircase will seat 14 passengers of which 8 are certified for takeoff and landing.
- Seating of the four Economy Sections will be separated into groups of 41, 100, 78, and 144 for a total of 333 — and a grand total including First Class of 365.

— *Between Ourselves* Extra, January 1970

Proudly Canadian: Air Canada 747 cabin crew in Canada-red colours.

movies, the third had movies but no smoking. The second and fourth had both. In economy, passengers sat nine abreast: two seats on the right, four in the centre, and three on the left. It took two captains, one flight engineer, one flight service director, twelve stewardesses, and two pursers to run the aircraft in flight. The stewardesses loved the 747 since the larger crew meant they only had to handle thirty-five passengers each on a full load as opposed to forty on a DC-8. The passengers loved the armrests, which had a twelve-channel selector for movies or music in both French and English. Economy passengers paid $1.50 for an alcoholic drink and $2 for headphones. There was an open bar in first class up the winding staircase with seating for fourteen (you had

to return to your seat for meals), but no bar in the rear of the economy class as American Airlines 747s had; it would mean a loss of eighteen seats for the airline. In later years the 747s would be converted to all economy, seating 429 passengers, the airline sensitive to the term "cattle class." Four more 747s were bought in the 1970s, with two of them "Combis" able to carry ten pallets and 275 passengers.

The debut of Air Canada's 747s was not without drama. The inaugural flight to Malton Airport from Montreal on March 28, 1971, was something of an embarrassment. Filled with airline "brass" and scrutinized by local media, the aircraft nosed up to the ramp, but halted twenty feet from it with engines off. It had to be towed closer

On February 19, 1973, Yves Menard, Air Canada's vice-president of marketing, and Ernest Fletcher, president of Commonwealth Holiday Inns of Canada (holding pen) sign an agreement to provide passengers with hotel space in the Caribbean.

by tractor, and the Air Canada staff deplaned by the old fashioned stairs, not the air bridge. The inaugural flight to Frankfurt on July 5 was worse; on entering German airspace, the authorities refused it permission to land and the Air Canada jumbo had to use Paris instead. This was more the fault of the Department of External Affairs than the airline — or lack of communication between both. In C.D. Howe's day, given the range of postwar airliners, Gander and Goose Bay were vital refuelling stops for European airlines seeking to enter the American market.

With the new jets, landing at Toronto's Malton Airport was the one card that Canada had in bilateral air negotiations — and External Affairs knew it. Citing runway construction at Malton Airport and ongoing air negotiations with the United States as the reasons, the Trudeau government stonewalled all bilateral air negotiations while it worked to channel the European airlines to Montreal, and specifically to the new airport at Mirabel when it was completed. Lufthansa, Air France, Alitalia, SABENA Belgian Airlines, SAS, Swissair, and TAP Portuguese Airlines had all been refused access to Toronto and its multi-ethnic market. "If we allow Lufthansa," said a spokesman for External Affairs, "we open the flood gate for all."

Air Canada would put all three 747s into service between April 25 and July, the first on the Toronto–Vancouver run, the second on Toronto–London and the third on the Montreal-Paris run. Vice-President of Marketing Yves Menard told the media that the 365 passenger aircraft needed a load factor of 40.3 percent on the Toronto–London and 44.4 percent on the Montreal–Paris flights to be profitable, and that summer the average load on weekdays had been 65 percent and as high as 92 percent on weekends.

———

By Love Possessed starred Lana Turner and was the first movie shown on a scheduled flight when Trans World Airlines screened it to first class passengers in 1961. Ten years later, when the 8mm film cassette and individual headsets were developed, Air Canada showed its first in-flight movie on the new 747. It was *Dirty Dingus Magee* and starred Frank Sinatra. But the movie screens used were no ordinary ones. The works of Canadian contemporary artists were displayed on their backs so that when not in use the screens could be turned around and the art showcased at 39,000 feet.

But by 1971, every airline CEO who had ordered the Boeing SST watched nervously as first the growing American environmental lobby, then Congress, and finally Charles Lindbergh, who sat on the board of Pan American, came out against the SST. By the time the government cancelled all funding that year, Boeing, already mortgaged to the hilt because of the development, was pleased to drop the whole project. By then Air Canada had already commissioned a study on the feasibility of the Concorde. "During the period mid-1970 to 1972, the Concorde people were aware that we were becoming very cold towards their airplane," remembered Clayton Glenn, "and pressure was being put on our marketing department to take part in studies in which BAC/SUD hoped to convince Air Canada that it should stay in the program." With the U.S. SST cancelled, the airline did not want to get locked in to buying aircraft that it could not use. Glenn and Yves Menard presented the board of directors with recommendations why the airline should pull out:

That the airline did not believe a two-or three-hour saving of time would attract a sufficient number of economy passengers to justify a reasonable frequency between Canada and Europe.

First, that in the interests of overall economics, the airline wanted its passenger aircraft to also be suitable to carry a sufficient number of low-yield passengers and be capable of carrying a large cargo load.

Second, when this was presented at the board meeting, there was no debate on the company's withdrawal; perhaps there was, Glenn thinks "a little sigh of relief." On July 6, 1972, Pratte cancelled the Concorde. Had the Concorde and U.S. SST been proposed after the 1974 oil crisis, Glenn concludes neither would have gotten off the drawing boards. Had Air Canada taken delivery of the supersonic aircraft it had on order, representing an estimated 24 percent of its total seat mile production, the impact on the airline's total fuel cost after 1974 would have been prohibitive. But it was able to get its down payment back in full, and its pullout, followed by all other airlines, made no political ripples either in North America or Europe.

———

On November 12, 1971, when Air Canada DC-8 Flight 812 with 115 passengers took off from Calgary for Toronto, almost immediately after takeoff the passenger in seat 2B asked for a screwdriver drink. Paul Cini was a small time car thief who had been drinking heavily for weeks before planning the hijack. He went to the washroom and changed into a wig, a trench coat, a hooded mask, and stepped into the lounge.

Now carrying a sawn-off shotgun and a bomb that had been made of sixty sticks of dynamite, he attracted the attention of Purser John Arpin and Flight Attendant Mary Dohey. He said he was a member of the IRA, demanded $1.5 million and wanted to be flown to Ireland. Pointing the shotgun at Dohey, he told the crew to follow his instructions "or she was dead." He then ordered her to hold apart the fuse wires that would explode the dynamite if they met. Then his shotgun accidentally discharged towards the cockpit, showering debris over the area. He apologized to Mary, saying, "I'm sorry. I didn't mean to do that."

With great courage she replied, "I know you didn't, dear. Would you like me to hold your hand?" She asked his name and made small talk with him, so much so that Cini later testified he began to weep under his mask.

Told they would need a navigator to fly to Ireland, the hijacker agreed to allow the plane to land at Great Falls, Montana, until Air Canada could fly in a navigator. Once on the ground $50,000 was brought to Cini, and Dohey persuaded him to release some of the passengers and crew. He said she could leave as well but she refused, risking her life for the safety of others. The company had a navigator waiting for them in Regina, and the hijacker ordered Captain Vern Ehman to fly there. When the flight was airborne, Cini asked for his parachute that had been stowed under his seat and then attempted to bail out with the money. But when he put his gun down to strap on the parachute, Captain Ehman managed to kick the shotgun away and Assistant Purser Philipe Bonny hit him on the head with the fire axe as four men overpowered him. Cini was turned over to the authorities and served his sentence in the federal penitentiary in Prince Albert, B.C., where he suffered from severe depression. "I guess I wanted recognition," he later said when asked about the hijacking. "I guess I wanted to stand up and say 'Hey, I'm Paul Cini and I'm here and I exist.'"

For their courage and sheer professional cool, Mary Dohey was awarded the Cross of Valour, the highest Canadian civilian medal for bravery, and Captain Ehman the

Medal of Bravery. Through eight terrifying hours they had remained calm. As John Baldwin would later write: "All of us in the Company felt half an inch taller because of the job done by the flight and cabin crew."

Two weeks later, D.B. Cooper was more successful, parachuting out of the rear door of a Northwest Orient Boeing 727 with $200,000, eluding capture to this day. His disappearance led to a number of copycat hijackings to which Air Canada was not immune soon after.

Forty-two-year-old Captain Donald Glendinning had begun his career flying for Queen Charlotte Airlines before joining TCA. For him, Air Canada Flight 932 Thunder Bay–Toronto on December 26, 1971, was going to be a quick turnaround, and he looked forward to being home in Winnipeg with his family for a New Year's Eve party. But twenty minutes before the DC-9 landed at Toronto a young man handed the flight attendant a note and told her that "they" had guns and grenades on board. The note said: "Take me to the captain in the cockpit. We are going to Havana, Cuba. This is no joke." The eighty-three passengers were unaware that it was a hijacking and the plane landed on schedule at Toronto, where they disembarked. Then it was refuelled and flown to Havana with all six crew members on board. During the flight the hijacker joked with the stewardesses, talking to them about his zodiac sign, the FLQ crisis, and the Black Power movement in the United States. On arrival in Havana he was taken into custody by the Cuban authorities. Since the extradition treaty that Canada had with Cuba then did not include hijacking, there was nothing Ottawa could do. Since he was a U.S. citizen, the FBI was called in and took his prints off a soda can the hijacker had used, matching them with those of Patrick Dolan Critton, a former New York elementary school teacher. Critton had just bungled a bank robbery in New York and then fled across the border and ended up in Thunder Bay because of a snowstorm.

Thirty years later, after a Toronto detective Googled him, Critton was found living under his own name in Mount Vernon, New York, working with underprivileged youth. It was September 10, 2001, and even as the world was focused on another aviation tragedy the next day, Critton was extradited to Canada, where he pleaded guilty to extortion and the kidnapping of the Air Canada crew. He was sentenced to five years and was deported to the United States. Testifying at his trial was Captain Glendinning, now retired. The whole crew had displayed great coolness throughout the incident and the captain was given a set of gold Air Canada cuff links inscribed with the hijacking date. After this, governments around the world brought in security measures at airports, and in the United States, sky marshals.

———

The introduction of the Boeing 747s only highlighted the airline's treatment of stewardesses as second-class employees. Females were barred from holding the new in-charge positions that the jumbo jet afforded. "For the senior flight attendants, it was a tremendous insult," remembered one. "Many of these were university educated or trained nurses. The situation was made more difficult by the fact that the males in charge were usually junior, and often less experienced." The airline now employed 2,600 females and 400 males, but all the top jobs of purser and director were exclusively for males. "Acting purser" was the highest a female flight attendant could aspire to, and male pursers got the prized international flights. Remembered CALFAA chairman Frank Fabian, "Some of the younger men, especially those from Europe, didn't like taking orders from women."

Air Canada was hardly alone in this — in most occupations men were usually put in charge of women, regardless of age or ability. Bill C-206, an act to amend the Canada Labour Code and the Public Service Employment Act with respect to discrimination in employment based on age, sex, and marital status, received first reading in the House of Commons in May 1972. Although it did not receive second reading before the House adjourned using its recommendations, CALFAA drafted proposals for their negotiations with Air Canada regarding the separate male/female seniority lists that the airline used. After what could only be described as contentious negotiations, the two lists were integrated into one cabin personnel seniority list, effective May 1, 1974. With this, Air Canada eliminated job discrimination among its male and female cabin crew, and female flight attendants no longer had to quit if married or "over-

The maroon coat that Air Canada pursers had worn for first class meal services was replaced in March 1969 by a terylene "Galaxy Blue" light-weight *maître d' avion* jacket with blue piping.

weight." Gone too were the strict regulations for "make-up," and, said one former flight attendant, the sameness of the "Barbie doll smiles." "Now we could all be ourselves."

When the CALFAA membership did ratify the settlement, there were outcries from both sexes. In an unsuccessful bid to overturn this, the all-male Purser Club fought seniority integration by hiring legal counsel, and there were many female flight attendants who thought that their union had not gone far enough.

The profession of flight attendant still exuded enough glamour to attract a steady stream of young women, and in 1975 the airline continued to receive an average of 400 applications monthly. The aircraft might no longer fly at 12,000 feet in bumpy weather, requiring the flight attendants to use their nursing training, pushing a drinks cart could be backbreaking, and layovers were fewer, but the reasons to join Air Canada were same as they had been for TCA in 1937: to travel, to meet people, to escape the 9–5 routine, and to be admired by all as you walked through the airport terminal. Base salary was $550 monthly to $15,000 annually with experience. At a maximum, she worked seventy-five hours monthly and on joining the airline was allotted two passes for her parents and/or her children. But said Christine Fahrenbruch, the company recruiter, "We want applicants to understand that being a flight attendant is hard work. It's not all glamour."

Unlike the airlines in the United States, where the swinging sixties had brought a form of sexual titillation to the profession, at Air Canada flight attendants never had to sink to the levels of "I'm Cheryl. Fly Me" (National Airlines) or wear paper uniforms (TWA) or shed layers of clothing during the flight for an "Air Strip" (Braniff) or hand out little black books so male passengers could get their phone numbers (Eastern Airlines). That was not to say that Air Canada's stewardesses were dowdy.

MONSIEUR DAVE DECLARES WAR ON THE INSTITUTIONAL LOOK headlined *Between Ourselves* in April 1969. "Women are individualists," M. Dave of D'Allaird's explained. "An outfit or a colour that looks well on one girl doesn't necessarily do anything for another. So I have tried to give the girls a choice when I designed the new wardrobe for Air Canada." In a series of five fashion conferences from Halifax to Vancouver, a multi-dress wardrobe for the Company's 1,400 stewardesses was unveiled on March 24. Two coats and a choice of four dresses comprised the in-flight ensemble, which consisted of an A-line mini dress in three basic colours: Jet Red, Galaxy Blue, and Sonic White. The red and blue dresses were both trimmed in white with a matching hat that completed the outfit. "We wanted to do away with the traditional uniform look," said Bill Fabro, director of passenger services. "And the new ensemble is designed to be contemporary, stylish and comfortable." The dresses were made of washable polyester, a new drip-dry wrinkle-free fabric that was supposed to hold its shape after months of wear. "These features are expected to make outfit care much easier during the jet-set life enjoyed by the stewardesses." The male pursers got a lightweight, *maître d'avion* Galaxy Blue jacket that replaced the maroon coat worn during all meal, bar, and snack services.

Through the more permissive seventies, for Air Canada stewardesses, uniforms remained modest, hemlines low, and dating passengers was at their discretion. If sporting a wedding ring was no longer grounds for dismissal, stealing company property like liquor miniatures, drinking alcohol on duty (presumably

The colourful new stewardess wardrobe unveiled in March 1969 consisted of an A-line mini-dress in three basic colours: "Jet Red," "Galaxy Blue," and "Sonic White," all in washable polyester.

those miniatures), and sleeping on the job were.

Passengers smoking in-flight had not been an issue for TCA cabin crew. All seats at that time had built-in ashtrays, and on special occasions in first class, souvenir cigarette lighters were handed out. But by the 1970s, before allocating seats, counter staff were asking "Smoking or non-smoking?" The airline soon reserved 25 percent of its seats as a non-smok-ing section (in DC-9s it was the first five rows), changing that to 40 percent by 1975. There were problems for cabin crew in enforcing the non-smoking regulations, especially when passengers who claimed that they did not smoke brazenly lit up in the non-smoking area. "What can we do?" asked Ted Morris, a public relations manager. "All we can ask is for him to stop. It's too high to throw him off the plane."

Between Ourselves was the fifteen-page newsletter for employees that Rene Baudru had mimeographed in his spare time beginning in December 1939. It was crammed with local gossip (hence the name), bad poetry, the odd drawing, and a few statistics thrown in for bulk. Later it would be edited by Norm Garwood and Bob Todd, with colour photos. Other employee newsletters also appeared through the years: *TCA News* (1939–40) *Transcanews* (1940–1) and *Liaison* (Air Canada Eastern Region Employee Newsletter (1980). In May 1972, *Between Ourselves* was replaced by *Horizons*, to be published every three weeks. In 2003, the printed version of *Horizons* became an online version and was renamed *New Horizons*.

Like McGregor, Pratte continually found himself at odds with the government of the day, especially with the "giveaways" of potential routes to Canadian Pacific Air, regional airlines, and Alitalia. In December 1972, in exchange for allowing CP Air to serve Milan (Rome and Montreal were already served by Alitalia and CP Air), the Italian airline was permitted to serve Toronto, with its large Italian population. It was more than just Milan — the Italian city was a jumping off point for destinations further east, and Pratte gratuitously began making public remarks about the lack of direction by the government on air transportation matters. The Air Canada president brought the

whole issue to a head when he threatened to resign. "Air Canada will disappear in ten years," he told *La Presse* indiscreetly on April 9, 1973, "if it doesn't get that route. It demonstrates that the government does not believe in Air Canada anymore." He said that after four years in office he had been unable to get a definition from the minister on what the government wanted Air Canada to be. "Does the government want it to be an enterprise with no interest in profitability? If that's what they want, let them tell us. It would be easy for us to cut fares by half on the domestic network tomorrow. It's not our money." This led to speculation in the media and Commons about whether Pratte would give up his $75,000-a-year job if his airline was not allowed to expand further.

In the West, CP Air president John Gilmer was also speaking publicly about the discrimination that his airline suffered, reminding that all of Italy had been allotted to his airline when Jack Pickersgill divided up the world. Minister of Transport Jean Marchand said that Milan was unimportant; he was more interested in putting Air Canada in a better position to compete with other airlines. He was working towards, he said, a policy where the crown corporation could borrow its own funds on the money market without a government guarantee — in effect a new regulatory framework for the airline to operate in. When asked if he and Pratte were on speaking terms, the minister replied, "I've got no fight with him." They spoke every day, he said — except the Air Canada chairman was in Barbados on vacation.

Although the Trudeau government had put former Deputy Minister of Transport John Baldwin in place as chairman to advise him, throughout his tenure Pratte worked determinedly to keep effective power from Baldwin, so much so that Trudeau himself noticed this and told journalists that he deplored it. Baldwin himself would allude to Pratte's problems, saying, with apologies to Shakespeare, "Uneasy lies the corporation that wears the crown." Left to writing the occasional article in *Between Ourselves*, the man who might have saved Pratte from himself retired in December 1973, capping an illustrious career in the public service with the C.D. Howe Award for his leadership in postwar Canadian aviation.

Baldwin was replaced with Ralph Vaughan, a lawyer and former Halifax newspaper editor. Having worked for the CNR and Angus McDonald, the late premier of Nova Scotia (and since 1971 as vice-president of the airline), Vaughan was said to be already a power in transportation circles. In 1968 Gordon McGregor had offered Vaughan a job with Air Canada, but Vaughan declined, saying that he "didn't know where the airline was going." Soft-spoken and normally reticent, in his first press interview Vaughan admitted that the company had problems. "We've got to sort out our financing. But I don't think you will see the airline go public in the near future as has been rumoured."

———

Air Canada did not receive its first 1011 from the Lockheed plant at Palmdale until January 14, 1973, and immediately put it in service on the Toronto–Miami run. Later, to compete with the long range DC-10-30, Lockheed brought out the L-1011-100 with fuselage tanks, and Air Canada bought five of them. But the U.S. airliner with British engines (a point not lost on Douglas, which had just brought out its DC-10 with General Electric or Pratt & Whitney engines) never recouped its developmental costs, and when Boeing launched its 747SP, the medium-range wide-body market dried up for both Lockheed and McDonnell Douglas, and the former concentrated on defence contracts from then on.

But if the L-1011 almost killed off Lockheed Martin and Rolls-Royce, its rival, the McDonnell Douglas DC-10-10, did much worse. The aircraft became known as the "Douglas Death Cruiser" because of a faulty latch mechanism on its forward-opening cargo doors that would blow open and cause the aircraft to de-pressurize in flight. CP Air would acquire a dozen DC-10s, but of the DC-10-30 version. Its public relations people dropped the Douglas name to call it a "10-30," which beat a "1011."

———

A mysterious explosion ripped apart Air Canada DC-8 CF-TIJ on June 2, 1973, on the tarmac at Toronto International Airport just as passengers were about to embark for a flight to Zürich and Vienna. Paul Jesin, a twenty-year-old dentistry student, was a summer employee of Consolidated Aviation Fuelling Services of Toronto and oversaw the refueling of the DC-8 with JP-4 jet fuel. He was watching the pressure and flow gauges when he heard an explosion. He looked toward the tail of the plane and "the wing seemed to have fallen down just behind my truck." He later said, "I just let go of the deadman hose and ran for the front of the truck." Jesin and Air Canada ground crewman Owen Nimmo were badly burned in the explosion. The Department of Transport inquiry suspected that the cause was the JP-4 fuel being used, which was considered more dangerous than the more commonly used JP-1 jet fuel. What did not burn were thousands of rocks in the baggage hold that were never claimed by anyone.

The Yom Kippur war in October 1973 led to the Arab oil-producing nations increasing the price of oil by 70 percent, and 1,000 gallons of Jet-A1 fuel, which had been $150.08 in 1973 climbed to $335.70 in 1974 and $429.41 the year after. Not only did this kill off the supersonic transport program, with the exception of British Airways and Air France, it also plunged the whole commercial aviation industry into recession.

Until 1970 fuel had represented 10 percent of Air Canada's operating costs, but by 1974 this had doubled to 20 percent — the highest single expense category excluding labour. Still, the airline fared better than its American rivals. Of the 450 million gallons of fuel that it used in 1974, 75 percent was purchased within Canada and of that only 20 percent originated in the Middle East. Through the oil embargo winter, Air Canada used its aircraft as partial tankers, especially those going to the

United States, where aircraft could return without refuelling. A good example was its Boeing 747, which could fly from Montreal to Miami and return without refuelling.

———

What damaged the airline more than any Arab oil sheikh was Elmer MacKay, the Progressive Conservative MP for Central Nova Scotia, disclosing in the House of Commons on April 17, 1974, that the marketing branch of Air Canada had made a $100,000 payment to one Robert McGregor, the owner of a Montreal travel agency. The Nova Scotian MP was the Tory opposition member for DREE, the Department for Regional Economic Expansion, and other than as a passenger he had no experience with Air Canada's operations. Asked by the media if he saw himself as a "crusading investigator," MacKay modestly replied that Bob (Stanfield) had assigned him some transport responsibilities, which led him to "take on" the national airline.

Claude Taylor had received advance notice of the disclosure in the House, and earlier that morning advised Pratte of what was about to happen. In response, the president handed Taylor the "McGregor file" put together the previous day by John McGill, vice-president, Eastern region. The opposition and media leapt on what promised to be a homemade Watergate, complete with shady cash transactions and high-level incompetence. The opposition asked Marchand to explain why Parliament had not been made aware of MacKay's revelations concerning letters of agreement with authorizations for expenditure from a Crown corporation to a travel agency. Caught off guard, both the transport minister and prime minister promised a full enquiry into the whole matter by launching a Royal Commission to look into the state of the national airline.

The government drew up Order in Council P.C. 1975-963 on April 25, 1975, and appointed the recently named Chief Justice of the High Court of Ontario, the Honourable Willard Zebedee Estey, to "inquire into and report upon certain matters related to the system of financial controls, accounting procedures, and other matters relating to fiscal management and control of Air Canada." Simply put, the government (and especially the opposition) wanted to know if Yves Pratte's Air Canada had strayed beyond the mandate of the 1937 TCA Act. The Inquiry was held mainly at the law faculty at McGill University, with poor Estey commuting weekly from his Toronto home. Critics pointed out that it was a task not normally given to a judge, especially one without a background in airline management — but by then everyone was looking for a scapegoat.

It had begun in early 1973 when Yves Menard had negotiated with two travel agencies, Robert McGregor Travel in Montreal and another in Vancouver, to involve Air Canada in the travel agency business. Other airlines already had their own resort accommodations abroad, to which they channelled their passengers, and Menard wanted to have these two agencies acquire a third one in Toronto,

the three becoming a national network of travel agencies into which Air Canada's customers could be directed. Led by Menard, the airline's marketing branch funded the venture. The board of directors approved this "general diversification" concept of involvement in the travel industry, but was never asked to approve any transaction involving McGregor Travel. Besides, the chances of the venture actually going anywhere were at that time considered slim.

———

The year 1974 promised to be interesting for Air Canada. Besides the L-1011s being temporarily grounded until an electrical fault in their automatic landing gear system was fixed, through April a spate of strikes crippled the airline's operations. Probably the only strike that didn't affect the airline was when the pilots on the St. Lawrence Seaway struck. Firemen at the larger airports struck, postal employees were on a "go slow," and the air traffic controllers voted 91 percent to strike through the busy summer period. Unfortunately, their ballots to do so were hampered by the postal strike. The airline was able to keep its DC-9s operating from the smaller airports but cancelled its DC-8 and L-1011 flights at the major ones, the company reservations centre coping with a record number of calls and putting 5,000 of its employees on temporary leave.

The distribution of complimentary passes always made for good press copy, and both Air Canada and CP Air had no qualms about to whom they gave them.

All members of the cabinet, the leader of the opposition, and former prime ministers like John Diefenbaker received them from the government airline. Both airlines also offered them to all provincial premiers and their wives. In November 1978, when told that he was the only premier to actually accept the airline passes, Alberta Premier Peter Lougheed was amazed. He had used them, he said, to visit his constituents. When it was pointed out that he and his wife had been to Haiti on an Air Canada pass and later Hawaii on a CP Air one, Lougheed said that he didn't think the people of Alberta would begrudge him taking a rest.

Both Air Canada and CP Air also curried favour with the government by giving Margaret Trudeau, the prime minister's wife, a complimentary first class pass so she could pursue her career in photography. This seemed to cause no controversy at the time, perhaps because it paled when compared to the thousands of dollars of camera equipment Mrs. Trudeau received as a gift from King Hussein of Jordan that year. When asked in the Commons about the passes, the prime minister's office claimed not to keep track of Mrs. Trudeau's "comings and goings," but Trudeau said that he would pay the airlines for all the trips that she had taken on unofficial business.

———

Initiated in 1972 by the minister for industry, Jean-Luc Pepin, to demonstrate Canadian expertise in Short Take Off and Landing (STOL), the federal government made available $16 million in funds for Airtransit. Using six de Havilland DHC-6-300 Twin Otters, the commuter airline owned by Air Canada would operate between Rockcliffe Airport, almost within sight of Parliament, and the former Expo 67 parking lot in Montreal, now designated in IATA code YMY. The two-year trial was to highlight not only the STOL abilities of the Twin Otter (and the larger four-engine Dash 7 to come) but also a complete STOL system from navigation aids, avionics, regulations, operating procedures, and support services. One hundred and thirty Air Canada employees were allocated, but because of union regulations fifty pilots were hired mainly from the military for their experience on de Havilland's other STOL planes, the Caribou and Buffalo.

Airtransit's president was the thirty-one-year-old Gary Vogan, who had joined Air Canada in 1967. Besides being used to demonstrate the whole STOL operation to potential Canadian operators (especially the Vancouver–Victoria route) and foreign buyers in dense urban countries like Japan, recovering the $16 million startup costs was not even considered, for on the tiny operation rode the future not only of de Havilland Canada but of the whole Canadian aviation industry. The Airtransit's Twin Otters were understudies for the Dash 7 to come, and Ottawa was pinning its hopes on the operation's success to recoup the $80 million that it had sunk into the latter's development.

Montreal, July 23, 1974. Minister of Transport the Honourable J. Marchand and Air Canada Captain A.J. Tonkin at the start of Airtransit (Short Take Off and Landing) STOL services between Rockcliffe Airport, Ottawa, and the former Expo 67 parking lot in Montreal, now designated in IATA code YMY.

The Twin Otters, normally configured to seat eighteen to fifty passengers, were modified to carry eleven only for the forty-minute flight, the reduced seating to cut weight in order to meet U.S. federal regulations criteria for steep ascent and descent. The fares were $20 each way, which included the minibus ride into town, and at its peak there were thirty flights daily. The customers mainly businesspeople. The service was to begin June 1, but this was delayed until July 18 because of the vocal opposition from residents of the very influential suburb of Rockcliffe — and the

unexpected methane gas that seeped out of the former Expo 67 parking lot, which had been built on a garbage dump. When both of these were settled, service began on July 24 and was scheduled to continue until the summer of 1976, when it was hoped that export orders for the Dash 7 would justify the whole demonstration.

———

There had existed informal preclearance arrangements between the United States and Canada at Malton Airport as early as 1952. But the signing of the bilateral preclearance treaty with the United States on May 8, 1974, would allow Canadians to clear U.S. Customs in the country's main cities like Toronto and Montreal, also opening up smaller airports in the United States such as LaGuardia in New York City and allowing the use of domestic terminals in larger ones. Unlike CP Air, Air Canada reaped the benefits of the treaty. Of the seventeen routes that came available, on August 2, Jean Marchand awarded the state airline the bulk of them. When temporarily out of office in later years, Marchand admitted (and later denied) that there was a split in the cabinet between East and West: there were ministers who wanted the Vancouver–based CP Air to be given more revenue-producing routes, and those in the east who felt that the Montreal–based Air Canada had not been given enough. There was an even a more fundamental question: which should be encouraged, private enterprise or crown corporations? The split in Cabinet wasn't only about Air Canada and CP Air....

____

In anticipation of the cross-border windfall, Air Canada had the perfect aircraft. The Boeing 727-100 trijet had been rolled out as early as November 27, 1962. With many parts, including an upper fuselage, identical to the veteran 707/720, the 727-100 had not been difficult for Boeing to design as competition with Douglas and its DC-9 in the short haul market, and Eastern Air Lines was quick to put the 727-100 on its shuttle service by 1967. Its appeal was its innovative high lift wing system,

which allowed for a high cruising speed but low landing speed and short takeoff run on shorter runways. In May 1971, Boeing announced the passenger version of a lengthened 727-200 series and American Airlines, Trans World Airlines, Delta, and Continental Airlines placed orders, especially for their inner city routes. What made the airliner distinct was its "air stairs" at the rear of the cabin that allowed easy access at even the smallest airports.

"If You Are Late For Your Rapidair Flight — Relax. You're Right On Time For The Next," shouted the magazine ad in bold red. One television commercial showed a Rapidair B727 arriving at a railway station. A model of a plane (two inches away from the camera lens) was photographed against the backdrop of a full-scale station. The first 144-passenger B727-200 to join the company fleet landed in Dorval on September 30, 1974, and four more arrived in October, with one entering the Rapidair service and the Montreal–New York route on October 27. The 132 passenger aircraft were configured in twelve first class and 120 economy. By this time, the aircraft was already in service with sixty airlines.

"From the outset we had to examine a wide range of technical, operational and economic factors," said Ian Macdonald, Air Canada's director of fleet planning. He had become involved in a feasibility study of the trijet in early 1972. "A key objective," he continued, "is to maintain fleet flexibility. Because of the mixed market and route structure we have, we need to be able to interchange aircraft in a way that is

At $8.3 million each and a range of 2,500 miles, the eleven Air Canada 727-200s were mainly associated with the Rapidair shuttle.

economical." At $8.3 million each and a range of 2,500 miles, the eleven 727-200s that Air Canada bought could easily fit all of the airline's present North American routes and over water to the Caribbean. On the short haul, intercity high-density routes, the 200 was more economical than the older DC-8s then in use. With its one class seating of 144, it had more capacity than the DC-9's ninety-five seats.

"Even the name 'Rapidair' was selected because it registered with our typical Toronto–Montreal traveller," said Victor Emery, marketing development director, and that it had obvious similarities to the CN's Rapido fast train between the two cities. Based on Eastern Airline's shuttle between New York and Washington, and also using Boeing 727s, Air Canada's service aimed at the businessman comprised of eighteen daily nonstop flights between Montreal and Toronto in each direction. Lounge 1 at Montreal and Lounge 50 in Toronto were designated for Rapidair with full check-in services, telephones, newspapers, and bar service. Departure times were regularized to every thirty minutes during peak hours and every hour in non-peak.

————

In 1973, Canadian couturier Leo Chevalier was hired to create a new wardrobe for stewardesses "in line with today's lifestyle." Chevalier replaced the old "uniform"' tradition with a fifty-one-piece wardrobe in red, blue, white, and brown that had 300 style combinations in polyester skirts, acrylic rayon sweaters, camel's hair winter coats, and a distinctive belt with Air Canada buckle. The interchangeable outfits could be mixed and matched to create a variety of ensembles. The smocks had been introduced in 1972 to be worn over the uniform of stewardesses-in-training. Designed by Phyllis Amoruso, fashion coordinator for the company, they were made from printed pique of cotton and polyester and sporting a pattern of various flowers of blue, red, yellow, and green scattered on a white background with black piping, adding, said the brochures, "a splash of color to the cabins."

The male pursers wore slim trousers with white shirt and regimental striped tie, except on 747 and L-1011 flights, where the director wore a red blazer.

———

As was to be expected, Pratte had agreed with McGregor in closing down the Winnipeg maintenance base and rationalizing everything in Montreal. But unlike McGregor, he was indiscreet with his opinion about it. "Our mission," he told the *Montreal Gazette*, "is not to provide jobs for Canadians — we do not exist to give employment. Our mission is to provide transportation."

With the new maintenance facility in Dorval now servicing not only Air Canada aircraft but those of other airlines as well, Pratte made his position very clear: all of the airline's maintenance would be done in Montreal. Besides, with the new Boeing 727s slated for use by Rapidair, the Montreal–Toronto shuttle, it made sense to have them serviced in Montreal. In this he was supported by the machinists' union, the IAM, which had more members in Montreal than in Winnipeg and stated that the government should stay out of the airline's management.

As a boy, Winnipeg MP James Richardson had watched as his father lost out to TCA in 1937 concerning the airway monopoly. Now minister of defence, just as the air force acquired five Boeing 707s for its transport fleet, Richardson campaigned to have them serviced in Winnipeg, along with the Air Canada Boeing 727s. In this election year, if Air Canada could return to Winnipeg for its maintenance, Western criticism about the Liberals would be stalled. Richardson's allies in this were CAE, which could only profit from such a contract, and, surprisingly, Prime Minister Trudeau and Jean Marchand, both of whom as Quebec members of Parliament were sure to lose votes in their own ridings if this occurred. Former Prime Minister Diefenbaker lost no time in reminding all that he had fought to keep the Air Canada base in Winnipeg in 1962. Arrayed against them were all the other Quebec MPs, led by the powerful Madame Jean Sauvé, minister of science and technology.

With the election looming, a compromise was worked out between Charles

Drury, the president of the treasury board, and Richardson on May 18. The government would allow some of the overhaul work for the Boeing 727s to be moved to Winnipeg, specifically the "A", "B," and "C" checks, but the major "D" checks would be in Montreal. There would be no jobs lost in Montreal, and no one would have to move to Winnipeg if they did not want to. In what the media termed "prime pork barrelling" or "priming the parish pump," Trudeau caught an Air Canada DC-9 to Winnipeg to make the announcement on May 27, adding that a $15 million hangar would be built to accommodate the 727s. Since all maintenance on Air Canada aircraft had to be done by the machinists' union, CAE would not be servicing the aircraft, but the airline would lease from that company its former facilities. When asked his opinion, Pratte bravely said that the airline would respect the government's decision and would work to implement it. The *Montreal Gazette* wondered why he was such a "pushover" and the *Ottawa Journal* pointed out that the capital cost of the Winnipeg base coincidentally just happened to be exactly the amount of profit that Air Canada had struggled to make in the two previous years, and put the whole affair down to "shabby interference in the airline's business." No one could have known that there was worse to come.

———

That June, when it looked as if Menard's proposal for the travel agencies was disappearing into obscurity, he contacted Ray Lindsay, the managing director of Venturex Ltd., a CN subsidiary used by the airline, to participate in the new ABC charter market. How much money, he asked, would it take to keep McGregor still interested? Venturex was already in the travel business and since July 1973 had been the lessee of a group of villas, condominiums, and apartments in Barbados known as "Sunset Crest." The leases were somehow then taken over by the airline, but it was not until April 30, 1974 that the board of directors approved them, electing to renew them through the calendar year of 1975.

Lindsay thought that $100,000 would be enough for McGregor, and Menard directed that funds from the airline's marketing branch be used. For this sum the travel agent would represent Air Canada's interests in discussion with the Province of Quebec concerning forthcoming travel agency legislation. There was (McGregor later said) also an unwritten gentleman's agreement whereby Air Canada would have an option on a percentage of the McGregor Travel shares exercisable for a nominal consideration. The marketing branch drew up Letters of agreement and Authorization for Expeditures (AFEs) to do this.

Three cheques totalling $100,000 were personally delivered by Lindsay to McGregor on November 29, 1974, and charged to the branch budget. The travel agency owner later testified that he called John McGill, the airline's vice-president of the Eastern region, who had been aware of the deal since 1973, for advice on what to do with the cheques. "He kind of laughingly said 'I hope you cashed them,'" McGregor said.

When it became known that Menard had not been making mortgage payments on the villa he had bought (and at which Pratte had been a guest), the vice-president of marketing denied any wrongdoing. He explained that he had not wanted to begin payments until he received full title of the villa — and then he would pay full price. But Menard's protestations, made public in the middle of a severe Montreal winter when a lot of taxpayers wished they had a villa in Barbados, led to the vice-president resigning on February 28, 1975.

Menard also acknowledged that on two occasions he had introduced Jean Charton, the president of Herdt & Charton Limitée, to John McGill and Bryce Buchanan, successive directors of Air Canada In-flight Operations, who were responsible for the purchase of wines for the airline. Following this, Herdt & Charton Limitée bid on and was awarded a contract to supply wine to the airline. In February 1972, when Lelarge Inc., an importer of fine food and a subsidiary of Herdt & Charton Limitée, invited Menard to become a director, he did so — without telling Pratte.

McGill warned McGregor on April 15 that the Sunset Crest deal was going to be revealed in the House, and knowing there must have been frantic meetings taking place at Place Ville Marie, McGregor demanded to see Pratte on the seventeenth, but the chairman was going to a testimonial dinner for Menard. McGregor later said that Menard phoned him and warned, "You know, Bob, if you don't say you intend to perform those consulting services as stated in the memoranda of agreement, you'll be ruined for life." When told that his testimonial dinner was cancelled because of the revelations in the media, Menard expressed surprise. "I don't know why we should cancel it? The whole thing is perfectly simple. It's a tempest in a teapot. We do deals like this all the time." Pratte denied that he had asked Menard to resign, but said that his decision was "a proper one in the circumstances."

After months of hearing testimony, the Estey Inquiry concluded that, as the marketing vice-president reporting directly to the chairman, Pratte had not followed his work, although he had the opportunity and the means to do so. Chairman Ralph Vaughan told the inquiry that he had known a year before Menard's resignation of the Barbados villa purchase but saw no conflict of interest there.

Menard's continuing relationship with his previous employer, Herdt & Charton Limiteé, was a definite conflict of interest and would have offended the corporate policy and guidelines that the airline's board of directors adopted on May 27, 1975. These specifically precluded any person in a position of responsibility with Air Canada from accepting a directorship that might have a prospective business relationship with the airline. But those guidelines were not in effect when Menard was director of the Herdt & Charton Limitée — and Pratte was unaware of this.[1]

The marketing branch had also failed to alert the finance branch to the imminent expenditure, and the sales and service branch was never consulted, even when the mounting losses in connection with the villas appeared. In the marketing of the accommodation, Air Canada lost approximately $1 million, which was charged to "promotion" in the marketing branch budget. The forecasts available by April 30, 1974, also showed a loss of about $500,000, and a similar loss was forecast for the year 1975. Much smaller amounts were included in the marketing branch budget for the Sunset Crest venture in these years, and the gross rental obligations of Air Canada under these leases were not reported in any budget. Nor was this project mentioned in any of the minutes of the weekly executive committee meetings. The investigation by the finance branch was seen to be "lethargic and accomplished very little until shortly before public disclosure of the deal."

The commission sympathized with McGregor, having found no evidence that he had made "untrue or improper representations." In his defence, McGregor stated that he never agreed or intended to perform such services. He had no reason to believe, he said, that that the Air Canada representatives he dealt with were not acting within their proper authority, and he had signed the documents they put before him.

The evidence against the company made public by the media was damning. Justice Estey called Menard "reckless and negligent in signing obligations without reading them, adopting a grand indifference to the rules." But the report was especially harsh on Pratte, who he said had isolated himself, even from his vice-presidents. "It

cannot be believed that the large number of officers involved in these two transactions deliberately withheld information from the Chairman. It can only be concluded that within the airline there is a widespread insensitivity to the necessity of keeping top management informed. The management style adopted by the Chief Executive Officer and some of the Vice-Presidents might also have contributed to the reduced flow of information." The chairman had been unaware of this transaction until at least January 1974, when Mr. Allen, a member of the Air Canada board, had casually mentioned to him a rumour that he had heard while in the Barbados about Air Canada's ownership of some kind of accommodation on that island.

In a three-day testimony before the inquiry in July, Pratte testified that he knew nothing of the $100,000 payment to McGregor until it was made public in the Commons. This was in direct contradiction to the testimony from Michael Cochrane, the airline's vice-president of finance, who said he had told Pratte about this on March 7, 1975. Pratte then gave what the media termed a "litany of complaints" that centred on the poor treatment that the airline had received from Ottawa and specifically the minister of transport and also the prime minister. The national airline, he said, was either ignored or opposed by Ottawa, and he complained that he had never received clear guidelines on what the government expected from Air Canada. Marchand refuted this, replying that the guidelines were in the Air Canada Act and he had personally met with

Pratte several times in the last year. "What does he want?" the minister asked. "To see the prime minister every day?" It was no secret that Marchand wanted to replace Pratte with Pierre Desmarais, another French Canadian but one who knew something about Air Canada since he was already on the board.

Despite his all his woes, Pratte said that he still liked the job, "but didn't know what he and the national airline were to do. It is normal that there should be some tension between the airline and the federal government," he told the press. "What is not normal is that they wanted us to fly nonstop between every town and city … and they want us to earn a good rate of return." The chairman hastened to add that he wasn't challenging the government to fire him — he only wanted it to establish clear guidelines and to judge its performance by those guidelines. Marchand had promised a new Air Canada Act and the chairman said he had been consulted as to what it should contain. Scapegoat for the Crown corporation's woes and Liberal political patronage, it had often seemed to employees that Pratte was flying the airline solo.

Prime Minister Trudeau, who had chosen Pratte, was then busy thwarting attempts by the RCMP and CBC to question Marchand about the controversial Skyshops concession in 1972 at two airports where Liberal party fundraisers in Quebec had made a fortune out of minor investments. Negotiating his way through the complex bureaucracy of the department of transport had never appealed to Marchand, and on September 25, 1975, Trudeau relieved his old friend of his burden, later to make him the minister of the environment. He appointed Otto Lang (Liberal, Saskatoon-Humboldt), at that time the attorney general and minister of justice to the position. Marchand would resign his seat in the House of Commons in October 1976 over a disagreement with the government's position regarding the use of the French language by air traffic controllers in Quebec.

Mr. Justice Estey found no evidence of dishonesty among Air Canada officials, saying only that some had acted in "cavalier disregard of the ordinary rules of business," and the whole affair might have ended there except that Otto Lang announced that there would be two reports made of the Estey Commission: one public and one confidential that only cabinet members would see. The opposition was incensed at this, and Elmer MacKay, who had begun it all, now urged Lang to bring forward legislation to implement some of the recommendations in the report. The prime minister, the Nova Scotian MP said, had not been giving Air Canada the attention it deserved, and the airline had fallen into the worst of both worlds: poor management at the top and the lack of government policy direction. There was talk that MacKay was using this as a springboard to throw his hat into the ring for the leadership of the Conservative party. Unfortunately, his motion to debate the Estey Report in the House failed since other members were uninterested.

The official opening of Mirabel Airport, October 1975. Air Canada CEO Yves Pratte flanked by Quebec Premier Robert Bourassa and Prime Minister Pierre Trudeau.

Not so Don Mazankowski (MP for Vegreville), the Conservative Party chairman of the caucus committee on transport, who demanded that all reports of the "Air Canada fiasco" be tabled immediately. Unlike previous holders of the position, "Maz," first elected in 1968, was a rarity — like C.D. Howe he was an airline aficionado. A former car and farm implement salesman, he held a private pilot's license, was an avid reader of *Canadian Aviation* magazine, and had definite plans for both Air Canada and airports in the country. Diefenbaker and Robert Stanfield had both recognized this and encouraged the young man to serve on the Commons transport committee. It was then that he met Claude Taylor, nicknamed by the *Financial Times* the airline's hired gun (i.e. lobbyist), and well into the night the two would discuss the future of commercial aviation in Maz's tiny office.

If it did nothing else, the whole Pratte affair did spotlight the calibre of the Air Canada board members and answer the question as to why they did not counsel Pratte to the pitfalls of Menard's venture. Long accepted in Ottawa circles was that an appointment to a seat on the airline's board was a political plum for party hacks, only one rung below an appointment to the Senate. With the financial honorarium came an airline pass anywhere in the world for the lucky board member and his family. It was not surprising then that party (and prime ministerial) loyalty was put before a knowledge of (or interest in) the airline industry or that board members were quick to side with the government rather than Air Canada's CEO.

OPERATION BABYLIFT

"Operation Babylift" was the name given to the evacuation of thousands of orphaned babies from Vietnam in April 1975 before the Communist troops entered Saigon. The first flight using a massive C-5A Galaxy aircraft had ended in disaster when a bomb destroyed the aircraft, killing 153 of the 328 orphans and attendants on board. Canadian military C-130s carried the orphans to Hong Kong in what was the largest rescue effort in history, and Air Canada employees volunteered to transport Vietnamese and Cambodian orphans to their new homes in Canada.

One of Pratte's last official functions was to attend the inauguration of Mirabel International Airport (YMX) on October 4, 1975. The first aircraft to land at Mirabel was an Air Canada B747 carrying the chairman and VIPs from other airlines for the opening ceremonies. Members of the crew were Captain Bill Benson, Chief Pilot 747, Toronto; Phil Pawsey, second officer supervisor 747; and Kent Davis, VP-flight operations. The cabin crew were flight attendants Renata Schmidt, Claire Gosselin, Elizabeth Burns, Paulette Couture, Vivian Case, Gloria Boucher, and Andrea Berthiaume; Serge Woolley, purser; Carlos Arriola, flight service director; and Bernard Claudel, flight attendant Supervisor.

———

In the early days of flying cargo by jet freighter, shipments were loaded onto flat pallets, fastened down with nets, and then rolled into position on the aircraft by roller conveyors. This was hardly an improvement from the North Star era, and it was inevitable airlines realized that if cargo could be packed into containers the exact shape of the aircraft's hold, it would rationalize space and increase security. ULD (Unit Load Devices) were introduced, nicknamed "igloos," and airlines invested heavily in building up their own inventory. Problems of getting one's own ULD back in record time were negotiated in 1972 by IATA, allowing airlines like Air Canada to offer their customers freighter service routes extending to any point served by its partners — as long as their ULDs were compatible. These were used on the DC-8 freighters that served the Montreal/Toronto–Europe route and supplemented by the airline's new B747-200 Combi.

Configured to twenty-eight in first class and 148 in economy, it had nineteen pallets of freight in the rear. The Combi flew Toronto–Heathrow (London) four times weekly. Its special 8x8x8-foot containers had been built to the meet the aircraft's requirements, each holding up to 15,000 pounds of cargo. In November 1975, Don Richardson, the airline's general manager, cargo, said that about half of Air Canada's total cargo revenue came from the Combis alone.

———

That October, even as the Trudeau government introduced wage and price controls to tackle rocketing inflation, the *Air Canada Inquiry Report* was published. It exposed a company that had lost its soul, that intangible belief in itself and its mission midwifed by Howe and cultivated by McGregor. The common purpose and high morale that the pair had instilled in TCA/Air Canada had been buried under Pratte's reorganization and Ottawa's indifference, and this translated into poor customer service at ticket counters and on board. The public was also tired of seeing its tax dollars going to perpetuate what was a charade of a national airline. But alternatives to Air Canada, especially in domestic travel, were still limited.

In resource-rich Alberta, Progressive Conservative Premier Peter Lougheed was maneuvering to buy PWA before a British Columbia company did, a deal that would not only make the province the "gateway to the North" but give its citizens some alternative to Air Canada. But in August 1974, when Alberta bought 93 percent of PWA's shares, the Trudeau government took it to the Federal Court of Appeal, saying that according to the Aeronautics Act, the province had to obtain approval from the CTC before it could own an airline. The Federal Court supported Ottawa in this, but Alberta's lawyers argued that the regulations applied to a "person," not a province. The Supreme Court agreed, and on February 22, 1977, it upheld Alberta's claim, and PWA's head office was moved to Calgary. To prevent provinces from investing in interprovincial transportation, the federal government would later introduce Bill S-31.

The bloodletting within Air Canada began on November 5, when twenty-three senior marketing executives were fired. On November 27 an Air Canada spokesman announced that Pratte had resigned as chairman and chief executive officer, effective December 1. In a lengthy letter of resignation submitted the next day to Otto Lang, Pratte said that the government had failed to defend Air Canada's senior management against allegations in Parliament of "incompetence and inefficiency." The establishment of the Estey Commission was a clear indication, he said, that the government had lost confidence in his stewardship. He wished his successor well. "I know that he will have the support of the employees of Air Canada; I only hope that he will have that of the Government." Pratte left office and returned to private practice, working for the law firm of Desjardins, Ducharme. Trudeau did eventually take pity on him and in 1977 appointed the former Air Canada CEO to the Supreme Court of Canada, the same day that he appointed Willard Estey, who had chaired the inquiry, to the same bench. Pratte would resign from the Supreme Court on June 28, 1979, because of ill health, ironically just as Transport Minister Don Mazankowski asked Air Canada for a report on the pension given him when he left the airline. There were rumours that he had received a pension based on twenty years of service with Air Canada when he had served only seven.

How did the company employees feel about Pratte? Clayton Glenn worked under CEOs Gordon McGregor, Yves Pratte, and Claude Taylor, and taking just fleet planning an as example of each one's management style, he would write that McGregor was known to have favoured British-made aircraft but always supported the recommendations made by his technical team, led by Herb Seagrim. "With Yves Pratte," he would write, "things were different. No fleet decision ... could be made without Pratte becoming intimately involved. He 'nickeled and dimed' each recommendation from his management team, and each decision bore his mark."

There was an unexpected rush of sympathy for Pratte — all from outside Air Canada. Renowned journalist Douglas Fullerton devoted a full page in the *Montreal Gazette* to Pratte, comparing him with Sir Henry Thornton, who reorganized the British railway system during the First World War and then came to Canada to build the CNR. Forced to resign because of a scandal manufactured by his political masters, Thornton died soon after a broken man. "A man has been wronged," Fullerton wrote of Pratte, "and we are all the poorer for it." Perhaps the best summation of Pratte would come from Robert Stewart in "The Redemption of Air Ugly," in *The Canadian*, September 3, 1977. "He seemed incapable of communicating effectively. His shyness emerged as stiffness ... and as trouble grew around him the media treated this lonely man roughly, dwelling simplistically on the assumption that he was a political appointee chosen to show that French Canadians could aspire to high management jobs in Crown corporations."

But that wasn't the last of the Pratte family connection with Air Canada. Yves' son Guy served as lead counsel in 2005 in hearings before the Standing Committee on

Access to Information, Privacy and Ethics, and the Oliphant Commission, which inquired into allegations between the Right Honourable Brian Mulroney and Karlheinz Schreiber. The investigation was in relation to a government contract involving the purchase of Airbus aircraft by Air Canada and where it was alleged commissions had been paid to Schreiber with portions set aside for the former prime minister.

Pratte's appeal as a French Canadian from an historic law firm had suited Trudeau in 1968. With federal-Quebec relations even more strained eight years later, the prime minister needed another eminent French Canadian lawyer, but this time one who also knew the transportation business. Pierre Taschereau was from a family of Quebec City lawyers that could trace its political origins to advising Prime Minister Wilfrid Laurier on legal matters. A lawyer for the CNR, he had been chosen by Jack Pickersgill to oversee the CTC's legal affairs. Appointed the railway's chairman in 1971, it was then that Taschereau met Air Canada's public relations vice-president, Claude Taylor. During Howe's time, CNR president S.J. Hungerford had also been the president of the national airline, and reverting to this, Trudeau appointed the CNR president to be Air Canada's acting president.

With Ralph Vaughan's resignation in December, Air Canada ended 1975 without a president and CEO or a chairman. It thus befell Taschereau to announce that that Air Canada expected a loss of $10 million for 1975, a decline from the previous year. There

was almost no growth in cargo and passenger revenue, and although the company had cut costs by reducing its workforce by 3 percent, this had had no effect. "Because of the airline's national commitments," he explained, "operational capacity could not be cut back proportionately. The reduction in employees provided no financial savings because of inflation, higher wages and the fuel bill which had risen by 23 percent to $32 million." There could only be better days ahead.

CHAPTER FOUR

CLAUDE TAYLOR AND THE SUMMER AFTERNOON

After the very public humiliation of Pratte, it was going to be difficult for the Trudeau government to find someone who wanted to run Air Canada. Drafting legislation that would free Air Canada from the CNR and eventually offer shares in it to the public required someone who knew the airline business — and his way around the corridors of Ottawa.

Learning nothing from choosing Pratte in 1968, cabinet members Jean Marchand (the minister of transport) and Marc Lalonde (the minister for national health and welfare) insisted a French Canadian should succeed him. They had two candidates in mind: Maurice d'Amours, who was already employed by the airline as a vice-president in sales, or the eminent geographer Pierre Camu, the former vice-president of the St. Lawrence Seaway Authority. Possibly to forestall them, in

December 1975 Transport Minister Otto Lang offered Donald Watson, the president of Pacific Western Airlines (PWA) the choice of either job: president and CEO or chairman of the national airline. Watson considered it for a week before declining. Then the minister offered it to another favourite of Marchand who was already on the Air Canada board, Outremont mayor, Pierre Desmarais — no relation to Paul Desmarais of Power Corp. At the last minute, Desmarais also turned it down, catching Marchand and Lang by surprise. Somehow the transport minister then managed to convince Trudeau that Claude Taylor was the only choice for the job, and on February 16, 1976, he was named the president of Air Canada.

Moving to the president's office on the forty-first floor of Place Ville Marie, Taylor said that he never had any inclination to be president and hoped it would change his life as little as possible. He and his wife continued to live in the modest house in Cartierville that they had bought in 1967, but for security reasons Taylor had to take a chauffeured company car to work rather than the commuter train. He now had to drop some of his volunteer activities such as the YMCA and Boy Scouts. A devout Baptist and a former deacon in his church, he continued his religious duties. For recreation, the new president still puttered around his garden, and when he had nothing to do he went over to his daughter's home to see there was anything he could fix there.

It could be said that Taylor's childhood had elements of either Abraham Lincoln's or Horatio Alger's. Born in 1925, he grew up on a New Brunswick farm during the Depression, his father dying when he was ten. To make ends meet, the boy rode the family horse on a circuit around the other farms, selling copies of *Maclean's* magazine. With the money earned, he bought fifty chickens and sold the eggs at the market in Moncton, hitching a ride on the milk truck. He also bred silver foxes and said that if pressed he could still pelt them. "You grab it with tongs and smash it on its head," he said.

Previous president, Gordon McGregor, had been regarded as a demigod by his managers, and Pratte was always an outsider, but Taylor always retained the common touch and was living proof that nice guys don't always finish last. Longtime TCA/Air Canada employee Clayton Glenn was quoted as saying that on hearing the appointment "morale in the company had risen 1,000 times," and had it not come from within, he and many others would have resigned. If further proof was needed, subordinates who had addressed Pratte as "Sir" called the new president by his first name. On that February morning, across the airline every employee knew that one of their own was now running the company.

The announcement was also greeted with universal applause outside the company. CBC Radio's Terry McKenna spoke for many when he said: "For Air Canada employees the gift of Claude Taylor is like the winner finding an Aladdin's lamp. He looks and sounds like he has been made to order for the job. He is good looking, soft spoken, and he remains a man with few enemies." The usually irascible radio commentator Gord Sinclair announced: "Lang is to be congratulated. There is no question that Taylor is one of their own." Even Ian Gray, president of CP Air, welcomed his opponent. "Taylor is a fine and experienced airline man and a worthy competitor." As for the man himself, on the first day on the job, the fifty-year-old Taylor said, "My challenge is to give the 20,000 employees of the airline the feeling that they have a role to play."

Perhaps to block a political appointee replacing Ralph Vaughan, Taylor asked that former Acting President Pierre Taschereau be made chairman. He and Lang both knew that the CNR president was looking forward to retiring soon, but Taylor recalled, "I felt … that I needed some help and he was a very wise person and I used him as a mentor almost in those early days." The government listened to him (this time) and Taschereau was appointed chairman.

————

The sound of the red Airtransit Twin Otters over the Rockcliffe suburb of Ottawa ended April 1, 1976, three months ahead of schedule when the budgeted funds had run out. With the Twin Otter aircraft losing $3.00 per passenger on each flight, the Air Canada-run STOL experiment had lost $2 million in its first year of operations. As a "demonstrator of STOL," Airtransit had a poor success rate. The Dash 7 aircraft that it was set up to feature had greater capacity and used less fuel than the Twin Otters and could have operated at a profit of a $1.00 per passenger on the Montreal–Ottawa route. But only eleven Dash 7s had been sold since the service began, and of that only three in the vital U.S. market. There had been no sales for the Vancouver–Victoria route, and the only interest came from Nordair, which wanted to buy Dash 7s to operate on the Montreal–Toronto–Ottawa STOL triangle — but only with government financing. Critics of the whole Ottawa–Montreal STOL scheme pointed out that the money spent on Airtransit could have been put to better use in improving rail service on the Quebec City –Windsor corridor.

Air Canada was often attacked because as a government owned corporation it was seen as a whipping boy, Taylor said in an interview with *Business Week* on April 26, 1976. "We have that cross to bear. It's the people's airline. And Canadians being what they are, like to be critical of anything

Canadian. Every time something happens to a customer, he feels quite entitled as a shareholder to suggest to us what we ought to be doing." The new president wanted the CN's hotels, travel agencies, and catering businesses to migrate to the airline. Now that so few people used the railway to travel, the airline was where they should be. His ambition, he said, was to staunch the operating losses that stemmed from the political interests that forced Air Canada serve communities in what were uneconomical short haul routes (one half of the airline's 10 million passengers flew short hops), an average of 598 miles compared with CP Air's 900 miles. This was what regional airlines were for. But most of all, as a former accountant, Taylor wanted the airline to keep its own books in order to insulate the commercially viable routes from the uneconomical ones.

His Achilles heel (in the Trudeau years at least) was that the new Air Canada president spoke no French. Many wondered if Lang had been aware of that when he offered Taylor the job. "If I had my life to live over again and someone asked, 'What would you do differently?'" Taylor once said, "I would say: 'Nothing really, except learn more languages.'" Sadly, it was his misfortune to be the head of the Crown corporation in what Prime Minister Trudeau called the most divisive dispute in Canada since the Second World War conscription crisis.

In April 1976, management issued a memo stating that the use of the French language in the cockpit was not permitted. Gerry Lareault, Air Canada's regional public affairs director, said that nothing had really changed since 1972. The memo was circulated to clarify company policy on the matter and to avoid future misunderstandings. Seven percent of Air Canada's pilots spoke French and they protested in writing, saying that they were forced to speak in English while in the cockpit, even to order a cup of coffee from a French-speaking stewardess. Attacked in the House by Quebec MPs, Lang's office quickly did damage control, saying that the Air Canada memo "was never intended to stop casual or ordinary conversations in French between anyone."

The language controversy could not have come at a more explosive time for Lang as he moved to avert a strike by air traffic controllers on the very issue of bilingualism in the air. The Trudeau government had proposed expanding bilingualism among the nation's 2,200 air traffic controllers by initially allowing French to be used in five small Quebec airports. Fearing this would go further — like Montreal's two airports — the Canadian Air Traffic Control Association (CATCA) called for a strike. The remainder of the Air Canada pilots and the air traffic controllers claimed the new practices would create unsafe flying conditions.

In Quebec City, the Quebec Airline Employees Association claimed that Air Canada showed "scorn for the French language," and *Montréal-Matin* columnist (and future Conservative politician) Solange Chaput Rolland wrote on May 13 that "trying to make Air Canada French is like trying to make the Vatican Protestant." Quebec Premier Robert Bourassa threatened to disallow Quebec provincial civil servants from flying the national airline, and Official Languages Commissioner Keith Spicer proclaimed that the Crown corporation had been a failure at bilingualism — then retracted the statement.

Interestingly, neither the CNR nor Air Canada had any plans to pay their employees a bilingual bonus, despite the federal government's decision to grant one to its employees. But Taylor gave his promise to Pat Carey, the president of the Anglophone Canadian Aviation Fellowship, that no employee would lose his job because of language policy. However, he would not comment on the Fellowship's demand to move the airline's main office to Toronto.

The Canadian Air Line Pilots Association (CALPA) and CATCA chose June 20, the eve of the 1976 Montreal Olympics, to strike. This time the issue was bilingualism in the cockpit. In solidarity, members of the U.S. Air Line Pilots Association stopped flying into Canadian airports, citing a "threat to safety in Canadian airspace." Commercial aviation came to a halt in Canada as representatives of the two unions were flown on Ottawa military flights to talk with federal officials. The language issue soon spread to other professions in the airline — chiefly members of the IAM. Of Air Canada's 4,500 maintenance workers, 1,200 were French-speaking, and they claimed that because all the manuals and courses of instruction were in English (the aircraft manufacturers were either American or British), they were at a disadvantage. They insisted that all manuals be translated into French or

131

Perry: Mr. Taylor, can anything be done to save Air Canada? I mean, the problems are horrendous.

Taylor: There are some problems, but the main one is that the airline is a totally a debt-financed organization. Most airlines are financed on the basis that there's about 50 percent or 45 percent of equity participation. That means that people own shares and take their risks on whether the corporation is going to earn a profit or loss. The other 50 percent is money that they borrow from banks. In Air Canada's case, it's almost 98 percent debt-financed. In other words, we pay fixed charges, interest charges at commercial rates of interest. We get no breaks at all.

Perry: So even if you have a profit that will get eaten up in the interest, you have to pay the loan?

Taylor: That's right. If we had a normal debt, which we call a debt-equity ratio, instead of having a $ 12.5 million loss this year, we would have had a $200,000 profit if we hadn't been paying interest charges on about 50 percent or 60 percent of our debts. We are a totally debt-burdened organization.

Perry: Right now you are a subsidiary of the CN. Are you going to get out from under that completely?

Taylor: Yes, our stock, our shares are held by the CNR on behalf of the government — even though we report directly to Parliament and have to appear each year before a parliamentary committee. We're looking forward to the new legislation that the Minister of Transport Otto Lang has promised us in the next few weeks that would create a new act for Air Canada that would give it its own status as capital structure and greater freedom to operate on as a commercial corporation.

they would also strike. When the French-speaking pilots took the airline to court on September 7, 1976, Chief Justice Jules Deschênes of the Quebec Superior Court ruled that Air Canada's English-oriented policy contravened the Official Languages Act and ordered all manuals be translated into French, and company regulations that stipulated all cockpit conversations be in English only be abolished. On September 30, Taylor agreed to abide by the decision and promised a greater use of French at the Dorval maintenance base, and a massive operation to translate all technical instruction manuals began immediately. It was public knowledge that the airline president wasn't bilingual himself, and Pierre Jerome, the airline spokesman, denied rumours that Taylor had offered his resignation to Otto Lang if it would help ease the government out of the bilingualism problem.

Because of the controllers' strike, the country prepared to live without commercial aviation that summer. Some airlines began busing their passengers across the border to get their flights, while Air Canada began laying off 12,000 unionized employees because of the strike.

Nine days later, the government agreed to postpone implementation of bilingualism until a special commission had ascertained whether the use of French in the cockpit would endanger safety, and the strike was called off. But CALPA members were unconvinced and promised to resist bilingualism, even as the Quebec branch of the Canadian Air Traffic Controllers Association said it would not participate in

Before in-flight entertainment meant personal television viewers, passengers read the magazines supplied by the airline. In 1976, besides *Time* and *Newsweek*, the airline also stocked *Playboy*. Strangely, only the last was regularly stolen by passengers.

the commission's study. The following year the government proved more decisive in dealing with the air traffic controllers. At the height of the tourist season, on August 6, 1977, to press demands for a 12.6 percent pay increase, CATCA called for a strike by its members and grounded all commercial aviation in the country. This time, when the government dispatched military aircraft to bring MPs back to Ottawa to enact legislation to order the controllers back to work, the strike ended in three days.

——

What didn't require any translation from English into French were the *Playboy* magazines onboard Air Canada flights. Before in-flight entertainment meant drop-down LCD screens and PTVs (personal television viewers), passengers chatted or looked out of the window, or read the newspapers and magazines supplied by the airline. Depending on the demographic, the type of magazines onboard was important, and Air Canada bought up to 2 million copies of a variety at 5,000 per edition. William Grant, Air Canada's manager of Air Canada Interiors and Service Development, said he was not particularly concerned about the theft of *Playboy* magazines, which always occurred on flights where there were a high proportion of businessmen. "We provide magazines as a service," he said, "and can understand that people sometimes don't have time to finish the article they're reading before the plane lands." Besides the staples *Time* and *Newsweek*, in 1976 the airline also stocked *Canadian Geographical*

Journal, Saturday Night, Canadian Review, and *Canadian Forum*. Strangely enough, only the copies of *Playboy* were stolen.

——

The Estey Inquiry and the parliamentary enquiries into the Atomic Energy Commission and Polysar Ltd. had brought to light outdated and questionable business practices in Crown corporations that embarrassed the government. In addition, the Auditor General's Report for 1976 was critical of the financial and accounting management of these corporations in general. This prompted the federal government to reorganize the financial structures of a number of Crown corporations, one of which was Air Canada. Transport Minister Lang introduced Bill C-17, known as the Air Canada Act, on October 29, which was designed to remove the airline from the CNR's jurisdiction and put it squarely under the Canadian Transport Commission (CTC). In the committee hearings on the separation from the CN, both Taylor and Don Mazankowski tried hard to insert a phrase into the act that would dictate that the airline be run "in anticipation of making a profit." But only the two of them, it seemed, shared this view of its future. The political powers of the day still saw the company as more an instrument of social engineering than a private profit-making enterprise. "My attitude towards the government at that time," remembered Taylor, "was not that we were a Crown corporation, but that we had a single shareholder that we tried to ignore as much as possible."

Servicing the smaller population centres, regional airlines had been hardest hit by the rising fuel prices. To remain solvent, especially in the winter, the federal government encouraged the operation of regional airlines — as long as they had no ambitions to begin transcontinental scheduled operations and compete with Air Canada, or merge with each other. In the West, when PWA's president Rhys Eyton applied to the CTC to buy the Winnipeg-based Transair for its Winnipeg–Toronto route, Air Canada held him off by trading with him its routes between Calgary–Regina–Winnipeg.

The very antithesis of the flamboyant Grant McConachie was Ian Alexander Gray, who became president of CP Air on February 1, 1976. If Claude Taylor's style was unpretentious, then that of his counterpart in CP Air was even more so. As a young engineer Gray had had the temerity to advise McConachie against buying the ill-fated Comets. Even as president, Gray drove a small red station wagon, always flew economy class (sometimes on Air Canada) and hated to be met at airports, CP Air he said was "being shafted by Ottawa" and would never be profitable if confined to 25 percent capacity of the transcontinental market. But through the 1970s, capacity restraints were gradually relaxed so that by 1978 CP Air's transcontinental share had been increased to 35 percent and Gray looked to replacing his DC-8s with wide-bodied DC-10-30s.

A more serious threat to Air Canada than CP Air's incursions were the futures of Nordair and Quebecair, two politically important carriers in central Canada. Being based in Ontario and Quebec, both regional airlines would always be overshadowed by Air Canada. Shut out of the most heavily used triangles in the country, that of Montreal–Toronto–Ottawa and Quebec City–Montreal–Ottawa, both Nordair and Quebecair's prospects were limited.

Although the only Francophone airline in North America, because it had been bought in 1969 by Howard Webster, a prominent member of the Montreal Anglo oligarchy, Quebecair was kept at an arm's length by the provincial government in Quebec City. It was only when taken over a decade later by the Francophone Alfred Hamel that North America's only French-speaking airline was elevated to the status of a cultural symbol, and its demise would be embarrassing to the Trudeau government. Now financially assisted by the Parti Québécois government, Quebecair attracted great public support in its province. There was even a concert at the Montreal Forum to raise money to keep it flying. But the damage from the Webster days, the use of British-built BAC 1-11s instead of B737s, for example, hampered its growth.

Nordair employed 850 people who maintained and flew a fleet of 6 B737s, one DC-8-61, five Fairchild F227s, and two Lockheed Electras that were used on ice patrols. Sharing Montreal's Dorval Airport with Air Canada, it was caught between Quebecair and EPA in the east and Transair and PWA in the west. Its only expansion was along the Seaway to Kingston, Hamilton, Windsor, and Pittsburgh. As a result, Nordair made most of its money on charters, its blue aircraft sent as far away as war-torn Biafra, Cuba, and Europe.

Without hope of getting the mainline routes, Nordair's chairman James Tooley saw little future for his airline — especially with the Parti Québécois victory in November 1976, which he knew would favour Quebecair. What enam-

---

Vivianne Lacoste had been a flight attendant with Air Canada for thirteen years when she agreed to be interviewed by *Weekend* magazine, December 16, 1978.

"For me flying's like going to the office. You're so busy you don't have time to be frightened. When the aircraft is full you're busy all the time. You've got the bar, the meals, the boutique which they've introduced in the last few years selling duty free goods such as liquor and perfume. And after you've got the movie.

"On flights within Canada the majority of the passengers are businessmen and they can be unpleasant. They want something and they want it now and they think they're the only ones there. We don't get hustled as much as men think we do. In the 13 years I have gone out with two passengers. A few flight attendants have married passengers but that doesn't happen often. A few girls have married pilots or male flight attendants, but I wouldn't say that the percentage is high. It's just not what people think. A pilot may phone one of the girls to go out on a layover, but a lot of the times it's just for companionship. It's for no other reason.

"At first I was afraid that they wouldn't take me as a stewardess because I thought you had to look like a movie star. But when I went on the training course I realized that you didn't have to be glamorous. They teach you about make-up and hairstyles, but mainly because of the lighting in the aircraft. It's a different type, and they want you to look as though you had a little colour. They want to you to look neat and tidy because you are serving food. The main objective of the training course is to teach you emergency procedures: what the escape chute is like, where the survival kit is kept and how to use it. We're given first aid training too, because you never know what can happen on board. I've had two persons have heart attacks on my flights, one so severe that we had to make an unscheduled landing. Hyperventilation is also something I've had to deal with. We have to write an annual exam on emergency procedures and we have to get a passing grade which is 100 per cent.

"I can fly now until I'm 60. I don't think I will; I just don't think my health could take it. For the last ten years I have worn support stockings. They really help, particularly on a long flight. Because of the pressure changes you often feel that someone's sitting on your head and you're sinking through the floor. The Lockheed is very bad for the backs of your legs because you seem to be flying at an angle and it's like you're walking uphill all the time.

"Being a stewardess has some very good benefits. I've had some trips which I couldn't have taken if I hadn't been with an airline. I feel lucky. I'm content with my job."

Unlike the airlines in the United States where the swinging sixties brought sexual titillation to the profession, in Air Canada flight attendant uniforms remained modest — pleated skirts, long-sleeved brown jackets, with white sweaters, as shown here in Old Montreal.

oured Nordair to suitors was its Montreal base and that it was an "Anglophone" airline, both assets that made it doubly attractive to CP Air, Calgary-based PWA, and Eastern Provincial Airways (EPA) from Gander, Newfoundland. Otto Lang wanted Air Canada to buy Nordair and rationalize the Montreal base and fleet, and Tooley encouraged a group of shareholders to approach Air Canada to ask if it was interested.

Having been spurned by Wardair when it tried to buy that charter airline in 1973, Air Canada saw an acquisition of Nordair as a good investment. Besides, if Nordair closed down, essential air services to places like Frobisher Bay and Hall Beach in the North would be cut and the government might order the Crown corporation to provide them. Then there was also speculation among aviation analysts that if Nordair wasn't taken off the market, Air Canada would soon have a third competitor on the transcontinental route. PWA had just applied to the CTC to buy Transair, and if the sale was allowed, it would bring the British Columbia airline closer to the Eastern markets.

Taylor approached the CTC on January 6, 1977, for permission to buy Nordair. Air Canada offered the regional carrier's board of directors $11.50 per share ($4.50 over market quotation), which represented a total investment of $25 million. Of particular interest to Air Canada (the press release said) were Nordair's "Tour Charter" flights to Europe and the south. As expected, there were objections to the purchase. The media wondered if a national carrier owned a regional one, would this result in a restriction of competition? To the Conservatives in opposition this was typical of the government airline further increasing its monopoly on commercial aviation in Canada. The Air Canada pilots refused to consider integration of their Nordair counterparts into the seniority list, calling them (it was alleged) "a bunch of cut-rate pilots, lacking the expertise that they [the Air Canada pilots] possessed." To which Nordair senior pilot J.S. Patterson pointed out that as a matter of routine in the North, his pilots landed on gravel strips that were too short with little or no approach facilities and yet there had not been a single accident — unlike the performance of Air Canada pilots at Sainte-Thérèse, Ottawa, or Toronto.

At the CTC hearings, Taylor promised to run Nordair as an independent subsidiary of Air Canada, allowing the airline its own board of directors and management. There would be no conflict of interest, he said, since only 7 percent of Nordair's operations competed with Air Canada's. And he promised that his company would not buy any other regional airlines.

———

At the end of 1976, Taylor's cost-cutting program had paid off. The airline had lost $10.5 million that year, but only the pilots' strike had prevented Air Canada from returning to profit. His second public announcement as president had been that he planned to increase fares, reduce staff, and end the politically prestigious runs to Vienna, Prague, Moscow, and Brussels. "The first thing I set out to do was to eliminate the criticism that we're running an inefficient airline," he said. On hearing about the number of Air Canada employees who used first class, one of the first things Taylor did was cut off such privileges except for those employees who had it written into their contracts. Only someone with his personal prestige could have pulled it off, and the staff cuts were not without incident. When eighty-four Air Canada ramp workers were laid off at terminals in New York, Cleveland, and Chicago with generous severance allowances, they retaliated by picketing the airline and handing out leaflets to boycott Air Canada.

The company celebrated its fortieth birthday on April 10, 1977, in an optimistic mood. Veteran retired pilot Frank Smith was chosen to tell the airline's history to service clubs, students, and the media. But as Claude Taylor discovered speaking at the celebratory dinner in Winnipeg, the media were less interested in the airline's past than the present. They wanted to know did Air Canada have any contingency plans if Quebec separated? (No) and was Margaret Trudeau still getting free flights? (No) Was the airline planning to buy the STOL Dash-7 now being built by the government-owned de Havilland Aircraft of Canada? (No) Taylor replied that the economics of effective STOL operations had not been proven.

When Air Canada introduced "Charter Class Fares" in February 1977, its domestic charter class fares for the summer season were sold out until Labour Day, forcing the airline to place ads in newspapers across the country to turn off the flood of requests coming in. By mid-April all charter class Canada fares for Christmas 1977 were also sold out. "We've just been too darn successful, darn it," said Norm Garwood, an Air Canada spokesman. Transcontinental service was rising — in 1976 Air Canada got 72 percent of the business, in 1977 it expected 76 percent. Best of all, with the busy summer season, the labour front was quiet. Two major union contracts were signed with the IAMAW and the Canadian Airline Employees Association, and in July Air Canada's 1,500 pilots approved a contract that included a 6.1 percent wage increase, allowing the average salary to go from $38,000 to $40,000.

That June the cabinet put the finishing touches on the new bill for Air Canada, the ministers trying to get it ready to present to Parliament before the summer recess.

As the bill received its second reading, the Conservatives pushed for various changes; they wanted the airline to appear before the Commons transport committee and also to have some regional representation on its board. The Air Canada Act would allow the airline to write off about $365 million of its long-term debt — now close to $1 billion, and cut its connections with the CNR, becoming a separate Crown corporation in its own right. The capital restructuring would provide a more normal debt to equity ratio (like 60 percent debt to 40 percent equity), which put the airline in the same range as other carriers. With this more normal capital structure, the financial markets might look at Air Canada in a favourable light when one day it went to them for financing. Said a pleased Taylor, "The bill states specifically that the airline is to be managed on sound business principles in anticipation of a profit."

Parliament passed the Air Canada Act on November 2, 1977, and it came into effect on April 19, 1978, where the debts of Air Canada and the Canadian National Railway Company were rearranged and the minister of transport now assumed ownership of the airline. Part of the long-term debt was refunded, and 329,009 equity shares were issued to a single shareholder: the government. The equity investment at year-end was 42 percent of the total capital employed — a normal commercial ratio in line with other airlines' balance sheets. By December 31, long-term liabilities amounted to $562.6 million and the fixed interest commitment was now more manageable.

139

The passage of the act significantly altered the relationship between government and Air Canada, preparing it for privatization that would occur ten years later. Forty years after its birth, the airline was to be managed as a "sound business" and operate "in contemplation of profit," something that Mackenzie King and C.D. Howe could never have envisaged. No longer able to rely on the government as a source of borrowed capital (there would be no government guarantees of the company's debt instruments), Air Canada was now firmly in the private sector. It would have to live or die on its balance sheet as it would attract the most competitive rates for loans, because over the next decade Air Canada was looking to borrow over $1 billion. By April 1978, when the recapitalization had come into effect, the company was back in the black, reporting a profit of $41.9 million.

And it wasn't only Air Canada that altered. In a way Taylor was the best friend that CP Air ever had. For all the years that the private airline had attacked Ottawa over TCA/Air Canada's special status, arguing for a level playing field, it was only when he told Lang that C.D. Howe's child could fly by itself that the federal government acknowledged that CP Air had a legitimate role to play in commercial aviation. The Air Canada president was the first to admit that he didn't do this out of altruism. He had been keeping a close eye on deregulation in the United States and the wave of consumer pressure (and anger) that was drowning in the CAB's restrictions.

It might be said that the deregulation movement was inevitable; even before the oil crisis of 1973 and the introduction of wide-bodied aircraft, the United States government had begun dismantling government regulations, first with the telecommunications industry in 1968, then finance in 1970, and finally transport in 1978.

Deregulation killed off what British aviation swashbuckler Freddie Laker called "Panamania," making sure that Pan American Airways (or British Airways or Air France), their nation's de facto chosen instruments — while hopelessly mismanaged — remained flying as symbols of national prestige. Economist Alfred Khan was appointed by President Jimmy Carter to head the CAB to dismantle the wall of regulations that had protected and restricted commercial aviation in the United States since 1938. By 1977, Congress had deregulated the air cargo industry, and on October 4, 1978, it passed the Airline Deregulation Act. This took power from the bureaucrats and gave it to consumers — and they wanted lower airfares. Airfares fell dramatically as the protected dinosaurs like Pan American Airways, Braniff, and Eastern Airlines disappeared and discount airlines like Air Florida and People's Express started up — and sometimes also disappeared.

In 1984 the CAB, with little to regulate, was abolished. Deregulation gave birth to several innovations in the industry, such discount fares, hub and spoke fortresses, frequent flyer points, code sharing between airlines, and computer reservation systems

CLAUDE TAYLOR AND THE SUMMER AFTERNOON

(CRS). Studies in the United States demonstrated that when an airline owned a CRS, travel agents using that CRS tended to favour that airline when booking customers — the "halo effect," the battle for customers moving to cyberspace. When British Overseas Airways Corporation (BOAC) and British European Airways (BEA) developed their own computer reservation systems independently of each other, so confusing did it make air travel in Britain that the British government was forced to mash them together in 1972 as British Airways.

Canadians watched the deregulation process across the border closely, increasingly taking advantage of it by driving across the border at Buffalo or Burlington to fly People's Express to Florida. They knew that to keep TCA/Air Canada from bankruptcy, Ottawa had hindered competition. They also wondered if deregulation would work in Canada. Max Ward, Canada's answer to Freddie Laker, certainly thought so.

———

Twenty-four year old Judy Cameron from Edmonton was chosen in May 1978 from 1,800 applicants to fly for Air Canada. Her initiation to flight had occured on a two-passenger Cessna 150 when the pilot asked if she wanted to see a pencil float from the front of the aircraft to the back. Cameron agreed and the manoeuvre was so much fun that she took up flight training soon after and graduated from Selkirk College. Cameron was the first female pilot in the company. The only other female in the cockpit in Canada at the time was F/O

Rosella Bjornson, who had been hired in 1973 to fly for Transair. The airlines knew that public and political pressure was going to force them to hire women as pilots, whether they wanted to or not, and this was especially the case with a government airline. Between 1978 and 1980 Air Canada received 1,728 applications but only twenty were from women. Of the 500 pilots hired in these two years, five were female: Judy Cameron, Gwen Grant, Britt Ferst Irving, Glenys Olstad Robison, and Barbara Swyers. Many years later, Air Canada President Pierre Jeanniot would compliment Captain Charlie Simpson, the head of flight operations, for shattering the "glass ceiling" in pilot recruiting. "He hired the first group of female pilots," Jeanniot would say, "a group of twelve who were immediately labelled in Air Canada, 'Charlie's Angels.'"[1] In October 1990, history was made when Barbara Baerg and Diane Bourdon, two of the airline's now nineteen female pilots, flew together.

As a private airline, CP Air was not under the microscope as much and would only hire two in the same period: Sandra Lloyd in 1979 and Kathy Davenport Zokol in 1981. Wardair would hire none. For the media there was an even better story: "Stew makes it from the back to the front." Britt Ferst Irving had been a flight attendant with Air Canada before she took flying lessons. She was hired by Air Canada in 1979 as second officer on a DC-8, later transferring to a Boeing 727. While the airline did as much as it could to shield them, the media attention that she and the other four female pilots got, to say nothing of the resentment from some male pilots, only added to their problems. When the women proved as adept as the men at flying, it all came down to maternity leave. Airlines were leery about pregnant employees, whether pilots or flight attendants.[2]

As second officer on a B727, Cameron would be paid $1,100 for a maximum of seventy-five hours monthly. She was married to a company mechanic, and if she became pregnant she would have to notify the airline and cease flying three months before giving birth. When she did become pregnant six years later, she told the airline her contract had nothing about maternity leave. "The FAA had no ruling on pregnant pilots flying, and I pointed this out to Air Canada. However, I did not want to make it difficult for Air Canada so they wouldn't hire other women pilots. I applied for a waiver from the Ministry of Transport aviation doctor. I flew until the end of my fourth month. I didn't tell any of the guys because I was worried about their reaction. I just kept letting my pants out."[3] During her career with the company, Judy Cameron would go on to pilot the L-1011, the DC-9, the B767, the Airbus 320, and in 2012, she was captain on the B777.

While the airline was coming to terms with maternity leave for its pilots, another more serious problem was being dealt with, that of alcoholism among pilots. In 1980, it was estimated that an average of twenty-four of Air Canada's 2,100 pilots were annually receiving treatment for alcoholism. Dr. Peter Vaughan, the director Air

Canada's medical services, said, "What we do with pilots with alcoholism is refer them to the Donwood Institute, Toronto, for a twenty-day in-patient treatment program. And in most cases we are successful. Of the twenty-four or so, only about 5 percent cannot be rehabilitated."

———

Seeing the warning light in the cockpit, Captain Reginald W. Stewart tried to abort Flight 189's takeoff. It was June 26, 1978, and C-FTLV was about to lift off from Runway 024R-06L at Toronto International Airport. The Air Canada DC-9-32 was on the Ottawa–Toronto–Winnipeg–Vancouver run with 107 passengers onboard. At approximately 8:15 a.m., as it attempted to become airborne, one of the tires burst and chunks of rubber were taken into the landing gear. By the time the captain decided to abort the takeoff, an Air Canada spokesperson later said, the DC-9 was already two thirds along the runway and moving at between 160 to 170 mph. But it needed 181 mph to get airborne. Witnesses said that the pilot had managed to hold the aircraft level after the blowout but that he had simply run out of runway. In full view of Toronto-bound commuters on Highway 401, the DC-9 skidded down the sixty-foot embankment into Etobicoke Creek, narrowly missing a dozen navigational pylons on which approach lighting was mounted. Had it hit them with full tanks of gas, a spokesperson from the Ministry of Transport said, the DC-9 would have exploded.

Appointed chairman of Air Canada by Prime Minister Trudeau in December 1978, Bryce Mackasey joked, "I'm in good company. The governor general, all sorts of ambassadors. They're all political appointees...." President Claude Taylor was not amused.

The aircraft broke into three pieces and came to rest (near where twenty-seven years later an Air France A340 would also fail to stop in poor weather on the runway) and burst into flames. There was initial confusion, passengers said, but once they realized what was happening everyone calmed down, some managing to get out through the gaping holes in the plane. There were two fatalities: Irwin Theodore Childs, forty-three, and J. Frank Scrase, seventy-five, but the other 105 passengers were taken to local hospitals. The airline offered out-of-court settlements to some of the passengers but did not accept blame for the crash.

————

In April 1978, PWA was given permission to buy Transair but on condition that it would discontinue service east of Winnipeg. Air Canada was finally permitted to buy 86.46 percent of Nordair in November 1978 — but with the proviso that it would not merge with it and would return it to the private sector within a year. To help its bottom line, Nordair was awarded the routes Toronto–Sault Ste. Marie, Thunder Bay, Dryden to Winnipeg, and the Golden Triangle, Montreal–Ottawa–Toronto.

From 1978 onward, Air Canada did well leasing its high-density seating DC-8s and 747s for use on the Hajj flights, flying pilgrims from Africa to Saudi Arabia. The federal government also chartered the high density DC-8-63s (227 seats) to fly Vietnamese refugees to Canada from Kuala Lumpur through 1979–80. Made possible by the changes in federal legislation, Air Canada was given government approval to take over two associate companies, Airline Maintenance Building Ltd., which had built the cargo facilities for Air Canada at Toronto's international airport, and Venturex Ltd. Using funds advanced by Air Canada, CN Realty had originally invested in both companies, and because of the Air Canada Act the airline could now buy up the remaining common shares it owned.

Federal approval was also given in 1978 to buy three ten-year-old Boeing 727-100s from United Air Lines so that Air Canada could expand its small package delivery service, Courierair. The 727s would be dedicated to next-day package deliveries under the trade name of Airvelope and for parcels up to fifty pounds in weight called Expedair. Federal Express Ltd. of Memphis had built one of the largest cargo airlines in the world using this concept, and how it would fare in Canada was anyone's guess.

————

Taschereau retired in November 1978, and Christmas came early for Lang's old friend, former labour minister and postmaster general, fifty-seven-year-old Bryce Mackasey. Ottawa needed a bilingual chairman who would be acceptable in the province of Quebec but still able to talk to the rest of the country. Mackasey had been mentioned in 1976 as a candidate for the position, and now he had suddenly become available, having just lost an election in the supposedly "safe" Liberal riding of Ottawa South. On December 14, he was appointed the airline's chairman for the next seven years with the proviso that he would serve at the "pleasure of the government" in power. The annual salary for the post was variously reported at between $52,000 and $90,000, and the perks were unlimited passes and a chauffeur-driven Lincoln Continental. Veteran journalist Charles Lynch wrote that the appointment was Trudeau's decision alone. Air Canada and Transport Minister Otto Lang said they were unaware of the appointment thirty minutes prior to Trudeau's statement. The announcement had been made at a weekly cabinet meeting without a vote, a cabinet source said. Mackasey, who had heard he was getting the job a few minutes before Trudeau's news conference, said in good humour, "I'm in good company. The governor general, all sorts of ambassadors ... they're all political appointees ... that doesn't mean they can't do their job." The newspapers reported that when Taylor heard of the appointment, he immediately phoned Lang to say that he would not tolerate any interference from the chairman's office.

A board meeting hastily called on January 8, 1979, effectively stripped Mackasey's position of all of its powers, making the job entirely ceremonial. A director who asked not to be identified said, "We made sure that he [Mackasey] will be an expensive figurehead and that's all. The only operating function he'll have will be the hiring of his own secretary." The next day Taschereau stated that no director had spoken to the media about the new chairman and expressed his "grave disappointment that such an erroneous state-ment would be printed." As a long-time politician Mackasey said that he was not offended in the least. The new chairman would then embarrass the airline by using his passes to fly the chef at the prestigious Beaver Club in Montreal to Paris, along with his wife and daughter. While there was nothing illegal about this, having it splashed across the papers served to antagonize airline senior management further.

The two men who ran Air Canada could not have been more different. Unlike the reticent, unilingual Taylor, Irish-Quebecer Mackasey spoke excellent French, having grown up in the working class Montreal suburb of Verdun. With his background he said that he hoped to help solve the airline's problems with bilingualism. Neither Taylor nor Lang were available for comment, but opposition leader Joe Clark put the Air Canada chairman Number 1 on the Tory "Hit List."

At the same meeting, the directors centralized control of the Crown corporation under a small group of senior executives, all responsible to Taylor. Previously, some functions like legal affairs, the running of the subsidiaries, and the corporate secretariat had been under the chairman. Pierre Jeanniot, formerly vice-president of the Quebec region, was made senior vice-president in charge of cargo, all subsidiaries, and of government affairs. The former vice-president of public affairs, Jean Douville, took over the subsidiaries under Jeanniot's direction. Michel Fournier, one of the youngest senior executives in the company, left his post as manager of Western Europe to be vice-president of public relations. Jack Kantor, manager of in-flight services, was made vice-president of the same, and Air Canada's first female vice-president, Anne Bodnarchuk, was made vice-president of computer systems.

———

Air Canada crews were used to members of Parliament coming on board and saying: "We own you guys!" But there were individual parliamentarians who behaved as if Air Canada were responsible directly to them. In 1978, for example, Air Canada's schedulers decided to eliminate a 10:50 p.m. flight from Ottawa to Toronto because there weren't enough passengers to make the flight financially viable. The flight was a favourite of Toronto-area MPs, who used it on Thursday nights to return to their ridings for the weekend. The evening parliamentary session usually finished with a 9:45 vote, so once the 10:50 flight was cancelled, MPs were stuck in Ottawa until Friday morning. One of the disgruntled parliamentarians was the future minister of transport, David Collenette, then vice-chair of the House of Commons standing committee on transportation issues. Collenette urged his fellow MPs to sign a petition, and then he personally put in a call to Claude Taylor's office "suggesting" that the 10:50 flight be reinstated. It was.[4] At times like this Taylor must have thought that privatization couldn't happen soon enough.

Three years into his position, the cheerful, bespectacled president could be proud of his achievements. The company employed 20,964 people in thirty-two countries. It had 110 aircraft: six B747s, ten Lockheed L-1011s, twenty-seven Douglas DC-8s, fifteen B727s, and forty-six Douglas DC-9s. Plans were approved for the purchase of nineteen B727s and to retire the older DC-8s and DC-9s. Productivity had improved by 5 percent in available ton mile and 6 percent in revenue ton mile per employee. Taylor had taken the airline from a loss of $12.5 million in 1975 to a profit of $20 million in 1977, tripling that to $69.2 million in 1979. Based on these figures, the U.S. Import Export Bank approved an $88 million loan to Air Canada to purchase fourteen of the 727 airliners. In a survey of fourteen carriers, British food expert Egon Ronay had ranked Air Canada's cuisine second behind Delta Airlines and far better than British Airways or Pan American. In 1981, *Air Transport World,* one of the most prestigious magazines in aviation, honoured Air Canada with its Award of Excellence for Technical Management.

———

But the meals and balance sheet apart, there was a host of problems. On March 1, 1978, the Canadian Human Rights Act went into effect, prohibiting discrimination on the grounds of sex — but the act was vague about the pregnancy and maternity leaves that the airline forced on its female employees. It would not be until the act was amended in 1984 that discrimination on the basis of pregnancy was specifically prohibited.

The Human Rights Commission also claimed that Air Canada discriminated against unmarried couples, denying them family fare discounts (ticket agents could require a couple living under common law to furnish an affidavit signed by a notary public to the effect that they had live together for two years). Perhaps less moralistic, all that CP Air required was that the couple show proof they lived at the same address.

A Miss Nancy Bain of Vancouver was planning a trip to eastern Canada with a friend. On April 7, 1978, she phoned Air Canada and enquired about fares and any possible discounts that they could get. She was informed that if she was married and travelling with her husband she could get a discounted fare under the family fare plan. When she replied that she wasn't married and would be travelling with a friend, she was told that she could then qualify for a reduced fare if she and her friend were living together as a family. On April 21, Miss Bain filed a complaint with the Canadian Human Rights Commission against Air Canada for discrimination on the basis of marital status. The federal court of appeal ruled on January 4, 1982, in Air Canada's favour, saying that it was not guilty of discrimination when it refused two unrelated adults travelling together taking advantage of the airline's family fare plan.

But the airline was also fighting battles on several fronts: a $30 million lawsuit launched by Diners Club over credit card monopoly, and seven provinces, led by Manitoba, were taking Air Canada to court to prove it was

THE BOEING B-727

Air Canada was a late bloomer to operating 727s — the type had been around two decades by then. We bought the latest model 727-200 which had been stretched and proven in the field by years of operations by the Americans. You either loved it or hated it. It was a truly three-man operation. Actually a two-man operation. The Captain and the Second Officer. Rarely did a captain know exactly what the second was scheming back at the "oiler panel," and a student physiologist could have a field day analyzing the interaction between the two of them. For here, the all knowing, all seeing Captain of our good ship had to admit some things were not in his control. And the absolute glee some of the "oilers" derived from this could be truly comical. To have a young, newly hired kid tell him, master and commander, that he, the lowest of the low on the seniority list, that he wasn't ready for takeoff was enough to light up the red veins in his nose!

— Captain Bud Olson

subject to provincial laws when over their airspace. And CALPA was planning on a strike vote. The airlines' 1,700 pilots were 15 percent behind their U.S. counterparts in wages, and the gap would soon be 25 percent. Their wage parity demands had been rolled back by the federal anti-inflation board in 1976, and it looked as if they would be again in 1978.

Taylor's assumption that Air Canada was the national whipping boy was never better illustrated when the wine growers of St. Catharines, Ontario, wanted it to provide more domestic (i.e. their constituents) wine on foreign flights, instead of just asking passengers if they wanted white or red wine. Taylor replied that when the airline did introduce Canadian wines, it was asked to keep the price below that of imported wines — which implied it was of lesser quality than foreign wines.

Then, in the role of perfidious Albion, the British government ordered Air Canada to move from Heathrow Airport to distant Gatwick Airport with its single runway and few connections. This was so it could find slots for a host of new Middle Eastern and Asian airlines. As TCA, Air Canada had been flying into Heathrow Airport since it was a tent city. The airline, which had first landed at Heathrow on September 16, 1946, using a ten-seater Lancastrian, now flew in 3,000 passengers daily in peak months, using five wide-bodied aircraft to serve eight Canadian cities from Heathrow. In vain did Taylor protest that 30 percent of passengers connected at Heathrow for other destinations and would be unable to do so at Gatwick. There would also be serious losses in revenue from the cabin grooming that Air Canada did for other airlines, and moving the cargo facilities and Air Canada flight kitchens, where 600,000 meals were produced annually.

Then there was the Air Canada staff at Heathrow who lived nearby. Brian Sygrove, the airport manager at Heathrow, had been there for twenty-four years and spoke for all when he said: "We are consistently among the top runners here, and the reason is quite simple — people. Pride and willingness to work for the airline which flows right down from the top." This was echoed by the Maple Leaf Lounge hostess, the legendary Jessie Bates, who twenty-three years before had come over to England for six months and liked the job so much that she had remained.

So serious was the move to Gatwick considered to Canadian interests that in January 1979, when negotiations between London and Ottawa broke down, the British were given an ultimatum on March 15: either leave Air Canada at Heathrow or face the possibility of being shut out of Canada completely. In April 1980, British Trade Secretary John Nott then instigated an 85 percent increase in landing fees against all airlines that used Heathrow in the hope that they would voluntarily leave for Gatwick. The airlines formed the British Airports Action Group, and with Air Canada withheld 46 percent of the increase.

While this was going on, British Airways was lobbying for landing rights to Calgary and Vancouver and was soon joined in this by Cathay Pacific Airlines from the Crown Colony of Hong Kong. With rights to London and Prestwick, Canada had no interest in any other British cities and was in no mood to grant permission. The airline's principal negotiator, Pierre Jeanniot, suggested that in exchange Air Canada be allowed Fifth Freedom rights so that the airline could pick up passengers from London and carry them to Asian destinations. At this, the British threatened to abrogate the bilateral air agreement that would prevent both

Air Canada and British Airways countries from landing in each other's countries.

It was brinkmanship at its finest and had a precedent in C.D. Howe's day, when the minister called a similar British bluff by threatening to consign BOAC (the predecessor to British Airways) to Quebec City's airport — which everyone knew did not have a large enough runway. This time Ottawa used its trump card: it withdrew from the 1944 International Air Services Transit Agreement, which would end British Airways' privileges of over-flying Canadian air space en route to the U.S. This brought the British negotiating team hastily back to the table. The dispute was settled in 1980, allowing Air Canada to remain at Heathrow and to fly Toronto–London–Mumbai and Montreal–London–Geneva–Nice. British Airways was given access to Vancouver, Calgary, and Edmonton, and Cathay Pacific to Vancouver. It was a victory for both countries, and Jeanniot was promoted to executive vice-president and chief operating officer. Six years later British Airways would claim that the Fifth Freedom rights of Air Canada serving Bombay and Singapore were unfairly weighed in its favour and wanted Whitehall to terminate the agreement. It took the personal friendship between British Prime Minister Margaret Thatcher and Canadian Prime Minister Brian Mulroney, both of whom had privatized their nation's state-owned airlines, to negotiate a mutually agreeable air service in June 1988.[5]

When Lang proclaimed his "Open Sky" policy on March 23, 1979, ushering in unfettered competition between Air Canada and CP Air on the mainline routes, the old C.D. Howe commercial aviation monopoly was transformed into a duopoly. All capacity restraints were removed from CP Air's share of transcontinental air traffic, and it was given a license to provide domestic transcontinental flights. No one was happier than Taylor when he heard the news. "I'll tell you what delighted me," he laughed. "At last the crutch has been yanked out from under those scoundrels. For years CP Air has squeezed every drop of juice they could at playing the underdog. But from now on they and the Canadian Chamber of Commerce can look for another scapegoat." If he had opposed "Open Skies" he would have been a "dead duck, PR-wise," Taylor later said. "I think the timing was just right, although I had a little trouble convincing the more socialistic members of my board." It was a significant shift for the federal government. Instead of one transcontinental airline, Ottawa had sanctioned two, and it didn't take CP Air long to apply to the CTC to fly into Halifax, thus making it truly a coast-to-coast airline.

If the Canadian public thought that deregulation meant cheaper airfares, as in the United States, Canadian carriers were less impressed. Canada was unsuited to the hub-and-spoke system; unlike the airlines in the United States, Canada's operated on an East–West axis in a very narrow, linear market. There were only two real urban hubs: Toronto–Hamilton and Montreal–Ottawa–Quebec City, and all were within driving distance of each other. Canada did not have the population centres that the Americans did, which had allowed the deregulation "babies" like People's Express or Valujet to take wing. And as Guy Chiasson, Air Canada's vice-president of marketing, pointed out, since deregulation went into effect below the border, airfares had risen on average by 20 percent. The average fare increase in Canada was, by comparison, 9.5 percent.

Besides, Air Canada had only just accepted CP Air as the second national airline. And Grant McConachie's former company, having fought hard to get to its privileged place, didn't want to lose it to the up-and-coming, aggressive PWA. With Nordair awarded the Toronto–Winnipeg route on February 1, 1979, even PWA feared more competition. Ever cautious, when Don Mazankowski became transport minister in June 1979 he announced a policy of "controlled deregulation." More significantly, he and Taylor began to discuss when — not if — Air Canada would be sold. A private airline became for the Air Canada president "more and more of a passion." The company needed money, and he needed a free hand to create a competitive global operation. "We had to have a change of ownership. And Mazankowski was very much a part of that."[6]

The only Canadian airline that had no fear of deregulation was Wardair, its founder Max Ward the strongest and most vocal advocate of free and open competition in the country. "What's the difference between airlines and groceries?" he asked. "Transportation is no different from food, shelter, clothing, so why isolate it? How

much protection is enough?" Both Taylor and Gray were aware that Ward wanted to join the exclusive transcontinental club — and both were prepared to resist Wardair's attempts to become the third transcontinental carrier. If his airline was to survive, Ward knew that it had to get access to the economy fare passengers that the scheduled carriers now had. When temporarily thwarted, Ward set his mind on scheduled flights to Europe. But the recession of 1981–82 intervened and he almost lost his company, barely clinging on through a bitter strike by the Wardair flight attendants.

Canadians discovered that deregulation only went as far as the border. In 1979, when American Airlines and United Airlines attempted "super saver" and half fare discounts for their Canadian flights, Ottawa blocked them to protect its own airlines. As a result, when Air Canada offered discounts of between 46 to 60 percent on flights into the U.S. (the reduced fares would allow Montrealers to go to Miami for as little as $189), American and United leaned on the CAB to have them disallowed. Because these were international flights, the CAB lobbied President Carter, who upheld their decision, causing Air Canada to scrap the seat sale. In 1982, the House of Commons Standing Committee on Transport recommended a "go slow" approach to deregulation: continued regulation but with room for greater competition.

———

Like CP Air, Air Canada was planning to replace the DC-8s and buy its next generation of aircraft for the 1980s. In May 1979, Chairman Bryce Mackasey announced that Air Canada was purchasing six Boeing 727s and six Lockheed L-1011-500s, dubbed the "Dash 500," as part of its $3.5 billion fleet renewal for the 1980s. The wide-bodied aircraft would seat 244 passengers in comparison to the 429 that the 747 seated, and with spare parts cost $49.6 million each, bringing the total cost of the six to $300 million. The compatibility with the airline's ten L-1011-1s purchased in the 1970s was a big factor in choosing the aircraft, Mackasey said, over the McDonnell Douglas DC-10, although the latter had more seating and its wings were built in Toronto. But the L-1011-500's range would permit it to fly from Vancouver to Frankfurt non-stop. "After some early Rolls engine delays were overcome," recalled Captain Ray Bicknell, who flew them for five years, "the bird settled into a very solid performing aircraft that was a delight to fly and had great passenger appeal. The autoflight system was state of the art, based on a three-autopilot system that was capable of zero visibility landings. The aircraft's operation allowed landings in 1–4 mile visibility. The 'Star had a wide-track gear that could handle large crosswind capability coupled with a braking system that was the best of anything that pilots had ever been supplied with before."

The L-1011s served the airline well; the only incident took place on March 22, 1982, when Air Canada Flight 933 took off from Miami bound for Montreal. The pilots noticed excessive vibrations overheating one of the engines. It was shut down and

Glen Hansen, Air Canada station agent, Regina, did not realize how strong an influence his job had on his youngest daughter.

"After being in kindergarten for a month my wife and I asked Leanne how school was going. Her comment was 'Pretty good, except the hardest thing is learning that prayer and the Air Canada song.' Talk about a brainwashed Air Canada employee's child. For a month she had been singing 'Air Canada' instead of 'O Canada.' We are still wondering what the teacher thought."

the aircraft circled the Everglades, dumping 20,000 pounds of fuel. Twenty-five minutes after takeoff it landed safely and all 287 passengers were put on another plane to Montreal. The ground crew found that the engine under the wing had partially disintegrated. "We don't know what caused it," admitted an Air Canada spokesman, "but the engines overheat and fly apart because of too little lubrication." The year saw a rash of engine shutdowns with the L-1011s — and this would be the sixty-first.

———

The Ottawa rumour mill claimed that to improve trade relations with Germany and France, the Privy Council was pressuring the airline to order the European-made Airbus A310. European aircraft manufacturers had never lacked ingenuity, having flown the first helicopter and jet fighter aircraft during the Second World War and the de Havilland Comet and the Concorde after it. But encountering the same prejudices that Japanese auto manufacturers initially did, they had little success in breaking into the North American market. In the late 1960s, former rivals Aerospatiale in Toulouse, CASA in Madrid, Messerschmitt-Bölkow-Blohm in Hamburg, Fokker in Amsterdam, and British Aerospace in Bristol, realized that if they were going to take on Boeing, Lockheed, and Douglas, they had to stop competing against each other and consolidate. In May 1969, with commitments from their governments to subsidize Airbus Industrie, the partners launched the A300, each national company building parts for it in their own factories, with the complete plane assembled in Toulouse.

Although the governments involved had carried the financial burden for the launch of the A300, the aircraft encountered severe difficulties entering the market. For one thing, parts, maintenance, and training did not fit into the contemporary fleets, which had American-built aircraft. Airbus knew that to stay in the race it had to supply a complete family of aircraft and did so, from the wide-bodied long range (A310, A330, A350, and A340) to the short- and medium-range (A320 and A321), and the European state-controlled airlines bought enough of the airliners to keep the assembly lines open — but only just.

After meeting with German and French leaders in 1977, Prime Minister Trudeau had asked Air Canada to consider the Airbus A310 as one of the alternatives in its next aircraft purchase, which Nova Scotia MP Elmer MacKay pointed out was political interference. After a thorough evaluation of all alternatives, Air Canada's team, headed by Ralph Vaughan, chose the Boeing 767 and sent the decision to Cabinet for approval. At this, Taylor received a personal letter from de Montigny Marchand, deputy secretary to the cabinet, calling for a delay in the decision to buy a North American aircraft until a committee was set up to evaluate the airline's choice. Like McGregor before him (and Pierre Jeanniot after), Taylor held that the choice of aircraft for the airline should be made on technical and commercial, not political grounds. Unfortunately, the airline's chairman, Bryce Mackasay, did himself no favours by now preferring the A310 and telling anyone in Air Canada who would listen that it would be the cabinet that would make the final decision, not Taylor and the airline's team.[7]

Chaired by Jacques Desroches, deputy minister of supply and services, the special committee made up of civil servants from various government departments heard from both Boeing and Airbus, but not from Claude Taylor, who refused to appear before it. It was the first time that a committee of government officials had ever reviewed the choice of aircraft, and it was a brave Air Canada president who faced up to such undisguised bullying from the airline's only shareholder. Fortunately, a federal election intervened and the Liberals fell from power. By the time Desroches submitted his report, it was to Joe Clark's Conservatives and perhaps seeing which way the wind was blowing, the committee endorsed the airline's choice for the B767 — and not only because it included a $145 million contract to Canadair from Boeing for work on the aircraft.

Air Canada held off announcing the purchase until after the election in July, when the airline made public its decision to purchase twelve Boeing 767s with delivery beginning in 1982. Like the A310, it was wide-bodied and twin-engined but more economical for longer flights. No longer deputy minister, Desroches would become president of the Aerospace Industries Association of Canada (AIAC).

—

The federal election in spring 1979 was a boon for the airline. Ever since Pierre Trudeau had rented a company DC-9 in 1968, the 102-seat aircraft had become the aerial platform of choice for the candidates with all three parties, each paying $6,000 daily for the aircraft, which included landing fees, crews, and fuel.[8] Revisions to the Elections Act since the last election in 1974 had increased taxpayer subsidies to electioneering — no doubt good news to the parties since in the previous election, the rental of the prime minister's DC-9 had cost the Liberal party $136,750. The reporters who travelled with the leaders were billed $4,300 on the average for their airfares on the thirty-three-day campaign, and all were familiar with the stage setting.

While Progressive Conservative leader Joe Clark and the NDP's Ed Broadbent (whose DC-9 for some reason was nicknamed "Frigid-Air") loved to "shmooze" with the media, Trudeau characteristically sat up front, solitary in pensive pose,

sending cryptic messages (sometimes in Latin) to the journalists via his staff. The television crews sat immediately behind the prime minister's entourage, followed by the French-speaking media and their English-speaking counterparts in the rear. As one reporter commented, it was two solitudes, even at 30,000 feet.

As much as possible, the same Air Canada cabin staff worked on Trudeau's flight, always led by senior steward Ray Nantel, who had served on the first Trudeau DC-9 in 1968. When asked if he had seen any changes, Nantel said that back then the only person drinking Perrier water was Trudeau, but now it was hoisted onboard by the crateful for his staff. The only incident of note concerning the Air Canada aircraft during the 1979 campaign occurred on May 11, when Joe Clark's DC-9 "lost" an engine; a bearing had come loose in the turbine as it pulled out of Toronto for Prince Edward Island. Realizing that there was no such thing as bad publicity, Clark, unfazed by the hasty return to Malton, enjoyed the next day's headlines: WHITE KNUCKLES ON AIR CLARK and TORY LEADER STARTS DAY OFF WITH A BANG! He later signed a letter to Claude Taylor commending the aircraft's five-member crew for their efficient handling of the situation.

Clark must have counted himself fortunate that he was not a passenger on Flight 680 on September 17. Fifteen minutes after leaving Boston for Yarmouth, Nova Scotia, the Air Canada DC-9 C-FTLU levelled off at an altitude of 25,000 feet when the entire tail cone fell off, leaving a gaping hole in the rear. In what could have been worse, only a beverage cart was sucked out into the Atlantic Ocean before the aircraft landed back at Logan Airport.

When Canadians went to the polls on May 22, they elected Clark as prime minister and in June he made Don Mazankowksi his minister of transport. Destined to go down in Canadian history as the best minister of transport since Howe, the forty-four-year-old "Maz" quickly gained the admiration of senior civil servants in his department. "The man is like a breath of fresh air," one told *Canadian Aviation* editor Hugh Whittington. "Not only does he have an open door but he has a completely open mind." Interestingly, when in opposition Mazankowski had objected to the sale of Nordair to Air Canada, but now in power was not prepared to return Nordair to the private sector. In the short time the Clark government was in power, to whom Nordair should be sold, whether a Quebec or Ontario buyer or buyers, occupied much of his time — and this suited Air Canada.

Calling the Mackasey appointment by the Liberals "blatant political patronage," one of the first actions the new minister took was to meet with him on September 17, and over a three-hour dinner told him that he was to resign. Mackasey had only been chairman for eight months, and Mazankowski was aware that breaking the seven-year contract was going to cost the taxpayers a lot of money; the speculation was the figure was $500,000. But the old street fighter refused to resign and it took a specially convened board meeting for the directors to endorse the government's decision to fire him. And so, like Pratte before him, Bryce Mackasey left Air Canada unhappily, blaming Clark's "vindictiveness."[9]

The new minister of transport and prime minister were expected to pick their own candidate to succeed Mackasey, but wisely they asked Claude Taylor for his recommendation. Taylor recalled later, "They said, 'Who would you like to see?' And I said, 'I'd like Taschereau back.' And Joe Clark and Mazankowski agreed to my wishes." Taschereau would return as chairman.

———

The Air Canada Act had allowed the airline to broaden its corporate earning base by selling its services to a number of clients. In early 1980, the company paid $9 million to purchase 29 percent in the aircraft broker Guinness Peat Aviation (GPA) Ltd. of Shannon, Ireland. Air Canada planned to sell off forty aircraft and GPA would help get the best prices. Using the equity method of accounting, this brought in $0.9 million. Other moneymakers were maintenance contracts with other airlines that had grown steadily since the 1960s, and by 1980 Air Canada performed twenty major contracts with various airlines, one of which was Air Lanka, which had leased two of Air Canada's L-1011s. The airline had led the world with its ReserVec computer system and now with ReserVec II and the addition of MAC (Mini Administration Computers), thousands of travel agents and airlines like Time Air of Lethbridge, Eastern Provincial Airways, and

Air Jamaica were linked into the airline's data processing and communications systems. Within the company, a prototype automatic ticket-issuing machine, "Tickematique," was tested at Montreal and Toronto airports, allowing passengers to use their enRoute credit card to make reservations and pick a ticket from the machine.

In May 1980, Air Canada revamped its dedicated package delivery service after a loss of millions of dollars. Bernard Gillies, the new vice-president of cargo, took the three 727s out of service and said that future parcel deliveries would be made by regular Air Canada flights. Two years before, the airline had overestimated market demand in Canada. "Both our estimates of the size of the market and the amount that we could capture of that market were wildly overstated," Gillies said. He recommended to the Board that the 727s be sold immediately, and they went to Interstate Airlines in October 1981. The courier service continued using the passenger flights, and in March 1980 the DC-8-63 freighters were converted to all-cargo aircraft.

Air Canada earned a profit of $57 million in 1980 after providing for corporation income taxes of $48.3 million. The federal government, its single shareholder, contributed $329 million to equity capital, the book value of which was $501 million in December 31, 1980. Good news for air travellers was that a Christmas strike was averted on December 19, 1980, when a new contract was hammered out between Air Canada's 3,500 flight attendants and the airline. The new contract would raise the monthly salary of a flight attendant with seven years seniority to $1,793 from the present $1,401.

———

Renting an Air Canada DC-8 was not only prohibitively expensive for an individual but also disruptive for the airline that had to take it out of service. When Lady Beaverbrook, the widow of Max Aitken, the New Brunswick–born billionaire publisher Lord Beaverbrook, hired a company DC-8 on October 6, 1976, to fly herself, her sister, and her two puppies from London to Halifax and back, it raised a few eyebrows. A scheduled flight would not do because the dogs would have been put in the baggage hold. But since Lady Beaverbrook had donated millions of dollars to her late husband's alma mater, Dalhousie University in Halifax, Air Canada considered her a valued customer.

Not so the next person to rent one of its DC-8s. Juvénal Habyarimana, the president of Rwanda, was on an official visit to Canada in October 1980. Because he was considered an influential ally in Francophone Africa, the Department of External Affairs wanted nothing to displease the president on his visit. While meeting with the Department in Ottawa, Habyarimana mentioned that he heard of a Michelin five-star restaurant in Quebec City. When he asked to be flown there for lunch on October 4, External Affairs had the Department of Transport's JetStar put at his disposal. But because Habyarimana also wanted to take his entourage of thirty

155

to lunch with him, this was beyond the JetStar's seating capacity. Air Canada was contacted and a DC-8 was sent down from Toronto to fly him and his staff to Quebec City and back, before returning empty to Toronto.[10] Try as they might, the press was unable to discover who paid for it.

———

Clark's term in office would end abruptly in March 1980 — as would Mazankowski's. When the Liberals returned to power, Trudeau gave his old friend Jean-Luc Pepin the opportunity to be minister of transport. Then on November 1, 1981, the prime minister appointed fifty-five-year-old Quebec City lawyer René Amyot as chairman of Air Canada. Already an airline board member, Amyot was well connected in his hometown and sat on several boards, so much so that he had been the honourary Belgian consul in Quebec City since 1966. After the Mackasey political appointment, Taylor was prepared for this and had carefully pruned the chairman's duties down to that of a part-time position — but one which still paid a handsome $95,000 annually.

However, Amyot's appointment as chairman was not favourably greeted by Pepin, who had his own candidate in mind for the position. The transport minister would be remembered for effectively ending subsidized rail passenger service in most of Canada. The *Ottawa Citizen* called him "the worst thing to happen to railroads since Jesse James," and now he was planning to do the same to Montreal's Dorval Airport. The *Montreal Gazette* cal-

culated that by 1981 the federal government had sunk about $600 million into Mirabel Airport, which was losing $50 million annually, almost exactly the same amount of money that Dorval Airport was making in profit. To recoup some of the $600 million, the minister began pressuring both Air Canada and CP Air to move their flights from Dorval Airport to the underused Mirabel. The plan, dubbed "Minus Six" by Transport Canada, would mean that the Crown corporation and CP Air could only fly out of Dorval to three locations: Ottawa, Toronto, and Quebec City. Rather than dealing with the expense and inconvenience of using "Miserabell" (as it became known), foreign airlines like Scandinavian Airlines Systems, Aero Mexico, and Aer Lingus applied to Ottawa to land at Pearson Airport. When they were refused permission, they left Canada. Air Canada employees, reluctant to move, held that Mirabel was going to be saved at any cost because it was in the riding of MP Francis Fox (Argenteuil-Deux Montagnes) who Trudeau had appointed as secretary of state and minister of communications.

In a confidential memorandum, Clayton Glenn, vice-president of the airline's fleet capacity planning, wrote: "We were appalled to find that Transport Canada had not taken into consideration the desires of the travelling public, nor the impact on the airline industry." Both Taylor and CP Air president Ian Gray strongly resisted the pressure from Ottawa to move. Unaffected in the "Minus Six" plan were regional airlines like Nordair and EPA, whose passengers could still enjoy convenient connections from Dorval to Halifax. "The day may come," said Taylor "when Mirabel will have some kind of rapid transit or road system, but that day isn't here yet." Passengers, Glenn said, preferred to use the already congested Pearson Airport than pay $45 for the hour-long bus ride between Mirabel and downtown Montreal.

Like his predecessors, Pepin also tackled the Gordian knot that was the regional airlines — at the expense of Air Canada. The logical solution would have been for the ailing Quebecair to merge with either thriving Nordair or Great Lakes Airlines, as Jack Pickersgill had once hoped. Nordair was being courted by both Great Lakes Airlines and the Quebec government. Considering their company an "Anglophone" airline, Nordair's employees were set to fight any shotgun marriage with Quebecair tooth and nail. Claiming to be insulted by Nordair's CEO, who said that because of the restrictive language situation in the province he would rather sell the airline, the Quebec provincial government yet bought 11 percent of its shares and then sold them to the Regionair group. Although it suffered a strike from July 25, 1982 to January 24, 1983, Nordair managed to rebound in 1983 with a $2.7 million profit, making it even more attractive to suitors.

Not so Quebecair, which was relying on its B737 charter flights to Fort Lauderdale to get it through the winter of 1981–82. When Air Canada introduced low excursion fares to Florida using its L-1011s, it nudged Quebecair to the edge of bankruptcy, prompting Michel Clair, the Quebec minister of transport, to begin confidential talks with his counterpart in Ontario, James Snow, to merge Quebecair with Great Lakes Airlines (renamed Air Ontario) in April 1981.

Flying ex-Allegheny Airlines Convair 580s, Great Lakes Airlines (which earned it the name "Great Shakes Airlines") had been losing passengers to Air Canada's DC-9 flights. But cash-rich PWA saw the potential in its Ontario routes, and with the Deluce family, which owned Austin Airways, invested enough in Great Lakes Airlines to keep it in the air. Clair threatened to end financial assistance to Quebecair unless Air Canada cancelled several services in the province of Quebec, particularly its flights to Sept-Îles, and to give Quebecair a monopoly on the route. To the minister and most Quebecois, Air Canada was the principal villain in the piece since it had destroyed Quebecair's Florida charter business and was now doing the same to its main scheduled routes. The Quebec minister of transport hoped that the threat of Quebecair's demise would stir enough nationalistic sentiment in the province to force the Trudeau government to take action.

On hearing the Clair-Snow proposal, Claude Taylor declared it unacceptable, as did Nordair's new president, Jean Douville. It was in Air Canada's interest to keep regional airlines from becoming a threat if it wanted to maintain its dominance in the domestic market. With a weak Quebecair and a controlling interest in Nordair, the situation suited the government airline. Pepin responded with his own plan: that Quebecair be liquidated and a new "Quebecair II" formed that would be evenly owned by Air Canada and the Quebec government. The resulting uproar to the Clair-Snow proposal both in the House of Commons and the Quebec National Assembly (and no doubt in the Air Canada boardroom) forced the minister to rethink this, and no Air Canada concessions occurred. In June 1983, to maintain essential air services in the province, the Quebec government purchased stock in Quebecair and began looking around for a buyer. Vancouver-based CP Air knew that. That airline had traded away its eastern routes to TCA in the 1960s, and under its new CEO, Daniel Colussy (who saw what the absence of a domestic network had done to his previous employer, Pan American Airways), looked to buy a domestic network that would feed into its Toronto and Vancouver hubs.

———

Taylor was pleased to leave 1982 behind. The airline had lost a DC-9 on June 2 when it was destroyed in a hangar blaze in Montreal. The airline had finished its worst financial quarter in its forty-five-year history. In its first loss since 1976, the airline had incurred a loss of $32.6 million, representing a negative turnaround of $72.8 million over 1981, when it had recorded a net profit of $10 million. Passenger traffic had fallen 21 percent from the previous year, and reductions in weekend services between

Toronto–Windsor, Toronto–Sudbury and Calgary-Vancouver were made on December 21. The airline president attributed the disastrous news to the worldwide recession and warned of a 5–10 percent drop in passenger traffic through 1983. While the gas-guzzling older DC-8s were being retired from passenger service as quickly as possible, the new fuel-efficient B767s were sitting idle on the tarmac at Montreal and Toronto because of a pay dispute with the pilots, who wanted to be paid for flying them as wider-bodied aircraft than the DC-8s.

The very last DC-8 was retired from commercial passenger service on April 23, 1983, when Flight 140 left Calgary at 1740 and landed at Toronto at 2310. The airline had taken delivery of its first DC-8-40 in February 1960 and operated the aircraft through to the DC-8-54 and DC-8-63 series. On average, the number of flying hours for each one was 40,000, with 17,000 landings. The record was held by DC-8 Fin Number 812, which flew 55,859 hours and landed 25,354 times. It was a good time to retire the DC-8s since new U.S. and Canadian noise and air pollution regulations would have meant that all DC-8 engines would have to be replaced by 1985. The aircraft were either stored at Marana in the Arizona desert or re-engined to use as freighters, with two DC-8-73CFs allowed to operate out of Pearson Airport in the early hours. Others were sold off to ATASCO USA Ltd. or Air Eagle of Iceland or wet leased around the world, to Thai International, Arrow Air, Air Haiti, and Quebecair.

WHERE DOES THE MONEY GO IN AIR CANADA?

In March 1983, *Horizons* magazine calculated thus:

FUEL: A B747 gulps down 9,200 litres on take off alone. Air Canada spends $1.64 million daily on fuel. That works out to $68,000 an hour and $19 a second. Flying a L-1011 Halifax–Vancouver is a $20,000 fuel bill. Miami–Toronto $10,000.

PERSONNEL: The 23,000 employees receive $773 million annually, which is 35 percent of the airline's operating cost.

USER CHARGES: Landing and take off fees, air traffic control fees, use of taxiways, parking, security, baggage handling cost Air Canada $12 million annually. Landing fees vary. Heathrow in peak summer costs Air Canada $11,397 to land a B747. In Tampa the same aircraft costs $111.

SOVEREIGN AIRSPACE: An Air Canada aircraft flying from Toronto–Frankfurt must pay $3,000 in total to fly over Ireland, UK, France, Netherlands, Belgium, and Germany. This cost is calculated by the weight of the aircraft and the distance covered. Europe has the most expensive airspace to fly over. For a B747 to fly over one thousand kilometres of German airspace is $ 1,935. In Belgium it is $1,575.

PRICE OF FLEET: In 1983 a brand new B767 was $54 million.

WHERE DOES THE REVENUE COME FROM?

Air Canada gets 80 percent of its revenue from the sale of tickets and depends on 23,000 travel agents to sell them. Their annual commission is $140 million. They use the airline's flight schedules and printing the brochures cost $1 million. Postage to mail brochures is $20,000.

Other revenue sources:
Charter: $33 million.
Freight: $225 million.
Service contracts to other carriers: $146 million.

One DC-8 would feature in an international drama when through Guinness Peat Aviation on September 9, 1983, Air Canada leased DC-8-61 C-FTJX to the Syrian government, which promptly seized the plane at Damascus, allowing the Air Canada crew to leave. It would take months of diplomatic negotiations before the aircraft was returned to Montreal on November 28 and sent off to Arizona. It would not be until April 1986 that the last of the Air Canada DC-8s would leave Marana, to be sold to United Aviation Services.

———

The airline was in the news through the summer of 1983 — and for dramatic reasons. It began on May 12, in the worst spring blizzard in a century on the prairies, and Flight 234, a DC-9-32 C-FTLJ from Vancouver, slid off the runway at Regina Airport. All fifty-seven passengers were safe.

Not so fortunate were the passengers of the next DC-9 incident. On June 2, 1983, DC-9 C-FTLU Flight 797 left Dallas for Montreal. It was at cruising altitude when the three aft lavatory flush circuit breakers tripped. Captain Donald Cameron tried to reset them from the cockpit, and when they didn't, he sent the first officer, Claude Ouimet, back to check the lavatory. Soon a strange odour filled the rear of the cabin and tendrils of smoke began to emerge through the seams of the lavatory walls. Flight Attendant Sergio Bennetti used the CO2 bottle to try and put the fire out, and passengers overheard a flight attendant

say that someone might have thrown a lit cigarette into "something." When the toilet door felt hot to touch, the first officer advised Cameron to descend immediately. The captain had already radioed Indiana Air Traffic Control, and noticing other circuit breakers popping, issued a mayday call. He put on smoke goggles and his emergency oxygen mask and began the 33,000-foot descent to Cincinnati Airport, as ordered by air traffic control. During the descent the DC-9's interior began filling with smoke as the cabin crew advised passengers to move to the front of the cabin.

"There was absolutely no panic," one of the passengers said later. "Absolutely nothing. Nobody screamed or yelled. There were no cries. It was dead calm." With acrid smoke filling the cabin and the aircraft descending rapidly, passenger Graham Wright of Toronto heard one woman nervously say, "Everyone think nice thoughts." Jim Lanagan, the supervisor of the Cincinnati rescue unit waiting below, heard the pilot's last words to the control tower: "I can't see anything."

The smoking DC-9 landed on Runway 27L with blown tires, the fire engines beginning operations as soon as the plane stopped. The exit doors were opened by the flight attendants, but as soon as they did so, a flash fire enveloped the aircraft's interior. Eighteen passengers and the three flight attendants got out through the forward doors and over-wing exits, the captain and first officer escaping through the cockpit sliding windows. But twenty-three passengers could not get out in time and rescue workers found bodies strapped to the seats and in the aisles, some burned beyond recognition.

Survivors credited the Air Canada crew with saving their lives. Besides Captain Cameron, who one said brought the DC-9 down "like an elevator," and First Officer Ouimet, whose uniform was reported to be on fire as he escaped, flight attendants Sergio Bennetti, Judi Davidson, and Laura Kayama were also commended. "They took charge, and there's no doubt in my mind," said Wright, "that if we had one more minute in that plane, none of us would have survived."

The National Transportation Safety Board (NTSB) was less kind and determined that the probable causes of the accident were "a fire of undetermined origin, an underestimate of fire severity, and misleading fire progress information provided to the captain. The time taken to evaluate the nature of the fire and to decide to initiate an emergency descent contributed to the severity of the accident."

The disaster was destined to be one of the plane crashes that changed aviation forever. In the past year the NTSB had counted twenty-five lavatory fires on aircraft in the United States alone. Governments around the world subsequently mandated that all aircraft toilets be equipped with smoke sensors and automatic fire extinguishers. As well, all aircraft interiors were retrofitted with fire-retardant materials in the seats soon after, and floor lighting that would lead passengers to the exits was installed.

The five-person Air Canada crew was awarded the Gordon McGregor Trophy by the Royal Canadian Air Force Association, something that the airline's first president would have agreed with. This letter to a newspaper said it all:

Maybe the coffee ain't so great,
Sometimes the baggage gets lost.
And maybe it takes too long to check in,
But give me guys like Cameron and Ouimet
And I'm flying Air Canada.

———

There is a saying in aviation that fuel in the tanks is limited but gravity is forever. This was never better proven than on July 23 at Gimli, Manitoba. A hundred miles from Winnipeg, the abandoned air force airstrip was now used for drag and motorcycle races and that Saturday was "Family Day" for the Winnipeg Sports Car Club. There were about 150 people camped along the runway, mainly weekend racing drivers and their families in tents, vans, and trailers. They were treated to the spectacle of a giant twin-engined Air Canada aircraft descending directly towards them. What was eerie, one later recalled, was the complete silence of it — as if it were a glider.

The Boeing 767-200 C-GAUN Fin 604 was on a flight from Montreal to Edmonton via Ottawa with sixty-one passengers onboard. The aircraft was usually fuelled by the FQISP (the Fuel Quantity Information Processor), which controls all internal pumps and lets the pilots know the amount of fuel available. But that day, the FQISP was inoperable and the fuel load being poured into the tanks was measured the old fashioned way — with a dipstick.

The B767 was the first Air Canada aircraft that measured fuel in kilograms instead of pounds. Using a unit conversion measurement of 1.77 lbs/litre instead of 0.8 kilograms/litre that should have been used, the pilots calculated that they needed 20,400 pounds of fuel to get from Montreal to Edmonton. The aircraft computer interpreted this as 20,400 kilograms, or 20,160 lbs. Captain Robert Pearson and First Officer Maurice Quintal calculated the figure three times and decided to go.

At 41,000 feet over Red Lake, Ontario, the cockpit warning system chimed and almost immediately after that a fuel light indicated that the left engine had failed. Pearson made to divert to Winnipeg for a one-engine landing, but attempting to restart the engine, the right one stopped and all the instrumentation in the glass cockpit died. Nothing like this had ever been practised in a simulator, and an Air Canada engineer who was a passenger began looking through the aircraft's operating manual for instructions. Without electrical and hydraulic power, Pearson was now gliding the 767 toward Winnipeg, without knowing how fast the aircraft was sinking or its airspeed. The Winnipeg air traffic controllers used the "blip" on their radar to calculate the 767's airspeed, and with that Quintal was able to figure out

that Flight 143 had lost 5,000 feet in ten nautical miles. They were not going to make Winnipeg. When in the RCAF the first officer had been posted to Gimli and calculated they had the speed and height to make his former base — unaware that it was now used as a racetrack.

Pearson saw that they were coming in too high for the Gimli runway, and as an experienced glider pilot he executed a perfect "forward slip" to increase drag and reduce altitude. The main landing gear dropped down by gravity, but the nose wheel would not lock. The 767 levelled off, and using the main gear only, touched nose-down on the tarmac. For the screaming spectators at the end of the runway it looked as if the aircraft was making straight for them. The captain braked as heavily as he could, blowing the tires, and the 767 stopped only a few hundred feet from the runway's edge. The sixty-one passengers scrambled out, exiting on the rear emergency slide. When the aircraft had halted, a few of the spectators grabbed the fire extinguishers located along the racetrack to spray the smoking undercarriage.

None of the passengers suffered injury except one elderly lady who was taken to hospital for shock. All were bused to Winnipeg and put on another Air Canada flight to Edmonton. Only seventy-five litres of fuel were found in the aircraft's tanks. In Montreal, an Air Canada spokesman said that the airline would ground its four 767s, the airline's only fully metric plane, whenever routine inspection

The Gimli Glider: There is a saying in aviation that fuel in the tanks is limited but gravity is forever. This was never better proven than on July 23, 1983, at Gimli, Manitoba.

revealed that their electronic fuel measuring systems were not working. Air Canada sent a repair crew from Winnipeg (legend has it that they too ran out of fuel on the way), and within two days the 767, known henceforth as the "Gimli Glider," was flown out.

Air Canada's investigation found Captain Pearson and First Officer Quintal as well as the mechanics in Montreal at fault for running out of fuel. Captain Pearson was demoted for six months to first officer and FO Quintal was suspended for two weeks. However, the Canadian Air Safety Board (soon to become the Transportation Safety Board) differed and ruled that Air Canada was at fault, commending the pilots for "professionalism and skill" in making the landing.

The fuel shortage had occurred, the board said, because of a mix-up between the Imperial and metric systems of measurement, to which Canada had recently converted. This was compounded by a failure of the airline to properly change operating procedures and reassign the fuel checks to the first officer after the third flight crew position, the flight engineer, was no longer on the standard crew manifest. Pearson and Quintal would be reinstated and eventually complete their careers, flying C-GAUN many times more until it was retired to the Mohave desert on January 24, 2008. Both of them were onboard for its last flight from Montreal to the Mohave, when air traffic control in Canada and the United States dubbed the aircraft's call sign "The Gimli Glider."[11]

Pearson and Quintal were onboard for C-GAUN's last flight to retirement in the Mohave desert on January 24, 2008, when air traffic control in Canada and the United States dubbed the aircraft's call sign "The Gimli Glider."

———

Away from the cockpit, another Air Canada embarrassment brewed up. The company was then searching for a new head office since its lease at Place Ville Marie was due to expire in 1985. In the depressed Montreal real estate market, fifteen possible sites were considered before being whittled down to two: First Quebec Corp., a complex on McGill College Avenue that hadn't been built yet, and Place Beaver Hall, at Dorchester Boulevard and Beaver Hall Hill.

The real estate firm of A.E. Lepage was asked to evaluate both properties, and its Quebec City subsidiary Racine, LaRochelle, Bernard & Associates Ltd. completed a report in August 1982 which chose the yet unbuilt complex, First Quebec Corp. Air Canada chairman René Amyot who made no secret that he favoured that site and delivered copies of this to Pepin and Trudeau in late October. But Amyot was unaware that the month before, A.E. Lepage (this time of Toronto), completed a second report that chose Place Beaver Hall as more suitable. It was two blocks from Place Ville Marie and closer to Central and Windsor stations for commuting airline staff than First Quebec Corp. Also, since it was being constructed by the Trizec Corporation of Calgary (which also owned Place Ville Marie), there would be no penalty if the airline moved before the lease ended. Taylor would later say that the first was only a draft report and the second one was the final one.

Things took a murky turn in November when, after receiving what he called "information from top Air Canada officials," Pepin asked that the RCMP investigate Amyot. Taylor and Amyot were both interrogated by the RCMP separately, and at a hastily called press conference on December 8, Taylor said that he was not going to comment on rumours concerning possible payoffs regarding the decision. Amyot was conspicuously absent from the conference. The Air Canada board unanimously decided to buy ten floors of Place Beaver Hall on December 9, 1982, for $31.7 million, and the building was renamed "Place Air Canada."

By April the following year the RCMP had found sufficient evidence to raid Amyot's home and his Quebec City office. In the House, Justice Minister Mark MacGuigan was asked by the Conservative opposition to provide details of the police investigation but declined to do so. At the annual transport committee hearings in May, members of Parliament watched amazed as Taylor and Amyot fought it out, contradicting each other on the choice of the airline's head office. Amyot said that he had been excluded from consultations by a "dirty, whispering

THE BOEING 767

I have yet to meet a pilot who has flown the 767 that didn't like it. For here was the line pilot's introduction to the term "GLASS COCKPIT" — the standard now in cockpit instrumentation. A simple description for glass cockpit, you ask? Basically, instead of individual gauges and instruments, the majority of information is displayed on small TV screens in LCD display.

But forget the culture jump for a minute. That the 767 may be remembered primarily as the giant leap in technology, but undoubtedly she is still a Boeing designed-and-built aircraft. Everything done in-house, unlike today's subcontracting aerospace organizations.

So even though her "raison d'être" was efficiency for cost saving, she had all the attributes to make her a "pilot's airplane." Her cockpit and instrumentation were designed by pilots for pilots. Here was an aircraft that easily handled the blizzard conditions of St. John's, Nfld., and could fly the oceans of the world on two engines — and with only two pilots.

Plenty of power, great brakes, excellent controllability, and dinner in Paris after you were finished! It did not get any better than this.

— Captain Bruce Olson

campaign" in Air Canada. Taylor defended the choice of head office, saying that the chairman's job was only "part-time" and that after Bryce Mackasey, Amyot was only a figurehead. The atmosphere between the two was made worse on May 2, 1983, when the *Le Devoir* newspaper revealed that Taylor had asked for the second report and changed the criteria to favour Place Beaver Hall.

Using his parliamentary immunity, Patrick Nowlan, the Conservative transport critic from Wolfville, Nova Scotia, added fuel to the fire by accusing Amyot in the Commons of being involved in the selection of the First Quebec Corp. complex with Montreal real estate developer Isaac Gelber, Montreal businessman Bernard St. Jacques, and Quebec City lawyer Pierre Jolicour. The three had supposedly received "secret kickbacks of $3.6 million." The revelation suited Nowlan's party just then since it was in the midst of a leadership race between former Prime Minister Joe Clark and newcomer MP Brian Mulroney (Central Nova). Elected leader of the Conservative Party on June 11, Mulroney promised to remove a "decaying and unprincipled group" from office, even as his campaign organizer Frank Moores cabled businessman Karlheinz Schreiber in Germany to open a file on Air Canada and political donations.

Having angered Western farmers with his railway legislation, Pepin left Transport Canada in August to become the minister responsible for Francophonie, and Trudeau parachuted in Lloyd Axworthy, his only minister from the West, in his

place. On settling into his new job as transport minister, Axworthy was handed a seventeen-page report from the RCMP outlining several conflicts of interest Amyot had been involved in. In September, when the Quebec Justice Department informed Amyot that he would not be prosecuted for any evidence uncovered by the RCMP's investigations, the Air Canada chairman must have breathed a sign of relief. But Axworthy acted immediately on the report and on November 2 called a meeting of Air Canada's board. Amyot was summoned to Ottawa immediately after and met the minister in a downtown hotel. The outcome of that meeting led to Amyot handing in his letter of resignation the next day. In his farewell speech he advised Air Canada to make the position of chairman a full-time one. He was relieved, he said, not to be prosecuted and happy to be leaving immediately because "his health would be better if he did so." Amyot failed to mention that so would his bank account since his severance pay was estimated to be a year and half's salary — approximately $135,000. Geno F. Francolini, CEO of an export packing and warehouse customs brokerage corporation and chairman of the Liberal party's financial management committee, was appointed interim chairman of the airline. In October the airline moved into its new offices, with Taylor inaugurating the opening by planting trees before the entrance.

In December 1984, 450,000 pounds of Christmas gifts including blankets, food, and medicine were sent to Ethiopia to avert famine. The airlift used the entire Air Canada cargo fleet and remains the largest of its kind for the airline. Many cargo fleet members gave up their Christmas vacations to help.

History was made at the new headquarters on June 27, 1985, when a monument was unveiled on the main floor to the late Gordon McGregor. Officiating at the ceremony Taylor said, "Air Canada people are a proud group, and we are doubly proud of our history. Next year Air Canada will begin celebrating our 50th anniversary and as we gather here, there is one name that has gone down in history as the great builder of TCA and Air Canada. 'G.R.,' as many of us knew him, would have been the first to remind us that no builder creates anything alone and I am delighted to welcome back a select group of people who helped make this airline, along with G.R."

He then introduced G.R.'s secretary, Beth Buchanan, "the one person who was closest to him," Don McLaren, the airline's first employee, and executive vice-president and chief operating officer Herb Seagrim, who, when former Prime Minister Trudeau appointed Yves Pratte, took early retirement. Seagrim was, said Taylor "a man who exemplified everything G.R. wanted the airline to be." It was perhaps the last gathering of the legends who built the airline, since present were George Lothian, Lindy Rood, Jim Bain, John Baldwin, Jack Dyment, and Walt Fowler. The plaque read in part: "Who can think of Pan Am without Trippe, KLM without Plesman, American Airlines without C.R. Smith, United without Patterson, Eastern without Rickenbacker? And Air Canada without Gordon McGregor?" No one doubted that Taylor had a hand in composing the text.

Ten years before, when Ernie Sykes, a former Air Canada employee and aviation buff, was at the Texas Confederate Air Force Fly-In and photographing a Lockheed 10A Electra in the U.S. Army Corps livery, he saw something that shouldn't have been there. The sun reflecting off its fuselage showed the ghostly image of the letters "CF-TCC." Of the five L10A's owned by TCA, only CF-TCA was left for the public to enjoy, as a static exhibit in the National Aviation Museum at Rockcliffe, Ontario. Word of Sykes' find spread through the airline, and with the airline's fiftieth anniversary coming up in 1986, it was seen as an opportune time to reclaim this piece of Canadian aviation history. Bud Clarke, the aircraft's owner, was cooperative, and on January 12, 1984, Captain Ray Lank arrived at Brooksville, Florida, to fly home N3749, the former CF-TCC. With him were Sykes, Ted Morris, and Air Canada Chief inspector Al Scammel.

The three-day flight in the 10A from Brooksville–Memphis–Omaha–Winnipeg was 1650 nautical miles and took twelve hours, ten minutes. Despite its age and use, the only repairs requiring attention were a wheel assembly repair and a feathering button that vibrated loose and landed on the floor between the rudder pedals. Once they arrived at CF-TCC's former TCA base, the following message was sent to Air Canada's VP Flight Operations: CF-TCC ARRIVED SAFELY HOME JAN 14 1984. THE ADVENTURE IS UNDER WAY.[12]

Led by R.D. Perras, between normal shifts volunteers of all trades at the Air Canada Winnipeg maintenance base worked on the necessary repairs through 1984–85, including a new paint job to make TCC operational for the airline's fiftieth anniversary in 1986. Their only compensation (other than the enormous personal satisfaction from working on a piece of aviation history) was a limited edition TCC crest. Old and sometimes lost trade skills were needed, and the Lockheed archives were researched extensively. Most of the 10A's skin was redone from new sheet metal using the "crown roller technique" of the 1930s. The landing gear was completely cast and then milled in the Air Canada machine shop. Many parts that were unavailable, like the landing gear clutch motors, had to be re-manufactured in-house. Most rivets and bolts were replaced to current specifications. The original simple 12V electrical system was kept but upgraded with modern components. Since the original seats did not meet existing fire retardant and G force standards, the interior was completely refurbished with nine B727 seats (vs. ten original) installed, along with cabin soundproofing and modern lightweight trim panels. Cockpit modifications included a new avionics package donated by King Radio.

Rebuilding the 10A, Lank said, was like locating a priceless old one-of-a-kind wooden jigsaw puzzle in your parents' attic, but then finding that many of the pieces were damaged and several were missing. All wiring was upgraded and instruments, controls, handles, switches, and knobs were refurbished as close to the original as possible. Pratt & Whitney donated the R985 450hp Wasp engines plus spares and feathering props (the early L10As had 400hp engines with non-feathering props). Since the original de-icer boots were no longer in production, a custom set was manufactured and donated by B.F. Goodrich. Other industry participation for the anniversary flight included fuel from Shell and Esso, as well as waived landing and navigation fees. CF-TCC's test flight would occur on March 18, 1986, and Rank trained pilots Joe Prime, John Racey, Jean Gilbert, and André Clermont for the cross-country flight to celebrate the anniversary, which would coincide with Expo 86 in Vancouver that summer.

———

A common theme in the 1984 federal election was that all parties wanted to liberalize airline regulation in Canada. As early as 1977, the federal government, the airlines, the provinces, and the public had taken part in hearings on aviation sponsored by the Standing Committee on Transport. Its report, titled "Domestic Air Carrier Policy," was tabled in 1982 and formed the basis of cross-country hearings conducted by the CTC on air fare reforms in 1983–84.

Axworthy distilled the concerns into his "New Canadian Air Policy" issued on May 10, 1984. Applying only to mature air services, i.e. below the fiftieth parallel from the Atlantic to the Ontario/Manitoba border and north of the fifty-fifth parallel to the Pacific, it specified that with the approval of the CTC, carriers could now fly on routes formerly reserved for Air Canada and CP Air. Removed were all license restrictions that had prohibited or limited the frequency of nonstops and turnaround services and maximum size of aircraft to be used. The Air Policy ended the Air Canada/ CP Air duopoly and recognized that other airlines were concerned Air Canada would use the public purse to protect its market share with higher frequencies and lower prices, and to allay their fears the minister instructed the government airline to operate "on sound business principles in contemplation of a profit," to sell off Nordair, and to refrain from competitive pricing. Asked if the airline was to be privatized, the minister replied not just yet. Air Canada with reluctance divested itself of its shares in Nordair in 1984 as promised, so that 65 percent of its shares were now owned by the airline's employees, the remainder by Innocan, a private venture company, and by the Quebec government.

Soon after, Air Canada reported a $19.6 million first quarter loss and Taylor warned of a difficult year ahead. On May 22, 1984, the minister announced that Claude Taylor would become chairman of the board and Pierre Jeanniot president and CEO, effective June 1. The position of executive vice-president previously held by Jeanniot was abolished, and in the future Taylor would be responsible for recommending to the board the strategic orientation of the corporation, i.e. to concentrate on privatization.

Jeanniot had contributed directly to the development of the first flight recorder, or "Black Box," and pioneered wide-body twin-engine operations over the Atlantic. When he first joined Air Canada in 1955, landing a job as a quality-control technician, he described the airline as "very much an operational company … we didn't have to go and advertise too much about the seats because they were being gobbled up." When he became senior vice-president of marketing in 1979, the first seat sale came to him, he recalled, "from the white linen sales of January in the big stores."

The Alberta government returned PWA to the private sector in 1983, just as CP Air lured the regional airlines EPA and Air BC into its fold that year, integrating them into its own schedules and (for Air BC) its Vancouver hub. Taylor suspected that it would not be long before CP Air's new president, Donald J. Carty (who had once worked for Air Canada), would make an offer on Nordair.

When Brian Mulroney was elected on September 17, 1984, as a solution to the neverending recession, privatization of government-owned institutions was in the air — and not only in Canada. In Margaret Thatcher's Britain, it was believed that "denationalizing" the major industries would make them more productive, and British Aerospace, British Telecom, and British Steel were privatized, with British Airways soon to follow. Mulroney initially said that such crown jewels as the Canadian Broadcasting System and Air Canada were not for sale, but to Taylor's delight, he mused "… there were some persuasive arguments in the case of Air Canada … in regard to the disposition of equity."

———

Three days after Mulroney was sworn in, Air Canada was honoured to fly Pope John Paul II from Ottawa to Rome, concluding the first ever visit to Canada of a reigning pontiff. Accompanying the Pope on the charter flight were thirty-two Catholic Church officials, forty-six media representing world news outlets, and eighty invited guests of the Canadian Conference of Catholic Bishops with clergy from Canadian cities that the Pope had visited. The L-1011 Fin 555 was flown by Captain Tom Thususaka, Montreal, Captain Frank Chowhan, Toronto, and Second Officer Reg Greening, Montreal.

The aircraft was to be equipped with a bed for the Pope, and many Air Canada employees at the Dorval base were involved with this. "This is not the first time I have been involved with such a project," said Fred Spriggs, manager of interior development. "I have made beds for the Queen and for Pierre Trudeau. But this time is unique in many respects. The Pope has never visited Canada before, and Air Canada is honoured to be chosen to fly him back to Rome. As well, we had never installed a bed on an L-1011-500 aircraft before and had to redesign the ones made for the DC-8s and DC-9s," he added.

The sleeperette cabin was positioned where Seats 1A and B were located, and the Pope's bed was covered by a Hudson's

Bay blanket. A "passenger control unit" was installed in the headboard, and along with the usual radio and light controls, as a personal and much-appreciated touch, Air Canada employees had built in a switch that illuminated a crucifix. For posterity, the airline employees that made the Pope's bed were Mike McHenry, acting general clerk, and Karl Bohl, development technician, who drew up the bed's design. Dennis Guay, a mechanic from the finishing shop, cut and sewed the upholstery. Others involved were Helmut Hemmerich, foreman of the finishing shop, and mechanics Jimmy de Palma and Laurent Brazeau.

The eight-hour flight left Ottawa one and half hours late because of delays on the Pope's final day in Ottawa. One hour before landing at Rome, His Holiness walked through the cabin meeting everyone, and Leo McIntyre, senior director, payload operations and control, presented the pontiff with a model of an Air Canada B727 on behalf of the crew that had been unable to perform his Edmonton–Fort Simpson–Vancouver flight due to a last-minute fuel leak. Rémi Lafrenière, general manager, Ottawa, presented the pontiff on behalf of Air Canada a National Film Board book titled *Call Them Canadians*. Flight Operations gave him a model of the L-1011, and In-Flight Services the Hudson's Bay blanket from his bed.

———

About to celebrate its fiftieth anniversary, what was the state of Air Canada's finances? The company had total assets of $2.589.5 billion. Flight equipment, including aircraft, had a net book value of almost $1.807.2 billion, and flight equipment under lease had a net book value of $91.7 million, with spare parts and material accounting for $89.6 million. Contrary to what was still widely believed, the $23.9 million in start-up and postwar subsidies from the federal government had ended as early as 1962, and the airline had paid $50 million in dividends — almost three times the amount it had received. In addition, since 1978 government loans of $129 million had been repaid along with associated interest payments of $148 million. Air Canada improved its capital structure in 1985 by launching a bond issue on the Tokyo stock market to the amount of 15 billion yen (CDN $80 million) and was about to do the same in 1986 by launching two Swiss perpetual bond issues worth U.S. $336 million. Now, at the end of 1985, it incurred a net loss of $14.8 million, compared with the $28.1 million net profit the year before.

Labour problems, debt, deregulation, political interference ... through the years, the man at the controls of the national airline continued his simple lifestyle. Claude Taylor put in his usual eleven- to twelve-hour days beginning at 7:30 a.m., meeting the executive group at 8:15 a.m. His greatest joy, he said, was nightly strolls with his first grandchild, eighteen-month-old Kimberly. The Air Canada CEO always flew economy "to see what's going on and to talk to the crew." His guilty pleasure, he confessed, was removing his shoes after boarding and getting stuck in an Agatha Christie novel. An avid gardener, Taylor would write in the employee newsletter: "Henry James said that the two most beautiful words in the English language are 'Summer Afternoon.' It conveys the alluring warmth that God is in his heaven and all is well." For Air Canada employees and Canadian air travellers in the turbulence that loomed ahead, the two most beautiful words in the English language might have been "Claude Taylor."

CHAPTER FIVE

PIERRE JEANNIOT AND THE SERPENT'S TOOTH

Introducing Jeanniot to the airline's senior managers at the Bonaventure Hotel in Montreal on July 30, 1984, Claude Taylor warned of what was to come: "When we go public, I said 'when' and not 'if,'" he told them, "the new shareholders will want to own a valuable asset. But getting there will mean increases in productivity and sharing the rewards of success. Profits made will be shared among employees before a dividend is paid."

Jeanniot, the decision maker, would run the day-to-day operations. Taylor the diplomat would deal with the government and the airline's future. But unlike Pratte and Baldwin (or Taylor and Mackasey), Jeanniot and Taylor seemed to work well together.

The two had met three decades before on — where else — an Air Canada flight, and Taylor never forgot the young man's enthusiasm as he talked about a "black box" to trace pre-crash glitches. Both had come from humble origins (their fathers had died when they were young). Born in France, Jeanniot spent his childhood in Somaliland, where his father had been a railway inspector. On his death, the family moved back to France and endured the German occupation. Immigrating to Montreal after the war, Jeanniot went to school in the working class neighbourhood of Saint-Henri and didn't know any English until college. As vice-president in 1970, he would be the first francophone to reach that level in the airline's history.

Both men also had sons in the company at that time and had heard the whispers of nepotism. Jeanniot's was a union activist for Air Canada ground crews, and it must have made for interesting family dinners. Their tempos differed; Taylor was open and relaxed, forgetting his next appointment until reminded by his secretary. Jeanniot was more guarded. "He's the good guy. I'm the bad guy," Jeanniot told a journalist. "Claude is the great diplomat. I'm more direct. He's more patient. I'm more brusque."

Both admitted to sometimes failing to see eye to eye. "We've never screamed at each other," confessed Taylor. "We've had differences but we've never gone out of the office, slamming the door."

As Taylor had done, Jeanniot began a series of cross-country station visits to meet employees and reassure them about the spectre of privatization on the horizon. And the fear and rumours of what was to come weren't confined to Air Canada staff. On his return, Jeanniot responded to a report issued by the francophone pilots

group "Association des Gens de l'Air" (The Association of Men of the Air). When privatized, would Air Canada decamp from Montreal to Toronto? The new president assured them that the company had no intention of reducing its presence in Montreal or transferring its technical and administrative expertise outside the province of Quebec. "The question of relocating some of the flight operations training to Toronto is currently being re-examined," he said. The airline had just completed two facilities at the Dorval Technical Centre to handle the B767 and L-1011-500. The new pneumatic and digital avionic shops, he said, made Air Canada one of the few airlines in the world that could do 98 percent of its own maintenance.

Montreal, 1985. In the airline's new headquarters, Pierre Jeanniot, president and chief executive officer, with Claude Taylor, chairman, at his right.

To stem the tide of Canadians who drove across the border and took advantage of lower fares brought on by deregulation in the United States, in July 1984 CP Air imported "Travel Bonus," its frequent flyer program, from the United States, which rewarded passengers' loyalty with free or reduced-cost air travel if sufficient mileage had been accumulated. This was followed by the perks of "Attaché Class" aimed at businesspeople. Air Canada launched "Aeroplan" the same month, an incentive program offering frequent travellers an upgrading of cabin class and free tickets; part of the airline's strategy.

———

With the Conservative victory, all airlines hoped that Don Mazankowski would be reappointed to his previous portfolio, and Prime Minister Brian Mulroney did not disappoint them. On September 17, 1984, "Maz" was back as minister of transport. The media called him a "fixer," a "water walker," and "the grand poobah from Vegreville," and the former car salesman was all of that — and more. Like the character in the Gilbert and Sullivan opera *The Mikado*, Mazankowski collected positions like other ministers did campaign buttons. When Canadian Airlines was bankrupt in 1999, he would defend his two-airline policy, saying that the Jean Chrétien government then in power should have begun a national debate on maintaining Canadian Airlines while looking at policy initiatives, like rethinking foreign ownership and limits on share restrictions. In later

years, when tainted by the Airbus scandal, Mulroney's popularity sank, Mazankowski's did not, and he remains today one of the few Canadians to be awarded the honorific "The Right Honourable," joining the first minister of transport, C.D. Howe.

Partisan (to Albertans at least) Mazankowski would give Max Ward the glittering prizes that he and Grant McConachie had always wanted: on May 10, 1985, Wardair was permitted to serve both London and Paris as Canada's second scheduled airline to Britain and France. CP Air grumbled that the government said it wanted competition and then gave these routes to an airline that didn't have the aircraft to serve them, but by then Max was off shopping for long-range wide-body aircraft. Air Canada could take some comfort in the fact that because of British and French restrictions on Heathrow and Charles de Gaulle airports, Wardair was confined to Gatwick and Orly airports, but with its in-flight service on Royal Doulton china and steaks cooked to individual taste, no one doubted that the national airline had a serious rival to London and Paris.

Ironically, the most vociferous defenders of the state-owned Air Canada were its employee unions, forgetting that they had consistently crippled it with strike actions. "You propose to sell out not only our members but all Canadians in disposing of our national assets," accused the IAMAW, the Canadian Union of Public Employees (CUPE), and the Canadian Auto Workers (CAW) in a three-page letter to Mulroney. The unions rightly feared that to attract investors, a privatized Air Canada was about to downsize its work force and rely more on part time non-unionized employees. Cheryl Kryzaniwsky, head of the Air Canada's ticket agents' union, said she feared for her members' jobs. "The only costs left to cut are labour costs," she said. When Mazankowski retorted that the union leadership did not reflect the views of its rank and file, Victor Blais, president of Local 148, said that the IAMAW had polled 8,000 of its members who worked for Air Canada, and they were all opposed to privatization. This was challenged by Edward Godin, the chairman of the Air Canada Employees Ownership Committee, a group of Air Canada workers for privatization. The fear was that any one group within the airline, for example the pilots, would buy enough shares to hold a controlling interest in its future.

Calling the sale "a triumph of blind ideology over common sense," the unions claimed that accountability to the public and especially safety would be eroded in a privatized Air Canada. "Safety has nothing to do with privatization," Benoit Bouchard, the new transport minister, insisted. "Does it mean that Canadian Airlines and Wardair do not have the same safety standards because they are not Crown corporations?" NDP transport critic Les Benjamin warned that a privatized Air Canada would drop the money-losing routes to small communities and keep only the "gravy" ones. But anti-privatization rallies held in Halifax, Toronto, and Winnipeg were sparsely attended, fuelling hopes that most employees were willing to consider taking a stake in the airline.

Fighting the closure of Air Canada reservations offices in Regina and Saskatoon in August 1984, CALEA, the Canadian Airline Employees Association, sought to merge with the CAW, the Canadian division of the giant United Auto Workers. Negotiations between CALEA and the airline on a new collective agreement began in the fall of 1984, the two sides becoming increasingly deadlocked on several issues.

The 2,900 ticket agents saw the airline as trying to squeeze cutbacks in salary, beginning with a 22 percent rollback in starting salaries and introducing a longer pay progression scale. "As well," author Craig Chouinard wrote, "they wanted concessions which would allow them to hire an unlimited number of part-time workers and have non-CALEA members do jobs … as well as hinting at the wage freeze."[1]

Charles Duhamel, the CALEA Constitution Chair, thought this was the first step to eliminate full-time positions. "About 60 percent of our membership are women," he said. "It's one of the few jobs where women get equal work for equal pay. What Air Canada is trying to do is create a part-time ghetto. It's a direct assault on women." The airline said it needed concessions to remain profitable in the face of increased competition caused by deregulation, and bargaining continued through December with a break for Christmas. With the cushion of ample strike funds and support from UAW leaders Bob White and Buzz Hargrove, CALEA management were able to get a mandate on February 21, 1985, to strike. Even Labour Minister Bill McKnight appointing a mediator was of little help, and on April 28 CALEA ordered its members out. Picketing began at all Air Canada bases, with rallies at the larger ones.

Well prepared for a strike, Air Canada had trained supervisory and non-union staff to replace the counter agents and flight attendants, keeping service going in a pinch. Passengers would be checked in with the use of simple manual procedures, and seat selection would only be offered on transatlantic flights. With J.R. Bouchard, the airline's director of labour relations, mailing a letter to each agent, the company invited ticket agents to drop the strike. While many passengers complimented the temporary flight attendants for pitching in, others griped that they were unable to order a cold rum and coke "because of the strike" or that they had to subsist on sandwiches instead of a hot meal or that the cabin crew looked as though they had slept in their uniforms or that overhead bins were not closed during flights or the toilets were out of paper....

Dave Pember, public affairs manager, Halifax, would later write of his time as a volunteer flight attendant: "I took this special assignment because I believed the company's future was at stake. I was called names — some of them not too complimentary. But I can live with that. I might have been a name caller too if I'd been on the picket line. But now I know where you, the flight attendants, are coming from. Illegal layovers, short turn-arounds on long hauls, beat up galley equipment that sometimes left my hands bleeding. Whoever

said a flight attendant's job is glamorous? It's a hard, difficult job characterized by sleepless nights and aching joints. My level of appreciation for you and your job has gone up tenfold."

Striking Montreal flight attendant Pauline Perreaux responded thus: "I must object to Mr. Dave Pember's description as a 'volunteer.' He agreed to cross a picket line, for which he received financial remuneration. Mr. Pember goes to lengths to describe his appreciation ... of our working lives yet by his actions he threw his support behind the side which would have us leave the bargaining table to work longer days and longer months...."

On May 18, Air Canada conceded in some of its demands and a tentative agreement that included a 4 percent wage increase over one year was reached the next day. The next month CALEA, which had begun in the struggle for TCA stewardesses to get taxi fare to Malton Airport in 1946, became UAW Local 2213 on July 1, 1985.

———

With his old friend in power, these were salad days for Claude Taylor, and the pair could be spotted together at their favourite Ottawa restaurants like Hy's and The Place Next Door or at Montreal Expos games, either in the corporate box or in Taylor's own seats above third base. Now there would be nothing to stop the steamroller of privatization — except fate. On his way to the office in December 1984, Taylor stepped off the curb at Dorchester and Peel streets. A bus hid the car hurtling towards him and Taylor flew through its windshield. Taken to the Montreal Neurological Hospital, he was diagnosed with fractures to his collarbone and both shoulders. Hundreds of letters and cards were delivered to his bed, which he said brought him a great deal of pleasure at a time when he most needed cheering up. Dr. Olaf Skjenna, senior director at the hospital, reported that the chairman was responding very well to physiotherapy, and three months later he could work from home. But he would not be on his feet until the following summer.

———

The New Year of 1985 began well for Air Canada. The travel agency P.J. Lawson Travel chartered one of its B747s to take 224 Canadians around the world, showing the Air Canada "flag" in such exotic places like Bali, Rio de Janeiro, Mauritius, and Cape Town. The airline's Fifth Freedom service began on January 15 as it reached out to the Orient with scheduled flights.[2] The L-1011-500 took off from Toronto at 2225 local time on the first leg of the airline's longest route: London–Bombay–Singapore. Two Air Canada DC-8 freighters had already supplied the stations at Bombay and Singapore with commissary and catering goods. Thereafter, these would be carried by the regular flights each month — especially 19,000 pounds of food unavailable in Bombay. Captain F. Richards, First Officer R. Ashleigh, Second Officer J. Ryntjes, Flight Service Director Gilles Lacaille, and In-Charge

Jeannette Forbes were part of the crew, and Flight 858's passengers were given a rousing sendoff at the departure lounge where members of the Hong Kong Kung Fu club performed a lion dance. The first passenger to be booked all the way from Toronto to Singapore was student Jackie Tan Yu Ling, who was presented with a box of chocolates. But the London connection was still the priority, and in case anything went wrong with the aircraft, there would always be a back up L-1011-500 ready.

At Heathrow Terminal III, Air Canada passenger agents in saris and Chinese dress greeted them. As the aircraft pushed back for what would be a "first" for the airline, Flight Service Martin Fleet addressed the passengers. "It's a proud day for Air Canada," he said. "For the first time we welcome you to the continuation of Flight 858 bound for Bombay and Singapore."

At Bombay Airport, Canadian High Commissioner John Warden greeted the flight, and new crews took over, led by Captains Sherman Everard and Les Hems, and Second Officer Bill Donaldson. Midnight supper was Kashmiri chicken and Lychees Imperatrice. In the morning, as Flight 553 made its descent into Changi Airport, Singapore, the flight service director announced: "I hope you are excited as we are about the first arrival in Singapore for Air Canada." It was now two days later (10:25 a.m. local time) for the Toronto passengers and at the tarmac to greet the now bleary eyed passengers were the Canadian High Commissioner George Seymour and the Commercial

Counsellor, Otch von Finckenstein. Air Canada's longest route (10,457 miles) had been inaugurated. The return flight at 22:10 that same day was to allow for maintenance checks and local connections.

———

On March 29, 1985, the following notice was distributed to all staff:

"It was observed on our inaugural service to Bombay/Singapore that employees traveling on business and on a personal basis seemed to monopolise the time of the flight attendants. Their time could have better been spent attending to the needs of fare paying passengers. Movement of employees up and down the aisles and blocking them was also reported.

"Most employees in Bombay and Singapore have only been with Air Canada a few months and their observations of employees and their family members on this flight ... will have a lasting impression on the newest members of the Air Canada family.

"Here are some don'ts from the 'Welcome Abroad' brochure:

- Loud talk, especially about being able to fly anywhere for only a few dollars.
- Drinking to excess.
- Inappropriate dress.
- Unkempt appearance.
- Entering the galley or monopolizing the attention of the flight attendants who do not have the time to talk shop.

"Let's remember, good sense fosters goodwill — let's use it!"

While Taylor was learning to move again, Maz was laying the groundwork for an Air Canada sale. First to go was the board of directors — the decades-old haven for Liberal political patronage. It came as no surprise when Mazankowski announced the resignation of all directors, with the exception of Taylor and President Pierre Jeanniot. To ensure that there would be no bumps on the road to privatization, a likeminded board was put in. In March 1985 he appointed thirteen new members effective June 1, among them Frank Moores, former premier of Newfoundland and now part of the Ottawa lobbying firm Government Consultants International (GCI), Fernand Roberge, manager of Montreal's Ritz-Carlton Hotel, and Gayle Christie, former mayor of the Toronto suburb of York. To the media, it was seen as the Conservatives' turn to get at the Air Canada trough. Brian Mulroney had campaigned on ending the patronage sleaze that the Trudeau government embodied, especially with such patronage plums as seats on Air Canada's board. When it was revealed in September that Airbus, eager to sell its aircraft to Air Canada, was also a client of GCI, Taylor called Mazankowski and Mulroney to have Moores resign from the board.

The White Paper "Freedom to Move — A Framework for Transportation Reform" issued on July 15 was Mazankowski's own salvo to deregulate the airline industry in Canada. With the passage of legislation in December, it would no longer be necessary for a carrier to establish that its service was required by "public convenience," only that it had to be "fit, willing and able" and sanctioned by the Department of Transport safety regulations — and Canadian. Much of the paper found its way into Bill C-18, the future National Transportation Act with its emphasis on market forces controlling the airline industry. In it, the 25 percent foreign ownership limit of airlines in Canada was copied from the current U.S. limit.

"Freedom To Move" caused more frantic partnering in the airline industry than the last dance at the high school gym. When prevented by regulation from dumping money-losing routes to spread the loss around, airlines had historically resorted to merging. Now, with deregulation and the relaxation of government control, the airline industry in Canada changed overnight. The two main airlines acquired stakes first in the larger "regionals" and then the smaller, family-run ones. On November 8, 1985, Don Carty shared a press conference with Nordair's president Jean Douville to announce that CP Air had bought the 65 percent of Nordair owned by the airline's employees for $17 million. The employees said they were relieved not to sell to the Quebec government. That provincial government would finally acknowledge the inevitable, and Quebecair was sold to Nordair/CP Air on July 31, 1986. CP absorbed its $64 million debt and renamed it Inter-Canadian.

When Air Canada dropped Lethbridge from its network in 1967, local rancher Stubb Ross began Lethbridge Air Services, operating a collection of aircraft that progressed from Beech 18s to Fokker F28s.

Renamed Time Air from the slogan "Time Flies — Why Don't You?" Stubb's operation gradually rivalled PWA in Alberta and Saskatchewan, and in 1978, to counter PWA buying Transair, CPAL first took a minority interest in Time Air, and then in 1993 as PWA Corporation the parent company of Canadian Airlines, all of it. By 1990, with Canadian Regional Airlines, Canadian Airlines had pieced together a national feeder network for itself that rivalled Air Canada's.

The "sleepy giant," as the media labelled Air Canada, had the most to lose from the competition that deregulation had fostered, but it still controlled 55 percent of the domestic market. In the face of CP Air's acquisition of regional airlines, it responded with its own shopping spree. It had to demonstrate that by pulling its unprofitable DC-9 jet service out of smaller cities like London, Sault Ste. Marie, Stephenville, Gander, Sept-Îles, and Yarmouth, that "connector" airlines could take over with their cheaper Dash 8 aircraft. In August 1985, Air Canada joined with PWA to buy 49 percent of Air Ontario and in September 1986 signed a joint agreement with Trillium Air of St. Catharines, Ontario. To rival EPA in the Maritimes, brand new Air Nova took flight on July 14, 1986 as the Air Canada connecting carrier, all Air Nova flights having the "AC" (the Air Canada designator). Although courted by CP Air, Austin Airways, the small Ontario airline owned by the Deluce family, sold out to Air Canada for $40 million on October

30, 1986. With Nordair/Quebecair in the rival camp, Air Canada set up Air Alliance in the province of Quebec, but because of a lack of Dash 8s was unable to start a commuter service, the shortage a result of the de Havilland strike the previous summer.

At the south end of Vancouver International Airport was Air BC, its staff of 385 working out of school portables. In 1979, when British Columbia's resource industry was doing well, the Jim Pattison Group amalgamated five small coastal airlines that made up Air BC. But the recession that followed combined with labour problems in 1981–82 almost bankrupted Air BC. Iain Harris, who trimmed aircraft and staff and even took on CPAL on the lucrative Vancouver–Victoria run, turned the company around. Using turboprop aircraft rather than expensive jets, Air BC was soon flying to Seattle, Bella Bella, Kamloops, and Castlegar. It became CP Air's feeder line into the British Columbia interior, the larger airline integrating it into its own CRS, taking over baggage handling and passenger boarding. In 1985, Harris started flights over the Rockies to Kamloops and Kelowna, with PWA's territory in mind. Looking for a coastal toehold, in November 1986 Air Canada made Air BC an offer to become their "connector." Harris informed CPAL of this but since they were about to be bought by PWA, they heard nothing back and Air BC became one of Air Canada's connectors.

To counter PWA's northern network to Cambridge Bay, Resolute, and Inuvik, Air Canada struck back with its own "North of 60" foray in November 1987, buying Northwest Territorial Airways Ltd. for $12.6 million. They soon changed its name to NWT Air, and Northwest Territorial's Lockheed Electras and DC-3s served Rankin Inlet, Iqaluit, Coppermine, Pelly Bay, and Yellowknife, tying into Air Canada's network at Edmonton and Winnipeg. By 1988, the Air Canada Connector system operated eighty-seven aircraft providing more than 230 connections with the Corporation at thirteen airports. Agreements to coordinate flight schedules through ticketing, boarding passes, and ground handling had been made with each connector airline, the stylized Maple Leaf logo and Air Canada livery on each of their aircraft. It seemed that contrary to what Jack Pickersgill had hoped, market forces and deregulation had solved the regional airline puzzle.

———

CP Air reinvented itself in January 1986 by formally changing its name to Canadian Pacific Air Lines (CPAL) and dropping the now dated 1960s orange livery for "Pacific Blue" and "Sky White," both separated by a stripe of "Corporation Red" to underline its aggressiveness, Carty said. Air Canada was not far behind with its own image remake, designed to attract business people. Called "road warriors" or astronauts (because they spent so much time in orbit) business travellers made up 60 percent of Air Canada's passengers, and its marketing strategy was aimed at getting more. The 1986 advertising campaign led off with

"The Dawning of a New Era in Executive Travel," headlining a dramatic photo of a B767 flying up the side of a glass office building and the byline "On Your Way to the Top." In a television commercial, a station attendant was shown guiding in … not a plane but a skyscraper. Once it is eased into place next to the other buildings, people begin walking in and out and the voice over says, "Around the world every day, thousands of business people count on Air Canada to get them to work and to get them home again."

Executive class on the B767s was redesigned with reduced seating, from sixty-three to forty-eight, and Avio Italian seats. Once seated the businesspeople were plied with fine wines and elegant cuisine, and allowed two-minute check-in and priority baggage retrieval. Introduced in February 1986, the "cashless cabin" was welcomed by everyone but especially by the flight attendants. Economy class was renamed "Hospitality Class," and free bar service, free audio, and free movies were made available to all passengers. Only the new "Airfones" with which passengers could call anywhere in North America cost $9.50 for three minutes.

————

Leapfrogging over the traffic between the airport and downtown has always been a time-constrained businessperson's dream. The first all-helicopter airport shuttle in history was New York Airways, which in 1965 began shuttle flights between JFK Airport to the top of the Pan Am building in Manhattan. Air Canada's public relations man Pierre Jerome said, "Businessmen want to get downtown in a whistle." And catering to the business market, on August 11, 1986 Air Canada contracted with OB Maple Leaf Helicopters to offer a high frequency shuttle using AS350 helicopters to link Terminal II at Pearson Airport with Cherry Beach heliport in downtown Toronto. Its only competitor was the STOL service operated by City Express from Toronto Island Airport. In theory, the whole trip from Pearson Airport to the Westin Hotel was ten minutes, with first class passengers free while those in executive class paid $15 and full fare economy $20. Everyone else paid $45. The AS350 did thirty-four daily flights every twenty minutes, and when rain prevented operation, the airline provided a bus. Because of poor load factors and the traffic congestion from Cherry Beach (the airline tried to get a closer heliport), Air Canada ended its helicopter service on June 27, 1987.

————

The first airline to ban smoking in Canada on all its flights was tiny Air Maritime before it was bought by Air Atlantic, but on April 27, 1986, Air Canada became the first major airline in North America to introduce complete non-smoking flights, initially on its Montreal–Toronto and Toronto–Ottawa runs. "Although this may not seem like a significant aviation contribution," Jeanniot would later say, "the introduction of the first ever non-smoking flights on a commercial airline turned out to be a bit of a landmark.

I took the decision — despite the strong negative recommendation of our Commercial Department who, by coincidence, were mostly smokers. The threatened, rather vocal boycott by the entire tobacco industry — growers, manufacturers, distributors — gave us tremendous free publicity, and we gained approximately five percent in market share on the Montreal–Toronto corridor." The decision was backed by a 1985 Statistics Canada survey that recorded that more than half of the smokers on aircraft said they would welcome tighter regulations in the hope that it would help them stop smoking. Smokers would be allowed to change their flights — full fare passengers at no fee. "We were still at the time a Crown corporation," Jeanniot concluded, "and the federal government decided to take some credit for the results and progressively extended the smoking ban to all domestic flights. As far as influencing worldwide the non-smoking movement, the rest is history."

All offices at Place Air Canada would be smoke-free on May 2, 1988, the company allowing for a three-month adjustment period when smoking was permitted in a special room on the twentieth floor next to the cafeteria. The Non-Smokers' Health Act came into effect in July 1990, making Canada the first country in the world to adopt such measures and forcing all Canadian air carriers to prohibit smoking on all flights, domestic and foreign. But as smokers switched to airlines that still let them to smoke onboard, Air Canada estimated that it lost $40 million in cancellations. This was especially the case on Air

Canada flights from Athens and Zagreb (from where 80 percent of the passengers smoked), and the airline was competing against Olympic Airways and JAT, the national airline of Yugoslavia, neither of which had banned smoking onboard.

———

Lee Koepke had flown his Lockheed Electra around the world between July 7–10, 1967, to commemorate Amelia Earhart's ill-fated flight thirty years before. His navigator, William Pohemus, had once been an Air Canada employee and on his return he informed the company that the Electra was the former CF-TCA, one of the "Five Sisters" that began the airline. Air Canada bought her on March 11, 1968, and repainted and registered as CF-TCA, she was flown to the National Aviation Museum on October 14 by Captain A.W. Ross and Herb Seagrim, who had first piloted her in 1937.[3] No longer airworthy, there she rested until 1985, when the little aircraft was to become the star attraction at the Air Canada pavilion in Expo 86. Her wings clipped, CF-TCA was loaded onto a flatbed truck and transported in fourteen days across the country from Ottawa to Vancouver.

But for the audio-visual presentation of the TCA Lockheed in operation in 1937, Air Canada needed to record the authentic sounds of Pratt & Whitney Wasps wheezing and coughing into life and taxiing, taking off, and landing. The other Electra CF-TCC was being rebuilt in Winnipeg and could not be used for taxiing or taking off. Then some-

When the airline celebrated its fiftieth anniversary in 1986, "CF-TCC," one of the five L-10As that began the airline, was flown across Canada by pilots and stewardesses, sometimes wearing their original uniforms from half a century before.

one recalled that the Beech 18 used by the RCAF after the war had the same engines, and the Vancouver chapter of the Canadian Warplane Heritage Museum made theirs available. The "takes" recording the sounds of a Wasp were done at Boundary Bay Airport, a sound engineer hooking up a microphone in front of the engines, careful not to let it be it sucked in or blown away by the prop wash.

By the airline's fiftieth anniversary in 1987, the pilots who had flown CF-TCC across Canada for its twenty-fifth, Lothian, Rankin, Giguere, and Rood, were past flying, but CF-TCC wasn't. Completely refurbished by Air Canada, it was to be the centre of a last hurrah for those men and women who had begun the airline half a century before, and to coincide with Expo 86, an extensive "Sentimental Journey" was planned. In the TCA livery of 1938, on April 10, 1986 at 12:00, the Electra took off from Saint-Hubert Airport, Montreal, its crew guided in the engine start-up procedure through a voice hook-up with the now retired Lothian and Rood, who were sitting in CF-TCA in the Air Canada Pavilion. The 10A would cross Canada, going to Moncton, Summerside, Charlottetown, Sept-Îles, Bagotville, Trois-Rivières, Quebec City, Dorval, Mirabel, Ottawa, Toronto, Windsor, London, Toronto, Muskoka, Val-d'Or, Rouyn, Earlton, North Bay, Sudbury, Timmins, Kapuskasing, Sault Ste.

Marie, Thunder Bay, Winnipeg, Brandon, Yorkton, Regina, Prince Albert, Saskatoon, Swift Current, Medicine Hat, Lethbridge, Edmonton, Calgary, Vancouver, Victoria, Seattle, Everett, and Washington, ending at Vancouver on May 10.

With the two pilots on each leg were the stewardesses who had flown in CF-TCC almost half a century before. Sometimes wearing their original uniforms or replicas, they were TCA's first steward-ess Lucille Grant (Montreal), Peggy Brown (Vancouver), Annette Donovan (Toronto), Katherine Deyman (Halifax), Ruth Heenan (Toronto), Pat Maxwell (Vancouver), Leila McKay (Winnipeg), and Margaret Turnbull (Ottawa).[4] At every stop along the way, a stewardess in the current airline uniform was on hand to present flowers to her pre-decessor in the 1938 one.

Ruth Heenan wrote this of her experience:

The memory of Air Canada employ-ees invaded my mind and fifty years disappeared for me. Voices and faces of former crews crowded back. Then the big moment — bending low and trying to be nonchalant — holding your precious cap — set-tling down. Then the memory of unfolding the jump seat, getting it set up into the floor slats, hooking up the safety belt, the feeling of a fast jog down the runway. Pratt & Whitney engines being adjusted and synchronized again, with trees, rocks, and lakes hurrying by below.

At only 5,000–6000 feet I even had a guilty feeling, I should be distributing my Pall Mall or Sweet Cap cigarettes and TCA logo match packs, packs of gum … pointing out town as transmitters, our guides to our next destination. The next thought about duty was to get the pilot's bulletin on speed, altitude and arrival times to circu-late; my gosh, better check those lunch boxes. What surprises are there in store this trip? Exploded chocolate marshmallow cookies, bananas shrivelled to black worm-like shapes, overflowing wax cups of tomato juice. Did they load the vacuum of milk onboard or was it two water and one coffee? Guess that's why we are the survivors.

Terry Denny, the fortunate employee communications coordinator, flew with CF-TCC and kept a diary of the trip, also capturing on more than 7,500 frames of film the amusing and the poignant. Naturally, Chairman Claude Taylor and Transport Minister Don Mazankowski made sure they took part, joining the Mirabel–Ottawa leg on April 20. A pilot himself, Maz could not resist getting into the 10A's right seat and flying CF-TCC for fifteen minutes, after which Ray Lank presented him with a set of Air Canada captain's wings.

At cities and towns, crowds turned out to pay homage to the little aircraft who, with her four sisters, had begun it all, and the crew and passengers were met by air cadets and local dignitaries, the airline retirees called the Pionairs, a Dixie band that played (what else?) "Those Magnificent Men in their Flying Machines," a 1929 Hudson automobile, and in Everett, Washington, a theatre company in 1930s dress. Along the way the Electra was escorted by flocks of Canada geese, a CF-18 fighter aircraft (at close to its stalling speed) from CFB Bagotville, and a Beech 18 of the Canadian Warplane Heritage Museum from Hamilton. Lank, who was met by his family in Toronto (his grandson carrying a sign that read "I'm proud of you Grandpa"), summed it up thus: "The very essence of Trans-Canada Air Lines and Air Canada combined to realize a dream."

As for CF-TCC, Captain Mason takes up the story:

Since the 1986 anniversary flight, TCC has continued 'flying the corporate image' during the summer, returning to her winter home at the Western Canada Air Museum each fall. A lot of this time has been spent promoting the Air Canada Employee Charity "Dreams Take Flight," an employee initiative that allows special needs children to visit Disneyland or Disney World. Air Canada supplies the aircraft, but the employees volunteer with fundraising events and securing sponsorships throughout the year to cover all other expenses. Since the first trip numbering seventy children in 1989, over 10,000 happy faces have experienced their wish.

As with "Dreams" all TCC operations are voluntary. The results of both these projects pay tribute to the dedication of Air Canada employees. The most experienced TCC pilots still active (at that time), Capt. Ken Patry (since 1988) and Capt. Alan MacLeod (after eleven years retirement), continue to demonstrate how this aircraft still can bring out the passion of aviation today.

____

The CEO of PWA, Rhys Eyton, was known for playing his cards close to his chest. In 1983, when the Alberta government returned PWA to the private sector, he masterminded the airline's privatization and then sold sixteen of its B737s to Guinness Peat Aviation, leasing them back. Without long debt, $300 million in shareholder's equity, and an asset base of $400 million, Eyton now offered to sell PWA to either Air Canada or CPAL as part of their feeder network, but both refused, and as late as November 1986, Eyton told the *Calgary Herald* that he looked to align PWA with Air Canada, CPAL, or Wardair.

At some point after that, the PWA CEO transformed himself from seller to buyer. On December 2, for $300 million, Eyton purchased Grant McConachie's airline from the railway monarchs at Windsor Station, Montreal — the canary swallowing the cat. In doing this, Eyton had taken on CPAL's high debt load and employee integration problems but also got routes to the Far East that were second to none. Mazankowski and Jeanniot said that the takeover did not represent a threat to Air Canada, and Max Ward too shrugged it off, saying it was one less competitor in the deregulated market. Hugh Riopelle, Air Canada's director of government and public affairs, thought that the CPAL takeover could only help. "To compete with them equitably we would have to operate under the same rules, and that means privatization." It was an historic moment for Canadians; for the first time they had a choice between two airlines of almost exactly the same size. But anxious about the changes to come, Taylor and Jeanniot began a media campaign to get the government to take away CPAL's Far East routes and form a single international carrier.

Eyton waited until February 26, 1987, when the Canadian Transport Agency had approved the purchase, to unveil the PWA/CPAL airline's "Wings Across Five Continents" look. He then moved the headquarters from Vancouver to Calgary, and followed that up on March 24 with renaming CPAL Canadian Airlines International Ltd (CAIL), perhaps harkening back to James Richardson's Canadian Airways. Don Carty had left by then, returning to American Airlines as senior vice-president.

———

Air Canada celebrated its fiftieth birthday on April 10, 1987, its final year as a public company. Its employees, unsure about their future, were in a sombre mood. There were some victories since two concerns that had

plagued the airline for decades were somewhat ameliorated. The Supreme Court agreed that the airline could sue the province of British Columbia for taxes it had collected on aviation from 1937 to 1974. Ordered to repay nearly $7 million to Air Canada, that province had admitted that its taxing law was unconstitutional because it amounted to a type of indirect taxation reserved for the federal government. The ruling opened ways for both CP Air and PWA to sue the province as well.

The Commissioner of Official Languages, D'Iberville Fortier, presented a positive report on the state of bilingualism in the airline. Forty-five percent of the customer service agents were now bilingual, as were 58 percent of the 3,417 flight attendants and 98 percent of the public announcements. With the Official Languages Act about to come into force, the government wanted to ensure that even when privatized, essential institutions like VIA Rail and Air Canada would retain their language obligations. Speaking before The Joint House Standing Committee in Parliament, Jeanniot took pride in this, saying that it only made economic sense when the Francophone market accounted for $600 million in the province of Quebec — and there were the French, Swiss, and Belgian markets to consider.

———

The dogfights between airlines were now no longer fought with duelling aircraft but computer code — and who had access to the greater system. Airlines rely on computerized reservation systems (CRS) to display fares and routes quickly so that travel agents can make bookings. Agents were locked into a particular airline's CRS, and in the deregulated market, whoever manipulated the information displayed on the terminal controlled the airline's reservations.

In the United States the two dominant systems then were SABRE, used by AMR (the American Airlines holding company), and United Airlines' Apollo. Air Canada had pioneered CRS with its ReserVec, but it was a "stand-alone," and CAIL's Pegasus 2000 system had been even less successful. Introduced north of the border in 1986, SABRE quickly captured 20 percent of all reservations made by Canadian passengers. Neither Air Canada nor CPAL could afford the huge start-up costs to create a similar system, and in May 1987, they put aside their differences to integrate their computer reservations systems. Called Gemini

PASSENGER FEEDBACK 1970–1990 (AIR CANADA ARCHIVES)

I wish to commend your employees Alain Gérard Duffieux and Kathy Frittenburg, who added a level of style, grace and tasteful playfulness which cannot possibly be duplicated on American Airlines or any of your competitors. If you could clone these people, Air Canada would never have an unsold seat.

Do something about the hideous cuisine: salmon the thickness of rhino hide, bread rolls that could be used to storm a castle and carbon dated lettuce. Please stop describing your calcified poultry as "cordon bleu." Have some respect for the chicken — and the French language.

You Found It! Here is a picture of my favourite blanket that my dumb dad left at Edmonton Airport when I went on your airplane. I was very unhappy and could not sleep until your manager in Calgary found it and put it on the next airplane marked "RUSH." — John Manning (2 years old)

A few years ago, the company spent several million dollars on reconfiguring the DC-9s, removing four revenue front seats to install cabin storage compartments. At the same time, one of rear toilets was taken out to provide in-flight crew use. Has there been a policy change that now allows in-flight crew the use of these storage compartments? I cannot believe the company removed revenue seats to accommodate crew baggage. Why can't the crew check their bags in the cargo compartment as do our customers? Or alternatively use the reconverted toilet for their coats and luggage?

Considering that Air Canada won the much-coveted Passenger Service Award three years ago, I find it hard to believe that the in-flight meal service has deteriorated as much as it actually has in such a short time. In Y class, dinner/lunch is now a casserole, which appears to be a sloppy mess, the contents of which are difficult to determine. Breakfast is now a plastic box, which looks unappealing and certainly lacks style.

Tell the flight attendants to stop acting as though passengers are demanding their firstborn child when they ask for another coffee.

Distributions Inc. of Toronto, its operational facilities were in Winnipeg, and employing 300 workers from Air Canada's ReserVec system and 200 from CAIL's Pegasus 2000 system, it leased fibreoptic lines that ran to 15,000 Gemini travel agents across the country. Gemini's president was Paul Nelson of CAIL, with Air Canada's Anne Bodnarchuk the chairperson. Ironically, although the Consumer Association of Canada thought that this lessened competition, the Competition Bureau approved the arrangement, as did Wardair, which was eventually forced to join Gemini as well. United Airlines let Apollo die and set up Covia, which would be integrated into Gemini.

The CRS wars were soon worldwide with airlines joining either Covia/Gemini (or in Europe Galileo) or SABRE. Gemini would later partner with PARS, owned by Trans World Airlines and Northwest Airlines, adding 6,500 more travel agencies. But the biggest coup for Air Canada's CRS was when PARS was selected by Abacus, owned by Singapore Airlines, Thai International, and Cathay Pacific. The combination of Gemini/Covia/PARS/Abacus would be the world's first truly global CRS.

Customer reservations were not alone in being tracked by computers. Two sophisticated in-house computer programs were introduced in 1987. ACCESS II tracked all of Air Canada's cargo shipments with terminal facilities in Vancouver, Saskatoon, and London, UK. PROMIS (Product Management Information System), completely designed by Air Canada mainte-

nance personnel, catalogued, tracked, and managed the scheduling of work required when aircraft came in for maintenance, prompting interest from other airlines around the world.

————

"We felt it was time to introduce a new wardrobe," said Connie Bastien, the airline's wardrobe and grooming manager. "It's been nine years since the previous uniform was introduced, and its life span was expiring." The company began working on uniforms for the fiftieth anniversary in 1984, hiring Montreal couturier Leo Chevalier, who had previously designed uniforms for Bell Canada, the Toronto Transit Commission, and the 1976 Summer Olympics. He was given the task of designing a uniform that would dress 7,000 people all alike in a manner that would be suitable for their jobs and also reflect the company's image. The first designer to be honoured with the Order of Canada, Chevalier aimed for a double-breasted style and crisp professional look.

Designed and manufactured entirely in Canada, the new wardrobe featured a double-breasted look in navy blue and burgundy. It would be worn by all "public contact" people, including flight attendants, sales and service personnel, as well as baggage, cargo, and load agents. For women, the new uniform consisted of a mid-calf-length navy blue skirt and double-breasted navy blue straight-cut blazer and pants. Cabin personnel would wear a burgundy background with navy stripes, ground employees a navy background with

PIERRE JEANNIOT AND THE SERPENT'S TOOTH

burgundy stripes, and supervisors equal navy and burgundy stripes. A white blouse or shirt complemented the outfit (raisin chambray for cargo, baggage, and load agents) along with a navy bow. Navy blue raincoats in a cotton/polyester blend along with accessories of scarves, gloves, belts, and gold electroplated brevets featuring the Air Canada insignia completed the uniforms.

Previous uniforms were made from a wool/polyester blend, and Warren Reeves, product and appearance manager, explained. "This time we are introducing 100 percent wool fabrics, which feel and look better and are more comfortable. This is also the first time that we have introduced uniforms simultaneously to all 'public contact' employees and we can establish a common inventory and reduce costs." The uniforms were "weather tested" by employees over a three-month trial period to provide input as to durability, comfort, and appearance after cleaning. The design team could only hope that the new look would be "fitting" for the years ahead.

———

Northern Transportation Company Ltd., de Havilland Canada, Canadair, Canadian Arsenals, Teleglobe Canada … the list of Crown corporations to be privatized by the Conservatives grew with every year they were in power, and there could be no doubt that the high-profile Air Canada was on it. In June 1986 the prime minister would elevate his "fixer" to be simultaneously government house leader, deputy prime minister, and president of the Privy

Council, and Mazankowski would hand the transport portfolio to John Crosbie. "Maz being deputy prime minister gave some added weight to it," Taylor admitted.

For his part, Mazankowski said, "To suggest that we were forced by the management of Air Canada [to do this], I could say if we were forced why did it take so long?"

The privatization campaign was transferred to a new ministry under Barbara McDougall, who did not share the vision and passion that Maz and Taylor had for the airline.[5] Taylor, who met monthly with McDougall, thought her motivation in a sell-off was purely political. "She wanted to have a politically successful privatization of a major Crown corporation."

Dominion Securities was hired to advise McDougall and walk her through the steps before the airline could be sold part or whole to the public. Air Canada brought in its own advisors, Wood Gundy Inc. and the U.S. investment banker Morgan Stanley & Co., and sought advice from the British investment house S.G. Warburg, which had presided over the British Airways privatization. The approach in the United Kingdom had been to sell two thirds of the British Airways' 720 million shares to the airline's employees, institutions, and foreign investors, with the remainder offered to thousands of small British investors. Although 1986 was a bad year for travel with the bombing in Libya and the nuclear accident at Chernobyl, Colin Marshall, British Airways CEO, managed to salvage the airline's credibility with a massive publicity campaign.

The selling off of corporations like Canadair (to Bombardier) and de Havilland (to Boeing) were privately negotiated. In a niche market, the aircraft manufacturers would never be able to stand on their own, and sales to an existing private sector entity were seen as their salvation. Canadair became a wholly owned subsidiary of the Bombardier Aerospace Group on December 23, 1986, and a year later launched a stretch version of its Challenger executive jet, which would evolve into the Regional Jet variant. But since Air Canada (like Petro-Canada, Cameco, and the CNR) was in highly competitive environment and stood a reasonable chance of survival alone, it could be sold through public markets. McDougall drew up a short list of Crown corporations to be successfully privatized, and Air Canada was at the top.

Initially, Taylor's goal was a total sell-off. The airline had not received an equity infusion since 1977 or government subsidy since 1962. It carried between 30,000 and 40,000 passengers daily and by now accounted for 56 percent of the domestic air travel market, with CAIL at 39 percent and Wardair at 3 percent. But its $1.05 billion debt hampered any fleet modernization plans that he and Jeanniot had. In a major speech in January 1987, Taylor said: "As a Crown corporation, Air Canada's ability to raise capital is limited because the government has given every indication that there will be no new equity, and we do not have access to private equity markets." There was some consolation that securities legislation in Canada would limit the overt hype that

characterized the sale of shares of British Airways and British Petroleum (BP); the latter's sale had caused enough turmoil to crash the stock market in Britain. But in February 1987 Her Majesty's government successfully sold off British Airways for $1.4 billion and Colin Marshall was rewarded with a knighthood. Watching from this side of the Atlantic, Taylor must have wondered how he could do the same.

Could selling off Air Canada in two tranches work? So close to the end now, at first Taylor would not settle for partial privatization. "Right up to October 1987," he later admitted, "I would have shot anybody who suggested partial privatization." Asked by a reporter if his motivation for a complete sale was because the airline desperately needed $3 billion to buy new aircraft in the next decade, Taylor snapped, "The issue isn't about money at all. I've done a little exercise with people who say the only reason you want to be privatized is because you need money to buy planes. The government could easily solve that problem. They could give us a cheque for $300 million. And I would still be unhappy."

Then Mulroney seemed to have second thoughts. At a cabinet meeting in Edmonton in early July, the prime minister remembered that he had once said Air Canada was not for sale and that Canada needed a national airline. Taking its cue from that, the government would only say that the sell-off was under review, and even Taylor began to believe that nothing was going to happen in 1987. But when Bill C-18, the National Transportation Act, received Royal Assent in August (to come into effect January 1, 1988), the prime minister made Maz the minister responsible for privatization, and the Air Canada sell-off was on again. His political clout and personality was enough to give the sale the push it needed to get it through the House of Commons committee hearings. An old hand at working the rooms, Taylor was at home here.

In October, the government redefined the international routes for both airlines. Canadian Airlines was designated for Germany, Denmark, Sweden, Norway, the U.S.S.R., Mexico, Central and South America, Indonesia, Taiwan, and India. More significantly, it was reaffirmed as the official Canadian carrier to the Pacific. Air Canada was given Cairo and the former CPAL destination of Tel Aviv, Korea, Malaysia, and the Philippines, but not what it really wanted: Hong Kong and Tokyo, where it already had an all-cargo service. Since 1985, besides Singapore and Bombay, the Air Canada network had grown to Vienna, St. Lucia, and Santo Domingo, and later Lisbon, Madrid, Athens, Nice, and Birmingham. After the signing of the bilateral agreement between Canada and Jordan in April 1988, Air Canada reserved a block of twenty-five seats on the Royal Jordanian Airlines L-1011 leaving Mirabel Airport twice weekly for Amman. To fit into Air Canada's systems, a fictitious airline, "A9," was created with flight numbers running from 001 and 099. Seoul was added that year, its use as a base in the Far East to compete against CAIL. On April 6, 1989, the airline began flying

three times a week to Zagreb, Yugoslavia (the inaugural flight receiving a congratulatory letter from the prime minister), where it had Fifth Freedom rights between Zurich and Zagreb.

The year 1987 was one of strikes, as two postal unions shut down Canada Post and railway workers the country's rail system. Contract talks between the IAMAW and Air Canada went on through the summer, the union wanting pension benefits indexed to inflation and a one-year wage increase of 7.2 percent. The government voted back-to-work legislation in the postal and rail strikes but hesitated with Air Canada, appointing a federal mediator instead. The airline offered 4 percent increases in each year of a two-year contract but balked at the pension indexing demand. By October the federal mediator had failed to bring both sides to the table and talks broke off on November 15, when workers staged a "phantom strike" using the threat of a walkout to divert passengers to rival airlines.

———

Because of the one-hour turnaround at San Francisco Airport on November 6, Captain J. David Robinson and F/O George Christie remained in the L-1011 cockpit completing their paperwork for the return flight to Toronto. The door suddenly burst open and a man, brandishing an axe kept in the cockpit, took the two men hostage. Two weeks before, both Robinson and Christie had undergone a routine training program for just such an ordeal. "Little did we know at the time," Robinson said, "that we'd soon have to use it. And it worked!" The would-be hijacker, claiming he was "underworld prey," allowed Christie to leave the cockpit, but for three and a half hours held Robinson hostage until surrendering to FBI agents outside. The FBI later discovered that the thirty-seven-year-old man had several false identities and mythical relatives, but a very real criminal record. Interviewed later, Robinson said that he was just glad that the would-be hijacker would receive the care he needed.

___

On November 25 at Pearson Airport, Montreal, Ottawa, and Vancouver, the International Association of Machinists and Aerospace Workers (IAMAW) called on 8,500 aircraft cleaners, cargo agents, mechanics, ramp attendants, and baggage handlers to walk off the job, saying "This action is being taken with deep regret because we are fully aware of the inconvenience and hardship it will present to our customers." Jeanniot locked out all the members and shut down the airline. Bob McGregor, the chief union negotiator, told a news conference that the airline was being "negative" and "irresponsible to the public." "I don't believe that those airplanes can be up to the maintenance standard that existed when our members were locked out," he said.

Union members staged a noon-hour pep rally, snaking around Terminal 2 at Pearson chanting "Jeanniot must go!" and singing "Jingle bells, jingle bells, jingle all the way; our kids won't have a Christmas, Jeanniot took it away."

The strike put in jeopardy the recently signed $20 million contract with a cargo charter company to Hong Kong, as well as plans to serve Egypt, Portugal, Spain, and Venezuela. Losing an estimated $7.9 million a day, the airline was grounded into the busy Christmas season before an agreement was reached.

Except for the strike in the fourth quarter, Air Canada had had a financially good 1987. It earned a net income of $45 million, a $5.3 million increase over 1986, and analysts put its book value between $600 million and $800 million. Much of this was because of the buoyant world economy and the relatively weak Canadian dollar. No one could guess that it would be another ten years before the airline saw another such profit....

But there were dark clouds on the corporation's horizon even then. Like Pratte and McGregor before him, Jeanniot must have wondered at the lack of protection that the federal government afforded its national airline. For specious political gain, the Mulroney government was encouraging Wardair to expand into Europe, giving Max Ward the lucrative routes to London and Paris while at the same time denying Air Canada's attempts to develop routes into the Far East. Any possibility of a cease-fire between Air Canada and CAIL after the PWA purchase died as the latter was being lured away by American Airlines, the both to gnaw at Air Canada's cross-border traffic, beginning by interchanging passengers at Terminal III, Pearson Airport.

And as always in the airline industry, there were new kids on the block. During the strike, Quebec tour wholesaler Traffic Voyages formed Air Transat, its own charter company at Mirabel-Montreal. It leased a L-1011 from Air Canada on November 12, in time to launch its first charter flight to Acapulco. A second L-1011 was leased in May 1988 that allowed Air Transat to begin charters to Europe. Michel Leblanc, described by the media as a "serial airline entrepreneur," began Intair, the first of his many airlines, and when that failed, Royal Aviation Inc. The British airline Air 2000 began Canada 3000, its own Canadian charter airline, at Pearson Airport in 1988, selling its ownership the following year to the Deluce family and Adventure Tours. Run by the entrepreneurial Angus Kinnear, Canada 3000 soon rivalled Wardair for charters to Florida, Mexico, and Europe.

Less successful was Nationair, a charter airline begun by former employees of Quebecair, Nordair, and Air Canada in December 1984. Based initially at Montreal-Mirabel, it would evolve for a brief period by fair means and foul into the third largest player in the Canadian airline business, providing UN, Nigerian, and Hajj charters, and was somehow given permission to operate a short-lived scheduled service to Europe. If ever there was a textbook case of how not to run an airline, it was this, and Transport Canada bore much of the blame for allowing Nationair to continue. By the time it bankrupted in 1993, Nationair had gone down in aviation history for the worst crash of a Canadian airline when 261 people, including fourteen Canadians, were killed at Jeddah Airport, Saudi Arabia.

———

Two men who had played historic roles in TCA/Air Canada passed in the summer of 1988. At age sixty-three, former CEO Yves Pratte died of a heart attack on June 26, at his home near Bromont in the Eastern Townships. Chairman Claude Taylor, who had succeeded Pratte, said his career had been marked by many challenges and many successes. "Yves Pratte guided the company through a changing and often turbulent era."

Don MacLaren, Air Canada's first employee, died aged ninety-five on July 4. Born in 1893, MacLaren had been a World War I air ace who, after the hostilities ended, purchased a Curtiss Jenny to make a precarious living taking adventurous Vancouverites flying around English Bay for $5 a head. Joining Canadian Airways, Don had actually gone down to the Lockheed plant at Burbank, California, to pick up the Electra CF-AZY. In a historic photo, on July 6, 1936, MacLaren posed before the Electra, the first modern aircraft in Canada, in the company of Herbert Hollick-Kenyon, the trans-Antarctic pilot, and aviation pioneer Lieutenant Colonel Jimmy Doolittle. It was MacLaren who had recommended to Howe Phil Johnson from Boeing to get the airline off the ground. He retired as director of passenger services in 1958 to paint and teach the Bahá'í faith. He had seen the Concorde in

Paris and was glad that Air Canada had not purchased any; the world, he said, was travelling fast enough without supersonic speed. MacLaren's death marked the passing of an era, not only in the airline's history but of Canada itself.

Mazankowski announced on April 12, 1988, that Air Canada would be sold to the public as "market conditions permit" with an initial treasury issue of up to 45 percent of its shares. The sale would be subject to several conditions that were placed into the enabling legislation. The Air Canada Public Participation Act was approved by Parliament on August 18, 1988, and a week later, on August 25, the company filed its first preliminary prospectus for an offering of common shares that it expected to generate $300 million. The proceeds of the offering would be used for capital expenditures like the acquisition of new aircraft and to pay down debt. Air Canada appointed RBC Dominion Securities and Wood Gundy Inc. to lead the underwriting group responsible for the share sale. They included among others Scotia McLeod Inc., Nesbitt Thomson Deacon Inc., and Burns Fry Ltd. Eligible employees would be able to buy shares through the Employee Share Plan administered by the Royal Trust Company.

The act stipulated that:

- the company's headquarters would remain in Montreal, Quebec;
- the airline, for the indefinite future, would maintain major operational and overhaul centres at Winnipeg, Manitoba, and in Montreal and Toronto;
- that no more than 45 percent of the company's shares would be sold and the proceeds would go to the airline, not to the government;
- that employees would be given the first chance to buy shares in the company, small shareholders the second opportunity, followed by institutional investors and, finally, foreign investors;
- that no individual shareholder would be allowed to hold more than 10 percent of the company's shares, and foreign ownership was limited to 25 percent of the initial offering;[6]
- that the government's 55 percent holding in the company would be voted in accordance with the private sector shareholders to give the company an arm's length relationship to the government;
- that a privatized Air Canada would continue to operate both in English and in French, subject to the Official Languages Act.

Deemed a cautious piece of legislation by financial experts, the act was the work of bureaucrats who chose to ignore the increasing globalization of the aviation industry. In management's favour, the 10 percent limit on the company's shares ensured that senior management could run the airline without interference from any one shareholder. But being tied to a Montreal head office in a politically divisive province, having operational centers in heavily unionized Canada, the 10 percent and 25 percent share ownership, the language issue — for a privately run airline now susceptible to market forces to do this to itself would have been inconceivable in the United States. This was, to paraphrase Prime Minister Mackenzie King, "privatization if necessary but not necessarily privatization."[7] Air Canada had exchanged one set of shackles for another — of its government's making.

The company filed a formal summary of its stock on September 26, 1988, stating that its net income after taxes was $101 million for the year ended March 31, 1988. The Initial Public Offering was issued in October, issuing 30.8 million shares, which were 42.8 percent of the company's total and netting $225.8 million on the $246.2 million sale, with underwriting fees costing $12.3 million and the airline absorbing $8 million in discounts to its employees. The price of the stock was set at $8 per share, and all employee shares were sold out by October since more than 17,000 Air Canada staff system-wide (80 percent of the workforce) committed to buying shares and now owned 25 percent of the entire offering. D'Arcy Little, senior director, human resources, said that because there was no precedent to follow they had to create, invent, and innovate. It was the largest employee participation in the ownership of any corporation in Canada. Little confirmed that 20 percent of the airline's retirees had subscribed to the issue. While the numbers varied over the years,

Air Canada's shareholder base was usually comprised of the following: institutional: 78 percent; retail: 16 percent; and employees: 6 percent. Approximately 87 percent of the shares were held by Canadian residents, and 13 percent by non-residents.

——

Beginning in June 1988, the privatized Air Canada changed its public face, the changes implemented over the next five years. The "signature" was modernized with new lettering and use of upper and lower case letters (Air Canada instead of AIR CANADA). Public opinion polls had warned not to touch the Maple Leaf, and it survived unchanged, but the roundel on the aircraft's tail was made bigger. Added was a burgundy stripe under the red stripe on the fuselage of all aircraft. In urgent need of modernization were the cabin interiors, now dated by their "with-it" look of the late 1960s in what were described as "mustard yellow and pickle green seats, catsup red carpets, and candy stripe curtains."

Because the upholstery now had to be fire retardant, this was an opportunity to completely refurbish the whole aircraft interior. Colour consultant Madeleine Arbour was hired to create an environment that she said was going to be "elegant yet comfortable." Hospitality class was given raisin-coloured seats with burgundy accent stripes. In Executive class, soft beige tweed covered the seats and in first class the fully reclining seats were covered in soft brown leather. Carpeting throughout the cabin was navy blue with raisin flecks.

Speaking at the Empire Club in Toronto on March 17, 1988 (while striking Air Ontario pilots picketed outside), Jeanniot confirmed that the airline had asked Ottawa for $300 million in new capital. The *Globe and Mail* reported that analysts were bullish on Air Canada over the long run, and Steve Garmaise of First Marathon Securities Ltd. predicted, "Three to five years down the road, I don't see any problem. The price could easily double because there's been a lot of potential to cut costs." In the first phase of a financing plan for fleet renewal, the company completed a long-term, unsecured, floating-rate $400 million financing in November arranged by Citibank Canada and Citicorp Investment Bank. These would be drawn upon to pay for the new aircraft when they were delivered in 1990 with a $400 million line of credit with Canadian banks.

Air Canada shares began trading on the Toronto and Montreal stock exchanges on October 13, 1988, with Jeanniot and Taylor signing the official membership book at the Montreal Stock Exchange. The beaming Taylor considered this his crowning glory. "That's the one I'll put on my tombstone," he said, laughing.

Governor General Jeanne Sauvé (who in a previous life as a Quebec provincial minister had fought to have Air Canada close its Winnipeg base) awarded Jeanniot the Order of Canada on April 12 for "playing a key role in making Air Canada one of the ten largest airlines in the world." This

From its first flight to today, the Maple Leaf stylized several times over has always been Air Canada's trademark.

was stretching the point. In the volume of passengers, Air Canada was the twenty-fifth in the world, in number of employees (22,200) it was sixteenth, in fleet size (109 aircraft) it was seventeenth, in operating profit ($83 million) it was twenty-fifth. No surprise that Aeroflot led in passenger volume, employees, and fleet size.

By March 1989 the company's shares were trading at CDN $11.75 per share, to hit a high of CDN $14.83 in August. The former Crown corporation completed its privatization in July with the filing of a prospectus for its second issue of stock. The company sold 41.1 million shares, for a total of 57 percent of its equity in the filing, at $12 per share, the proceeds from that sale going to the government. "This day has been a dream of mine for many years," said Taylor. "It marks another significant milestone in a series of events that began on April 12, 1988." The airline's first Annual General Meeting (AGM) was held at the Montreal Convention Centre on April 26, and more than 1,200 of its shareholders attended (many of whom brought their children to witness history), including a number of retirees. "In the past as a Crown corporation, our annual meetings were held before a Parliamentary committee," Taylor recalled. This was certainly livelier.

A new board of directors was elected at the AGM. No longer political appointees rewarded for services to the party, they included captains of industry who would bring in investment, men such as William James, president and CEO of Falconbridge Ltd., and David A. Ganong, president of Ganong Brothers. Two women were on the board, Louise Brais Vaillancourt and Jean Wadds, the first female Canadian high commissioner to the United Kingdom. Former Prime Minister Trudeau said that Wadds had been one of the three women responsible for the recent repatriation of the Constitution; the other two were Her Majesty Queen Elizabeth II and former British Prime Minister Margaret Thatcher.

———

At 3:30 p.m. on September 24, 1988, with Air Canada Captain Bob Hill at the controls, a reconditioned Lancaster bomber took off from Mount Hope Airport outside Hamilton. Because the Second World War had ended as soon as the bomber had been completed at Victory Aircraft, Malton, Lancaster MK X FM 213 was put into storage. The RCAF would use it in a maritime search and rescue role until 1963 before declaring the bomber surplus. The Lancaster was then bought by the Legion post in Goderich, Ontario, to be mounted on three posts as a memorial. Donated to the Canadian Warplane Heritage Museum at Mount Hope, Ontario, it might have remained in a static condition had not more than fifty Air Canada employees overhauled thousands of its components between 1983 and 1987, the work done mainly at the Machine Process and Sheet Metal shop at the base in Dorval. The fruits of their labour were christened the "Mynarski Lanc," and it remains one of only two Lancasters flying in the world today. But by September 1988 the media, the government, and the public were engrossed in another Air Canada aircraft....

———

News of the airline's successful privatization was overshadowed in the media by the whiff of skullduggery, especially when it allegedly could be traced to the highest levels of government, even to the prime ministerial residence on Sussex Drive. Author Robert Ludlum could not have invented a better cast of characters. They included the RCMP, the FBI, the prime minister's office, CBC journalists, the U.S. ambassador to Canada, the lobbyist firm GCI, Frank Moores, former Trudeau cabinet members like Francis Fox, and German arms dealer Karlheinz Schreiber.

In the largest civilian aircraft order in Canadian history, on March 30, 1988, Air Canada's board of directors approved the purchase of thirty-four Airbus A320s and parts for a total of $1.8 billion. It also took an option for twenty additional A320s that could be converted in "stretched" versions. That it was followed by the announcement to privatize the airline on April 12 led to much speculation. "Was it a coincidence," wrote Globe and Mail journalist Harvey Cashore, "that Mulroney changed his mind about privatization ... only days after the Crown airline committed to the Airbus purchase?"[8]

Jeanniot said that the cost of the new aircraft would be offset by work placed in Canada by Airbus. This included a $1 billion contract for Canadair to manufacture Airbus parts. With Canadair rather than Bristol Aerospace of Winnipeg benefiting from the Airbus deal and a federal election and provincial one in Manitoba in the offing, the Mulroney government delayed the A320 announcement for as long as it could. The $400 million parts supply contract was made public on November 15, 1988, less than a week before the federal election.

There were many in the company who recalled the controversy when DC-9s were bought instead of the Sud-Aviation Caravelle in 1966. That the airline had chosen an American aircraft over a French one incensed French Canadian university students, who paraded before Place Ville Marie, yelling "Hang McGregor!" This time Air Canada had chosen a European aircraft instead of one built in the United States, and the reaction to its decision was historic or histrionic, depending on where one stood.

Aerospatiale in the 1980s reminded observers of Boeing in the 1960s: predatory, far-sighted, and lean, just at a time when the American giant was defensive, complacent, and provincial. Quite simply, Airbus had, to quote an Air Canada vice-president, "built a better plane." Its electronic flight display, the "glass cockpit," had done away with analog dials (and flight engineers) and left Boeing's B727s in the "steam gauge" era. American and Canadian airline pilots warned of computer blackouts at critical moments in flight, but in September 1984, Pan American World Airways, the airline that had historically been the unofficial chosen instrument of the United States, bought twelve A310s and sixteen A320s, taking an option on fifty more. In 1986, Northwest Airlines signed an agreement to buy ten A320s followed by a second one for A330s and A340s. Closer to home, in early 1987, Max Ward, who had put a down payment on B767s, changed his mind and ordered twelve A310s at a highly discounted rate of $42 million each and then went on to order twenty-four Fokker F100s instead of B737s for his feeder network.[9] This was followed by an order by CAIL for twelve A320s and Canada 3000 for thirteen aircraft. Receiving worldwide news coverage, a A320 was appropriately christened on Valentine's Day 1987 by Their Royal Highnesses, Prince Charles and Princess Diana.

Air Canada had been preparing for its choice of aircraft for years and had three teams evaluate the potential competitors, Boeing, McDonnell Douglas, and Airbus. One examined the bids, the second the aircraft's technical aspects, and the third its suitability to the airline's network. In June 1987, at his request Jeanniot took Transport Minister John Crosbie to the Paris Air Show, where the pair spent time looking at the A320. Back in Ottawa, in a scene that would have been familiar to Sir John A. Macdonald and the railway promoters outside his office, both Boeing and Airbus pestered Crosbie at every social function. Even former Minister of Finance Marc Lalonde was recruited to lobby for Airbus and on November 27, met with Jeanniot, only to be told that the selection was Air Canada's alone.[10] Referring to the lobbying for the A310 by the Liberals in

1979, Mazankowski stated in the House that unlike the previous government, this one did not interfere with Air Canada's decision on its fleet acquisition — that it was an issue resolved by its management and board alone. "The decision was made," he told the media in 1995, "by the people running Air Canada at the time."

Interviewed by *Maclean's* magazine, Taylor said that the federal government was deliberately kept out of the loop. "We never talked to them at any time, even when the government was the major shareholder." The Airbus decision was "clear-cut," he said, because Boeing and the other competitors had "nothing that could touch" its technology. (Later Karlheinz Schreiber would testify before the Commons ethics committee that he and Taylor "met often" but never discussed Airbus.) That was another myth, said Taylor. "I never met Karlheinz Schreiber. I never shook his hand. He has told people that he visited my office, but he never did."[11]

Crosbie was also determined that the government would not interfere in the choice of aircraft and called Jeanniot to Ottawa to brief him.[12] The Air Canada president informed the minister that the decision of the three teams was unanimous: the A320 was the most suitable aircraft, and he was sure that the board of directors would agree. Crosbie pointedly asked if there had been any pressure from the prime minister's office or lobbyists in the decision, and Jeanniot assured him that there had not. It was purely an Air Canada decision. To defray the cost of the Airbus purchase, the airline was selling off twenty-four of its DC-9s to Citibank plus twenty-eight of its B727s to Federal Express and would do a sale/lease back of four of its B767-200ERs.

The last non-American aircraft that Air Canada had bought was the Vickers Vanguard, an Edwardian oddity when compared with the stalwart DC-9. On June 26, 1988, at an airfield in Mulhouse, France, a brand new Air France A320 on a charter flight for the local flying club flew into the trees apparently out of control, the crash causing a major loss of confidence in the highly computerized aircraft. Air Canada pilots familiar with Boeing and Douglas aircraft lost no time in making much of what was thought to be a "cockpit blackout," especially when it was followed in 1990 by another A320 crash in India.

And as for the Americans, sharper than a serpent's tooth was an ungrateful client. Boeing's relationship with Canada was supposedly secure. In 1987, Boeing of Canada employed more than 7,000 Canadians and had revenues of $530 million in the country. The year before, it had also taken the antiquated de Havilland Company off the government's hands to invest millions of dollars in its modernization. Boeing's Ottawa representative, Mervyn Cronie, intensified his lobbying campaign, reminding the public and Air Canada that his company had always employed thousands of Canadians. Jeanniot in turn reminded Boeing that Air Canada had bought many of its aircraft and would continue to do so. In the

meantime, he told Boeing to lay off, a message the company ignored."[13]

With the billions of dollars involved, acquiring a fleet of aircraft has always had a whiff of scandal about it, and envious of the state subsidies given Airbus, Boeing had long claimed that the Europeans were using unethical means to obtain contracts.[14] They and the U.S. State Department saw a "fix" or a conspiracy in the A320 sale which could be traced as far back as former Prime Minister Trudeau pressing Air Canada to consider buying the A310 instead of the L-1011. When Air Canada opted the L-1011 instead, the Airbus Industrie group then focused on the medium-range A320 as the wedge to open up the North American aviation market. The State Department, which had acted for years in Canada as Boeing salesmen, insisted that Prime Minister Brian Mulroney had tilted the playing field away from Boeing and towards Airbus and that the decision to buy the Airbuses was a political one alone.

The reasons given were the promise of contract work to Bombardier by Airbus Industrie, and the politically explosive allegation was that the Conservative party got campaign funds and the prime minister's friends commissions from Karlheinz Schreiber for facilitating the deal. So that they would not impede the sale, it was claimed that Air Canada executives who were pro-Boeing were moved to other jobs and that instead of its older fleet of DC-9s, the company's five-year strategic plan made the replacement of the B727s scheduled to remain in service until the mid-1990s a priority.

An Airbus A320 in Toronto Raptors livery. Forever known as the aircraft that almost brought down a Canadian prime minister, the first A320 (Fin 201, C-FDQQ) was accepted by Air Canada on January 25, 1990.

The Airbus purchase controversy has been dealt with elsewhere, becoming the Canadian equivalent of Watergate. It led to scrutiny by the CBC television program *the fifth estate* (which also worked on the Bahamasair bribery scandal), the *Financial Post*, and *Maclean's* magazine. Not even the cancellation of the Avro Arrow has led to so many books, such as those by Stevie Cameron (*On The Take: Crime, Corruption and Greed in the Mulroney Years* and *The Last Amigo: Karlheinz Schreiber and the Anatomy of a Scandal*), William Kaplan (*Presumed Guilty: Brian Mulroney, The Airbus Affair and the Government of Canada*), and Harvey Cashore (*The Truth Shows Up: A Reporter's Fifteen-Year Odyssey*

Tracking Down the Truth About Mulroney). The burning question remains: if Air Canada chose the A320s without Schreiber and Moores' influence, why did Airbus pay both huge commissions?

When Jeanniot was later interviewed on *the fifth estate*, he was shown the secret Airbus contracts where International Aircraft Leasing (IAL), the Liechtenstein shell company, contracted with Airbus to receive the commissions. Into it flowed the 2.5 percent of the amount that Air Canada paid for each A320 for the first twenty aircraft and then being reduced to 2 percent from numbers twenty-one to thirty-four. The total, the CBC interviewer calculated, was a cool $20 million. Asked if he could use his personal contacts with Airbus to shed light on why $20 million Canadian taxpayer dollars went to IAL, Jeanniot said: "I've helped to the extent I can. I have an international association [he was then president of IATA] and I am not going to start diving into some specific issues that is really of concern between the morality of the Canadian public and a company."[15]

Even the purchase of seven Boeing 747-400 combination aircraft (three firm, one reserved, and three options) in February 1989 did little to mollify the anti-Airbus critics. The two pilot B747-400 Combi in a three-class 277 passenger configuration (sixteen first, fifty business, and 211 hospitality) had a range of 6,348 nautical miles that would enable to the airline to fly nonstop London–Singapore, Toronto–Seoul, and Vancouver–Seoul. It would accommodate twelve cargo pallets, seven on the main deck and five on the lower. Overall fuel burn was expected to be 18 percent less per seat than for the 747-200 being currently operated by the airline.

———

With their "connector" families, Air Canada and CAIL controlled 90 percent of the domestic market, and although the Conservative government had propped up Max Ward with scheduled flights, he couldn't offer his passengers the seamless connections to their hometowns that his rivals could. By December 1988, Wardair was $700 million in debt with the Fokkers and A310s unpaid for. Throwing it a lifeline, the government was about to designate

Wardair the second Canadian carrier to Hong Kong, a move that would have devastated CAIL and disappointed Air Canada. On January 19, 1989, Eyton bought the airline for an overly generous $248 million. Analysts pointed out that had he waited a couple of months Wardair might have withered away, its planes parked in the Arizona desert. Kinnear's Canada 3000 now filled the void left by Wardair, becoming the country's third largest carrier.

Max Ward had also received a merger offer from the AMR Corporation, the parent company of American Airlines with (because of the federal legislation that prevented more than 25 percent of foreign ownership) three Canadian banks as partners. Looking for foreign investment, both Air Canada and CAIL were unanimous in their drive to change this, with CAIL favouring a percentage increase of up to 49 percent. With the Wardair purchase, the PWA Corporation added another debt load and airline culture to its already unwieldy hodgepodge, but at last Grant McConachie's former airline had access to London and Paris.

The first A320 to arrive in Canada was actually in the livery of Cyprus Airways. It spent four days in March 1989 at NWT Air's Yellowknife base for the mandatory cold weather testing. The Air Canada team it carried included Dave Brooks (Montreal Maintenance), Brian Jensen and Bob MacCallum (Passenger and Operational Services), Terry Lelond (Winnipeg Maintenance), Don McLeay (Operations Engineering), and Earl Diamond (Interior System Engineering).

While a variety of sophisticated devices were used to monitor the A320's operating systems, some were elementary. "For the Transport Canada tests, we simply let the unheated aircraft sit overnight at temperatures of -35 degrees after draining its lavatories and drinking water systems," said Earl Diamond. "For the next test, three cargo doors and one passenger door were left open for a period of 90 minutes at temperatures below -30 degrees. This is typical of Air Canada's winter operations, when an aircraft stands with its doors open while passengers are boarding and cargo is being loaded."

At shareholder and employee meetings in April 1990, Jeanniot and Leo Desrochers, executive vice-president, marketing and sales, warned that although it had made a profit in 1989, this had come from the sale of its shares in Guinness Peat Aviation. "Even though we took in airline revenues of $3.6 billion in 1989, the profit from the airline itself is only $107 million. When you consider that we have $3 billion worth of aircraft on order, you can see that an operational profit of $107 million doesn't go very far in paying the bills. In fact, the bill for just one B747-400 is $150 million." Some financial analysts, he said, would like him to copy Canadian Airlines and "push a few thousand people out of the door. But that's not my style."

In a move that surprised all, Jeanniot tendered his resignation on August 3, 1990. There had been persistent rumours of a feud in the airline boardroom over Air Canada's future, but Jeanniot told the media that he believed the time was right for him to retire.

When Air Canada moved its passenger operations from Prestwick airport (PIK) to Glasgow's on May 16, 1990, it was the end of an era. The airline's first transatlantic flight from Montreal to Prestwick using the Lancaster bomber CF-CMS took place on July 22, 1943. The airport terminal building at Prestwick was the former Orangefield Hotel, where the poet Robbie Burns had once stayed. The following poem was penned by Jim McCall, Cargo Services at Prestwick.

Ode on the Passing of a Friend

In '47 came TCA, an airline from far away.
The journey from Canada took nearly a day.
But even though the fog was thick,
Their planes could always land at PIK.
A little airport, a handful of staff.
They worked long hours, but they could laugh.
Anyone who flew through this station
Knows for sure — the Scots are a friendly nation.

But sadly, like Burns, I have to say,
The best laid schemes gang aft a glae
The market is a changing place,
But we will still put on a brave face.
Our passenger service through PIK has come to an end
And hence this message, to you, we send.

To all our friends throughout the years,
Please think of us, but shed no tears.
We have had fun, your friendship too,
Do not forget us, we will miss you.

"I have done my time. A chief executive should not hang around forever." Taylor was close to retirement and many had expected Jeanniot to replace him as chairman. There was speculation that the board of directors, now made up of sharp-eyed business people rather than political appointees, thought that Jeanniot was not moving fast enough to create shareholder value. He did acknowledge that there was a disagreement between himself and the board over whether the airline should promote its executives from within or hire from outside.

Whatever the reasons, the resignation took effect immediately with Taylor combining Jeanniot's duties with his own. "Mr. Taylor will make it one of his first priorities to find a president and chief executive," said Air Canada official Francine Vallée.

It was not until January 30, 1991, that some light was shed on Jeanniot's sudden departure — by himself. "I could scarcely contain my indignation in reading the article," the former president wrote in a blistering letter to the *Globe and Mail*. In an article that had appeared in the newspaper's *Report on Business* magazine, Taylor had disparaged his managers in a "simply despicable" way, Jeanniot said. He charged that his former colleague had insulted the airline's dedicated executives by comparing some of them "to cockroaches who must be swept off the wall." Jeanniot challenged several statements attributed to Taylor in the magazine, suggesting that he should not have slashed service "on the backs of the customers and the employees." The former president said that Air Canada

employees deserved an apology and that Taylor had insulted his head office team by suggesting they were not interested in turning a profit. "The carrier is leaderless," Jeanniot accused, and "locked in a process which could destroy the soul of one of Canada's great corporations."[16]

An Air Canada spokesperson said Taylor had "no desire to comment." By then the chairman/president had other things to worry about. Desert Storm, the Allied military operation against Iraq, had begun on January 17, 1991, and led to skyrocketing fuel prices and empty aircraft as frightened business travellers and vacationers shied away from flying anywhere.

As for the A320, forever known as the aircraft that almost brought down a Canadian prime minister, the company took delivery of its first A320 (Fin 201, C-FDQQ) on January 25, 1990, at a special ceremony at Airbus Industrie headquarters, Toulouse. With a refuelling stop in Iceland, it was flown to Montreal on January 26 and entered service on February 18.

———

Interior design consultant Madeleine Arbour was made responsible for "arbour-izing" the A320 fleet. She chose a design that she said "would create a unified look and yet contrast with the red and burgundy stripes on the aircraft and the dark blue Leo Chevalier uniforms of the cabin crew." In the first class section there were luxurious caramel-coloured leather seats, in the executive class the thick, textured, rosewood herringbone upholstery was intended to give a smart, businesslike flair, and in hospitality class the seats were covered in a fine woven raisin-coloured fabric that conveyed a feeling of comfort. "I wanted to create a unified look," Arbour said "and yet a certain diversity and visual variation between the three classes."

Led by Michel Fournier, vice-president marketing services, and Jim Donaldson, director facilities design and chief architect, the Corporate Design Committee led the redesign of the aircraft exteriors, ground equipment, uniforms, and signage, from paper napkins to casserole dishes.

———

What began as a modest idea, taking a group of kids on a day's outing to Canada's Wonderland, blossomed into an ambitious undertaking for a group of Air Canada employees at Toronto's Terminal 2. "Why rent a bus when we could charter a plane and take the kids to Disney World?" reasoned Bob Kent, customer sales and service shift manager and one of the masterminds behind the "Dreams Come True" project that saw eighty underprivileged children take a one-day trip to Disney World on April 18, 1990. Turning their idea into reality took Bob, Kent Angus, Chris Dale, and Kathy Dutchak and many hundreds of volunteers from every area of the Air Canada Toronto operation a year in planning and a lot of volunteer time to accomplish.

"From the outset this was an employee-driven project," says Bob. "Many companies who heard about what we were planning, including our own, offered us

money. But we preferred to raise our own." In all $14,000 was collected, through bake sales, deli lunches, raffles, and draws, to cover such items as jet fuel, entrance fees, and meals at Disney World. Organizers also managed to obtain a variety of items from major organizations. Labatt supplied backpacks filled with "goodies." Kodak donated disposable cameras and there was even a man Bob calls the "mystery nice guy" who, having read about the project in the newspaper, contacted Bob and asked if he could give each child a hand puppet. Securing an aircraft for the one-day trip could have been a costly venture. But when Leo Desrochers, executive vice-president, marketing sales and services, heard about the project and found out that the group was dedicated to accomplishing its goal, having raised $7,000 already, he authorized to have a DC-9 made available. "We are truly indebted to him," said Bob. For arrangements in Orlando, the organizers were fortunate to have Tampa based customer service agent Mike Kelly. "This guy is something else," said Bob, "he and the Tampa staff donated buses and arranged all the catering, ground handling, terminal landing fees be donated. He even invited the local press to meet the plane."

Where were the children, aged between seven and twelve, all physically, financially, or emotionally disadvantaged, to come from? The organizers canvassed employees who came up with the names of ten agencies, including the Canadian Diabetes Association, Big Sisters and Big Brothers, The Children's Aid Society, and the Hospital for Sick Children in Toronto.

205

AIR CANADA: THE HISTORY

When they arrived at the airport by bus on April 18, some did not know that they were going to Disney World. "Some had never even been on a bus," said Bob. The excited passengers were all given ID cards, a backpack, and fluorescent green cap (courtesy of the Air Canada cargo staff). They gathered in the Air Canada Maple Leaf Lounge for a sendoff from none other than Chairman Claude Taylor, who had heard of the project and juggled his busy schedule to be there. The plane's flight crew (Captain Rick Morrow, First Officer Doug Evans, and Flight Attendants Rob Campbell, Donna McGilvery, and Yolanda Tsampalieros) had all volunteered to work on their day off.

"The day was great from start to finish," said Bob. "Although we were all emotionally drained by the end of the day, it was a heartwarming experience." Among his memories is one of seeing a little boy on the flight down to Florida who seemed very worried. When asked what the matter was, he replied, "I'm scared that this is all a dream and that I'm going to wake up."

———

Even before Iraq's invasion of Kuwait in August 1990, airlines around the world had been suffering from the effects of a lingering recession. Air Canada closed a dozen stations in 1989 and the following year those at Geneva, Sudbury, Timmins, North Bay, Windsor, Rouyn, Val-d'Or, Victoria, Havana, and the Dominican Republic followed with frequency to several others decreased.

Management implemented changes in October, 1990:

- Moving the headquarters from downtown to Dorval.
- Consolidating all pilot training in Toronto by moving all the simulators there.
- Suspending the Bombay–Singapore, Lisbon–Madrid and Zagreb, Nice, and Athens routes.
- Postponing routes scheduled for 1991 like Seoul-Singapore and Frankfurt–Delhi–Singapore.
- Selling the recently bought B747-400s.
- Selling the DC-8 freighters.

Despite such measures, in 1990 it posted a loss of $74 million. It did not help that Michael Wilson, Brian Mulroney's minister of finance, chose January 1991 to introduce the Goods and Services Tax, which further discouraged Canadians from travelling. In an attempt to staunch the flow of red ink, Taylor announced plans to eliminate routes and cut 2,900 staff, but by the end of 1991 the company had lost $218 million.

The situation was even worse at Canadian Airlines; its many acquisitions had financially exhausted it. The new CEO, Kevin Jenkins, had come from Wardair and understood that his airline's survival depended on attracting an alliance partner, and even hinted at a merger with Air Canada. Desperately looking for a massive cash infusion, he went cap in hand to Fort Worth, Texas, the AMR headquarters. The holding company for American Airlines

206

offered salvation but at a price — only if Canadian Airlines dropped its Gemini CRS and integrated into its own SABRE. Air Canada refused to release Canadian Airlines from its obligations to Gemini, and the CRS launched a $500 million lawsuit against both PWA and AMR, and also sued Canadian Airlines for $1.5 billion on the grounds that its negotiations with AMR had broken fiduciary trust between them. The Competitions Tribunal was called in to rule on the case.

And it wasn't only in Canada. By 1990, the third largest airline in the United States, Houston-based Continental Airlines, had already gone through its second bankruptcy and was heading toward a third. Continental announced drastic cuts in staff, service, and its aircraft fleet on August 21, 1991, hoping that the changes would help speed its move through bankruptcy reorganization. The next day, its CEO, Hollis Harris, resigned and in a recorded message he asked employees to pray for the future of the company. "God will show us the way to survive," he said. North of the border, Claude Taylor could only hope for the same.

An event that brought a tear to the eye of many pilots, airline presidents, passengers, and aviation historians took place on December 4, 1991 at JFK Airport. Taxiing through a farewell wreath of water by cannon, the *Clipper Juan Trippe* departed for Miami. While Pan Am employees stood at the gate in melancholy silence, the last Pan American flight made a low pass over the airport. Whether the legendary airline

had been killed off by deregulation, poor management, grasping unions, or excessive competition, it demonstrated that the airline industry worldwide was in desperate trouble.

CHAPTER SIX

TWO HOUSEHOLDS, BOTH ALIKE IN DIGNITY

Candidates for the presidency of Canada's national airline included former Canada Post Corporation CEO Michael Warren and Sir Graham Day, a Haligonian who ran the British Rover Group PLC. Taylor, the board, and the thousands of investors really wanted the former Canadian Airlines president and CEO, Don Carty. Now executive vice-president at American Airlines, Carty had his eye on his boss Robert Crandall's job, and on January 30, 1992, he gave Air Canada his answer. "I'm staying where I am."

The board then did the unthinkable. Railway presidents, Anglophile war hero, political appointee ... Air Canada had been run by each of them with varying degrees of success — but never a foreigner. With the passenger load factor that had been 70 percent in 1988 slumped to 63 percent and the airline losing $1.5 million

daily, they reached out to an American to rescue Air Canada.

Hollis Harris, former president and CEO of both Delta Airlines and Continental Airlines, was then biding his time in Atlanta. Harris had left Delta in 1990 to become the chairman, president, and CEO of Continental Airlines, then going through its second bankruptcy in a decade. After a disagreement with management as to how he could return it to profitability (he refused to slash staff and wages), the sixty-year-old left Continental a year later. Harris and Lamar Durrett, another ex-Delta employee, joined Air Eagle Holdings as consultants. Founded by Robert Milton, a young Georgia Tech graduate, the trio was attempting to launch a discount airline at Hartsfield Airport, Atlanta.

Deregulation and privatization around the world in the 1980s and 1990s had given birth to a number of low-cost airlines like

Ryanair in Europe, Valujet in the United States, and WestJet in Canada. These avoided "legacy costs," those costs that inevitably build up over time in mature businesses. Their employees, usually young, accepted lower salaries, had no seniority or pension plans, and were not unionized. Their planes were newer and usually of a single type, like the Boeing 737, reducing pilot training and maintenance costs. Like the dot-com industries sprouting with them, their start-up costs were small, the technology new, work rules were flexible, and route plans were rationally based on current market conditions rather than historic arrangements. Operating so close to the margin, many, like Vistajet and Intair in Canada, failed. Others, like Air Eagle, never even got off the ground. Although they lobbied hard, Harris, Durrett, and Milton failed to attract investors or political interest. Atlanta was Delta Airlines "country" and no one wanted to go up against it. It was while in Frankfurt looking for financing that Harris got a call from Air Canada.

Despite warnings from Milton that it would be a Sisyphean task, Harris was intrigued by the prospect of turning around Canada's national airline. None of the trio could understand why with only 1.61 percent of the world's passengers (compared with 42.57 percent in the United States, 27.23 percent in Europe and 22.22 percent in Asia/Pacific) the country promoted two carriers when a thin market justified one. Duplication of routes, airline fleets, and personnel, with self-serving politicians

behaving like popes dividing up the world for each airline — it was no wonder that Canada was the quicksand for privatized airlines. Even by airline industry standards, both Air Canada and Canadian Airlines were highly leveraged; 80 percent of their fixed capital base was encumbered by debt. About the only thing that both airlines agreed on was to work to change the federal legislation preventing more than 25 percent of foreign ownership, with Canadian Airlines favouring a percentage increase as high as 49 percent. Asked by Harris to do a study on the situation, Milton predicted that unless they merged, and soon, Canada's two largest airlines were fast heading into bankruptcy and oblivion. Privatized airlines could not be run this way; it was a lesson out of "Airline Management 101," Milton would later write.

Harris told the Air Canada board that he would accept the president's job, if he were also made vice chairman and CEO. These were positions he had filled simultaneously at Continental Airlines, and it was common enough in the U.S. aviation industry, but not at Air Canada, where they had been, until recently, political appointments. Given the sour history between the men who had occupied the chairman and presidents' positions in Air Canada, the board must have agreed to this with some alacrity. In effect, said an observer, they wanted someone who was quite different from the spirit that pervaded the airline's head office; someone without the cultural baggage that came with working for a former government-owned airline. On

February 20, Air Canada announced that Hollis Harris had been selected.

"There simply isn't a better qualified person to manage Air Canada," Taylor reassured the local media. "I personally feel very excited for the future of our company with Hollis at the helm. He is a quality airline man with thirty-seven years of hands-on experience. He has a strong feel for customer service, the bottom line, operating efficiency, and the interests of our employees." The sixty-eight-year-old Taylor finally stepped down in January 1993, accepting the position of Chairman Emeritus.

Hollis Harris's early childhood was spent on the outskirts of Carrollton, West Georgia, the mill town mentioned in Margaret Mitchell's *Gone With the Wind*. His grandfather had been a minister and his father later became a Methodist minister. When his family moved to Atlanta, he had his father take him to Candler Field, the original Atlanta airport, to watch the aircraft. After graduation from high school, Harris attended Auburn University, focusing on aviation administration but in 1951, after a year of college, he joined the army to help fight in the Korean War. Hoping to fly, he volunteered for the air force, but because of an enlistment freeze, was put in the Army. "I asked to be an airplane spotter in Korea, but they must have thought I was crazy so they sent me to Germany," Harris later said. After two years in Germany as a battery commander in the 567th Field Artillery Battalion of the 35th F.A. Group, Harris returned home and met his future wife. He was discharged in 1954 and got

a job at Delta Airlines. Like Durrett and Milton he also enrolled at Georgia Tech, shifting his focus from aviation administration to aeronautical engineering. During his junior year at Tech he began working on projects at Delta that could be done at any time, so the airline, he said, "let me go to school full-time." In 1961, Harris graduated from Tech with a bachelor's degree in aeronautical engineering.

When asked what he did at Delta, Harris said that he "moved around." His titles included transportation agent in the marketing division, aircraft engineer, and head of the aircraft-engineering department. He also held management roles in the facilities department, in-flight services, passenger service, and operations. "I always wanted to improve. I didn't want to design, I wanted to manage and I set my goals high," he recalled. "I wanted to be the CEO and president of Delta." In 1987 he succeeded, expanding Delta's network airlines by merging with Western Airlines, making it the fourth largest U.S. carrier. In a pattern he would later use in Canada, Harris looked to acquiring the ailing Pan American Airways for its historic overseas routes.

Then Air Canada came calling, the board offering Harris a five-year contract to turn their company around. An aging fleet, a lingering "state airline" mentality, too many employees for the network to support, the life-and-death struggle with Canadian Airlines, limited access to the trans-border market — the airline was in trouble. In March 1992, to raise some cash, Air Canada sold its enRoute credit

When the board hired Hollis Harris on February 20, 1992, to turn Air Canada around, many Canadians feared a "creeping Americanization" of the formerly government-run airline.

card business, worth about $300 million, to Citibank Canada. How could Harris pass up such a challenge? Except for Claude Taylor, he would have an inside track on decision-making. Taylor had every confidence that he could do it.

When it was said that he made decisions by scribbling on a paper napkin, Harris summed up his managerial style this way: Listen carefully to the people around you but don't rely on their support. "I've never been afraid to make a decision, even when I didn't have a full consensus," he said.[1] Besides the expertise, a few months later Harris also brought with him his two

colleagues from Air Eagle, Durrett and Milton. HARRIS HIRES PAL FROM GEORGIA; FILLS NO. 2 JOB AT AIR CANADA, the Montreal press proclaimed. "One year ago, Harris and Lamar Durrett left Continental after seeing it into bankruptcy protection. And now they're teaming up again to try to give money-losing Air Canada a boost."

Harris had interviewed Durrett for his job at Delta Airlines in 1967, and the former executive vice-president of administration and personnel moved with him to Continental, running its "System One" CRS. On May 11 Durrett began as Air Canada's executive-vice-president (technical operations and corporate services), overseeing aircraft maintenance and purchasing.

There were many at Air Canada who found the concentration of so much power in the hands of the "Georgia buddies" worrisome. "Now we're seeing Americans come in with some marvellous ideas about how to cut costs, and it's clear that they'll try to send some of our work to their friends down south," complained Michel Cyr, president of the IAMAW. "Hollis Harris came in and now he's bringing up his American friends. I don't know what's going to happen to our work, but there's no doubt we're seeing the Americanization of Air Canada."

The closeness between Harris and Durrett was not the reason for the appointment, said Air Canada spokesman Ronald White. Durrett had been chosen after an executive search across North America, and he was the best the airline could come up with. But he was an unknown, even to U.S. aviation analysts. "I'm really looking forward to get to know the people of Air Canada," Durrett said when interviewed in his Atlanta home with the same Southern accent as Harris.

As for Milton, it was said that he worshipped Harris with the fervour of a teenager for a rock star and would have followed him anywhere. But given the publicity with Durrett's appointment, Harris hired him on contract as a consultant to Air Canada's freight operations. Milton arrived at Dorval Airport on May 25 to a country that he thought of as "an oversized Switzerland" imbued with politeness,

safety, and cleanliness — and curiously, two airlines, and to a city with two airports, Mirabel and Dorval.

What, the public wondered, were Americans doing running the national airline? The hostility was apparent at the shareholders' meeting, when many stepped up to the microphone to pointedly begin their gripe with "Y'all," to be followed by proclaiming that *they*, at least, were proud Canadians. Those who did so had forgotten that TCA would not have been in the air so quickly had it not been for Americans like P.G. Johnson from Boeing and D.B. Colyer, O.T. Larson, and "Slim" Lewis from United Air Lines. And Harris's dictatorial style and "can do" enthusiasm would have gladdened the heart of another transplanted American — the airline's godfather, C.D. Howe.

"Believe me," Harris once said to an audience of Toronto businessmen, "I did not come up here to tell you how to fix your problems. I'm very sensitive to that. When the Air Canada board brought me up here, they gave me three very specific tasks. One was to help turn Air Canada around to profitability. The second was to use my experience in heading Delta and Continental to help Air Canada position itself for the future with alliance partners. And third was to develop a group of Canadian candidates to take over as CEO."

Air Canada was in the process of moving from its downtown headquarters to the Montreal suburb of Saint-Laurent. Scheduled to be completed by May 1992, the new offices, called La Rondelle (or The

Puck), adjoined Dorval airport and housed the headquarters complex with a seven-floor tower with training facilities on the first two floors and administrative offices on the other five. The two buildings were in a T-shaped configuration connected by a two-storey entrance hall that would also give access to the main base by tunnels. Typical of their CEO's independent streak was a refusal to take advantage of federal and provincial government offers of grants to upgrade the airline's Dorval maintenance base.

No one knew better than Harris that his former employer Continental Airlines was nose-diving into bankruptcy. The airline had 42,000 employees and 320 aircraft, roughly twice as many as Air Canada, and its major hubs were Houston, Denver, and Newark. But morale was said to be so poor that when in public its employees used to remove the Continental insignia from their uniforms to avoid answering difficult questions. Although U.S. restrictions on foreign ownership prevented Air Canada from merging with Continental, or even dictating its strategy, Harris knew that investment in the airline was a good idea. "It's a win-win situation," he explained, "since both companies will benefit from synergies in such areas as network coordination, information systems, and maintenance."

On August 28, 1992, Air Canada and Air Partners of Dallas (a pair of Fort Worth investors, James Coulter and David Bonderman) bid $400 million for a one-third interest in Continental Airlines. Others also thought it was a good investment, and on September 16 the German airline

Lufthansa, partnered with investor Marvin Davis, matched Air Canada's offer, starting a bidding war. When Lufthansa withdrew in November, Air Canada and Air Partners emerged as the front-runners. U.S. aviation consultant Andrew Nocella certainly thought that Air Canada would be getting a bargain. "Continental is a very large airline with some good assets. Its cost structure is lower than either American Airlines or Delta, and it has some good hubs."

Bluntly told by the board that his mandate was to put Canadian Airlines out of business, Harris then tackled Air Canada's perennial rival. With Canada's demography clustered around the border and U.S. carriers already serving 90 percent of its population (compared with Canadian carriers serving only 25 percent of the U.S. market), privatized commercial aviation in Canada, as James Richardson could have told them, was barely viable. There were just too many airline seats chasing too few customers. On domestic routes alone, overcapacity of 20 percent to 30 percent had led to damaging price wars that neither airline could afford. Even Durrett, recently arrived from Atlanta, marvelled, "How in the world can this country of 30 million people have two international airlines when only the United States and Japan field two international flag carriers? Sooner or later we're going to have to face up to that. And by 'we,' I mean the government, the industry." That and the lingering recession made it clear that only one airline could survive in Canada. The federal government was considering several options to help both

Canada's troubled airlines — and one was to merge them. But since this would eliminate an estimated 10,000 jobs, especially in Calgary and Vancouver at a time when the country's unemployment rate was 10 percent, it was not a politically viable solution.

As Gordon McGregor had hoped, Harris was convinced that a merger of both Canada's airlines would create a strong all-Canadian giant that could effectively compete on world markets. It was not only inevitable, but, he thought, immediate. The aviation system, he liked to say, was much like a city that clings to two airports. Both airports compete for the same business at almost any price, while other cities concentrate on one facility that can deliver better service at a lower cost. And as a result, both airports are weakened, both carriers are weakened, outside competitors gain at the expense of both, and quality economic growth is sacrificed to the illusion of choice.

It was an analogy that no native-born Canadian would have made. To its detriment, almost since Confederation the dominion had been crippled by dual overbuilt transportation systems, and since the days of Prime Minister Mackenzie King, whatever the party in power, government policy had focused at maintaining a fine balance between the CPR and CNR and now Canadian Airlines and Air Canada, with the hope that neither would monopolize transport in the country. And it wasn't only railways, steamships, and airlines. The Georgia trio's recently adopted city of Montreal was even then struggling with keeping both Mirabel and Dorval airports going.

In aviation, as in comedy, timing is everything, and combining the synergies of the two carriers with Continental Airlines just as the archaic rules restricting flights between the United States and Canada were being liberalized then was ideal. Bilateral air agreements negotiated in the 1960s allowed only direct service between eight Canadian and twenty-five U.S. cities, leaving many routes and smaller cities unserved. Faced with the increasing globalization of commercial aviation, in 1992 the United States signed its first "Open Skies" agreement with the Netherlands, eliminating government interference in routes, capacity, and pricing, despite severe opposition from the European Union.

Seeing the $10 million annual impact on the Tennessee economy that KLM Royal Dutch Airlines aircraft had by connecting its Amsterdam hub directly with that of Memphis, Canadian negotiators wanted a similar deregulated agreement. With 13 million passengers in 1993 generating $3 billion in revenue, the cross-border market was the largest between the United States and any country. To even negotiate an "Open Skies" agreement, the diplomats commuting between Ottawa and Washington had to fly via Montreal or Toronto, since an airline connection between the two capital cities was not allowed.

But Harris's merger proposal did not take into account the historic mistrust that had pervaded commercial aviation in Canada since the days of McConachie and McGregor. Like the Montagues and Capulets in fair Verona, relations between Air Canada and Canadian Airlines were blatantly poisonous. Rather than merging with fellow Canadians, PWA preferred courting AMR and begging for government handouts. And both airlines resented being chided by a foreigner. In a quote that would get much publicity at the time, Rhys Eyton would say, "I've had enough of the arrogance of a former Crown corporation, of a gun-slinger that arrives up from Georgia to tell us how to organize our Canadian structure."

Nothing demonstrated the historic mistrust more than the events of the year 1992, when loyalties shifted with the speed of a Renaissance court. Canadian Airlines and AMR announced on March 22 that they had signed a letter of intent under which AMR would acquire a one-third equity interest in Canadian Airlines and a 25 percent voting interest (the maximum allowed under Canadian law), causing Harris to file a formal complaint with the National Transportation Agency stating that control of a Canadian airline would henceforth be in American hands. In an attempt to scuttle the AMR/Canadian Airlines merger, he also made public that PWA had rejected a proposal from Air Canada that would have alleviated its financial crisis.

In it Canadian Airlines would continue to be managed from Calgary and Air Canada from Montreal. Each company would have its own president and there would be equal representation of directors from both companies on the board.

Duplication of routes both internationally and domestically would end, as would 6,000 jobs in a streamlining program that Harris promised would be "spread evenly between the two airlines." When analysts estimated that if Canadian Airlines and Air Canada merged, job losses among the combined 35,000 employees would be a lot higher, closer to 10,000, Harris promised that the holding company would ensure equal treatment of employees of both companies and minimize job losses. "This merger offer is viewed as a partnership to build a strong Canadian carrier for the future, and not as an Air Canada takeover."

Shareholders of both companies would receive one common share of the new holding company for each existing share. Canadian Airlines' shareholders would have 40 percent interest in the new company and Air Canada shareholders 60 percent. Subject to regulatory approval, the offer would expire on September 9. The proposal to merge the two carriers, promised Harris, was "a true partnership, not a takeover."

The Air Canada CEO was not alone in attempting to sabotage the AMR/Canadian Airlines deal. Struggling with its own unpopularity, the Mulroney government was aware how a takeover by a U.S. airline would play out in the polls. Their aircraft might be leased from Japanese, Swiss, and Israeli banks but airlines (like sports teams) could still evoke patriotism, and a Gallup poll showed that only 9 percent of Canadians favoured their two airlines merging with a U.S. carrier, and 25 percent wanted a government bailout of both Air

Canada and Canadian to prevent this from happening. Air Canada and Canadian Airlines were still national icons, however voters might gripe about them. The federal government refused a request from PWA for loan guarantees but told Jenkins that if he broke off all dealings with Fort Worth to replace their aging B707s, DND would buy three of the former Wardair A310s for $150 million.

The very public fight over which airline was to survive was played out in the nation's newspapers, where employees of both companies took out full page ads, Air Canada's promoting the merger and Canadian's asking "Air Canada, are you confused?" and stating that they were not going to allow a takeover by fellow Canadians.

By July, when Canadian Airlines couldn't provide AMR with adequate guarantees for servicing its operating cash flow requirements or its long-term debts, AMR left it standing at the altar and PWA returned to talking with Air Canada. Both airlines were suffering heavy losses and jettisoning jobs, with Air Canada eliminating 9 percent of its workforce and the PWA directors resigning over personal liability exposure in the event of the airline's insolvency. With more faith, the Council of Canadian Airlines Employees was formed to give PWA a cash infusion from payroll deductions.

On the deadline of September 9, Harris held a press conference to celebrate the imminent merger. "It's a historic day for the Canadian airline industry," he crowed. A combined Air Canada/Canadian Airlines

committee had worked on the details of a holding company formed on the basis of a one-for-one swap of shares with Air Canada shareholders owning 60 percent and PWA shareholders 40 percent. Public reaction to the merger was mixed. Besides the inevitable job losses, a single privately owned airline would have a monopoly on the most lucrative routes in Canada. The media labelled it "Mapleflot" after the Soviet Aeroflot.

By September, even as the Council of Canadian Airlines Employees made ready to invest $150 million in exchange for shares in the PWA/AMR deal, Harris was putting together a $100 million bridge financing for PWA, and on October 8 the combined airline committee submitted a pre-merger agreement to their boards of directors. "This is the best offer they're going to get from us," he told the media. "Air Canada and Canadian Airlines lost nearly $1 billion between them last year. That's like giving $40 to every person who walked up to a check-in counter over a twelve-month period."

But at Thanksgiving the mood had changed — at least in Montreal. Many on the Air Canada board feared the baggage that Canadian Airlines came with and the merger was no longer seen as viable. The merged airline, experts figured, would have a debt of $7 billion and equity of less than $600 million. Even Harris conceded that the combined carrier wouldn't make any money for a while. On October 28, overruling his CEO's proposal, Claude Taylor stated that unless Ottawa provided more than $1 billion in "rent-free capital," the all-Canadian mega-carrier was never going to fly. If the merger won approval, it would be hampered by Air Canada's political concession to maintain both brand names and operating headquarters and Montreal and Calgary. Besides, given its poor financial record, no one expected Canadian Airlines to survive until the following summer, and when that happened all of its Far Eastern routes would be available. Why get involved now? Air Canada walked away on November 3, leaving Canadian Airlines alone again (naturally?).

Hell hath no fury as an airline scorned, and PWA filed a $1.5 billion lawsuit against Air Canada, alleging predatory pricing, saying that this was all a bluff to prevent the AMR deal and that it never had any intention of a merger. Fort Worth wasn't particularly interested in pouring money into an airline that hadn't made any for years; the real prize was infiltrating the Canadian travel market with its CRS SABRE. For that and a 25 percent equity stake, AMR was willing to pump $170 million into Canadian Airlines, but only if its CEO Kevin Jenkins could convince Ottawa and the provincial governments to come up with some loan guarantees.

Asking taxpayers to put money into a failing enterprise was incomprehensible to Harris. Canadian Airlines should be allowed, he callously said, to go the way of Braniff, Eastern Airlines, and Pan American — i.e. into the dustbin of aviation history. Agreeing with their CEO (and with short memories of their

airline's own protectionist past), between November 14–19 Air Canada employees held rallies across Canada to protest any federal involvement. In agreement with them was the Royal Commission on National Passenger Transportation, which released its report on November 19, calling for the government to end subsidized transport in Canada.

But going into an election, the federal government wanted above all to keep competition in the airline industry alive and injected PWA with $50 million on November 24 (and in a wonderful example of corporate ethics, demanded that Canadian Airlines stop paying its creditors). When that was followed on December 18 with the governments of British Columbia and Alberta promising loan guarantees of $20 million and $50 million respectively, Canadian Airlines was taken off life support. In return for veto powers on the board, funnelling its Far Eastern traffic through the Vancouver hub and both airlines using SABRE, on December 29 Crandall and Carty provided it with a cash infusion. On the last day in a year of shifting loyalties, accepting its conditions for restructuring, PWA returned to the AMR fold.

At this turn of events, Harris asked the U.S. Department of Transportation to investigate whether the AMR/PWA deal was breaking any antitrust laws. For the benefit of the Canadian audience, he wrapped himself in the Maple Leaf flag and in an interview with the *Globe and Mail* warned of American Airlines' CEO Robert

Crandall: "I know him ... If Crandall is into an arrangement — 5 percent, 10 percent, 15 percent or whatever — he is going to be in control." Canadian Airlines, he said, would be reduced to a "feeder" status. The year lurched to an end with Air Canada losing $454 million and Canadian Airlines $543 million.

The New Year began well for Air Canada. On January 7, 1993, the U.S. Department of Transportation approved the proposed $450 million bid for Continental Airlines by Air Canada and Air Partners. "We are thrilled with this decision," said Harris. "Our investment in Continental is an important component of our corporate strategy to develop a global network of airlines." Air Canada then poured U.S. $235 million into Continental Airlines, with the now retired Claude Taylor looking after the investment. It would own 55 percent of Continental but have 65 percent of the voting rights on Continental's board of directors. Because of U.S. restrictions on foreign ownership of airlines, although Air Canada and Air Partners bought 27.5 percent of Continental's equity, Air Partners would have 41 percent of the voting stock, while Air Canada was limited to 24 percent.

Although an Air Canada spokesperson said that the Continental deal did not preclude a domestic merger with Canadian Airlines, both Canadian carriers then withdrew their merger application from the National Transportation Agency (NTA).

Harris's investment in his previous employer earned mixed reviews. The debt-rating agency Standard & Poor's Ltd.

questioned whether $450 million would be enough to improve Continental's competitive position in the U.S. market. Calgary-based analyst Gord Currie of Loewen Ondaatje McCutcheon Ltd. said Air Canada "should be spending the money to pay down their debt or cut their costs and leave global expansion to later." When Harris announced a two year 5 percent wage reduction for all employees on February 23, at a time when all Air Canada employees had seen their wages frozen for the last three years, spokesmen for the airline's unions voiced their opinion that the Continental investment would have been better spent paying down Air Canada's $4 billion debt and easing the impact of announced layoffs. About 560 Air Canada machinists, baggage handlers, and cleaners were losing their jobs as part of cost-cutting measures announced in July. While Air Canada's largest union, the International Association of Machinists and Aerospace Workers, welcomed the move because their workers had been promised that Continental aircraft would come to Montreal for maintenance, the union's president, Michel Cyr, said that the money could have been spent easing the impact of layoffs.

The $450 million infusion was too late to prevent Continental Airlines from a US$204 million deficit in 1994, but soon the money and its new CEO, Gordon Bethune, worked their magic on company morale, and in 1995 the airline returned with a profit of $202 million. Air Canada too had a good year, raising $480 million by selling Class A non-voting shares to a syndicate of Canadian underwriters and stock in Continental Airlines for $68 million.

The Continental investment meant more than cash and shared frequent flier programs. Like other non-equity alliances that Air Canada had just concluded with United Airlines and Air France, it gave Air Canada wider access to the United States, especially the south and southwest, Mexico, and Central America. Use of Continental's Pacific Rim routes, especially those of its subsidiary Air Micronesia, temporarily assuaged the struggle for Canadian's Pacific empire, and on May 3, Air Canada began flying non-stop into Houston, Continental's hub, its alliances allowing it to increase flights to Newark and Chicago. "The links with Continental, United and soon Air France will improve our business by offering more choices to our customers, without forcing us to add additional aircraft," predicted Air Canada vice-president Al Thompson. "The link with Air France will connect us with additional European centres and open up the Middle East and Africa to our clients."

On the transatlantic scene, Air Canada began non-stop flights on May 20 from Toronto to Düsseldorf, one of the airline's original destinations, and to Berlin. "We are doing a lot of shuffling around," Thompson added as he outlined the new routes scheduled for the summer. "Our goal is to make a profit. We now think we are on the right track." With maintenance work from Continental and Northwest airlines and selling off the older B747s, in 1993 Air Canada enjoyed a $16 million profit in its second quarter.

————

Barely five years after Canadair's privatization, its purchaser, Bombardier Aerospace, had become the third largest aircraft company in the world, mainly because of its phenomenally successful regional jets called CRJs. The fifty- and seventy-seat jets allowed airlines to bypass the old hub-and-spoke system by providing jet service directly into smaller cities. "Hub busters," Harris called them, and ordered twenty-six CRJs in 1993, accepting the first at the Farnborough Air show in Britain — exactly where Gordon McGregor had fallen in love with the Vickers Viscount forty years before. "With an operating radius of 1,000 miles they are ideally suited to as many as sixty-four Canada–U.S. city pairs," he said. "This is the right aircraft to grow the short end of our system. The trend is somewhat away from hub and spoke and more to point-to-point services. We will be able to go into markets of a maximum of 1,000 miles apart that are too small for a McDonnell Douglas DC-9 or Airbus Industrie A319, but perfect for the Canadair jet."

At the same Farnborough air show, the Air Canada CEO was asked what his company would do if the province of Quebec separated from the rest of Canada to form its own independent country. The sovereigntist Party Québécois, led by Jacques Parizeau, had just been elected, and unfazed by the flight of large corporations leaving Montreal, was intent on holding a referendum on whether the province should separate from the rest of Canada. As a Southerner who had grown up with the history of the U.S. Civil War, Harris, like Durrett and Milton, must have wondered what he had gotten himself into. Would Air Canada follow other companies and scout out office real estate in Toronto? Should Quebec separate, Harris replied, Air Canada would have no choice but to move. Under the terms of its privatization the airline was required to be based in a Canadian city, and if Montreal became part of a foreign country, it would be legally able to leave the city.

Harris's second mandate, that of putting Canadian Airlines out of business, was going nowhere, and on August 18, 1993 he once more proposed a merger. He offered $1 billion for Canadian Airlines' international routes. Air Canada had been operating Far Eastern routes since February 1987 with its DC-8F Jet Traders, circumventing the globe the opposite way with cargo charter flights from Montreal–Toronto–Brussels–Dubai–Bangkok. But it wasn't enough and Harris offered to buy Canadian Airlines' transpacific routes to Tokyo, Taipei, and Hong Kong for $200 million in cash and relieve it of $800 million in lease obligations of eight aircraft. It would, he said, "make the airline a powerful domestic carrier." Aware that the Asian routes were its dowry to any marriage, PWA rejected this outright. Eyton saw it as "a diabolical plot to kill Canadian...."

Canadian Airlines rank and file thought so too, and 97 percent voted to accept the AMR deal rather than Air Canada's. With the Gemini hearings scheduled for mid-November, Harris tried to get the Competition Bureau to consider his latest offer as new evidence to prevent Canadian Airlines from leaving the shared CRS — but this would be rejected.

With the on again–off again AMR/PWA merger, PWA had subjected Gemini to relentless litigation in their effort to dissolve the partnership to satisfy AMR's conditions. The CRS company would file a complaint with the Competition Bureau, accusing SABRE of predatory pricing in Canada, contrary to the Competition Act. In August, when PWA took Gemini to court to have it declared insolvent, Harris threatened to launch an anti-trust lawsuit against American Airlines. The winds were definitely not blowing Air Canada's way. On October 14, the Supreme Court ruled that PWA could transfer to SABRE, and if Air Canada would not release Canadian Airlines from Gemini within a month, the shared CRS should be dissolved. Elected on October 25th, 1993, Jean Chrétien's Liberal government seemed intent on propping up Canadian Airlines to preserve airline competition in Canada, rather than letting it die of natural causes. Air Canada officials bitterly complained that the Liberal Party had rented a Canadian Airlines B737 rather than an Air Canada aircraft when campaigning.

Choosing his cabinet, Prime Minister Chrétien asked the Don Valley East member of Parliament, David Collenette, what post he wanted. Collenette, who in 1978 had used parliamentary clout to get Claude Taylor to reinstate a Toronto flight so he could get home for the weekend, loved anything to do with trains and planes. He asked for the Transport portfolio, but the prime minister needed someone who could take the reforms begun with Mazankowksi's "Freedom to Move" to modernize Transport Canada and prepare it for the new century. Relying on Collenette's love of history, Chrétien placated him with the Defence portfolio — hardly high-profile after the Somalia embarrassment.

The new minister of transport, Doug Young, appointed former Mulroney prime ministerial aide Stanley Hartt to mediate in the Gemini/Canadian Airlines dispute. The Competition Bureau recommended on November 5 that its 1989 consent decision regarding Gemini be rescinded so that the Canadian Airlines–AMR deal could be allowed to proceed, conditional to that airline moving to SABRE. This was followed on November 24 by its ruling that Canadian Airlines should be released from Gemini, paving the way for that airline to close the AMR deal. "We strongly believe the international routes belong to the government of Canada and the Canadian people," Harris said, and on December 16, 1993, the Air Canada CEO made a final attempt to buy them and eight aircraft for $300 million and assume some $800 million of its debt. But as PWA had reported a profit of $38.5 million in the second quarter, Canadian Airlines' future looked brighter than ever, and the offer was rejected on December 22.

————

While SABRE's greater "halo" promoted Canadian Airlines and American Airlines across North America, for Air Canada, taking over a weakened and demoralized Gemini, network and all, would have entailed enormous ongoing cost and difficulty. It would have been embarrassing for the new Liberal government since the Gemini office was in the Winnipeg constituency of Lloyd Axworthy, now minister for human resources; if it closed the loss of 700

The first Canadian-built aircraft to be used by TCA/Air Canada since the North Star, there would be forty-eight Regional Jets (CRJ100/200) in Air Canada's fleet. With a length of 26.77 m (87 ft 10 in) and a wingspan of 21.21 m (69 ft 7 in), the CRJ 100 and 200 models cruised at about 804 km/h (503 mph) at 12,496 m (41,000 ft). Their maximum range was 3,000 km (1,864 mi) for ER models and 3,710 km (2,305 mi) for LR models.

Configured only to hospitality class, passenger reviews were:

- "Cramped and stuffy. The DC-9s of the sixties were better."
- "The legroom pitch is poor. Seat width fair and seat recline poor. It is time to sell these tin cans with wings to an African country."
- "Claustrophobic and cramped. Has to be the worst aircraft in the Air Canada fleet."

hundred jobs would be a poor beginning. A deal was brokered whereby if Canadian Airlines could be freed from its CRS contract, Ottawa might see its way of granting Air Canada rights to Japan, Korea, and Hong Kong. It worked out well for all parties: Air Canada dropped the litigation on January 27, 1994, and Pegasus, the Canadian Airlines CRS, moved to the SABRE database in Tulsa. Two separate companies were created to take over Gemini's operations: Galileo Canada (affiliated with Galileo International, the world's largest CRS) and Advantis Canada, a subsidiary of IBM Canada Ltd., which became the network provider for Galileo Canada and took over management of Air Canada's information technology systems, including voice and data networks.

Keeping its end of the bargain, in March the federal government designated Air Canada the second carrier to serve foreign markets, and Air Canada's first passenger service to the Far East was launched on May 16 to Seoul, code sharing from Toronto and Vancouver with Korean Air Lines. More historic was Flight 891 on September 20, when an Air Canada 747 took off at 2:15 p.m. from Vancouver for Osaka, Japan, inaugurating four-day-a-week service to the Far East. Osaka's Kansai Airport might have been an engineering marvel, but it was also the most expensive piece of tarmac to land on anywhere in the world, and airlines only accepted it when they couldn't get slots at Narita Airport in Tokyo. But for Air Canada it was all about the symbolism; Canadian Airlines' forty-year monopoly as the country's flag

carrier to Japan had finally been broken. Air Canada hired Japanese-speaking flight attendants to serve Japanese meals and beverages, and showed Japanese in-flight movies. "We're pulling out all stops to make this a success," said Harris, who was on the first flight, leading a group of Canadian business executives with the return flight from Osaka to Vancouver carrying a high-level Japanese delegation. "Air Canada's people have been waiting for years to finally see the Maple Leaf fly to Japan." Initially, the airline operated Boeing 747s on the route, switching to the Airbus A340 in 1996. For its trans-Atlantic and trans-Pacific routes, the airline bought six Airbus A340s at $120 million each, taking options for another three.

For Canadian Airlines, it was a bitter pill to swallow. At home, their Western territory was already under attack by discount airlines Calgary-based WestJet and Greyhound Air, which had been started by Dick Huisman, the former vice-president of marketing at CP Air. They didn't need the added competition to the Far East. "We are obviously disappointed," Vice-president International Ian Bootle said. "We have worked hard for forty years to develop the Japanese market and should have had the opportunity to take part in future growth. Landing slots have been constrained in the last few years and this is the only time it's been opened for additional frequency. We feel we deserved Osaka." Bootle said their outbound traffic had been slack in the last year or two with loads averaging about 70 percent, no doubt causing Canadian Airlines' deficit at the end of 1994 to be $291.8 million — but Air Canada's was worse at $326 million.

In July 1995, in a joint service with Cathay Pacific Airways, Air Canada cargo flights to Hong Kong would begin. It would not be until December 20 when Air Canada could inaugurate three passenger flights a week to Hong Kong, where it was known as Air Canada–Maple Leaf Airlines.

———

By now even their detractors had to concede that the Southerners had brought an entrepreneurial spirit with them to the Montreal airline. With the older B747s and L-1011 TriStars being retired, Air Canada was looking to renew its long-range fleet. While some of its L-1011s were sold to Air Lanka, in 1990 three had been parked in the Arizona desert, and there were many who thought they would never fly again. The L-1011s had been the mainstay of the Delta fleet, and the three Southerners had fond memories of the aircraft. "When I was at Delta, especially in the technical operations area, we had dealings with Air Canada — we both flew the L-1011," Durrett recalled.

Reactivating the fully depreciated airliner was a quick, inexpensive way to rebuild transcontinental capacity after the recession had ended. But every time a new idea such as this was brought up, Milton noted the airline's managers and their attitude of "We've always done things this way and there was no reason to change," always killed it. The L-1011s were too expensive to operate, required too much maintenance and were Lockheed-built, while Air Canada was a "McDonnell Douglas" airline. Milton suspected that the old guard, those whose roots extended back to the Crown corporation days, resisted using the TriStars because none of them had come up with the idea.[2] On the strength of his evaluation that they would be suited flying between Vancouver, Los Angeles, Montreal, and Toronto exclusively, Harris insisted that the remaining L-1011s be brought back to Dorval. Given a roomy 238-seat configuration that for three more years re-established them as customer favourites, the L-1011s operated only between those four destinations — and made money doing so.

AIR CANADA 1994	A319	A320	B747	B767	CL-45	DC-9	L-1011	TOTAL
Owned	0	21	5	11	0	26	5	68
Op.lease	0	13	4	11	44	9	0	41
In service	0	34	9	22	4	35	3	107
Orders	25	6	0	5	6	0	0	48
Options	10	0	0	5	38	0	0	56

With up to thirty-five DC-9s still flying, Air Canada had been selected by
Douglas Aircraft (now part of McDonnell
Douglas) as the North American modi-
fication contractor for its DC-9X modernization program. In June 1989 it had
signed a letter of intent with McDonnell
Douglas Corp. for a study on modernizing
the DC-9 fleet. The upgrading program
would cost half as much as replacing the
planes with new aircraft, said Ron White,
an Air Canada spokesman, and Harris
agreed, saying that the hush kitting and
airframe upgrades would extend the lives
of the DC-9s for up to fifteen years at a
very competitive price and under war-
ranty of the manufacturer. The program
would potentially include re-engining,
re-wiring, new avionics, and other system
upgrades with all work carried out at the
Air Canada facility in Winnipeg from kits
supplied by Douglas Aircraft.

It thus came as a surprise that on May
11, 1994, after intense trans-Atlantic competition among aircraft manufacturers to
replace its fleet of DC-9s, the airline chose
the A319. It would acquire twenty-five
A319 twin-engine, 112-seat aircraft, and
would take an option on an additional ten
aircraft. Air Canada did not announce a
price, but the A319 was listed in the Airbus
catalogue at $39 million each, which valued
the initial order at about $1 billion. The
deal gave Air Canada, which had bought
thirty-four of the slightly larger A320s,
the second-largest fleet of Airbus planes

in North America, after United Airlines.
A spokeswoman for Air Canada, Kym
Robertson, said the acquisition "makes a
tremendous amount of economic sense"
because Airbus offered 100 percent financing. "The salesmanship was very aggressive," she said. "Our position was that any
kind of proposal that we entertained had
to be cash-neutral or better." The A319
made a better fit than other planes because
it had the same engine, cockpit, and galley
as the A320 that Air Canada used. "The
bottom line is that the new aircraft would
be cheaper than refurbishing the DC-9s,"
Robertson said.

The United States government in
its dispute with Airbus reviewed the deal
closely with the Europeans about subsidies
granted to aircraft manufacturers to win
markets abroad. Given the fuss made over
the airline's previous choice of its sister
the A320, Harris took pains to emphasize
that the A319's selection was based on
"attractive acquisition terms for an aircraft
offering excellent operating economics and
increased revenue-generating capability."
Ordering the twenty-five A319s for introduction between December 1996 and the
end of 1997 wasn't a selection of European
over American; he particularly liked the
Airbus commonality advantages in crew
training and qualification, simulators,
ground handling, and maintenance. The
A319 also had longer range (almost twice
that of a DC-9), larger capacity (twenty-
two more seats than a DC-9), and much
greater fuel efficiency (29 percent less fuel
burned per seat mile).

———

In anticipation of the signing of "Open Skies" treaty, Air Canada announced plans to begin twenty new scheduled routes using its RJs, with direct connections such as Toronto–Columbus, Ottawa–Washington, Calgary–Houston and Toronto–St. Louis, increasing its U.S. market share by 30 percent within a year. Liberating airlines north and south of the border, Prime Minister Jean Chrétien and President Bill Clinton signed the Canada–U.S. Air Services Agreement, better known as the "Open Skies" treaty, on February 25, 1995. Canadian air carriers now had unlimited route rights to provide "own aircraft" services between points in Canada and points in the United States, and carriers of both countries were free to set their own prices for trans-border services according to market forces. This was followed in November 1997 with an agreement that allowed Canadian and U.S. carriers to code share to, from, and via one another's territory, with carriers from other countries (provided the other country allows code sharing and the carriers hold the underlying rights) to serve that country. It wasn't the hoped-for cabotage (the right to carry domestic traffic in the United States) but the next best thing. It gave Canadian carriers access to any point in the United States from any point in Canada while phasing in U.S. carrier access to the local hubs — Toronto, Montreal, and Vancouver — the "sporting chance" clause allowing both Air Canada and Canadian Airlines to establish footholds before the market was totally opened to U.S. airlines. Air Canada's "Operation Due South" began on March 6, when Toronto–Atlanta became the first of the "Open Skies" flights, to be followed on May 1 by Ottawa–Washington and an hourly shuttle on Toronto–LaGuardia (New York).

———

AIR CANADA AGREES TO STOP SERVING FRENCH PÂTÉ. The Washington-based animal rights group People for Ethical Treatment of Animals took credit for pressuring the airline to stop serving pâté de foie gras to its first class passengers but in reality by 1994 airlines worldwide were looking to trim costs, and the extras that customers had come to expect since the 1950s disappeared. Flights north and south of the border that once featured complementary meals, magazines, "kid's packs," and pillows now only offered peanuts, pretzels, and soft drinks. Charges for unaccompanied minors and excess baggage doubled, and on some routes there was little difference between travelling executive class or economy. While this trend was not peculiar to Air Canada, its employees who worked in customer service blamed the "Americanization" of the airline on Harris and his buddies. "Between the airline we had five years ago and the airline we have now, there's been a deterioration of service," one said. "We're the ones who have to face criticism. We're the front line. We get the anger and the disappointment of the customers, not Harris."

225

The year 1995 demonstrated that the world's major airlines had finally reaped the benefits of the massive restructuring that had begun in the industry three years before. The U.S. airlines, better managed and with significant progress in reducing unit costs, enjoyed their best year since deregulation, the top ten posting operating profits of $1.5 billion. The traditional hub and spoke airlines, feeling the pressure of the perky young discount carriers (American Airlines estimated that 40 percent of its domestic bookings were being impacted by Valujet and Southwest Airlines), tried to begin their own, Continental's CALite, United's Shuttle by United, and Delta's Song, to counter the phenomenon. Would Air Canada follow suit?

————

The Montreal airline was becoming concerned about the cloud arising in the West, no bigger than a man's hand. On February 29, 1996, Calgary businessmen Clive Beddoe, Mark Hill, Tim Morgan, and Don Bell launched WestJet. Unashamedly cloning Herb Kelleher's Southwest Airlines low-cost airline model, the four began what would become Canada's most successful discount airline. WestJet infused the first 200 employees it hired with passion, enthusiasm, and humour, all qualities the public thought lacking in Air Canada. It had profit sharing, share purchase, (and for pilots) stock options. It was said to be so egalitarian that its CEO took no salary but cleaned the planes between flights and searched for parking at headquarters like everyone else.

Although they paid for snacks and earplugs, passengers came to look forward to the hilarious announcements by WestJet cabin crew, which would have made standup comics jealous, and the legendary in-flight toilet paper races (in which Rows ABC competed with DEF) would have been inconceivable on Air Canada. Cheery and with a can-do attitude, WestJet staff seemed to embody the virtues of friendliness and community spirit that Canadians took pride in. But what must have made the management at Air Canada green with envy was that WestJet workers didn't have the right to strike — instead, 92 percent of them belonged to the non-union Pro-Active Communications Team (PACT). Beddoe's people were company owners, not adversaries, and passengers were "guests." The former government airline, with its rigid human resources policies, perceived customer arrogance, its heavily unionized strictures, mature counter and cabin staff, could not compete with WestJet — especially outside Central Canada.

Still, the WestJet "fun" culture wasn't for everyone. In late 1998, Beddoe, remaining on as executive chairman, appointed Steve Smith as president and CEO. Smith had run Air Ontario, and the perception was that he brought the Air Canada "cultural superiority" with him. Within a year, he had run afoul of the four founders and left.

Lower costs, a single aircraft type, cheaper airports, a young, enthusiastic workforce — start-up airlines had begun with all of that before, only to be shot down by red ink soon after. On May 11, when a

Valujet DC-9 crashed into a Florida swamp, the National Transportation Safety Board determined that that safety standards on discount carriers had not been adequately scrutinized. In September, Beddoe was forced to ground his three B737s because Transport Canada inspectors found that the airline had been following an incorrect set of maintenance manuals — which it had allowed before the launch. Calgary media saw a competitor's hand in this, and when WestJet resumed flying on October 4, Air Canada initiated a seat sale. Both events only ensured the discount carrier's success since Westerners, quick to see an Ottawa conspiracy designed to protect Air Canada, rallied around WestJet, what they considered their own airline. From 1996 onward, Air Canada could either fight WestJet — or merge with it. It would attempt to do both.

———

The PWA merger dead, Harris said that Air Canada would "continue with the strategic alternatives we are already pursuing." These were forming alliances with major airlines around the world. When the U.S. government granted anti-trust immunity on May 28, 1996, to the AMR/PWA merger, he hoped it would do the same for his choice of partners. Slighted by USAir (which chose British Airways for its partner), Harris aligned Air Canada with American Airlines' rival, United Airlines, the largest carrier in the world. He then allied it with Lufthansa, which dropped its code sharing with Canadian Airlines to do so.

The agreement was a comprehensive alliance with provisions that included, subject to government approval, code sharing, schedule coordination, and shared reciprocal participation in both airlines' frequent flyer programs like Air Canada's Aeroplan and Lufthansa's Miles and More. Air Canada and Lufthansa jointly began daily non-stop flights on June 15, 1996, with Lufthansa operating daily non-stop flights to and from Vancouver, on which Air Canada sold seats using an Air Canada code and Air Canada operating daily non-stop flights to and from Calgary, on which Lufthansa sold seats using a Lufthansa code. Alliances with Korean Air, All Nippon, and Swissair followed with Harris predicting that one day a handful of major world alliances would span the air travel world, offering the public "one-stop" shopping.

———

Air Canada reported a $38.2 million profit in 1995, a decline from 1994 but still the second straight profit after four years in the red. But although it still retained a 56 percent share of the domestic market, it too was feeling the effects of competition, namely WestJet and Greyhound Air in the West, CanJet in the Maritimes, and charters Air Transat, Royal, and Canada 3000.

On August 1, Harris opted to semi-retire, staying on as executive chairman, saying that he would leave Air Canada completely when his five-year contract expired in February, 1997. He wanted to either start up a new airline using the soon-to-be surplus Air Canada DC-9s or run a major U.S. carrier. Under him, Air Canada had made a successful though difficult transition from a bloated Crown corporation to a lean private-sector carrier, and he had won the grudging respect of many, including the unions. "I think most people would say he did a lot of good things to turn the airline around," said Cheryl Kryzaniwsky, CAW president of the local that represented 3,300 Air Canada workers. The heir apparent, executive vice-president and chief operating officer Jean-Jacques Bourgeault, credited Harris with instilling a "new pride" and "can-do" attitude at Air Canada, saying "He made people believe everything was possible at Air Canada."

Harris was credited with positioning the company for the advantages soon to become possible in "Open Skies" and the commercial aviation alliances like Oneworld, Star Alliance, and SkyTeam, the global empires developed in the mid-1990s to get around the foreign ownership restrictions that countries had to international mergers. In May 1997, Air Canada would become a founding member of the Star Alliance, launching code-shares with several of the alliance's members.

But as Robert Milton would point out, Air Canada was the only airline within Star Alliance that was restricted by its own government from flying to partner countries. It couldn't fly, for example, to Brazil, the home of Varig, its Star Alliance partner. Or to New Zealand, home of Air New Zealand, or Thailand and Thai International, other alliance partners. Ottawa had allotted all of these parts of the world to Canadian

Airlines, which in its enfeebled state could not service them. And as for Canadian's "Oneworld" partners, they seemed intent on taking advantage of its penurious condition. The American Airlines pilot's contract specified that any flying over a 6.4 percent operating margin on trans-border routes had to be conducted by American Airlines, their aircraft and pilots — not Canadian's. Since losing it to Grant McConachie in 1949, Air Canada had wanted to fly to Australia. Instead of flying Vancouver–Sydney as it had once done, Canadian had allowed its partner QANTAS to take the Sydney–Honolulu route, keeping only the low yield Honolulu–Vancouver part for itself.

———

Harris hadn't put Canadian Airlines out of business, nor had he found a Canadian to take his place. The board had been divided in choosing an heir to Harris. There were those who thought it time that a Canadian and veteran Air Canada employee be chosen. Bourgeault, a twenty-five-year veteran of the airline, had been expected to replace Harris. Others wanted the wunderkind Robert Milton, who in March 1995 Harris had taken off contract and made executive vice-president of marketing. Viewed by Harris as still too inexperienced to be CEO and by middle management and the pilots as too aggressive, Milton had streamlined the cargo and marketing divisions in the airline and redesigned the airline's entire flight schedule, adding more seats to the inventory without bringing in additional aircraft or aircrew. Harris warned that if the board chose someone other than either Durrett or Milton, they would lose both men.

Lamar Durrett had followed him in 1990 to Continental Airlines, and later, when offered a job to help organize the Olympic Games in Atlanta, had chosen instead to follow him once more across the border. Harris thought that such loyalty should be rewarded and exerted enough influence on the board that Durrett was appointed president and CEO on February 22, 1996. Aware of the criticism that was bound to follow the announcement of yet another American at the helm of Canada's national airline, the board took the precaution of separating the chairman's function from the day-to-day running of the airline. On Harris's departure in August, they appointed John Fraser from Winnipeg as chairman.

Those board members who had approved Durrett justified their choice. "He's got absolutely outstanding people skills," said Fraser, adding that he was the best choice because his experience with two major international carriers could only help Air Canada. Shareholders and employees were less forgiving and charged that Durrett had ridden Harris's coattails to the top Air Canada job.

Taking over on May 14, if he heard the snide remarks that Air Canada should be renamed the Confederate Air Force, Lamar Durrett was quick to point out that the present CEO of American Airlines was Canadian Don Carty. "So

it's really just a trade-off," he would joke. After having spent years in Harris's shadow, Durrett admitted that following him wasn't easy. Harris made decisions in a dictatorial fashion, scribbling them on a napkin. Durrett was courteous and cautious, Central Casting's idea of a mint julep–sipping Southern gentleman, always looking for a consensus of opinion before he moved. He had been responsible for some of the airline's recent successes. When Air Canada and Canadian Airlines were trying to negotiate new deals with the government on Asian routes, it was Durrett who had lobbied hard for Air Canada, earning him the nickname of "Darth Vader" among Canadian employees in Calgary.

"It's clear that my predecessor deserves a lot of the credit for the successes of Air Canada now," said Durrett, "but I've got to say [that] the execution of a plan is sometimes equally as difficult, and sometimes more so, than the planning of the plan. Hollis Harris always gave me along-the-road opportunities, but at the end of the day it's the person with the opportunities who has to prove that he has the capabilities to do the job. I am the president who is the executor of the plan."

As a boy growing up in Tate, Georgia, sixty miles north of Atlanta, Lamar had always been a "by-the-book" kind of kid, recalled his ninety-three-year-old aunt, Cora Durrett. "His mother adored him because he never gave him any trouble," she said. Durrett met his wife Barbara while was he working under Harris at

Delta's in-flight service department. She was a stewardess and remembers disliking her future husband on first sight as he and Harris set about trying to enforce rules only loosely observed by the flight attendants. "I thought he was prissy, walking around with his little rule book."

Unlike his mentor, who commuted between Atlanta and Montreal, ensuring that his stay in Canada was temporary, Durrett embraced his adopted country. He took up skiing in the Laurentians and applied for Canadian citizenship, studying hard for the oral exam, and hired a tutor

Unlike Harris, Lamar Durrett embraced Canada, taking out citizenship and learning French, but he failed to create shareholder value.

to learn French. The new CEO said that he wanted to speak the language when touring parts of the company that had a high proportion of francophone employees. Being profiled as a foreigner who had taken the job from a Canadian made him self-conscious. "I don't want to be remembered as the American who was president of Air Canada," Durrett once said. "It did bother me that for the first few years, everything ever written about me not only indicated that I was an American, but that I was a Southerner — whatever that connotation might mean." While admitting to keeping his U.S. passport in his back pocket, on May 27, 1999 Durrett became a Canadian citizen. His critics charged it was nothing more than a nationalistic ruse to better deal with Ottawa politicians, and Durrett himself conceded, "It feels much more comfortable lobbying for tax reductions [for the airline] and changes to fiscal policy as a Canadian." But he and his wife bought a house in the tony Montreal neighbourhood of Westmount and said

that they intended to retire in Morin Heights in the Laurentians.

———

Statistics Canada estimated that in 1995, 28 percent of Canadian homes had personal computers, and in June Air Canada launched its website with its home page address, www.aircanada.ca. Access command for its CompuServe forum was GO AIRCANADA. Almost eliminating the travel agent profession, the website gave customers twenty-four-hour online access to schedules, Aeroplan, and new routes — a far cry from the pre-ReserVec days when the progress of flights were charted across the country by a manually moved marker.

With company stock having fallen by 49 percent since 1990, from $12 to $4.87 per share in 1995, Durrett expected a rough ride from shareholders. Debt payments depressed profit, which fell from $129 million in 1994 to $52 million in 1995. In the first quarter of 1995, the airline showed a $7 million operating loss,

AIR CANADA 1995[3]

Total operating revenue	1994–95 percentage change	Total operating expenses (000)	1994–95 percentage change	1995 operating profit/loss
$3,290,110	12	$3,089,360	12	$178,120

CANADIAN AIRLINES 1995[3]

Total operating revenue	1994–95 percentage change	Total operating expenses (000)	1994–95 percentage change	1995 operating profit/loss
$2,292,638	5.9	$2,312,129	8.8	$40,150

the smallest of a first quarter since 1987, but the $88 million net loss was sharply higher than the year before. In the second quarter, the loss was $23 million compared with a $27 million the year before. It was only in the third quarter that the airline saw a record $179 million profit. Company shares that had bottomed out at $4.11 in June 1996 rallied at $6.60 in December. While this was partly because of a strong summer of international routes and retirement of the older L-1011s and B747s and because Air Canada was selling its stocks in Continental Airlines, it was viewed as a sign that the company had turned around.

When Doug Young left in January 1996, the prime minister appointed former Foreign Affairs officer David Anderson as minister of transport. As the senior federal minister from British Columbia, Anderson had a vested interest in keeping Canadian Airlines flying. It was a heady time to run Transport Canada since on May 29 the NTA was replaced with the Canada Transportation Act, creating the Canadian Transportation Agency (CTA), a quasi-judicial tribunal with the powers and rights of a superior court. From now on a Canadian air carrier could operate with whatever aircraft it chose, wherever it chose and as often as it wished, subject to certain financial requirements. In recognition of the de facto breakdown of national airlines and the emergence of truly global skies, the federal government's relationship with commercial aviation had matured dramatically — and finally.

On July 1, Anderson presided over the commercialization of civil air navigation services, transferring air traffic control from his department to NAV CANADA. Occurring even as the FAA began to levy air navigation charges in U.S. airspace, the introduction of such fees increased operating expenses of all airlines accordingly, both in the United States and Canada. If this weren't enough, it occurred at the same time that airport fees at Toronto's Pearson Airport would rise by $40 million.

The freedoms allowed by the Canada Transportation Act were too little and too late for Canadian Airlines. Had McConachie been allowed to operate more than one transcontinental flight in 1959, had CPA been given access to London, had Eyton been allocated unlimited transborder routes ... it would have been a different story. So dark was its future that when the reserved, soft-spoken Kevin Benson was made Canadian Airlines' new CEO on June 29, 1996, someone remarked "it is a bit like being given captaincy of the *Titanic*." Chosen by that airline's board of directors because he had brought Trizec, the property management company (which had once owned Place Ville Marie, the former Air Canada headquarters), back from bankruptcy, Benson warned that there was no Plan B.

As TWA, Continental, and America West had done, Canadian Airlines might have sought the protection of bankruptcy court, living out its time as a "zombie" while waging a nasty price war against Air Canada. Or Canadian's battered employees could make even more payroll concessions or the federal and provincial governments find even more money to prop the airline up, or in return for Ottawa easing foreign ownership restrictions, AMR could invest even more. If none of those happened, Canadian Airlines could go the way of Pan American.

But Benson had other plans. He opened discussions with Gerry Schwartz and his vice-president, Tony Melman, in 1996 about an infusion of capital. There are very few investors who can claim to have made any return on their investment in airlines. Most are lucky to escape with their portfolios — and reputations — intact. Virgin's Sir Richard Branson is famously quoted as saying: "If you want to become a millionaire in the airline business, start off with a billion dollars...." Billionaire Warren Buffett agreed, saying: "If a farsighted capitalist had been present at Kitty Hawk, he would have done his successors a huge favor by shooting Orville Wright down."[4] Industry analysts thought that there were only three men in Canada with enough money and chutzpah to restructure the country's fractured airline business: Gerry Schwartz, Jimmy Pattison, and Paul Desmarais. Said to be the fifth richest man in Canada, Pattison had once merged a number of west coast airlines together to form Air BC. But as much as he liked the glamour of aviation, in 1987 he was happy enough to sell 85 percent of Air BC to Air Canada and got rid of the remainder in 1995. The fourth richest man in Canada was Paul Desmarais Sr., who sixty years before

had transformed his father's single-route Ontario bus company into mighty Power Corp. Not only had the romanticism of buying airline stock escaped Desmarais, but as his son André was married to France Chrétien, the prime minister's daughter, the optics to do so now would have been poor. Or perhaps Pattison and Desmarais had taken Buffett's warning to heart.

Not so Gerry Schwartz. Known as the "leveraged buy-out king" to his admirers and a corporate vulture to everyone else, Schwartz was ambitious and savvy. His Toronto-based private equity company Onex Corporation either owned or operated dozens of companies as diverse as Beatrice Foods, Cineplex, Celestica Inc., Dura Automotive Systems Inc., and the aero catering firm SkyChefs. The Winnipeg native's modus operandi was to use debt financing to purchase undervalued companies and then restructure them into profitable operations. The year before, the Belgian company Interbrew, in a $2.3 billion hostile takeover bid, had beaten Schwartz for John Labatt Ltd. and its Toronto Blue Jays baseball team. Losing out on owning one national icon, he desperately wanted another — and what was more Canadian than either of the country's airlines? Schwartz and his wife Heather Reisman (of the Indigo bookstore chain) were also politically well connected, having raised millions of dollars for the Liberal party. Although he always protested that he hadn't sought any favours from the party in power, such was Schwartz's political clout that when Collenette was defence minister he had arranged for Schwartz the ultimate "big boy toy": a flight in a Canadian Forces CF-18 fighter.

———

But since 1997 proved to be a boom year for the airline industry worldwide, with even Canadian Airlines making a third quarter profit of $106 million, private investor money was not needed ... yet. For Air Canada, 1997 proved to be its best in its sixty-year history. As measured by operating revenue per employee, since 1992 productivity had improved an impressive 57 percent. Not counting its regional carriers, the company had an overall yield (the average revenue generated from each mile travelled by a paying customer) of 17.5 cents, while Canadian's yield was 13.94 cents. By the fourth quarter of 1997, Air Canada's yield had risen to 19 cents and Canadian's had sunk to 13.87 cents.

Now seen as his own man, Durrett could point to several successes: the debt had been pared by $600 million, mainly through the sale of the last tranche of Continental shares in early January. With the advantages of "Open Skies," Air Canada could now fly across the border at will, making the Continental connections superfluous. Other revenue-generating measures included in-house overhauls for B747s, exchanged for third party work on B767s, and led by Delta Airlines, travel agent commissions were capped through North America.

The airline celebrated its sixtieth anniversary in 1997 by paying homage to its past with the painting of a brand new A319 in the silver livery of Trans-Canada Air Lines. Claude Taylor, who had either witnessed or initiated much of that history, formally retired from the board of directors that year, ending a career with TCA/Air Canada that had begun in 1949. Given that he had been one of the earliest advocates of privatization, it was fitting that he left at such a high point in the company's history.

At the same time the airline confidently embraced the future. On February 22 Air Canada would introduce email specials and discounts with the launch of "GoAirCanada webSaver." Discount carrier Greyhound Air was gone, and Canadian Airlines' escalating woes had forced it to reduce domestic operations, allowing Air Canada and upstart WestJet to take up the slack. By now the Calgary-based no frills airline had reduced its airfares enough and expanded its routes, especially in Western Canada, so that Air Canada had difficulties competing. Except for wet leasing a B757-200 for flights to Hawaii, WestJet's CEO, Clive Beddoe, had no intention of competing with either Air Canada or Canadian on overseas routes. But what if it entered into an agreement with Air Canada to feed its short haul network into that airline's international flights?

When David Anderson left Transport Canada for Fisheries and Oceans, the prime minister looked for a replacement. His former minister of defence, David Collenette, was then serving his penance on the bank benches. Having successfully dodged the fallout when his Chief of

The airline saluted its sixtieth anniversary in 1997 by paying homage to its past with the painting of a brand new A319 in the silver livery of Trans-Canada Air Lines.

Defence Staff General Jean Boyle put the whole military on alert to search for the missing Somalia enquiry files, Collenette had resigned in October 1996 over a conflict of interest case with the Immigration and Refugee Board. In June 1997 destiny beckoned him when Chrétien appointed him to run the department that he had always wanted: Transport Canada. At a critical time in commercial aviation history he was given an opportunity to follow in the footsteps of such giants as Howe, Pickersgill, and Mazankowski.

———

The white elephant that Mirabel Airport had become — the airport that Pierre Trudeau predicted would be the gateway of the twenty-first century — closed to all scheduled international flights in 1997. Its slow death had begun with the 1970 recession followed by the 1973 oil price shock, decades of bickering between the various levels of government about a rapid transit system, and two wrenching separatist referendums. The political uncertainty and confused traffic sharing between Mirabel and Dorval airports that made flight connections difficult adversely affected the development of both airports, making Mirabel a hub without spokes — or passengers.

With Ottawa deciding to maintain domestic and trans-border flights at Dorval and the creation of Aéroports de Montréal (ADM) in 1992, air carriers were given the choice of operating scheduled international flights at Dorval or Mirabel, which closed to scheduled traffic in 1997 and charters in 2004. Following months of meticulous planning and sensitivity training for its Mirabel employees, Air Canada moved off all of its Mirabel assets by truck convoy to Dorval at midnight on September 14, 1997. Mirabel would handle only charters until 2004, the year that Dorval Airport was ironically renamed Montréal-Pierre Elliott Trudeau Airport after the prime minister who had attempted to strangle it.

Air Canada divested itself of Air NWT in June, most of its interests in Galileo Canada, and all of its interests in Apollo Travel Services. It still had twenty-eight DC-9s (the aircraft nicknamed the "Energizer") that were being hushkitted on a progressive basis. To replace the six B747-100 and 200s sold off, it added twenty-seven new aircraft to the fleet: four A340s, twenty-two A319s, and one CRJ, making the average age of its fleet 9.9 years. The regional airlines had a combined fleet of seventy-nine aircraft, the de Havilland DHC-8 the single largest fleet type by number (sixty-four), followed by ten British Aerospace BAe 146s.

There had been a labour disruption by the Air Canada's regional airline pilots early in the year that impacted the bottom line by $57 million. The corporation's

decision to reinstate tax losses by a repayment of fuel excise tax rebates from previous years had resulted in a $43 million charge to fuel expenses. On the horizon was the "Year 2000" problem (when all computer systems would be made incapable of handling two-digit year codes across the millennium change), and to make its systems "Year 2000" compliant, the airline had already spent $5 million.

But at the end of 1997 the price of Air Canada's common shares closed on the Toronto Stock Exchange at $14.75 per share, a 138 percent increase from its 1996 close, and operating income was an unprecedented $368 million, a 71 percent improvement over 1996. As of December 31, 1997, the airline had posted a $427 million year-end profit, the highest in its sixty-year history.

Historians would look back at the late 1990s as the last glorious years of the legacy airline industry. The beginning of the dot-com boom in 1997, combined with deregulation, had allowed the biggest airlines in the United States to erase years of losses, and like the energy giant Enron Corporation, inflate their book value and market capitalization to unrealistic proportions. Then, as airline executives have always done, they then went on a spending spree, buying hundreds of new planes in a frenzied grab for market share and allowing their unions fat contracts. By 1999, the technology bubble (as speculative as Enron's accounting) was imploding, erasing enormous personal fortunes and dragging down corporate profits. Airlines saw their pampered "Road Warriors," those free-spending business travellers that they had come to depend on, vanish, leaving only the budget-conscious leisure travellers who sought out low-fare carriers like Southwest Airlines, JetBlue, AirTran in the United States, Ryanair in Europe — and WestJet in Canada. The airlines were on course to lose billions of dollars and shed thousands of jobs in the new century, unless a major restructuring of the industry occurred.

———

Fredericton Airport and Air Canada's Canadair Regional Jets (CRJ) would be an unhappy mix on a few occasions. On February 8, 1996, as Flight 646 from Toronto landed on slippery runway 15 in darkness, the flight crew lost control of the aircraft at low speed and it yawed off, leaving the runway until its nose gear sank into the soft ground beside. There were no injuries — this time.

On December 16, 1997, C-FSKI, another CRJ Flight 646 with thirty-nine passengers onboard, attempted to land on the same runway. The weather was difficult, the pilots fighting blowing snow, fog, and darkness. Runway visual range was 1,000 feet and the ceiling and visibility was below the minimum published for an instrument approach. At 200 feet above the runway the captain approved the landing, and the first officer disengaged the autopilot. This caused the aircraft to drift off the runway centre line. The captain then ordered a go-around and the first

EXCERPT FROM AVIATION INVESTIGATION REPORT A97H0011 TRANSPORTATION SAFETY BOARD OF CANADA REPORT RELEASED APRIL 15, 1999

The flight attendant who was travelling as a passenger exited out the right side of the aircraft and quickly assumed a leadership role. She assembled the passengers around her in a group and had them "sound-off" to establish a passenger count. This process was repeated periodically to confirm that no one had wandered away. She stopped passengers from re-entering the aircraft while the engines were running and, given the strong smell of fuel, warned them not to smoke or light matches. When the engines stopped, she boarded the aircraft and gathered up coats for the passengers outside.

Later, as rescue personnel had not arrived, the occurrence flight attendant again exited the aircraft and instructed some passengers to take the flashlight and make their way to the runway. Most passengers made their way in small groups, some passengers without winter clothing or footwear. They shouted for help as they went, but rescue personnel could neither see nor hear them.

The three crewmembers stayed on the aircraft with the trapped passengers until rescue personnel arrived. Passengers who exited on the left side were surrounded by forest. They walked deeper into the forest, eventually making their way through the trees to the right side of the aircraft where there was a clearing and a route to the runway.

— Aviation Investigation Report A97H0011,

Transportation Safety Board, April 15, 1999.

officer advanced the thrust levers, but by then it was too late. The aircraft's right wing hit the runway, the nose landing gear broke off, and the CRJ slid into a snowy ditch. It then attempted to get airborne again, hit some trees, one of which entered the cabin through the door before coming to rest. The captain and eight passengers were seriously injured, but the two flight attendants (one was a passenger) and all others escaped with only minor injuries.

The Transportation Safety Board Report concluded that the aircraft had stalled because of an accumulation of ice on the leading edge of the wing. But the drama and the heroism were in the report's details — especially what it said of the professionalism of the Air Canada crew.

———

The Ice Storm of January 5 opened the new year of 1998, coating much of Ontario, Quebec, and New Brunswick with 7–10 cm of ice. The four-day closure of both Montreal and Ottawa airports forced the cancellations of hundreds of flights, unluckily for Canadian Airlines, which had got the contract to fly the Team Canada trade mission to Latin America.

With 22,837 employees, an 8 percent increase over 1997, mainly because of hiring customer service personnel (including call centre staff) and carrying more than 60,000 passengers daily, Air Canada was now the world's twelfth largest airline. It had just been named the world's best passenger service airline by *Air Transport World* magazine and awarded the prestigious gold

medal for best domestic long haul and silver for best North American business class by the travel information publisher OAG Worldwide. Its domestic market share was 59 percent and trans-border market share 43 percent. Internationally, the weak Pacific operations in 1998 were partially offset by increased Atlantic and Caribbean operations and revenues. It was time to strut — and also to win the hearts, minds, and pocketbooks of Canadians.

Raising their company's profile with advertising campaigns and restyling their liveries, Canadian Airlines staff brought out their "Proud Wings" Canada goose; it was one way to keep in the public's eye.

Leveraging Air Canada's brand on sports teams and arts festivals was another. Christening Toronto's new sports complex as the Air Canada Centre, painting an A320 in the logo of the Toronto Raptors, sponsoring the Air Canada Grand Prix Formula 1 racing event in Montreal, the Air Canada Championship PGA Tour event in Vancouver plus jazz and movie festivals, gave the airline an immediate payback in customer recognition far beyond the sports pages and television screens. How successful it would all be in the long run remained to be seen.

———

The four profitable years of expansion from 1994–97, when revenues grew faster than costs, did not escape the notice of the Air Canada pilots. Their union, the Canadian Air Line Pilots Association (CALPA) was as old as the airline itself. It had begun on December 13, 1938 when Captain "Jock" Barclay brought together thirteen TCA pilots in a Winnipeg hotel room to discuss the idea of creating a professional body to represent them. The more militant Air Canada Pilots Association (ACPA) had displaced CALPA on November 14, 1995 as the pilots' bargaining agent. The 2,100 Air Canada pilots earned between $20,500 and $128,200 annually, on average $100,000 a year — 30 percent to 50 per cent less, an ACPA spokesperson said, than the pay of comparable pilots in the United States and Europe. They had made wage and scheduling concessions through the company's rough ride from 1990 onward, and now with their contract expiring in April 1998, they demanded a 20 percent raise over two years.

And it wasn't only pay. The pilots' union said that Air Canada pilots averaged between seventy-eight to eighty-five hours of flying time per month compared with an industry average of seventy-five to seventy-eight hours and wanted more rest periods between flights and fewer days away from home. When negotiations between the airline and the ACPA broke down in July, the pilots voted 97 percent in favour of a strike.

On September 2, in their first strike in the company's sixty-year history, Air Canada's pilots walked off the job, grounding the airline and putting thousands of staff from baggage handlers to caterers out of work. "Our management has failed to address our concerns and we are angered," said Jean-Marc Bélanger, the association

chairman. "We are angry, dismayed, and displeased that we are forced into this situation." The strike left idle 9,500 flight attendants, baggage handlers, ground crew, and other Air Canada workers. Another 1,000 employees of Cara Foods, which provided flight meals, were also laid off. The union soon came down from its original demand of a 20 percent raise over two years to a 12 percent salary increase, which the airline countered with a raise of 9 percent, spokeswoman Priscille LeBlanc saying that the difference between the two salary proposals would cost Air Canada an extra $150 million over five years if applied to all employees. "This is a significant labour cost that would have made Air Canada uncompetitive in Canada, our largest market." The airline countered it could not afford another 3 percent for the pilots, especially since it would soon be negotiating contracts with other unions.

The airline had a contingency plan in place for the strike, allowing passengers with tickets between September 2 and 6 to delay their travel plans at no cost. Its regional carriers were unaffected since their pilots still belonged to CALPA, and the airline's partners, United Airlines, Lufthansa, Korean Air, SAS, and Royal Jordanian, took up the slack on international routes. But analysts estimated the strike was costing Air Canada about $13 million a day in earnings. The walkout ended September 14, with the pilots agreeing to a two-year contract that gave them a 4 percent wage increase in the first year and 5 percent in the second, the same as the offer at the start of the strike. Jean-Marc Bélanger said that the strike did produce gains "in the whole global picture." The pilots' strike had a $250 million negative impact on operational earnings, and although the airline rebounded quickly with a "kiss and make up" sale, the president thought it marked the end of Air Canada's five-year expansion.

Durrett said he was "not proud" that the first pilots' strike in Air Canada's history had happened on his watch or that the airline would report a $16 million loss by December 1998. While Air Canada had just added its fiftieth route in four years to the United States, "every time we look left, right, up or down," he complained, "there's a strong competitor there, and Canadian is one of them." His other concerns were spiralling fees at Toronto's Pearson Airport (and the planned replacement of Air Canada's Terminal II that the airline was expected to contribute to) and steadily increasing NAV CANADA fees that forced Air Canada to introduce passenger surcharges to defray their costs.

Canadian Airlines had also suffered collateral damage from the pilots' strike — and it could least afford to. Seeing the labour action as heaven-sent, the company quickly launched a media campaign to win over Air Canada passengers, putting its staff on overtime and adding extra flights. But at the end, the hard-won Air Canada customers, anxious to protect their Air Canada frequent flyer points, deserted and Canadian Airlines was left paying heavy overtime and maintenance fees, with no

permanent gain to show for either. And with WestJet's increasing inroads, it no longer was the only alternative on domestic routes. Worse was to come when the Federal Aviation Association grounded all early model B737s to inspect their Teflon-coated wiring systems. Canadian Airlines, which operated nineteen of the aircraft, was devastated as its customers scrambled to switch to Air Canada's brand new A319s. As well, taking advantage of a recently concluded bilateral air transport treaty between Japan and the United States, AMR didn't need their Far Eastern routes or Vancouver hub anymore. This allowed up to ninety round trip flights weekly for U.S. carriers and led American Airlines and Japan Airlines to enter into a code-sharing agreement that would divert most of American's feed away from the Vancouver hub.

———

By September, all six of the Air Canada Boeing 747-100 "Classics" and nine more DC-9s had been parked, the remaining DC-9s scheduled to be replaced by 2002. The original 747s, once called "Fat Alberts," had been like nothing else in the Air Canada fleet. They were the last aircraft to require three pilots and had their own pilot groups and large spare parts inventory. Fully depreciated by now, they would be missed for what they did best: earned big money in the summer. Not missed would be their enormous fuel and maintenance fees. The newer 747-400s would soldier on until October 31, 2004, when

AC873, the last Air Canada Boeing 747 flight, landed in Toronto from Frankfurt, ending thirty-three years of "Jumbo Jet" service with the airline.

The airline planned to replace the "Classics" with a combination of A340-300s and the new twin engined A330-300s, resulting in lower fuel, maintenance, and crew training costs. But the Asian recession, the slowing down of the North American economy and the worldwide commodity slump, all combined with the pilots' strike to give Air Canada a $16 million loss in 1998, which was little compared with Canadian Airlines, which lost $138 million that year.

But it was no surprise that after hitting a high of $15.40 in 1997, Air Canada shares closed at $6.80 that December.

——

As Toronto goes, so goes the national airline industry, and on January 2, 1999, when a snowstorm closed Pearson Airport's runways, all carriers were forced to cancel flights to and from Toronto, backlogging national service into the next week. With 45 percent of the traffic into Pearson Airport, Air Canada was the most affected, and when it failed to adequately communicate the cancellations to its customers

"Jumbo Jet," "Flying Whale," "Fat Albert": from 1971 to 2003, the Boeing 747 was operated by Air Canada in four variants, its wide-body configuration an instant hit with passengers and crew.

DREAMS TAKE FLIGHT

Very early in the morning I woke up with my brother, even before the alarm clock rang. I got dressed and we went to the Air Canada hangar. We all enjoyed the party while Air Canada prepared its plane for us. All of a sudden an alarm rang and the huge doors opened. Wow! Marianne and I boarded the plane to male my biggest dream come true. Thank you. Julian, age 7

My baby daughter Jamie is six months old with a number of allergies and symptoms. She has been hospitalized with a serious lung infection. I come from a small town where we have only one pediatrician and you can only do so many medical tests. Through Air Canada and Hope Air I was able to fly to Kelowna to see a pediatrician who specializes in allergies.
C.B., British Columbia

Hello,
My name is Claudia, and I would like to thank you for making my dream come true. I really thought I was dreaming when I saw Mickey and Minnie in the big hall where the airplane was. It was as if I was dreaming all day long and when I went home, I wanted go to sleep so that I could continue my dream. I love you a lot and I hope other children have the chance to experience the same thing I did. Claudia, age 8

Us kids, we need to have dreams and be able to realize them. You did more than that: you did realize our dream and you also made us enjoy it. I could never thank you enough, and this is from all the others and me. Thanks to you who made this project possible. Sincerely yours, Kristofer

in time, hundreds of would-be passengers fought through snow drifts to show up at the airport, only to be marooned there. Although the company insisted that the fault lay with Mother Nature and not its incompetence, its fuming customers were not consoled.

But Air Canada's troubles were nothing compared with its rival. There is a saying that all businesses go through good times and bad times, except for airlines, which go through bad and just plain awful times. A weakened Far East market and WestJet's growing incursions at home had left Canadian Airlines effectively bankrupt — again. When its board met in January 1999 to view the launch of the "Proud Wings" campaign, Benson broke the news. The airline had run out of cash and he of options. They authorized him to begin talks immediately with Durrett concerning a merger.

But in Montreal, Air Canada's directors were looking at handling a more dangerous threat than the faltering Canadian: WestJet. By reducing airfares and offering better service amenities, Air Canada had gotten rid of the pesky "mom and pop" competitors like Vistajet and Nationair. But financially stable, non-unionized and economically well run, by 1998 WestJet had gained an enthusiastic, loyal customer base, and was no longer confined to Western Canada. It was only a matter of time before Beddoe signed interline pacts with European and Middle Eastern airlines that could siphon off its domestic traffic. Weighed down with all its legacy airline baggage, Air Canada realized that it could never compete with

WestJet, and in a scenario dubbed the "Visions Project," Lamar Durrett looked to implement a strategic alliance with it.

At the close of the century, even the federal government realized that (like the imminently expected Y2K millennium bug) the two-airline policy had wreaked irreparable damage and could not continue. If domestically WestJet was providing Canadians with more choice, globally competing air alliances were siphoning off air travellers from both Air Canada and Canadian Airlines. Neither airline would ever be healthy if the other continued to exist. "While we fully acknowledge that at any time in the 1990s Canadian's performance has been less than acceptable," Benson would admit, "the truth is, Air Canada's has not been all that sterling either. Their operating margin, in fact, in the past five years has been about half that of the major U.S. carriers. Their stock had dropped some 14 percent over the past five years compared with the major U.S. carriers, whose stock had increased approximately 300 percent in the same period."[5]

Whatever the solution, it was no longer going to be confined within Canadian borders. In any merger, one airline would have to abandon its global alliance and join the other, and because AMR owned so much of Canadian Airlines and would insist that its SABRE CRS be used, the Fort Worth airline would have to be part of this as well.

Then there was the new minister of transport; would David Collenette bolster support for the Liberals in the West by allowing a merger and thus saving Canadian Airlines — and end the historic two-airline policy? With so many jobs at stake, especially in Calgary and Vancouver, the government had to be brought into this as soon as possible. And it wasn't only Transport Canada....

The 1985 Competition Act forbids competitors from talking to each other about prices, routes, or capacity, or taking any action that smacks of conspiracy, collusion, or anything likely to lessen competition in Canada. Mergers of all sizes and sectors of the economy are subject to review by the Competition Bureau, an independent law agency run at that time by its commissioner, Konrad von Finckenstein. Although its powers are limited to identifying competition issues and advising the government the means of mitigating them, failure to involve the Bureau is a criminal offence and its advice is taken at the highest levels of government. As finance minister, Paul Martin had taken the Bureau's advice on a prospective merger of banks in Canada — and disallowed it.

Having reviewed previous attempts at mergers: Canadian Airlines and Wardair (1989), the proposed Canadian Airlines and Air Canada merger (1992), the alliances between Canadian Airlines and American Airlines (1994), and between Air Canada and United Airlines (1996), the airline industry was well known to the Competition Bureau. Foreign airline industry models relevant to Canada had been examined. Australia too had once had a rigid domestic "Two Airline Policy": Ansett-ANA and Trans-Australia Airlines (TAA) and a single international carrier, QANTAS. When TAA went bankrupt, Ansett-ANA won a stranglehold on the domestic market as QANTAS did overseas. There were many Canadians who agreed with the Competition Bureau that as in Australia, competition in the national airline industry was fast becoming extinct and an Air Canada/Canadian Airlines merger, or the imminent Canadian Airlines bankruptcy, would leave Air Canada the dominant carrier in the country.[6] Von Finckenstein advised Collenette that the government should allow increased foreign ownership (up to 49 percent of the voting shares) in a Canadian airline and that foreign carriers be allowed to operate their own airlines in Canada. The commissioner was also aware that he had no choice but to accept whatever the minister of transport decided.

———

"Be careful what you pray for," Hollis Harris used to say to Robert Milton, "because someday you just might get it." And Harris ensured that his young colleague did. Within five years Milton's vaulting ambition had taken him from working on contract in freight operations to senior director of scheduling to vice-president, scheduling and product management to senior vice-president, marketing and in-flight service to executive vice-president, and finally chief operating officer in 1996.

Two years later, he put together a strategy team to review the company's business structures, asking the group, "How do we do something that will protect the employees and enable the shareholders to do well and the businesses to do well on a sustained basis?" The team looked at every facet of the airline and its operations. Air Canada did not own unrelated lines of business, such as hotels. Even so, it became clear that portions of the airline might be more profitable as stand-alone entities. The team concluded that the high-risk and low-return profile of the airline business was masking the investment value of certain segments. One option was to divide Air Canada up and monetize each piece separately, and by 1999 three businesses that could potentially be separated from Air Canada were identified, in addition to the regional airline with its separate union agreements: ACTS (the technical services group that handled major maintenance, repair, and refurbishing of the fleet), the air cargo business, and Aeroplan, the frequent flier program.[7]

His work earned Milton the prestigious "Top 40 Under 40" award for 1998 that recognized forty Canadians who had achieved significant levels of success in leadership and innovation before age forty. But within Air Canada, he had the reputation as Harris's "hatchet man" with little sympathy for the unions, which was why Durrett had kept him far away from negotiations with the ACPA during the pilot's strike.

Although the board had backed him in handling the strike, Durrett had come off badly through it, and his time as CEO was running out. Whoever was chosen as his replacement, Milton knew that he wouldn't have the latitude that both Harris and Durrett had given him. Again and again in freight operations, scheduling, and marketing, he had encountered fierce resistance to change, especially from middle management, who in his opinion did not want to take risks or make decisions. "Not Invented Here" (NIH) was the classic and constant excuse he heard — in his view one of the vestiges of working in a former "just break even" Crown corporation. There were times, he believed, when the entire corporation was dedicated to resisting change.

He also disagreed with senior management over the considered strategic alliance with WestJet. If Air Canada ceded its domestic market share to WestJet, Milton knew that it would never get it back — and its regional pilots were sure to strike. Full service airlines could never compete with the Ryanair wannabes that were springing up. Why not compete with WestJet on its own level, by starting up a discount carrier within Air Canada? Milton had developed the model when he, with Harris and Durrett, had attempted to make Air Eagle fly. Like WestJet it would be no frills — and no unions.

But Milton didn't see it that way. As much as he enjoyed being at Air Canada and his family living in Montreal, unless he could inherit Durrett's job, there was no reason to stay. Only as CEO could he implement the changes he saw were necessary. It was while considering his options in early 1999 that Milton was offered a position with Bombardier.

———

On February 4, at the Goldman Sachs conference on airline investment in Miami, Benson met secretly with Durrett, Chairman Jack Fraser, and American Airlines President Don Carty. Would Air Canada and AMR consider an Air Canada/Canadian merger? It would prevent Canadian Airlines from closing down, and in the long run gladden the hearts of both Air Canada and Canadian Airlines investors. Kept confidential from employees, media, shareholders, and alliance partners, the merger would be fleshed out again by the same parties in Toronto on February 11. With the consent of the others, including Air Canada senior staff, on March 12 Benson approached Collenette. He presented the minister with a document astutely titled "A New National Dream," a title sure to appeal to the minister's love of history (Collenette would be familiar with *The National Dream*, Pierre Berton's book on the building of the Canadian Pacific Railway). It was nothing less than a complete restructuring of Canada's two-airline policy. A merger would allow both airlines to streamline by dropping duplicated routes, older aircraft, and surplus employees by combining positions. There would be less competition or confusion at their Toronto, Vancouver, and Montreal hubs, and any short-term job losses were sure to be made up in the long term. The downside was that Air Canada would be adding Canadian's crushing debts to its own, and its global partners, especially Lufthansa, would object to changing alliances.

If Benson was desperate by the spring of 1999 and Durrett somewhat committed to a merger, Carty was less so. He was in the unique position of knowing the other players' cards. AMR had already invested too much in Canadian Airlines and as the senior creditor it was worth more dead to them than alive. Because of the 25 percent restriction in a foreigner owning an airline in Canada, AMR couldn't directly buy up a majority of Air Canada's shares and merge it with Canadian Airlines. Besides, the American Airlines pilots' union opposed further investment in the carrier. Having been employed by Air Canada and CP Air, Carty was also aware of the mindset and mistrust within both those companies. All Air Canada had to do was wait for its opponent to die off — and odds were that would occur by March. Why take on its debt load? He suspected that once back in Montreal, Durrett was too much of a gentleman to sell the idea to his people. Carty also understood that there would be no white knight from the private sector riding up to rescue Canadian Airlines. One that did so would have to buy back AMR's stock at a highly inflated price, many more times the value that the stock market was then giving Canadian's shares.

At a meeting in Chicago on March 25, Benson and Carty formally presented Durrett with the merger proposal. Air Canada would have to assume about $2 billion in debt and come over to Oneworld. Briefed by his board, Durrett rejected this outright. Benson would have to find someone else to invest in his airline before

they talked further. Because of the New Year snowstorm, Air Canada barely made a $3 million profit for the first quarter of 1999 — and that only because it sold off its investment in Equant NV, the Dutch telecommunications company. After the heady successes of 1997, its shareholders would be in an unforgiving mood.

At the Air Canada annual general meeting in May held at the Palliser Hotel in Calgary, the shareholders voiced their displeasure, taking it out on Durrett. Shares that they had bought a decade ago at $11.75 were valued at $6.00 and going lower. "There's no question our shareholders are not happy with the performance of Air Canada," he commented to the media. "Neither are we and neither is our board." Durrett was reprimanded for losing shareholder value by mishandling the pilot's strike. As well, Air Canada's management was faulted for allowing operating costs to rise 20 percent from 1996 to 1998. Compounding the disappointment was that the broader North American airline industry was booming. The airline did manage to post a $73 million profit in the second quarter, still down from $91 million the previous year. The embattled CEO had one piece of good news that he divulged to his senior staff: they could expect Carty and Benson to come to Air Canada with a merger offer more to their liking.

A sign of the government's increasing fear that Canadian Airlines was about to declare bankruptcy, leaving Air Canada with a monopoly on air transport, came in June when Collenette convened a secret cabinet committee made up of Justice Minister Anne McLellan, Environment Minister David Anderson (representing British Columbia), former Treasury Minister Marcel Masse, and Public Works Minister Alfonso Gagliano. The committee knew that Benson was not going to ask Ottawa for more taxpayers' dollars. A massive government injection of funds, as Benson had candidly observed, might please his company's 17,000 employees but would anger 26 million other Canadians. But knowing that a federal election was coming up, the politicians were also aware that those 17,000 jobs translated into $500 million in tax revenue and 35,000 votes, most in the Liberal-weak West.

But for a merger to occur, the airlines had to talk openly, and Benson asked that one of the rules in the Competition Act be suspended, specifically Section 47. This would suspend for ninety days the application of the Competition Act as it applied to airlines in Canada, thus allowing discussions to take place. Although Air Canada senior staff had signed off on the "National Dream" paper, they did not see the need or possibility of a suspension of competition rules.

Douglas D. Port, Air Canada's senior vice-president, corporate affairs and government relations, would later testify before the House of Commons Standing Committee on Transport:

We had been given a paper by Canadian Airlines called "The New National Dream," written by Canadian, and in that there were a number of propositions as to how Canadian Airlines, in going forward on a potential merger with Air Canada, could find mechanisms that would accelerate the approval process. That was because there was concern that a normal approval process with the Competition Bureau could take up to two years.

One of the propositions put forward in that paper was something called a Section 47, and although I'm in charge of government relations, I will confess at that time I had about four months experience in that role, having just arrived back from London, England, so I went to see the Associate Deputy Minister of Transport Margaret Bloodworth. I did not wish the transport department to be caught short with any news about a potential merger because we had learned from what happened with the banks that surprises with the federal government are not a great idea. So I decided to talk to Ms. Bloodworth. In that conversation I asked the question, what is a Section 47 and what impact would it have? That was the phraseology and the tone of the questions I asked. I was informed by Ms. Bloodworth, or her ADM, Louis Ranger, that such a measure was Draconian and would not have any impact on a potential merger situation because it was a short-lived venture.

That is the entire context of the questioning. There was never a request by Air Canada to in fact enact it. It was a question of what does it mean and what impact would it have.[8]

"We asked the Ministry of Transport [sic] about the applicability of Section 47, we did not ask for Section 47," Milton later stated. "We were told by the Minister's office that Section 47 was not applicable in the case of an airline merger."[9]

In June, when Collenette asked both airlines to discuss exchanging international routes, the Competition Bureau immediately announced that it would conduct an investigation to see if the airlines were colluding. The minister then quickly backtracked, saying that he was only urging them to "discuss items of mutual interest." His government, having propped up Canadian Airlines with a series of band-aids for so long, needed the airlines to initiate a suspension request. In this way, the Liberal government could mollify the members of Parliament in the House, especially from the Reform Party, about subsequent job losses in the West. The minister asked Durrett his opinion: what if the competition laws were relaxed so talks with Canadian Airlines could take place? Durrett was evasive but Milton smelled a trap. The merger was a good idea that Air Canada CEOs from McGregor to Harris had repeatedly lobbied for, but why was the Liberal government so keen now? On June 9, David Bell, Canadian Airlines'

treasurer, hinted at what was to come. "Canadian expects a major transaction in 1999, and American Airlines is going to be a big part of this."

By then Benson had already approached Gerry Schwartz again, this time with a plan to buy both airlines and merge them into a single all-Canadian carrier. The sheer audacity of it all must have appealed to Schwartz. With the AMR hold on it, he knew it was poor business sense to pump money into Canadian Airlines alone, but investing in an Air Canada/Canadian Airlines company was a win-win proposition. The idea of an Air Canada/Canadian Airlines merger under Onex management also appealed to AMR, which saw it as an opportunity to recoup some of its $246 million investment. In May, AMR managing director John Boettcher flew to Toronto to meet with Onex and Canadian Airlines at the Inn on the Park. Since federal law prohibited a foreign takeover of Air Canada, it was agreed that AMR would remain hidden in the bushes until the "kill" took place. The operation, called "Project Tornado," depended on Gerry Schwartz being able to sell it to the shareholders and public as an Onex-led initiative and a Bay Street solution that a cabinet minister from Toronto (i.e. Collenette) would be proud to present in Parliament. The only problem was that "Project Tornado" had to be carried out quickly, before Canadian Airlines began parking its planes in the Arizona desert, and without the involvement of the Competition Bureau. Benson was accordingly told that if Onex was to be involved, he had to convince Collenette to suspend Section 47. In anticipation of the merger offer, Schwartz set up a company called Arco, and through it between June 15 and June 23, Onex acquired $43 million in Air Canada shares.

That month Milton made his move. He would be turning forty in July and with the Bombardier job offer in his back pocket (and knowing that the board's faith in Durrett had been eroded by the pilots' strike), he asked the directors for a commitment that he would replace him as CEO. It was a bold move that might have backfired, but with the dismal condition of the airline's finances and Canadian Airlines' collapse looming, the board agreed. To allay any fears he might have had, they promoted Milton to president, the youngest in the airline's history. Jean-Jacques Bourgeault, a leading heir apparent, was on vacation. He returned to find Milton in the president's chair. Unlike Durrett's gentlemanly approach, Milton was blunt, straightforward, and seen as decisive. Those assets, combined with the rumblings of a hostile takeover, appealed to the board.

Saying that because there was a great deal of speculation about the contents of talks between the airlines, on June 24, Air Canada once again offered to buy Canadian's international routes for $525 million, take over $1.4 billion of its debt, and keep most of its employees on the payroll. In its proposal, filed with the federal government, Air Canada said a successful deal with Canadian Airlines would see:

- The Montreal airline buy Canadian's international routes, along with associated assets and liabilities;
- Code-sharing opportunities for Canadian Airlines on Air Canada's international routes;
- Canadian would keep its domestic operations to compete with Air Canada;
- Both airlines continue to operate within the Star Alliance and Oneworld networks for international travel.
- That Air Canada would provide the liquidity (cash infusion) Canadian Airlines needed;
- Canadian would keep its head office in Calgary;
- Most of Canadian Airlines staff would keep their jobs, while Air Canada would hire certain employees associated with Canadian's international business.

"We have studied the proposal, and Canadian has come to the conclusion it's just not acceptable," Jeff Angel, the Canadian Airlines spokesman replied. "Canadian's international routes are the most profitable part of our operation."

Three days after Milton saw Collenette to outline Air Canada's proposal, on June 27 the Canadian Airlines CEO showed up at the minister's door. Benson bore good news that a private sector solution had been found, and not a penny of taxpayer's money would be needed — but only if the Competition Bureau could be taken out of play. Secondly, as the minister responsible for the Bureau, Industry Minister John Manley, had to be briefed so that he and Collenette could be seen to act in concert.

By the time the Canadian Airlines AGM was held on June 29 (also in Calgary) speculation was rife that either British Airways (part of Oneworld) or Air Canada was about to provide that life-saving cash infusion. Every shareholder at the AGM was aware that if Canadian went into liquidation, they would not get a penny. The airline needed $200 million immediately just to remain in the air, and Benson admitted that he had opened discussions with Milton but said little more. It was a date, not a marriage, he told the media.

———

Milton's first major appearance as the new president of Air Canada took place on July 7 and he was facing a difficult audience in the main boardroom at Toronto's Air Canada Centre. They were hard-bitten securities analysts who knew the transportation industry and they were unimpressed with the performance of the airline's management and its share price. Air Canada stock was trading at $6.30 — less than half its value one year earlier, and the pilots' strike and the snowstorm fiasco still resonated. While still CEO, Lamar Durrett had run out of credibility with them and the investment firms they represented. The board hoped Milton could win them over. Never one to sugarcoat the issue, Milton told the analysts that Durrett had been stripped of the president's title because he had failed to create shareholder value. He assured the

audience that things would change under his watch. Labour relations would improve, costs would be cut, and the company would begin working for the benefit of shareholders, not only the customers and employees. The analysts appreciated the new president's candidness. While some skepticism remained, Milton had made a good impression. "He should have been put in place a long time ago," said Yorkton Securities analyst Jacques Kavafian. "Robert Milton is the only shareholder-oriented CEO this company has ever had."

Fortunately for Milton, a strike by Air Canada's 5,100 flight attendants was averted at midnight on July 8, minutes after the strike deadline had passed. A sure sign of the changing demographics among flight attendants was that the main dispute was over pension benefits. Pamela Sachs, the head of the flight attendant section of the Canadian Union of Public Employees (CUPE), was pleased that the union had negotiated improved retirement income, safer and healthier working conditions, and wage increases of 5 percent, 4 percent, and 3 percent over three years.

Meanwhile in Montreal Air Canada shares were being bought up at an alarming rate. Warned that a hostile takeover by Schwartz was in play, some of the airline senior staff like Durrett, who were aware of the regulatory barriers to such a move (especially the 10 percent limit on ownership of Air Canada), were disbelieving. As if girding its loins for the battle ahead, on August 6 Air Canada announced that Durrett would retire and Robert Milton was to be the new chief executive officer, taking over on the fourteenth. "There are many challenges ahead," said Durrett in farewell, "particularly in terms of satisfying our shareholders, and I believe the time is right for new ideas and new leadership to pursue these goals. Robert Milton is a clear star on our horizon, and he is ready and more than able to drive this company forward."

Although he had promised to seek the Competition Bureau's advice on the airline issue, Collenette knew that he would have to go over von Finckenstein's head and suspend the competition rules to prevent a complete collapse of Canadian Airlines. Any change in legislation to favour Canadian Airlines would require an Order-in-Council and full cabinet approval — the only way to implement policy without parliamentary consent. Taking such a bill to Parliament would ensure a heated battle from MPs with a concentration of Air Canada employees in their ridings, something that, with an upcoming election, the government could do without. The cabinet was meeting on July 28 and legend has it that Collenette personally walked his special Order-in-Council around to get the required signatures before presenting it. Whether by design or coincidence, his memorandum was introduced to cabinet the same day that Canadian's second quarter losses were made public. In a stopgap measure, Defence Minister Art Eggleton announced on July 30 that Canadian Airlines would be awarded a $96 million, three-year contract to provide DND with domestic charter services beginning April

1, 2000. Not enough to save the company, but certainly making it more attractive to potential suitors.

On August 4, four days before Benson actually asked for it by letter (and nine days before calling a press conference to announce it), Collenette's office abruptly informed the Bureau that it was going to suspend the competition rules.

Then, playing his part in the drama, Benson made the formal request to Collenette on August 9, asking him to suspend Section 47. The markets had closed when Transport Canada called a press briefing for 4:00 p.m. on August 13. Accompanied by Industry Minister John Manley, Collenette announced that the government had invoked Section 47 of the Transportation Act and suspended the powers of the Competition Bureau for ninety days. The two-airline policy was dead and the airlines had until November 9 to arrive at a solution. As scripted, Manley chimed in to say, "I'm committed to ensuring the outcome will be as pro-competitive as possible for the benefit of Canadian consumers." Done on a summer Friday afternoon when the press bureaus in Ottawa had closed, it was all suspiciously well-timed and no one asked the ministers how suspending anti-trust legislation so that both airlines could consolidate fares and divide up routes could be "pro-competitive."

Warren Buffett used to say that whenever he wanted to invest in an airline there was a 1-800 number he could call. He would then confess, "I'm Warren Buffett and I'm an aeroholic." And someone would talk him out of doing so. Collenette's action led to a frenzy of media speculation that a white knight was about to appear. *Globe and Mail* columnist Hugh Winsor was close to the truth when he wrote on Monday August 16, "Mr. Collenette and Mr. Manley are hanging their hopes that some outside (that is, not Air Canada) investor or investors can be persuaded to invest in some restructured entity which would be more attractive than either one of the two airlines in their present form."[10]

That same day, Collenette revealed that he was "considering" changing the foreign ownership restrictions, raising them from 25 percent to 49 percent. With this the share prices in both airlines jumped, welcome news for Milton now moving into Durrett's office. Three days later, Gerry Schwartz called him to announce that subject to the change in ownership rules, he was going to buy both Air Canada and Canadian Airlines and merge them together. Milton's baptism of fire was about to begin.

CHAPTER SEVEN

ROBERT MILTON: PARADISE WON

Robert Milton, Air Canada's chief executive officer, received a Christmas present on December 23, 1999 that his predecessors had craved for years: control of Canadian Airlines. Impossibly boyish, usually brash and blunt, he refused to gloat over the historic gift at the news conference.

"It's Christmas," Milton said. "I guess today I'm supposed to be happy and nice, so I'll try." Approval by the Competition Bureau on the deal with Canadian Airlines he had negotiated had just arrived. When asked if he felt vindicated by the victory after four months of struggle, his chubby cheeks broke into a smile. "There's no point dwelling on it," he told the assembled media. "We just get on with the future."

Milton was at the zenith of his popularity, admired for the skill and speed at which he had defeated a hostile bid from Canada's takeover king, Gerry Schwartz of Onex

Corp. and then went on to negotiate deals with Canadian Airlines, giant AMR, and finally the Liberal government, which had made no secret of backing Schwartz. In the new century about to begin, Milton faced equally difficult challenges. He had to merge two airlines that had been bitter rivals, pacify creditors, soothe employees' fears, and negotiate with militant unions that had extracted promises from Ottawa that there would be no layoffs in a restructuring of the Canadian airline industry.

Robert Milton had been preparing for a job like this since boyhood. Assuming command of an under-performing airline at a time of overcapacity, rising fuel costs, and a hostile takeover, he thought Air Canada, in his own words, a great airline but "with some lousy habits, most of them inherited from its days as a Crown corporation." By 1999, the flag carrier of Canada had consistently disappointed shareholders, employees, customers, and millions of ordinary Canadians. Many of his countrymen would have agreed with author Peter C. Newman, who said that if God had meant Man to fly, he wouldn't have invented Air Canada. "Back then, it used to be ABAC," remembered a former passenger. "Anything But Air Canada."

The third American to run the nation's flag carrier, Milton had the kind of childhood that aircraft-mad boys dream of. He first got "hooked" on aviation as a little boy — he was on a flight from the New York City area to St. Louis in an executive jet. "They let me up in the flight deck, and that did it." Milton was born in Boston, the eldest of three children. His father was a former State Department officer and now international businessman who moved the family around the world with regularity, from Boston to New York, Washington, Hong Kong, London, Beirut, Belgium, and Singapore. While other American kids grew up on their hometown streets, knowing only their neighbourhood, local schools, and McDonald's, the one constant in young Robert's life was airports and aircraft.

Even as a four-year-old, when he packed his suitcase to run away from home, he knew the exact airline he was going to catch to do so. David indulged his son's passion

Blunt, straightforward, controversial. Wunderkind Robert Milton merged Air Canada with Canadian Airlines, taking on Onex, AMR, and the federal government.

for aviation and when posted to Hong Kong in 1963 would take him to Kai Tak Airport to watch the aircraft skim over the Kowloon tenements on landing. Young Milton never forgot seeing his first Boeing 747 when the family moved to Belgium and later visiting the Boeing plant in Seattle where they were built. Even before he was a teenager he was familiar with the world of aviation, the airlines, their fleets, schedules, and routes. Other boys built model airplanes but Robert would also study flight schedules, pore over the specification sheets of each new airliner, and harass airline public relations departments for brochures and photos. As an adolescent in Singapore, he used to catch the bus to Changi Airport with his best friend Doug Green to spend hours watching airplanes. Listening to air traffic control instructions by radio and haunting the airport's runways to photograph aircraft and record their registration numbers got the two boys in trouble with the police. Doug wanted to become a pilot and would eventually fly for British Airways. But not Robert. "I was only interested in running an airline," he remembered.

To do that, he wanted to study business in university and applied to Georgia Tech in Atlanta. Not only was it his father's alma mater but Hollis Harris's as well. Graduating in 1983 with a Bachelor of Science degree in Industrial Management, the young man saw that, because of a downturn in the economy, there was little chance of being employed by a major airline. So when his father gave him $15,000 to buy a Jaguar, he began his own. Using their personal credit cards to pay for fuel,

he and a partner started Midnite Express, picking up contracts from the big courier companies for a small parcel business. Juggling schedules, dealing with employees, and maxing out their credit cards a few times, within five years the entrepreneurs were operating a regional feeder company in the southeastern United States with twenty-five aircraft, a perfect safety record, and a reputation for reliability. It was a better education than anything he had learned in college and by the time he sold Midnite Express in 1988, Milton, not quite thirty, had proved to himself that he could run an airline.

While he was working as a consultant for British Aerospace, a family friend introduced him to Hollis Harris. When Air Eagle failed, Milton followed Harris and Durrett across the border. Nothing demonstrated the government mindset in Air Canada for Milton better than what occurred one day when he was walking through the technical operations department. He noticed employees working in cubicles set against an outside wall. The windows that lined the wall were covered with brown paper. Was their view that bad? When asked for an explanation he was told that the employees along this particular wall were part of a compensation grouping level that did not qualify for a window at their place of employment; hence the brown paper. The arrangement, typical for a federal government department, was ludicrous to Milton in an airline no longer government-owned.

But while Milton loved aircraft, he never allowed the romance of aviation to obscure the impossibilities of making a "legacy" airline such as Air Canada profitable. "As much as I grew up loving airplanes and wanted to run the airline," he would say, "I realized that the airline was the worst business we had." With its international routes and business class, Air Canada might still command a premium, but saddled with baby boomer employee seniority, entrenched work rules, pensions, and operating costs, it would never compete with low cost start-ups like WestJet. Discount airlines were the future, Milton knew, but selling that to the employees of a former government airline would be difficult. He was also convinced that the various parts of Air Canada, if operated separately, could be worth more than the combined company and proposed that the company examine its various functional areas to look for divisions that could be stand-alone entities. Then Air Canada could consider each business for "carving out" (separately incorporating each subsidiary and selling a fraction of the shares) or "spinning off" (divesting through a distribution of all the new company's shares)."[1]

Officially becoming CEO on August 14 (the day after Transport Minister David Collenette's suspended Section 47), Milton looked forward to putting his "carving out" theory into practice and also contacting Kevin Benson to negotiate a merger. Even when he joined in 1992, he had always known that Canada's two major carriers would one day merge. "Ultimately, I thought it would happen," Milton explained, "but I had no idea when or how.

I sure as heck didn't guess the 'how' right."

But before Milton could contact Benson, Gerry Schwartz introduced himself by phone. "Hi, it's Gerry," he said. "Do you know why I'm calling?"

Milton had an idea but joked, "You want us to switch our in-flight catering from CARA to SkyChefs, right?" Aware that they were about to be thrust into the spotlight, the men then confined themselves to small talk.

With the approval of the Canadian Airlines board of directors for the Onex plan, in a televised conference in Montreal (significantly Air Canada's home base) on August 24, Gerry made public his "private sector" solution. "This is the time for a bold step," he announced. Onex Corp., with the backing of American Airlines' parent AMR, was bidding $1.8 billion to buy both Air Canada and Canadian Airlines and merge them into a single powerful entity. Once his AirCo had completed the purchase and merged them into a national airline, the new company would still be called Air Canada.

Based in Montreal, it would have projected annual revenue of $9 billion and rank as the twelfth largest in the world. The deal was valued at $5.7 billion, based on Air Canada's shareholder value ($1.5 billion), Canadian Airlines' equity ($54 million), and AirCo's debt ($250 million). AirCo would invest $1 billion with AMR, Onex, and related entities. AMR, which had agreed to invest $625 million, would own 14.9 percent of the new Air Canada and would take over the merged airline's reservations and accounting operations, but in time would sell these off. Onex would invest $250 million and own 31 percent but in time would also sell off its stake as well. The Canadian public would hold the remaining stock. Holders of Canadian Airlines common and non-voting shares would be entitled to receive either $2 cash per share or .24 common shares of AirCo. Holders of Air Canada common and Class A shares would receive $8.25 per share or one common AirCo share. The offer would expire on November 4 (later extended to the ninth), one day before the expiry of the ninety-day government suspension of the Competition Act. It would be conditional upon at least 66.6 percent of shareholders tendering their shares.

The only sour notes in Schwartz's proposal was that the new Air Canada would have to leave the Star Alliance and transfer to Oneworld, and an estimated 5,000 jobs would be cut because of duplication. Noting that both airlines had lost $2 billion since 1990, Gerry concluded: "This is an opportunity to stop the bloodbath." Later to gain public and political acceptance, he would also make what Milton termed "election promises" — major flight centres would be in Toronto, Montreal, and Vancouver, bilingualism would be upheld, and there would be a five-year ceiling on air fares and limits on employee reductions. In what was sure to gladden Air Canada and Canadian Airlines customers, Schwartz also promised to honour the frequent flyer points of both airlines.

Milton's memory of that August day

when Onex announced its plan to buy Air Canada was of Jürgen Weber, Lufthansa's CEO, phoning him to ask how he could help. "I didn't even get to watch the live press conference by the guy who's announcing he's about to take us over because Jürgen is on the phone: 'What can I do — where, when, how?' That's the kind of allies you need," he said. "Jürgen, who I consider to be the heart of the Star Alliance, asking what I needed for help." Having sold him SkyChefs, Weber knew Schwartz, aware that possibly his own money was being used to take over Air Canada.

Local media were not so kind. *Maclean's* reported that Air Canada was "blindsided" by Schwartz's announcement.[2] "Gerry Schwartz has the Right Stuff" applauded author Peter C. Newman in the same magazine. The *National Post* thought it akin to a Pearl Harbor attack, something that must have resonated among the airline's past and present American CEOs. "Hunkered down in their headquarters," the newspaper reported, "Air Canada's US-led management team was livid at yesterday's turn of events."[3] HOW THE MIGHTY HAVE FALLEN! was another headline.

Until August 24, Air Canada's management thought that they had the upper hand with their waiting-for-Canadian-to-die campaign. The Montreal airline knew that it had few friends in Ottawa, and after the mishandling of the January snowstorm even fewer elsewhere in the country. Who could blame it for being paranoid after the pre-emptive strike mounted by what looked like the Dallas–Toronto–Ottawa axis?

"A smart move — just like the old Gerry, the master of the leveraged buyout," applauded Bay Street. Fund managers who had made millions of dollars investing with Onex thought the deal very positive and recommended its acceptance to Air Canada's shareholders. Even the prime minister, no doubt relieved that a private sector solution for Canadian's perennial problem been found, got into the act. "We're not talking about somebody starting a new company here," Chrétien said. "Onex has been on the stock exchange for a long time.... He's not a guy who runs a nickel and dime store." Late night comics cracked that Milton was out shopping around for shark repellant.

Air Canada's initial public reaction to Schwartz's plan was to issue a pair of press releases that said: "It is difficult to see in the Onex proposal any benefit for Air Canada or its employees." It warned that should Schwartz succeed, control of the country's flagship carrier would be with AMR and Onex. After all those secret meetings, Air Canada senior staff was not a little hurt by Canadian's rejection of them in favour of a foreign suitor. Milton was especially disturbed by Benson and Collenette's summary dismissal of his last offer, made just three days before Schwartz's bombshell. "We felt that our proposal was a win-win-win situation for the issues facing American Airlines, Canadian Airlines, and the federal government," he said. "The rejection ... and the announcement of the Onex–American Airlines bid within days of the rejection make it clear that our offer

was not seriously considered. Based on our information, American Airlines would have had a veto over such a transaction, and presumably would have exercised it."

Schwartz countered that he had tried to arrange a meeting with Air Canada executives but had been turned down. Benson was surprised at Air Canada's lack of enthusiasm. "It's being offered to them under their own name, in their town, with them as CEO." he said. "Why are they turning it down?"

While everyone assumed Air Canada was busy assembling a counterproposal to the Onex bid, the airline was waiting to get the financial backing of its Alliance partners, Lufthansa and United Airlines. To buy time, the company adopted the "poison pill" strategy. This had been developed during the merger and acquisition madness of the 1980s, when Trans World Airlines was taken over and asset-stripped by Carl Icahn, so that it never recovered. To make future takeovers of this kind unpalatable, companies booby-trapped themselves so that corporate pirates couldn't convince their shareholders to sell them their shares. Air Canada swallowed such a "pill" on August 30, calling it the "Shareholder Rights Plan." In essence, it stated that lock-up agreement and voting arrangements in connection with a takeover bid over the 10 percent threshold would automatically trigger the pill. The airline issued one right for each Air Canada share outstanding. It gave the directors the discretion to call the "separation time," that is the rights were not exercisable until the separation time, which was the close of business on the tenth trading day after the date of the first public announcement of the acquisition of 10 percent or more of Air Canada shares and the commencement of an offer to acquire 10 percent or more of the shares. The "pill" stated that AirCo's August 24 announcement making the offer had triggered the separations time. Onex's lawyers knew that the poison pill would have to be neutralized, i.e. the courts would have to force the Air Canada board to remove it. This gave the Montreal airline time to mount a credible defense.

Milton scheduled a special meeting of shareholders for January 7, 2000, to consider the offer, the date two months beyond the Onex deadline and well past the Section 47 suspension window. AirCo immediately filed an application in Ontario Superior Court on September 7, arguing that its August 24 offer would fall victim to "serious prejudice" if the shareholders meeting was not held by November 8. Onex asked the Ontario court to force Air Canada to hold a shareholders' meeting by November 8, one day before its offer expired. To contest this, Air Canada hired as chief counsel Calin Rovinescu, known as a "takeover specialist" from the law firm of Stikeman, Elliott.

At Air Canada's September 2 board of directors meeting, Milton and a number of "designated senior management employees" were assured golden parachutes in a $1.95 million bailout package if they were fired or chose to resign if Onex succeeded in its bid. If for any reason he parachuted, Milton would be cushioned by thirty-six months of his base salary and bonuses. The

packages were tucked into Air Canada's thirty-five-page circular, mailed to shareholders who formally rejected Onex's bid.

All the players understood how power in Ottawa worked and that final approval for the Onex proposal rested with the cabinet. The government said it would rule on any proposed airline merger only after shareholders had approved it. Consequently, Onex and AMR lined up Ottawa's most powerful lobbyists to push for their takeover of Air Canada and Canadian Airlines. Within days of the bid being announced, according to filings with the federal lobbyist registry, Earnscliffe Strategy Group, Capital Hill Group, and Global Public Affairs Inc. were hired by Onex/Canadian Airlines to lobby MPs and federal officials and advise on how to sell the proposal to government. Canadian's board also had two key Chrétien loyalists among its members: Jean Carle, a former Chrétien aide, and Ross Fitzpatrick, a B.C. senator. The lobbyist connections were on top of the obvious links between executives at the two companies and the government. The country was going into an election and Schwartz was a well-known Liberal fundraiser. Against this, Air Canada hired the lobby firm of Government Policy Consultants Canada and brought in reinforcements in the person of the seventy-year-old Hugh Riopelle, its former "in-house House of Commons" lobbyist.

His predecessors had their problems with transport ministers — McGregor and George Hees, Pratte and Otto Lang ... but they were nothing compared with the antagonism between Milton and Collenette. Calling him two-faced, Milton would write that it was obvious the minister of transport was complicit in shaking down Air Canada on behalf of Onex and of all things American Airlines, in essence ceding control of both Air Canada and Canadian Airlines to the cowboys in Dallas.[4] Fearing that their boss had made too many enemies in Ottawa, Milton's staff hired Peter Donolo, the former communications chief to the prime minister as senior vice-president of communications. Fluently bilingual, the ever smiling Donolo had been Chrétien's spin doctor from 1991 to 1999 and was credited with "humanizing" the prime minister's image, making him more appealing to mainstream voters. Could he do the same with Milton?

For almost a month Air Canada was silent amid the fury of the Onex campaign. Milton would write, "Our silence unnerved Onex and American Airlines.... Without a response from us the Onex plan just lay there to be dissected and criticized by everyone with a point of view." Through these critical months Milton was seen as "combative," "abrasive," and "pugnacious" by the media. The new CEO later defended the way he responded to the Onex threat by saying, "When what amounts to your family comes under attack, you react in a certain way. The way I reacted was protective of people and a company I cared about. It was a very strange situation because there was a lack of clarity as to the law," he says, referring to the 10 percent ownership cap. "Because it was so strange, I think it warranted combativeness."

To his credit, Schwartz stumped the country like a politician, his let's-make-a-deal manner appealing to the battered Canadian Airlines employees and dismayed Air Canada shareholders alike. And his observation that those who had bought shares in 1988 "would have been better off burying their money in their backyards rather than investing in Air Canada" did have a ring of truth that many appreciated. On September 14, standing before the Haida Gwaii sculpture at Vancouver Airport, Schwartz spoke to employees of both airlines and later on a popular radio show took calls from appreciative listeners. Three days later he was in Montreal meeting with investors (including the Caisse), pointing out that the Onex proposal had already been responsible for increasing Air Canada's shareholder value to $12, almost double what it had been on August 24. Air Canada's attitude continued to baffle him. As with his other acquisitions, Schwartz expected that there would be offers and counter offers across a bargaining table. "What part of 'Yes' do they not understand?" he wondered aloud. "Under our proposal the headquarters of the new airline is in Montreal, the culture will remain fluently bilingual, the name will remain 'Air Canada', the senior management of the new airline will most likely come out of Air Canada."

But despite Schwartz's canvassing, Onex was still seen as the least trustworthy of all the players. In an Angus Reid poll taken between September 7 and 12, 54 percent of Canadians polled thought

Schwartz's plan to merge both airlines "unacceptable." Rightly or wrongly, Gerry was also seen as getting special treatment from his powerful friends on Sussex Drive in Ottawa. Hearing the political accusations, Schwartz snapped back. "There's all this innuendo about whether the 'fix' is in and did Gerry get a big favour from the Liberals? My reaction is really simple: look at our record. It is fantastic. I don't need favours from the government to succeed." A majority of Canadians thought the federal government, Air Canada, and even the cowboys at AMR more scrupulous. More than two thirds polled said that like opposition leader Preston Manning, they were reconciled to having a single national airline — but less than half supported the Onex bid. What was a surprise was that 33 percent of those polled thought that the minister of transport (i.e. the federal government) had completely lost control of the issue.

The airline's unions, Canadian Auto Workers (CAW), International Association of Machinists and Aerospace Workers (IAMAW), and Canadian Union of Public Employees (CUPE), were in an unenviable position through all of this since they represented the employees of both airlines. Judy Darcy of CUPE, for example, was responsible for 3,998 Air Canada and 2,565 Canadian Airlines flight attendants, and similarly IAMAW's Dave Ritchie led 19,000 baggage handlers, aircraft refuellers, maintenance men, and caterers of both airlines — including that of the Onex-owned SkyChefs.

CAW president Buzz Hargrove met with Schwartz and endorsed the Onex bid for control of Canada's skies on November 1, believing it to be the best security for his members of both airlines. The labour leader did not believe that Milton would meet the commitments that his union would get from Onex. Schwartz's Liberal connections, Hargrove thought, ensured that Ottawa would pour in millions of dollars to buy out the CAW members in the new airline. But Hargrove did not take into account the loyalty that Air Canada's CAW members had towards their airline. They accused him of selling out to Onex, and at a televised meeting on November 4, Air Canada workers roundly berated him. The decades of mistrust between both Canada's airlines boiled over, causing Air Canada employees, regardless of their union affiliation, to wear anti-Onex stickers and "Buzz Off" buttons to work, while their Canadian Airlines counterparts held rallies and chanted "Better dead than red" — red being Air Canada's colour.

Only the pilots of both airlines belonged to separate unions: Canadian's were part of the Air Line Pilots Association (ALPA), to which, ironically, United Airlines' (and soon Air Canada's Jazz) pilots also belonged, and Air Canada's belonged to the Air Canada Pilots Association (ACPA). After Schwartz said that a blanket approach would be taken to pilot seniority in any merger (Canadian Airline's pilots had more seniority), the ACPA refused to support the Onex bid.

Fed up waiting for the government to act, on September 3 Ritchie issued an ultimatum that Ottawa had thirty days to get directly involved and guarantee his members' jobs, or beginning September 27, his IAMAW brothers would "lay down their tools for as long as it took" in an illegal strike. Collenette, still busy denying that the Liberal government favoured the Onex bid, urged Ritchie to reconsider. The strike threat was called off when the minister assured Ritchie that whatever the outcome, his members' jobs would be safe. To his credit, during the air wars Milton kept close to Air Canada's employees by recording frequent messages to keep them abreast of developments, and inviting them to respond by voice messages or email. And he always replied to them, said company spokeswoman Nicole Couture-Simard.

Milton and Schwartz would meet on September 8 at the Toronto office of Stikeman, Elliott, where Air Canada formally received the Onex proposal. Milton would later write that Schwartz made a direct pitch to him to remain the CEO of the new Air Canada. "Robert," he said, "you're the guy who will be running things. I just want you to know that people who run companies for me make a lot of money. I can assure you that you'll be comfortable with this deal." Milton thanked him for the offer and said that he would think about it. The minutes of the meeting remain confidential, and all that was admitted was that no agreement was reached. Shortly after, Onex mailed the takeover bid to Air Canada shareholders so that they could consider it. Bay Street wisdom was that by playing a waiting game and postponing the shareholder's meeting until 2000, Milton was going to get the best deal

for his shareholders — better than the $8.25 that Onex had offered.

Frenzied trading began of the airline's shares by a new player, the Caisse de dépôt et placement du Quebec. Managing the pensions and savings of Quebecers, the Caisse was the airline's largest shareholder, already owning 19.9 percent of Air Canada's Class A non-voting shares. Because of its nationalist sympathies, the airline was hesitant to do business with (or publicize its connection with) the Caisse. But between September 8–10 the Quebec investment firm spent $80 million to buy 909,450 common shares, giving it a common share stake of 5.6 percent. Its mandate was to keep jobs in Quebec, and if the Onex proposal meant the loss of some 5,000 jobs (and many of those were thought to be at the main Air Canada base in Montreal), the Caisse was determined to use its $68 billion clout to prevent that.[5]

Air Canada fired its long expected opening salvo on Monday September 13, not at the bargaining table but in court. Challenging Ottawa's decision in the Federal Court of Canada to suspend the Competition Act, it wanted the bid subjected to a merger review by the Competition Bureau. Section 47, Air Canada's legal team claimed, was now useless because Canadian Airlines was "locked up." It could no longer share information with Air Canada, because due to its agreement with Onex, it could only talk to Oneworld members. Air Canada also attacked in two provincial courts. Proceedings were begun in the Quebec Superior Court challenging the legality of the Onex offer and an affidavit was filed in Ontario's Superior court to the effect that numbered companies linked to Onex had spent $43 million to buy Air Canada stock on June 15, one month before Ottawa had lifted the competition rules. Onex fired back that it was routine to quietly acquire shares in a targeted company so as to not to upset the market and that Onex had never tried to hide the acquisitions.

To prove that it was doing just fine without Onex, on September 17 Air Canada released its interim results for July and August. Not surprisingly, everything was up: operating revenue by 11 percent, passenger revenue by 3 percent, and passenger yield by 5 percent. Three days later, the company followed this with a director's circular that recommended unanimous rejection of the AirCo offer because it violated the Air Canada Public Participation Act, which limited individual holdings of Air Canada common shares to 10 percent. Then it also made public the details of the $2 billion offer it had made to Canadian Airlines on June 23.

What dogged Schwartz throughout the campaign was that he was seen as fronting for an American takeover of Canada's airline industry and of using his political connections to unfair advantage. Air Canada hammered home that the unsolicited bid by Onex, backed by AMR, was a back-door attempt by Americans to get control of Canada's skies. The media gleefully focused on AMR's "lock-up" clause, in which Canadian Airlines would have to pay American Airlines $500 million if

it were to break the business relationship between them. Collenette now admitted that while he knew that the Onex bid was in the pipeline before August 13, he had been unaware of the AMR "lock-up" clause. Milton thought it a landmine waiting to go off — what other booby traps awaited Air Canada if it merged with Canadian?

As the fight took on patriotic overtones, on September 22 Don Carty, the Canadian CEO of American Airlines, flew into Toronto to hold a press conference. Surrounded by Canadian flags, Carty (who hadn't lived in Canada for decades but maintained a cottage in the Ottawa Valley), accused Milton of being "an American CEO who's wrapping himself in the Canadian flag and turning this into a nationalist issue." AMR believed that the Onex proposal represented the opportunity to truly create a great airline, he said. His company had written off its investment in Canadian Airlines years ago. Yes, it was true that at first AMR would own 14.9 percent of the new Air Canada, while Onex would have 31 percent and other shareholders about 54 percent. But under the Onex merger proposal, Carty said, AMR would eventually sell its minority stake in the new airline. "The one weak part of our [American Airlines'] network is Asia and we intend to work with the new Air Canada to build Vancouver as the premier North American hub … there's nobody in Dallas interested in running a Canadian airline. We have 800 airplanes of our own." Carty's appearance only seemed to reinforce the public's anti-American view of losing what had now become a national treasure to Dallas.

Air Canada's directors issued a management circular on October 8, unanimously recommending that shareholders reject the Onex-AMR resolutions and forward their proxies for the vote to be held on November 8. The directors warned that under the AirCo offer Onex and AMR would own 38.1 percent of the new Air Canada. Meanwhile, the airline's publicity department launched a "Spread Your Wings" seat sale with reductions of 40 percent. It also offered special relief fares to earthquake-stricken Taiwan and made much of being the first to introduce the Airbus 330 to North America.

On the same day that Air Canada rejected the Onex resolutions, Schwartz held a news conference outlining his iron-clad commitments to the industry and the country to win support in the lead-up to the critical Montreal meeting of Air Canada shareholders — now a month way. Onex urged Air Canada shareholders to change their voting stock into restricted voting shares since this would allow them to skirt the 10 percent cap and tender to Onex's offer. The company could then go to the Liberal government and ask it to approve Onex's ownership of more than 10 percent of Air Canada. Schwartz said his company was committed to Canadian control, jobs, published airfares, service to smaller communities, competition, quality of service, bilingual service, seat sales, and frequent flyer points. "Upon completion of the merger, the shareholder rights that AMR negotiated with Canadian Airlines

in 1994 will terminate. Apart from a right to nominate two of the thirteen directors, neither American Airlines nor AMR will enjoy any special rights, controls or influence over the new Air Canada." In addition, Onex promised to appoint an ombudsman reporting to the new airline's independent directors to ensure that the commitments would be followed. "The new Air Canada will stand behind all its commitments for at least five years, which is well beyond the expected two-year integration period for the merger," Schwartz promised.

AirCo sent out its pink proxy forms to all Air Canada shareholders on October 13 to vote their shares against the "poison pill." The accompanying letter by Schwartz said: "This a unique time in the history of Air Canada and for you as an Air Canada shareholder.... We are committed to creating shareholder value. Who is going to look after shareholder interests, Onex or the same group that has been in charge for the last eleven years? Look at results and history, not just what they, or we, promise.... We invite you to join in the creation of a new Air Canada."[6]

Parliament was back in session by October 13, and given the media attention over the summer, strangely the airline debate barely figured in Question Period. This was because the Reform Party's MPs were from British Columbia and the West, where support for the Onex proposal was strong. It took the Bloc Québécois MPs to raise questions in the House whether Onex had known about Collenette's August 13 decision before the company acquired its

$40 million worth of Air Canada shares. While taking flak for this, the minister also found himself having to reassure members, especially those in rural ridings who would lose their air connections, that his government and not the private sector still had control over the nation's airline policy. "We want a Canadian solution," he said. "The market alone will not decide what is best for Canadians." His boss was more truthful. Asked on September 27 about the estimated 5,000 layoffs in the Onex proposal, Prime Minister Jean Chrétien sniffed, "We have never guaranteed everybody jobs. Even in the public service, we cut 20 percent of them."[7]

By now the suspicions of the Ontario Securities Commission (OSC) were also aroused. The timing of the Onex/AirCo purchase of Air Canada shares seemed too coincidental. If there was evidence that Schwartz knew of Ottawa's decision to suspend the competition rules before Collenette made it public, an OSC spokesperson stated, the commission would launch an investigation. Like a Greek chorus, federal officials continued to reiterate that Onex was not getting special treatment. The decision to suspend parts of the Canada Transportation Act until November 10 was based, they said, on many factors, chief of which was Air Canada's August 20 proposal to buy Canadian's international routes.

On October 15, just as Schwartz was meeting with Air Canada's financial advisors Nesbitt Burns Inc. to discuss his offer, the Star Alliance rode to the rescue.

Gathered in Tokyo that month to sign up All Nippon Airways and Singapore Airlines, the Alliance's CEOs understood that if they were to keep Air Canada in the group, something more than moral support was expected. The two most senior members, United Airlines and Lufthansa, announced that they had put together a rescue package consisting of a share purchase in Air Canada of $230 million, the lease of three Airbus 320s for $190 million, and the provision of a ten-year guarantee to Air Canada of $310 million. When the Canadian Imperial Bank of Commerce (CIBC) agreed to contribute $200 million, the two airlines also agreed to buy back up to 35 percent of Air Canada shares at $12 each to a total of $800 million. Finally, the Alliance CEOs had put together their own "poison pill" in the form of a departure tax to prevent any of their members bolting to Oneworld.

Air Canada's legal maneuvers were also beginning to pay off. On October 19, in response to the Federal Court application, the company got what it wanted from the Attorney General. When the Section 47 suspension ran out on November 13, so would the advantages it accorded the Onex proposal. In other words, any merger transaction would face the full weight of the Competition Bureau's review powers.

Four days later, buoyed by the financing from CIBC and the Star Alliance partners, Milton announced a $930 million bid to restructure the whole airline industry in Canada and also to launch a discount airline based in Hamilton.

Air Canada was to buy out Canadian Airlines at $2.00 a share, for a total of $92 million, then revive it as a distinct entity but with a smaller head office in Calgary. Canadian would be financially restructured, get out from under AMR's control, code share with Air Canada, and continue to operate its trans-border and international routes, where it would code share with all the airlines of the Star Alliance. Each of the companies would have a separate board of directors and management team. Existing service to all communities served by Air Canada, Canadian, or their subsidiaries would be preserved. Keeping Canadian separate would not only protect Air Canada from Canadian's debts but also keep its employees' wage gains and security intact. No shareholder would own more than 10 percent of the Air Canada voting shares. "We have taken the time to craft a plan that is practical and built on the untapped potential of Canada's airlines," Milton said. "Canadian Airlines is an airline with great people … its true potential has not been realized in recent years. Our solution is to unleash that potential."

Capitalizing on their strengths, the combined airline would be the tenth largest in the world. The two carriers would launch daily Toronto–Tokyo and Toronto–Hong Kong flights and also reactivate "dormant authorities" for routes including Vancouver–Shanghai, Vancouver–Sydney, Montreal–Milan/Rome, Toronto–Madrid, and Toronto–Amsterdam. Job cuts as a result of duplication would be half of those in the Onex plan. Only 2,500 employees from both airlines would be let go mainly through attrition, early retirement, and voluntary severance over a two-year period, but unfortunately Canadian would bear the brunt of them.

The plan was to be put to a vote by Air Canada shareholders on November 8, less than a week before the Section 47 suspension ran out on November 13. All were aware that any merger after that would face the scrutiny of the Competition Bureau. When asked for a response, Onex's Nigel Wright was sure that the shareholders would reject it. "At first glance it looks like the Spruce Goose — good on paper but it won't fly," he said.

Chaired by Stan Keyes, the MP for Hamilton West (who was teased by the other MPs that the discount airline would be called Hamilton Airways or Keyes Airlines), the hearings by the House Standing Committee on Transport on the future of the airline industry formed a backdrop to the Milton-Schwartz duel being played out in the media. Through October, the three main players in the drama, Collenette, Milton, and Benson, spoke at the hearings, the minister stating that the deadline for Parliament and all Canadians to give their views on the subject would be November 26.

The minister finally attempted to answer the questions that the media had plagued him with since August 13. The merger would be subject to a review by the Competition Bureau, and if Air Canada's shareholders did vote for the Onex proposal, Cabinet just might be willing to lift the limit on individual share ownership "to achieve a healthy Canadian-controlled airline industry." This last was fleshed out in the announcement on

October 26 detailing a restructured aviation industry. Called "A Policy Framework for Airline Restructuring in Canada," it was an attempt by Ottawa to level the playing field if Canadian Airlines failed and Air Canada became the dominant international carrier. Tabled in the House, under this "dominant carrier" policy, there would be:

- no reduction in the Canadian ownership and control requirements; the 25 percent limit on foreign voting shares would not be changed;
- government examination of the possibility of increasing the 10 percent limit of Air Canada's voting shares that can be held by one person;
- assurances that effective measures would be put in place to deal with predatory behaviour by a dominant carrier;
- government action to ensure that access to airport facilities would be allocated to enhance competitive domestic services;
- government requirement of commitments from the dominant carrier with respect to services to small communities during the restructuring process;
- government requirement of commitments from the dominant carrier that, during any major restructuring of the airline industry, employees would be treated fairly; and
- the introduction of legislation giving the government permanent authority over the review of any merger or acquisition affecting Air Canada.

Especially pertinent was the last point. It was further explained in the annex that any merger would be subject to approval by the governor in council on recommendation of the minister of transport and the commissioner for competition. Air Canada might no longer be a crown corporation but (its CEO felt) the government could still exercise control over it.

At the parliamentary hearings, Milton reminded the MPs that while he personally held that the 10 percent rule contained in the Air Canada Public Participation Act to be "shareholder unfriendly," he wanted to remind everyone that the Air Canada plan complied with all existing laws governing the airline and would not require legislative change in terms of either the 10 percent rule concerning individual ownership or the 25 percent rule concerning foreign ownership. Whatever money United Airlines and Lufthansa put in, they would get between them a 7 percent share of the non-voting stock. It was truly a made-in-Canada plan that respected the laws of the land.

As expected, at the hearings Benson called the allegations of AMR's subsequent control "fear mongering" and said that his hope was one day to see the slogan "Air Canada, a Canadian airline." Time, he warned, was running out for his airline, and as if to prove his point, Canadian Airlines reported third-quarter earnings of $71.3 million but a nine-month loss of $54 million. Perhaps nothing demonstrated Canadian Airlines' sorry state more than the sight of its eight beloved DC-10-30s being retired to Arizona, one of which was the famous *Spirit of Canadian* with its employees' signatures all over the fuselage.

AirCo raised the ante on October 28 by offering $13 for each Air Canada share, the company circular urging the shareholders to tender their shares to Onex. It also promised full national ownership, and control of the new Air Canada's AMR's rights would terminate on completion of the merger. Also, the merged airline would have the option of choosing AMR's SABRE as its information technology supplier. The circular derided Air Canada's offer as "totally and clearly unworkable" because "how would they finance $1 billion in payments and costs that would result from terminating Canadian's current relationship with American Airlines?" Two days later, Air Canada responded in a press release that the choice of SABRE came with a penalty of $250 million. How many more secret deals were there between AirCo and AMR? the release coyly speculated. Air Canada then applied to the Securities Commissions in Alberta, British Columbia, Ontario, and Quebec to force such disclosures.

While the unions in both airlines were furious that Milton was planning to start up a low-cost airline, which to succeed like WestJet would have to use non-unionized labour, Air Canada's CAW brothers were even angrier at their president. Hargrove did not think that Air Canada could meet the commitment that Onex had given him. There would be no involuntary layoffs, and up to 400 new jobs would be created in Montreal. Schwartz said that he had listened carefully to Canadians and would hold fares,

keep competition going, and keep services to smaller communities. That was enough for Hargrove, who on November 1 told a news conference in Toronto, "I am endorsing the Onex proposal to restructure the airline industry as the proposal that in the best interests of the members of our union." Milton, he said, had been given every opportunity to come up with wage and job commitments similar to those provided by Onex, and he hadn't come through.

Our trip was months in the planning and we were keenly looking forward to our trip (to England and Scotland). We missed our Manchester connection in Toronto due to mechanical problems with the aircraft from Calgary. At the gate in Toronto was Marija Brnardic, who helped us by confirming our re-booking to Manchester the next evening, walking us down to the baggage area to ensure our flights and tickets were in good order, and finally to get hotel and meal chits. The agent who served us there was Yusuf Sunar. By the time we left T1, we were outnumbered by your staff helping us! The next day, Dennis Bates was at the ticket counter, who was there the previous evening. He gave us confirmatory information and thanked us for our good-natured approach to the matter by increasing our class of service for the flight to Heathrow. Marija, Yusuf and Dennis all demonstrated every one of the best personal and professional elements of customer care and courtesy that one could expect.

You can be proud to have them working for Air Canada.

— D.M., St. Albert, Alberta

In its battle with Onex, Air Canada would hire as chief counsel Calin Rovinescu, known as a "take-over specialist" from the law firm of Stikeman, Elliott. Chief restructuring officer during the airline's 2003–04 restructuring, Rovinescu was appointed president and CEO on April 1, 2009.

Coming up to the November 8 deadline, both sides worked feverishly to woo the shareholders to sell their shares to them. The bids could not be compared per dollar since Air Canada offered to buy back only 35 percent of its shares and the Onex offer would be paid out of a combination of cash and stock. Now flush with cash from the Star Alliance, on November 2 Air Canada raised the stakes to $16 per share for up to 68.7 million common and non-voting shares, representing 36.4 percent of outstanding shares and generating a cash payment of $1.1 billion to its shareholders. But Onex countered with a bid of $17.50 per share, conditionally open for ten days, only if Air Canada left Star Alliance.

The Air Canada team knew that finding more cash wouldn't be easy; Lufthansa, United Airlines, the CIBC, and the airline's own coffers had given what they could. The only alternative was to go back to the Caisse, a politically controversial move for the nation's flag carrier. Through Thursday, November 4, Stikeman, Elliott's Calin Rovinescu and Rob Peterson, the airline's chief financial officer, negotiated with Caisse officials for more money. They came to an agreement early on Friday, November 5, with a $150 million loan and an option for another $150 million.

That Friday, while waiting for a ruling from the Quebec Superior court (which could go either way), Milton assembled his team in the Raptors Room (named because it contained an Air Canada A320 in Toronto Raptors NBA livery) near his office to go over the strategy of under-

mining the Onex offer. Then they heard the news. Justice André Wery of the Quebec Superior Court announced that while Onex's ploy for getting around the Air Canada Public Participation Act was "ingenious," it was also legally specious. Temporarily removing certain voting rights of the airline's common stock would allow Onex to skirt the 1988 Act that limited ownership of the airline. But the proposal was illegal because to temporarily convert its voting shares to non-voting shares (and also to retain the power to replace the Air Canada board of directors) contravened the Air Canada ownership limits.

"Onex is disappointed in the Quebec court's conclusion that shareholders cannot accept our offer," Schwartz said in a news conference carried live over radio and television. "Naturally we will respect that decision and accordingly have instructed counsel that our offers and resolutions be immediately withdrawn." Surprising many, Schwartz did not appeal the ruling, using neither his influence in Ottawa to end the 10 percent limit on individual share ownership nor adapting his proposal so that AirCo would never have more than 10 percent of the shares. Nor did he say if Onex would make another bid for Air Canada again.

His legal team could have appealed the Quebec court's ruling but it seemed that Schwartz had lost the will to drag on what promised to be an increasingly bitter and expensive fight. "We hope that Air Canada and Parliament will now act to remove this restriction [of the 10 percent rule]," he said. Having spent $28 million at $5.77

on average per share to acquire its foothold stake in Air Canada, it could now sell its shares at the current price of $9.90 for a net gain of $18 million. But the legal and lobbyist fees were sure to eat into that, and Nigel Wright concluded, "It's probably a wash. The gain is spent money." In the end, like every good gambler, Gerry Schwartz knew when to fold and walk away from the table. The ten-week very public brawl over the future of Canada's skies had ended.

Milton held that Schwartz's inability to win Air Canada over was because his lack of understanding of the airline industry, making "election promises" that he could never keep. Nor did he understand AMR's intentions when it gained control of Air Canada — later proven when American Airlines took over and gutted TWA in January 2001. Instead of attacking Air Canada with the hostile takeover bid, had Schwartz opened negotiations with him, especially since Air Canada's chairman Jack Fraser was a friend, who knows what might have happened? The real winner in all of this was thought to be the Caisse de dépôt et placement. Not only had the Quebec nationalist institution fought off a Toronto takeover, but also it kept Canada's airline industry in Montreal.

While all around him were popping corks and relishing victory on December 21, Milton was deflated. Just when they had gone cap in hand to the Caisse, Onex had conceded defeat, and it was a Quebec judge and not Air Canada that had defeated them. Milton had played a cautious waiting game, taking on Onex, AMR, and

Ottawa, and with help from his friends in the Star Alliance, he had thrashed them all. But the dogfight for Canada's skies should have been decided in the shareholders meeting, he thought — not in court. In a press release, Milton called the judge's ruling a victory and said that Air Canada's own proposal to its shareholders remained. At a news conference at the Dorval Hilton he told reporters that the brawl had been a wasteful ordeal that never should have happened. Instead of devoting his first months in the CEO's chair to running the airline, he had been diverted to fending off what he termed was "a supremely confident takeover specialist operating in partnership with one of the most aggressive corporations in airline history, both benefiting from the backroom machinations of the federal government." It had all been a waste of time and money, he felt. Since the Air Canada shareholders were no longer required to vote, the Air Canada CEO called off the special shareholders meeting scheduled for November 8.

Milton was very aware of what had occurred when Rhys Eyton took over Wardair, with its crippling debt. He was under no obligation to go through with the offer to accept Canadian Airlines and its monetary liabilities, obsolete aircraft, AMR shackles, and disparate groups of employees — all hostile to Air Canada. Had the merger not taken place, the Air Canada accountants later discovered, Canadian would have closed down on December 14 and in a free market economy would have followed TWA, Braniff, Swissair, and

Pan American into the dustbin of aviation history. As the victor, Air Canada could then pick clean the carcass, taking over the Far Eastern routes and favoured landing slots at Pearson Airport. In its annual report for 2000, Air Canada would piously state, "From the civic point of view, Air Canada's acquisition of Canadian Airlines was preferential to the latter going out of business. The collapse of Canadian would have ripple effects on the economy; over 16,000 employees would have been out of work and communities out of air service." The report then went on to conjure forth doomsday visions of stranded travellers, empty resorts, and cancelled hockey games.

But with all the jobs (and votes) at stake in Western Canada, Milton was convinced that the Liberal government had no intention of allowing Canadian Airlines to quietly die. If Air Canada did not take it over, warts and all, Ottawa would prop it up, keeping it alive zombie-like to wreak havoc on the already fragile airline industry ... or worse.

———

On hearing that Onex had pulled out, the transport minister must have suffered some palpitations. The federal government's scheme had failed. Speaking in Toronto on November 8, the minister vowed to put the whole messy airline business behind him. But a few days after the Quebec court ruling, Duncan Dee, Air Canada's manager of government relations, got a call from Randy McCauley, Collenette's chief of staff. Apparently the Canadian govern-

ment had made it clear to United Airlines (Air Canada's main source of financing) that Milton had better go through with merging with Canadian.[8] United Airlines was and remains the largest airline in the world, but even it did not want to go up against the government of a sovereign country. The message was clear. In a private conversation, Milton was made aware by Collenette that Canadian Airlines' Pacific routes and Pearson landing slots were the property of the government, which could if it wanted give them away ... say perhaps to Air Transat or Canada 3000. Or to a wealthy Liberal fundraiser who with the lucrative routes and slots could then start up his own airline. Milton would sourly conclude, "We had to catch a falling knife."

Others were not so sure. The *Globe and Mail*'s Matthew Ingram would write: "It was Mr. Milton's choice to take over Canadian Airlines, and the debt that he took on in order to do so — not to mention the restrictive union agreements he signed in order to secure government approval — weighed the airline down to the point where it could barely maintain altitude, let alone start to climb. It's clear that the Air Canada CEO and his team figured that with a virtual monopoly on the Canadian market, the company couldn't help but win."[9]

Watching it all unfold with interest that summer was Konrad von Finckenstein, the commissioner of competition. Impotent for ninety days, a week after Onex conceded, his office got its regulatory powers back. Collenette had stressed that for the government to approve any merger, it would first require the Competition Bureau's blessing. If Air Canada went through with its October 18 proposal to take over Canadian Airlines, would von Finckenstein approve it? If he disallowed it, Canadian would die and disappear. Whatever he did, it would mean the death of airline competition in Canada. The commissioner met with Milton in mid-November, reminding him of the restructuring policy tabled by the government in regard to competition — service to small communities, airport slots, treating employees fairly, etc. Unless he could extract some concessions from Milton, von Finckenstein threatened to prevent the merger. As for Canadian Airlines, left at the altar by Onex, its shares fell 18 cents to $1.44.

The suspense on its fate was broken on November 17. In a lengthy circular sent to Canadian's shareholders, Air Canada said that not only would it step in with emergency financing during the restructuring of Canadian's debt but agreed to buy the airline for $92 million, or $2.00 a share, through a numbered Alberta account, 853350 Alberta Ltd. This was 90 percent owned by former CIBC debt-restructuring specialist Paul Farrar and 10 percent by Air Canada. The offer for Canadian's 46 million common shares, at a cost of $102 million would expire on December 7.

There was speculation that American Airlines might refuse to sell its 25 percent share in Canadian to Air Canada. When Carty suggested that severing his company's ties with his former employer would cost

Air Canada at least $1 billion, in words that would return to haunt him, Milton said, "Canadian Airlines is losing $500,000 a day. The figure of $1 billion is pretty far-fetched and the sooner we can get on with sensible business-like discussions the better."

Canadian Airlines admitted on November 29 that the Air Canada bid was fair financially, but refused to recommend acceptance by its shareholders, asking instead for "clarifications." Was this a stalling tactic until AMR and Oneworld could come to its rescue? The Oneworld alliance CEOs meeting in New York at that moment put out a sanctimonious statement that Canadian Airlines was an important part of their network. Benson made a personal appeal to them, especially to AMR, to better Air Canada's offer. But when asked, Carty said that American Airlines wouldn't hang onto its stake in Canadian at any price. "Is [Canadian] a critical piece? No. No single piece is. This is not an issue that is critical to us, our alliance or anyone's alliance." On December 2, Benson returned from New York empty-handed. Bleeding $2 million daily, Canadian had been abandoned to its fate.

On Saturday morning, December 4, the last CEO of Canadian Airlines made a conference call to the airline's board members. The next day, worried about their own liabilities, the board recommended to the shareholders that Air Canada's $92 million offer be accepted. It was going to be a close thing since they would have one working day to convert their "share entitlements" (which were 20 percent of the airline's

When one compares Air Canada to other North American carriers, it is clearly on top. However, all North American carriers are truly deficient when customer service, in-flight services and overall passenger comfort are compared to European airlines (such as Virgin) or Australian and Asian airlines.
R.W., Thornhill, Ont.

When I wanted to make a change in my reservation (in Toronto), the person who answered my call treated me like a criminal. She told me that I should call their office in Mexico City (!) because that's where I bought my ticket. When I asked her for help, she hung up on me. Maybe she didn't like my accent. I will NEVER fly with Air Canada again.
A.L., Guadalajara

In some cases a flight on Air Canada may cost more, but in my opinion it is generally worth it. The planes are well equipped, lots of legroom, free newspapers, many direct flights, staff is always very pleasant and I have found the food good as well.
D.A., Hamilton, Ont.

I keep hearing how bad Air Canada is. I have never had a bad flight, bad service.... From what I could see on any flights that there have been any regrets, it is the rudeness of some of the passengers who think that they have a license to abuse the AC staff simply by purchasing a ticket.
J.A., St. Catharines, Ont.

shares) into the common shares that Air Canada needed. Air Canada extended the deadline for the takeover bid to December 23 while it negotiated with AMR.

Now that Oneworld had abandoned Canadian Airlines, Carty was forced to come to an agreement with Milton. "I wasn't entirely surprised," Milton said when he did. "Canadian was in a tough spot. American correctly came to the realization that without Air Canada participating, they could not fix Canadian Airlines. Oneworld knew that once Air Canada was free of the takeover attempt, they had to fix Canadian Airlines and that was too difficult."

American Airlines settled for a payment of between $55 and $60 million and some non-monetary issues. The potential payoff for AMR was that it would continue to supply some airline management services to Canadian, with Air Canada promising $83 million in windup and un-amortized startup costs if it cancelled these services. To provide Canadian with interim funding, Air Canada bought its access to Narita Airport Tokyo on December 14 for $25 million, purchased, leased back the A320 simulator that had Canadian had bought in September for $7.5 million and three of its Dash 8 aircraft for $13.5 million. It also increased Canadian's line of credit at the bank by $50 million. On December 8, Air Canada made public that it had gained control of Canadian Airlines and had also reached a deal with AMR to buy its stake.

Deputy transport minister Margaret Bloodworth negotiated guarantees from Air Canada that there would be no layoffs or employee relocation for a minimum of two years, and small communities would continue to be served. Also, to stimulate competition domestically, the regional carriers, Air BC, Air Ontario, and Air Nova (and soon to be acquired Canadian Regional Airlines) were to be sold off to private investors. This last Milton refused to do, agreeing only to unload Canadian Regional (if a buyer for its old F28 fleet could be found).

Following two weeks of negotiations, Air Canada and the minister of transport announced on December 21 that they had found "common ground" in the airline's bid to acquire Canadian. Determining that a merger was more pro-competitive than liquidation through bankruptcy proceedings, von Finckenstein also blessed the deal. Air Canada agreed to sell off Canadian Regional Airlines, surrender a number of slots at Pearson, honour all seat sales and frequent flyer points, and refrain from starting the discount airline until September 1, 2001. In addition it would continue to serve communities currently being served by both airlines and not lay off or relocate unionized staff until March 2002. Collenette, who had been the sorcerer's apprentice in creating the monopoly, mused aloud that he would be pleased to let foreign carriers from the United States or Britain's Sir Richard Branson in to fly domestic routes.[10]

———

Just forty years old, Milton had achieved what his predecessors Gordon McGregor, Claude Taylor, and Hollis Harris had wanted

for years: control over Canadian Airlines. The purchase also increased Air Canada's domestic market share from 65 percent to 80 percent. If he did not join the rest of his staff in popping the champagne it was because he realized that he had only won a battle in a war that was about to begin on two fronts: debt restructuring and employee integration.

"If Canadian were allowed to fail," he later said, "a big vacuum would have been created, which would have been very difficult for Air Canada to respond to quickly enough in terms of the capacity needed. We would have been in a tough spot. It also might have forced the government to allow foreign carriers in, in ways that really hadn't been needed previously. Who knows what would have happened? I liked the prospect of acquiring an operationally capable, customer service-savvy airline like Canadian and putting it under our wings and growing very quickly." After decades of accepting a duopoly — one private, one public — in railroads, steamships, as well as airlines, Canadians were not comfortable with a monopoly. Even Aeroflot now had domestic competition. Milton was aware that if he competed hard with an upstart airline, the Competition Bureau (to say nothing of the minister of transport) would scrutinize every detail. Because it wanted competition in commercial aviation, since Ottawa had kept Canadian Airlines in the air for years, so it would new entrants.

AIR CANADA KICKS GRANNY, 88, OFF PLANE: REGULATOR SAYS THEY WENT TOO FAR was a typical Air Canada horror story that year.

"They were very, very mean to me," Sarah Brownstein told the media from her home in Montreal.[11] The grandmother had just boarded an Air Canada flight from Montreal to Washington when the captain and flight attendant removed her from the plane (so roughly that she said she banged her head) and left her on the tarmac, all because she had refused to sit near the toilet. Deciding that she was not "self-reliant," the flight attendant wanted her to sit at the back so she could be near the washroom, but Mrs. Brownstein, who walked with a cane because of arthritis, preferred to sit at the front. The Canadian Transportation Agency (CTA) ruled that the captain and flight attendant had violated Air Canada policy and ordered the airline to hand over training reports on them and reimburse travel expenses incurred by Mrs. Brownstein's son-in-law, who had to fly up from Washington the next day to accompany her. Air Canada apologized and reimbursed the cost of the plane tickets for both Mrs. Brownstein and the son-in-law. But the airline defended the flight attendant's actions, saying that cabin crew are allowed to assess passengers who may be non self-reliant, adding that Mrs. Brownstein's limited mobility raised safety concerns since only one flight attendant was available for that flight.

This and other complaints led to the government establishing the office of the Air Travel Complaints Commissioner as part of the CTA. Collenette appointed former NHL referee Bruce Hood to the job. There was no love lost between Hood and Milton, and no surprise that in his first

year Hood discovered that 80 percent of the complaints concerned Air Canada. By the time he presented a scathing report on the airline to the House in May 2001, Air Canada had countered with its Customer Service Plan, in which it promised to report every fifteen minutes on the status of a flight, to provide meal vouchers, hotel and airport transfers in case of an unplanned overnight delay, and to resolve all complaints within sixty days.

———

Restructuring Canadian's $3.5 billion debt load, combining schedules, negotiating long-term labour contracts, and training thousands of Canadian employees on Air Canada systems must have been almost equivalent to the reunification of the two Germanys in 1990. The board of directors for Canadian Airlines resigned on January 4, 2000, and were replaced by Paul Farrar, Kevin Benson, Robert Milton, and Calin Rovinescu, the last now Air Canada executive vice-president, corporate development and strategy. On the same day, 853350 Alberta Ltd. acquired 82 percent of Canadian outstanding common shares and non-voting shares at a cost of $79 million. The convertible preferred shares from AMR were purchased the next day for $59 million.

Rupert Duchesne from Air Canada and Mary Jordan, Canadian's senior vice-president, were appointed to head the joint integration "QuickWins" team streamlining the operations of both airlines. Immediately changed were shifting capacity on some routes, especially where both airlines had competed. Through Air Canada and Canadian both flew A319s, the subtle differences in layout of cockpit controls meant that the pilots had to be retrained before flying the other company's aircraft. Symbolically, on January 30, Air Canada allowed a Canadian B737 to be brought into its Vancouver hangar for maintenance. A transitional paint scheme was applied to the exterior of all Canadian's fleet that included the Canada goose and red Canadian name on the white forward fuselage and Air Canada Maple Leaf on the green tail. As Chris Marshall, project leader of the Air Canada/Canadian transitional team livery project, said, "This is monumental when you consider the long-standing rivalry."

Paul Brotto, Air Canada senior vice-president, was appointed chief operating officer of Canadian on January 19. Brotto later remembered, "When I came in, Canadian operationally was running well: good service, good safety, and good on-time performance. But financially it was broke. It did not have enough money to meet the Christmas payroll."[12] Brotto was promoted to CEO on February 29 as Benson moved to Vancouver to become president of the Jim Pattison Group. Pattison was one of the three potential white knights that might have rescued his former airline instead of Gerry Schwartz.

Canadian Airlines filed for bankruptcy protection on March 24 and began debt restructuring under the Companies' Creditors Arrangement Act, Section 34 of the United States Bankruptcy Code, and the Court of the Queen's Bench of Alberta.

Beginning in February with negotiations with creditors until June, the process would take five months to complete. Secured creditors received 97 cents on the dollar, unsecured 14 cents. Securing the co-operation of the labour unions began on March 27, when the CAW reached a deal with Air Canada that took care of all of its members in both airlines, with ALPA following on May 31 and CUPE, IAMAW, and all other unions soon after. On June 1 Canadian officially left Oneworld and began code-sharing with Star Alliance, and the next day all Air Canada and Canadian operations were merged at Pearson Airport, with Canadian computer reservation systems moving from SABRE to Air Canada's ReserVec III.

It wasn't just the computers of both airlines that had to "talk" to each other. There were 22,991 full-time employees in Air Canada, 14,036 in Canadian, and their integration meant much more than offices being moved together, aircraft being repainted, and survivors donning the same uniforms. Terminal operations, city ticket offices, call centres, cargo warehouses, inflight services, IT systems, accounting, marketing job seniorities ... all had to be merged, pruned, and streamlined. Air Canada employees were prevented by their collective agreements from servicing Canadian's planes or passengers, who were now stampeding to Air Canada's ticket counters. And if the record number of bad weather days that summer were not enough, what took place at Pearson Airport was the height of chaos. With the help of the Greater Toronto Airports Authority, all other airlines were moved from Terminal 1 to Terminal 3 so that Air Canada/ Canadian Airlines could be consolidated at Terminal 1, which had to be refurbished and ready for operation by June 2. Toronto newspapers competed with each other in finding Air Canada horror stories: pensioners left stranded, high school students devastated when flights were cancelled, sports equipment lost, a passenger told by an Air Canada employee to shut up.... It was, Brotto said, the summer from hell.

The hero of the hour in December for taking on Onex and AMR, Milton soon discovered how fickle the public and parliamentary moods were. Appearing before the House Standing Committee on Transport through May 2000, he and Brotto endured the barrage of complaints from members of parliament who came armed with frustrations from their constituents, everything from price gouging to being left on the phone for hours to arrogant onboard service. Rather than the David who had battled Gerry Schwartz, Milton was now seen as the Yankee intent on defiling a national icon. "Mr. Milton, everything you do you just hurt, hurt, hurt," Liberal MP Joe Sekora postured, enjoying the press coverage he knew it would get him, " ... destroying cities, communities, businessmen, travellers, tourist bureaus...." Only orphans, widows, and kittens it seemed, had escaped the demonic foreigner's clutches. One media commentator remarked that not since the Americans burned York (present-day Toronto) on April 27, 1813, had such xenophobia been rampant.

The House grilling was a prelude to what the Air Canada CEO later faced at the AGM. Once thought to be the panacea for forty years of duopoly, the merger was now seen as unwieldy and unworkable. Milton took such a public flogging in Parliament, the media, and by shareholders that even Gerry Schwartz sympathized, saying that he bet Mr. Milton now wished Schwartz had won.

Following approval by the creditors, the Court of Queen's Bench of Alberta approved the plan of arrangement on June 27, 2000, so that Canadian Airlines could become a wholly owned subsidiary of 853350 Alberta Ltd. Subsequently, Air Canada acquired the remaining 90 percent of the common shares of 853350 Alberta Ltd. The court ruling approved the restructuring as "fair, reasonable, and equitable" because it saved over 16,000 jobs and preserved the integrity of the national transport system, allowing the Air Canada CEO to say, "With this ruling, we can implement the financial restructuring and close the purchase of Canadian Airlines by Air Canada."

Canadian Airlines, now a wholly owned subsidiary of Air Canada and no longer a Oneworld alliance member, could reinstate its direct service to Sydney, Australia from Vancouver on July 7, a route that its North Stars had pioneered in Grant McConachie's day. Shanghai, another McConachie prize, was added in November, the second entry into China. Canadian Regional Airlines was put up for sale as the Competition Bureau wanted, but when there were no buyers after sixty days, it was integrated

The de Havilland Dash 8s became the workhorses of the Regionals. Great Lakes Airlines morphed into Air Ontario to become an Air Canada Connector and finally Jazz.

into the Air Canada regional system. In 2001, with the labour agreements in place, Canadian Regional would join Air BC, Air Ontario, and Air Nova as Air Canada Regional (ACR), their fleets streamlined from the F28s and the Dash 8-100s to Canadair CRJs and soon Dash 8-400s. On May 27, 2002, ACR would be relaunched as Air Canada Jazz.

Merging in one of the busiest air travel summers on record invited chaos, frustration, and the weeping and gnashing of teeth. Worldwide, the economy was booming, and as a sign of what was to come, Air Canada's April 2000 traf-

fic was up 25.3 percent over April 1999, resulting in a passenger load factor of 75.7 percent. By June the passenger load factor had climbed to 78 percent with customers lured to Air Canada by the new Express Check-In kiosks, seat sales, and in-flight email and Internet services.

———

With Canadian's death throes as drawn out as Mimi's in *La Bohème*, airline entrepreneurs had ample time to fill the vacuum, each entrant seeking a niche market to lure passengers away from competitors. In 1995, Ken Rowe, the Maritimes millionaire, bought Air Atlantic in a fire sale from British Aerospace and allied it with Canadian Airlines. Looking to expand, in August 1998 Rowe issued an ultimatum to Canadian Airlines for more jets to more places, or he would shut it down. Canadian Airlines called his bluff and Rowe was forced to close Air Atlantic down. But by May 2000 he was so impressed with WestJet's model and success that he began an Eastern Canada version called CanJet Airlines, based in Halifax. Losing heavily on its Moncton–Toronto route, by February 15, 2001 CanJet joined in accusing Air Canada of "capacity dumping" and predatory pricing.

After the profit of $140 million the year before, Air Canada ended the year 2000 with a loss of $82 million. Signalling stormy weather ahead on December 22, Milton announced that he would cut 3,500 jobs and that higher fuel costs would force a 6 percent fare hike. It had been a tumultuous year; with the merger the airline had grown 44 percent and now controlled 70 percent of the domestic market and over 50 percent of the Canada-U.S. trans-border market.

That any start-up airline in Central Canada would go up against such odds was lunacy. Two Toronto-based charter carriers, Angus Kinnear's Canada 3000 and Michel Leblanc's Royal Aviation Inc., entered the scheduled market. Perhaps no one epitomized the discount airline mania better than Michel Leblanc, who in his lifetime would run seven airlines, having once been instrumental in merging Nordair with Quebecair to form Inter-Canadian,

later Intair. Transitioning from a charter to a full-service airline had been a bridge too far for Max Ward. Analysts wondered how Kinnear and Leblanc would fare. With the approval of 94 percent of its shareholders in March 2001, Royal Aviation merged with Canada 3000. The following month, Ken Rowe was relieved to sell CanJet's assets (but not the name) to Canada 3000 for $7.5 million.

Now the second largest airline in the country, Canada 3000 sought to challenge Air Canada on the Toronto–Montreal–Ottawa triangle, called the "Bermuda Triangle" in the aviation world because so many start-up airlines had disappeared into it. Canada 3000's CEO, Angus Kinnear, also looked to capitalize on Toronto's Asian market and to fly to India using an A340. His airline had become the poster boy for competition in Canada, the government hoping it would, as Canadian Pacific Air Lines had once, serve as a check on the dominant airline.

Most bizarre of all entries was Roots Air, launched by the Toronto charter company Skyservice Aviation. Its CEO, Russ Payson, believed he could raise enough capital to start an airline that would give businesspeople an alternative to Air Canada's unpopularity and WestJet's basic service. Using Branson's Virgin Atlantic Airways as a model, in June 2000 Payson gambled on the glamour of the athletic clothing company Roots Canada and actor Dan Aykroyd to "brand" his airline Roots Air. Aykroyd was known to Canadians for, amongst his many other prominent roles, playing Avro boss Crawford Gordon in a television movie about the ill-fated Avro Arrow — a poor omen for what was about to take place. Even before it had flown, Roots Air added its name to the list of airlines that accused Air Canada of predatory pricing. By the time it was launched on June 7, 2001, investor capital had dried up but Payson was committed. If a former record store promoter like Richard Branson could take on British Airways through his panache, why not him? Roots Air's initial route network was modest enough, Toronto–Calgary–Vancouver and hopefully one day Los Angeles. Its fleet of Airbus A320s was divided into Gold, Silver, and Bronze classes, like Olympic medals. Roots "Class" service was to be everything that Air Canada and WestJet weren't: luxurious, friendly, and hip.

But the sheep were in the wolves' territory, and Milton and Rovinescu worked the alchemy of yield management to their advantage, matching or undercutting all entrants' fares and offering Aeroplan points as well. Roots Air was the first to die, ceasing operations on May 4, barely forty days after launch. A faltering global economy was slowing business travel to a crawl, and once the darlings of the airlines, businesspeople were now working the Internet for bargain fares, unwilling to pay for the amenities that Gold and Silver Class offered. Besides, there were a total of twenty-one Air Canada and WestJet daily flights on the Calgary–Toronto route. It wasn't only passenger loads that were disappointing; lack of availability of aircraft meant that one of the aircraft that Roots Air was forced to use was an old ex-Greyhound B727. Payson

said that the decision to suspend flights "was the fiscally responsible thing to do ... made after consideration of the dramatic changes in the airline landscape in Canada." But there was a "strategic arrangement" in place to cushion the abrupt landing.

Almost immediately after announcing a first quarter loss of $168 million, Air Canada then found $15 million to buy a 30 percent stake in Skyservice Aviation and a 50 per cent voting/35 percent non voting interest in Skyservice Airlines, the carrier saying it would also honour all Roots Air tickets issued on its own flights. It seemed that by using Skyservice's non-unionized workforce Milton had his discount carrier after all, and service was scheduled to begin in July. It didn't take long for Clive Beddoe, WestJet's chairman, and the Air Canada Pilots Association (ACPA) to object strongly to this. But when July came, the ACPA allowed Milton to begin an internal discount airline with its pilots being paid less, and Skyservice was dropped.

———

For Milton (as for the airline CEOs of legacy carriers around the world) it was a race against time; the discount start-ups were snapping at his heels. To compete with WestJet and now Canada 3000, his low-fare alternative had to be seen by the travelling public as dramatically different from Air Canada. Modelled on JetBlue in the United States, it was to be called "JetRed" and be based in Calgary, West-Jet's home base. But creating a brand new airline would mean beginning the glacially slow process of getting an operating certificate from Transport Canada. Designing a low-cost carrier within Air Canada by cannibalizing planes and using his own airline's personnel was quicker. "Why does a full service airline need a discount brand?" the company's annual report explained. "The same reason why full service grocery chains also have no-frills stores where customers pay for bags or brings their own.... Discount carriers are consistently profitable. It's time to join them." This version of "JetRed" would be based at Pearson Airport and fly between mainline cities with a few Florida destinations thrown in.

As with Roots Air, it was all about branding: different logo, fleet livery, and customers' expectations from the mother airline. The only problem was that JetRed would still have to use expensive unionized staff, both onboard and off. Cabin crew was cut to a minimum; the number of flight attendants allowed by Transport Canada was one for forty passengers, which ensured cost savings there. To be launched in the fall of 2001, the low cost carrier, now christened "Tango" (from "Tan and Go"?) was a point-to-point service with limited frequencies, no baggage interlining privileges, cheaper but nonrefundable fares, fewer Aeroplan miles, and completely e-tickets with 80–85 percent of its sales from *flytango.com*, the rest from its own call centre. When the ACPA allowed him to move twenty aircraft to "JetRed," Milton ensured that they were fuel efficient, low-maintenance A320s. The A320s would have nineteen more seats crammed into them than the same aircraft

on the mainline (but with the same legroom as their mainline sisters), and as on WestJet, customers would have to pay for snacks and headsets.

What fascinated observers was that Tango was to compete head-to-head with Air Canada on all its mainline trunk routes out of Pearson Airport. It didn't have to make more money than Air Canada, just lose less. Milton described Tango's operation like an accordion. "In tough times there will be more Tango and less green airplanes and when times improve, more green, less Tango."[13]

Across the river from the Parliament Buildings, the Competition Bureau's von Finckenstein ensured that Air Canada, like Caesar's wife, had to be above suspicion. When WestJet chose to make Hamilton its Eastern hub for Maritime expansion (the underused John C. Munro Airport was cheaper than Pearson and in the middle of the "Golden Horseshoe," the densely populated western end of Lake Ontario), Air Canada took swift action, not only against WestJet but also CanJet (now part of Canada 3000). Milton was determined not to yield market share to Beddoe. Fares were slashed and extra flights and larger aircraft were put on between Moncton and Pearson Airport. The fares for all three airlines on the same route were close enough, but WestJet and CanJet couldn't match the frequent flyer points and worldwide connections that Air Canada could give its customers. Nor did passengers like being dropped so far out of Toronto without access to connections at Pearson Airport.

WestJet couldn't compete and joined the chorus in accusing Air Canada of predatory behaviour. A year later, when Bill C-23, an act to amend the Competition Act and the Competition Tribunal Act was discussed in the House, Beddoe appeared before the committee to explain how it was done: "Air Canada was charging $605 one way between Moncton and Toronto. They announced they were going to cut 20 percent of capacity out of the route. We announce we're going in there. Air Canada immediately adds 50 percent more capacity and drops their walk-up fare because ours was at $350 versus their $605. I'm not suggesting they can't match our fare, but there are two things: adding capacity and undercutting. They turn around and cut their walk-up fare to $250, add 50 percent more capacity, and add double and triple mileage points on top. For what purpose? Then they have the audacity to suggest they're making money doing it."[14] In January 2004, WestJet moved the focus of its Eastern Canada operations out of Hamilton to Pearson Airport.

In July, the federal government would pass legislation to govern the burgeoning competitive airline environment by increasing the powers of the Canadian Transportation Agency (CTA) on domestic airfares. Following complaints filed against Air Canada, the Agency determined that the lowest return fare offered by Air Canada between Prince Rupert and Vancouver was unreasonable when compared with lowest return fares on a comparative route. In October, the Competition Bureau required Air Canada to cease offering competitive discount fares on certain CanJet routes, and in early March 2001 would prohibit the airline from engaging in anti-competitive practices with WestJet as well. It was a slap on the wrist, Beddoe thought, and wanted the tribunal's powers strengthened so Milton would think twice about repeating this. It would not be long, he knew, before Air Canada came after WestJet.

———

Much to the relief of Paul Brotto, Air Canada no longer needed to operate Canadian Airlines as a separate entity — something promised during the Onex war — and the Canadian Airlines brand could be dropped within a year. Keeping Canadian on life support had been costing Air Canada $2 million daily, the aircraft fleets were, with the exception of the A320s incompatible, the 2,500 voluntary early retirement packages that had been offered to the employees of both airlines cost $100 million, and those Canadian employees staying on saw their wages increase to parity with their Air Canada colleagues. On October 5 Laura Cooke, Air Canada's manager of media relations, explained. "The airline changed course when it realized just how bad the financial situation was at Canadian when it acquired it in January. We developed the blueprint without having access to Canadian's true financial position.... It quickly became clear that Canadian was not viable as a stand-alone company."[15]

Now the three million members of "Canadian Plus" frequent flyer program could be integrated into Air Canada's Aeroplan. Online services moved from *www.cdnair.air* to *www.aircanada.ca*, and Canadian's aircraft switched from SABRE's Flight operations System (FOS) to Air Canada's Flight Management and Integration System (FMIS). Mutual code sharing with Canadian and Air Canada operating out of different terminals in Pearson until June created for confusion among passengers and taxi drivers alike. It would not be until September 25, 2002 that the Canadian Industrial Relations Board declared that Air Canada and Canadian to be a single employer with respect to all bargaining units, allowing for a complete intermingling of their workforces.[16] Canadian Airlines would disappear seventy-five years after James Richardson began its ancestor, Western Canada Airways. On May 31, 2002, the Air Canada ID/travel replaced the ID/travel cards of Canadian employees and retirees. For the public, Canadian Airlines vanished on the weekend of October 21–22, 2002, when all tickets were issued in the name of Air Canada only and airport information monitors no longer listed Canadian Airlines flights.

The legislative action necessary to allow the merger was contained in Bill C-26, An Act to Amend the Canada Transportation Act, the Competition Act, the Competition Tribunal Act and the Air Canada Public Participation Act and to amend another Act in consequence, which came into force on the 5th of July.

With it, the historic duopoly that had begun with the Air Canada Act in 1977 was effectively extinct.

———

By the second quarter of 2001 the airline had lost $108 million. Its biggest corporate client, Nortel Networks Corporation, was steadily collapsing, its stock going from $46 to $12 in months. Business travellers were looking for lower shares online.

To raise funds, on May 15, Aeroplan, Air Canada's frequent flier program, would be converted into a wholly owned subsidiary for eventual spin-off to attract investors. If things weren't bad enough already, in June the airline would be fined $1 million as part of settlement with securities regulators.

One of the legacies of its Crown corporation days was that at the end of 2000, the average number of Air Canada employees per aircraft totalled 165, excessive when compared with the U.S. industry average of 137 employees. On July 4, Milton sought to cut payroll costs by asking employees to voluntarily take a leave of absence or work reduced hours.

The "unbundling" program so dear to Milton's heart was sure to bring in some cash. Jazz, its unprofitable regional airline, was a prime candidate for sell off (as the government had hoped), as was Airport Ground Handling Services and Air Canada Technical Services, which would be transformed into a standalone profit centre with a mandate to begin a third party maintenance, repair, and overhaul (MRO)

A Canadian Airlines Boeing 747 on final approach at Hong Kong's Kai Tak Airport. For Air Canada, landing rights for Hong Kong, Osaka, and Seoul were all it wanted from its rival.

business.[17] When airlines are in trouble they sell and lease back their aircraft, and Air Canada did just that, going from ownership of 47 percent of its fleet in 1997 to owning just under 4 percent by February 2003. With the slowing economy, job cuts, and Canada 3000's success, there was not going to be any growth in 2001.

———

To negotiate aircraft financing with British banks, on the evening of September 10, Milton caught the flight to London. He must have been quite pleased with himself. A few days before, *destina.ca*, the airline's Internet travel services portal, was launched. It would cut down on the commissions that the airline paid travel agents. Next month the discount carrier Tango would begin operations. All in all, he was looking forward to a break-even third quarter. Arriving at Heathrow Airport the next morning (where as a boy he had spent golden hours watching aircraft movements), he checked in at the airport's Renaissance Hotel, which overlooked a runway. He was napping before the meeting began when his secretary called. An aircraft had crashed into the north tower of the World Trade Center in New York. Milton switched on the television in time to watch the second airliner hit the south tower and explode.

He called Rob Giguere, then executive vice-president of operations in Montreal, to have the cockpit doors on all Air Canada aircraft locked immediately, and even before NAV CANADA did, he told the pilots to land the aircraft. Sixteen Air Canada planes with 110 crew and 2,200 passengers were soon to be stranded outside Canada, some in locations where the airline had no facilities, their flight crews becoming their custodians. Then he sat down on the bed to watch incredulously

On May 27, 2002, Air Canada Regional would be relaunched as Air Canada Jazz. Spun off in 2006, its latest incarnation would be as Air Canada Express in 2011.

with the rest of the world the crashes into the Pentagon and a Pennsylvania field and the Federal Aviation Administration halting all flight operations across the United States for the first time in history.

In Canada at 10:00 a.m. EDT, on the order of the minister of transport, NAV CANADA directed its operational facilities to ground all air traffic. The Notice to Airmen (NOTAM) issued to pilots at 10:43 a.m. read: "Due to extraordinary circumstances and for reasons of safety, all departure services from NAV CANADA served aerodromes are ceased effective immediately. Due to closures of U.S. airports and airspace all National Traffic will be recovered in Canada." At 12:28 p.m., the minister of transport ordered the closure of Canadian airspace. NAV CANADA was to recover any aircraft flying, both domestic and international, as soon as possible. Typically, about 1,500 aircraft would be flying in Canadian-controlled airspace at the time the order was issued.

In what would be called "Operation Yellow Ribbon," some 220 foreign aircraft were ordered to land at sixteen Canadian airports, from Whitehorse to St. John's. At most locations, Air Canada was the only operator capable of offloading the 44,000 passengers from those planes and providing maintenance for their aircraft. Wherever they were, the airline's employees rose to the occasion, assisting their own grounded passengers and those of other airlines. Many cancelled their vacation plans to help, some working twenty-four hours for the four days that all aircraft were grounded. They

opened their homes to strangers, provided supervision to unaccompanied minors, and brought coffee, donuts, and sandwiches to the airports. It was, Milton would later write, "human nature at its best, a sterling silver lining on the dark cloud that hung over humanity that fateful Tuesday morning in September."

Wayne d'Entremont was the safety and regulatory auditor at Halifax Airport that day. With four other Air Canada employees from the Atlantic region, he was about to begin de-icing training for the upcoming winter season. "None of us realized what was about to unfold on that fateful day." Shortly after the morning session began they were told to gather their marshalling equipment and meet the airport duty manager on the ramp. There was no time to explain as they began to set up the Emergency Command Centre to deal with whatever was happening. "The news was now clear, the United States, namely New York, was under attack." They met with the waiting airport duty manager on the ramp and in the short drive to runway 15-33, now designated as a parking lot for up to 100 aircraft, he briefed them on what was taking place and what was going to be required. Said d'Entremont:

We had approximately twenty minutes to come up with a plan on how to park what eventually became forty-seven wide-body aircraft, with the ability to get service and emergency vehicles to any in case they were needed. We figured that

287

if we put them in a herringbone pattern, wing tip to wing tip, that we could fit literally 50 percent more aircraft in the same space. We just started parking them. They came in one right after the other. The term I've used in the past is 'It's raining aluminum.' Once all the aircraft were parked, the passengers remained onboard for many more hours until the authorities figured out what to do with them. Nearly 8,000 passengers were now stranded in a province they had never heard about.

When the passengers finally disembarked and entered the terminal, Air Canada staff were on hand to greet and assist them. Many of the airline's Halifax Sales and Management team spoke other languages, a talent was not wasted on that day. What amazed the staff greeting the passengers were how calm they were despite the many hours stuck in an aircraft. They were grateful to be on safe ground and taken care of. The city of Halifax prepared for the invasion of passengers, not knowing how long they would be here, as the air space was closed to all air traffic for an undetermined amount of time. Schools, church halls, auditoriums, and private homes were opened to welcome the unexpected guests.

Wayne brought home two stranded fellow Air Canada employees from out of town and gave them each a room for however long it took.

"In a time of crisis," Wayne concluded, "it is amazing what can be accomplished when Air Canada employees work together in conjunction with the Halifax Airport Authority and the other handlers at the airport in time of need and help stranded passengers, regardless of who was on board or what dangers may have been present at that time."

Although he had complete confidence in his staff in Montreal, Milton knew that he had to get home. With all transatlantic flights grounded, he called Bombardier and was able to hitch a ride to Montreal on a Challenger that was in Germany. He caught it at Luton Airport outside London with Calin Rovinescu, who had been vacationing in Spain on September 11. The flight was only possible because Minister of Transport David Collenette had used his influence to obtain clearances from the British, American, and Canadian authorities to do so.

As usual, Milton, the consummate aircraft buff, sat with the crew in the cockpit of the Challenger. Flying the Atlantic with fighters patrolling the skies made him nervous. "I asked the pilot if he felt comfortable about the flight, and he shrugged and said, 'I've got a fax here that says it's okay. If a fighter shows up off our wingtip, I guess I'll just hold it up to the window and let him read it."[18] What was strange about the flight across, Milton recalled, was the complete silence on the airwaves — no chatter from pilots or air traffic control, "Perhaps the first time," he mused, "this had taken place since Lindbergh had flown the Atlantic." But while the public may have applauded his action, because Milton was in an aircraft not flown by an Air Canada pilot, contrary to union agreement, the ACPA filed a grievance against him.

The events of September 11 had a significant adverse impact on the airline industry worldwide, and the International Air Transport Association (IATA) estimated that in the following week the world's airlines lost $10 billion. Historic national carriers like Swissair and SABENA (the latter had begun in 1923) vanished, as did Ansett-ANA, Australia's second carrier. North American airlines, already in financial trouble with the weak economy, were now on the brink of bankruptcy and laid off thousands of their employees. Even as the tragedy unfolded, insurers were already withdrawing coverage from all airlines. Before September 11, the chances of a terrorist act in the air were considered so remote that aviation insurers wrote insurance for third-party liabilities from acts of terrorism and war at no additional charge. The cover for damage done to people and property on the ground was part of airlines' "all risk" insurance, which also covered the aircraft and its passengers. Because the events of September 11 caused billions of dollars of damage to third parties, cover for third-party terror risk became the hardest to get and the most expensive of all insurance policies for airlines.

The first post 9/11 Air Canada flight took off on September 13, and it would be six days before the airline was operating at something approaching its normal schedule.[19] The four days that all of its aircraft were grounded cost $100 million in lost revenue. The fourth quarter operating loss, $308 million, and fourth quarter passenger revenue would be down by $440 million, or 20 percent. Domestic passenger revenue was down $552 million, or 13 percent, and international passenger revenue by $150 million, or 6 percent. The U.S. transborder market was the most adversely affected, with fourth quarter passenger revenues down 30 percent. On the other hand, because of reduced flying, staff layoffs, cost savings, and favourable fuel prices, the corporation also saw a major reduction in operating expenses compared with the fourth quarter of 2000. Also, alternate revenue was generated when four B767s-300s with crews were leased to QANTAS as that airline coped with Ansett's bankruptcy.

The world's airlines lost $15 billion, and the six largest full-service airlines in the United States alone (Air Canada's peer group) lost $5.1 billion in the fourth quarter of 2001. Canadians watched on television as President George W. Bush promised his country's aviation industry a $24 billion bailout package. Would Ottawa do something similar for the airlines in Canada? The answer was quick in coming. On September 19, little more than a week after 9/11, Milton announced on the CBC–TV's *The National* that he wanted between $3 to $4 billion in taxpayer dollars for Air Canada alone. It was an ill-timed interview and the figure sounded arbitrary. To the public he was using the tragedy of 9/11 to paper over the cracks evident in mismanagement before that fateful day.

The CEOs of other airlines in Canada were appalled. Air Transat was about to lay off 1,300 employees, and John Lecky, Canada 3000's chairman, announced that unless it received immediate aid the airline was applying for bankruptcy protection. Only WestJet seemed unaffected by 9/11; Clive Beddoe had just moved into his new hangar and head office at Calgary's airport. Without international routes in 2001, WestJet would generate $37.2 million, a 23.0 percent increase in net earnings from $30.3 million in 2000.

For Milton it was all about levelling the playing field. WestJet, Air Transat, and Canada 3000 didn't fly across the border — only Air Canada did, and soon it would be competing with the resuscitated American carriers. On September 25, Ottawa threw him a bone and rescinded on its "no layoffs pledge" at Air Canada. The next day Milton announced that 5,000 employees would be terminated. Because of the integration of Canadian Airlines, the staffing levels had made for a bloated company. On October 2 the government announced that a $160 million bailout package would be approved — for the whole Canadian airline industry. Air Canada's share of that was a paltry $100 million, and lest Milton appear ungrateful, by April 2002 this was reduced to less than $70 million.

The American CEO's confrontational attitude towards Jean Chrétien's government distressed the airline's board and his own senior staff. Former Air Canada CEO Claude Taylor would have schmoozed his way through the corridors of power, winning over politicians and bureaucrats with his charm and sincerity. But Milton came across like a carpetbagger in the Reconstruction South, exploiting the events of September 11 for his own purposes.[20]

The launch of Tango (which had been in the pipeline since early 2001) on November 1 was unfortunate. Taxpayers wanted to know how Milton had the gall to demand billions one day and launch an airline the next. In vain did he argue that terrorist attacks and the subsequent fall in airline traffic were the major reasons for doing so. "In the post-September 11 world of depressed demand, a move in this direction is all the more necessary, as we need to aggressively promote all consumer incentives that encourage and stimulate travel," Milton said.

In direct competition with WestJet and Canada 3000, initial one-way fares were bargains and would range from $79 for the Toronto–Ottawa route up to $299 for Halifax–Vancouver, with no minimum stay or advance purchase requirements, and the new service would be offered in Toronto, Vancouver, Calgary, Edmonton, Winnipeg, Ottawa, Montreal, and Halifax, and between Toronto and Fort Lauderdale, Orlando, and Tampa, as well as Montreal to Fort Lauderdale and Orlando. Milton touted it as part of his "unbundling," but there were many (including the Competition Bureau) who suspected Tango had been created to kill off Canada 3000.

The company's plans were still on track for a short-haul, low-fare airline, Milton also said, which, unlike Tango, was to be based in western Canada. To be called "Zip," it would be headed by former WestJet CEO Steve Smith.

Passengers weren't fooled by Tango. The aircraft might be white with a purple tail, and while they were paying less to sit in cramped cabins, without free food, and with nonrefundable tickets, they knew that Tango was part of Air Canada and they still expected Air Canada service. The "airline within an airline" arrangement wouldn't work for United Air Lines with its "Shuttle," Continental with "Continental Lite," U.S. Airways with "MetroJet," Delta with "Song," or British Airways with "Go," and was seen as a strategic error on Milton's part, a sign of Air Canada's desperation to combat climbing fuel prices, increasing domestic competition, and a labour-heavy workforce.

——

One of the other names for the low cost carrier had been "Jetz." Air Canada had dropped out of the sports charter market years before because it couldn't provide specially configured aircraft for the teams' road trips on an ad hoc basis. When Sport Hawk International, their charter carrier, went bankrupt, teams like the Toronto Maple Leafs, Toronto Raptors, and Edmonton Oilers looked around for a replacement. With the merger, Milton had the aircraft and crews available. Three former Canadian Airlines B737-200s about to be retired from mainline service were reconfigured from 120 seats to forty-eight executive class seats. With their low ownership cost, one dedicated mechanic, and two pilot crews (compared with the three on the B727s usually used by charter companies), the B737s were ideal for sport team schedules — and it wasn't just the National Hockey League. In the 2004 federal election campaign, Stephen Harper and Jack Layton would both use Jetz aircraft for their cross-country tours.

On November 9, a week after Tango began flights, two days after the United States began bombing Afghanistan, and hours before his aircraft were to be seized at airports, John Lecky announced that Canada 3000 was grounded. The $7.4 million that it was due from Collenette's bailout (and the onerous conditions that came with it) would not be enough to save it. With Canada 3000's demise, Air Canada would end 2001 with 80 percent of the market and a record $1.25 billion net loss. But it had almost $1.1 billion in cash primarily through the sale-leaseback of Airbus aircraft, engines, and computer equipment, and its average of employees-to-aircraft had fallen to 148.

The year 2002 began with some hope. Fuel and crude oil prices had declined and remained below the unprecedented levels seen in 2000–01. In February 2002, federal legislation came into effect removing the 15 percent limit on individual ownership of shares in Air Canada, but the 25 percent restriction on foreign ownership remained. The Air Canada Regionals, Air BC, Canadian Regional, Air Ontario, and Air Nova, were formally merged on March 27 as "Jazz," and in September "Zip," the Western-based discount carrier, would be launched.

———

I find that people who complain the most about Air Canada are the people who do not fly outside Canada. If they did they would be surprised to find that our national airline has a global reputation for excellence in safety and service. My fellow American business travelers always request Air Canada over their own American airlines.
M.V., Toronto

I was flying from Vancouver to Toronto and when the meal cart showed up, I asked for water because the meal was incredibly dry: the usual concrete bun, mummified chicken and solidified apple sauce. I was told to wait for the beverage cart but when that arrived they were only serving alcohol and I do not drink. The steward told me to wait for the non-alcohol cart. I could not eat the dry meal so I waited and waited ... until the steward took my tray away and said they couldn't serve any drinks as we were landing.
H.C., Toronto

I arrive alive with my belongings intact. That's enough to make me a happy customer. The enormous list of other wonderful things that Air Canada does for me is icing on the cake.
K.T., Toronto

Unlike the previous such occasions, Air Canada's sixty-fifth anniversary on April 10, 2002, was a sombre event. Passenger loads were strong but ongoing labour problems, rising fuel prices, WestJet adding capacity and moving east, expenditures for new aircraft, and looming pension shortfalls all made for poor liquidity. Watching the dwindling cash reserves, Milton and his chief restructuring officer, Calin Rovinescu, must have wondered if there would be a seventy-fifth anniversary in 2012. With passage of the Air Travellers Security Charge Act on March 27, the government had saddled it with collecting fees up to $25.91 to fund air travel security. The company's stock at $8 a share in 1988 (and for a brief moment in May 2000 soaring to above $21) was in April $6.49 — the airline was a pitiful investment. There were rumours that Michel Leblanc, the former chairman of Royal Aviation, was about to launch his own discount airline. Could Milton and Rovinescu turn a one-time national monument mired in outdated restrictions into a lean, debt-free organization? Having seen airlines in the United States (and notably Canadian Airlines in this country) die because they had failed to restructure in time, they were aware of the consequences.

Creditors, labour unions, potential investors, the federal government, the airline's rank and file — and the Canadian public — could only wonder what Air Canada's flight path in the coming years would be. But that is for another book.

THE DREAM CONTINUES

"My goal was always to fly for Air Canada," remembered Mike Hillier. When he was four years old, his dad, with a "fresh" private pilot's license, became a partner in a Cherokee 140 — and that's when Mike's passion for aviation began. "We would spend the weekends either flying, or when we couldn't fly, washing the airplane. A great deal of our family road trips didn't involve hitting the open roads, it involved the open skies. The smells, the sounds, the views, I just couldn't get enough."

At fifteen, Hillier attended Ottawa Aviation Services (OAS), the private pilot ground school at Ottawa Airport. "This was my way in." he knew. "I had to study hard to grasp the concepts at the time, but knew this was what I wanted to do, so it wasn't hard to keep at it." In 1996, he took advantage of a high school co-op program that placed him in OAS, a work environment that interested him. "I was able to keep up with my flying lessons during school hours, to make some money and to learn about maintenance schedules, bookings, moving planes, and fuelling them." Like thousands before him, Mike was besotted. "I loved being on the ramp, the smell of gas, the sounds of the props spinning and the roar of First Air's Boeing 727 blasting off runway 14 in the mornings."

On completing his commercial license and instructor rating at OAS, Hillier was promptly offered a job to instruct at the school. In the year and a half he was at OAS, he met people from all walks of life who he says "simply wanted to learn how to fly. I enjoyed being able to get up in these planes everyday and call it my job. The first flight in the early morning was always the best. Fresh air, dew still on the wings, and the air was so calm."

But to get that coveted job with Air Canada, Hillier knew that he needed the experience of flying bigger aircraft, twin engined and/or turbine powered. In 2000, with his instructing qualifications in hand, he hit the road, driving through all of Ontario, north and south, visiting airports on the way. He was successful in Winnipeg, when Ministic Air hired him to work in dispatch. "I had barely learned my new role when one of the company's pilots left and the chief pilot came into the office in a panic. He needed a pilot right away to fill the vacancy for their medevac operation. I didn't know him, and he didn't know me, but I raised my hand and said that I was a pilot. Twenty minutes later, we were in his office going through King Air 100 manuals. The next day I was airborne, starting my King Air flight training."

Hillier was sent north to Island Lake, Manitoba, to live with the other medevac pilots. It was an exciting life, he recalled. They would fly throughout northern Manitoba and Ontario, into small communities, landing on short, gravel runways, sometimes in the middle of the night. "I did this job for about a year and gained a great deal of experience. But the days were numbered for Ministic Air because of financial difficulties, and it was time to seek employment elsewhere."

Still with an eye on the golden ring, Mike watched as Air Canada took over Canadian Airlines, making it the sole full service air carrier in the country — but then because of the downturn caused by 9/11, it froze the hiring of more pilots. In 2001, Mike found a job at West Wind Aviation in Saskatoon. "I was part of a big family there and had the opportunity to fly many different types of planes. My first job at West Wind was flying a Cessna 401 as a single pilot on cargo runs. The flights were very short in duration, but flying single pilot IFR was one of the toughest jobs out there for a young pilot, especially at nighttime in bad weather. You had to be very diligent because you were on your own, so no one was there to pick up on your mistakes. I flew doctors to small communities for medical clinics in the Cessna 402 and charters throughout North America in King Air 200s."

Hillier remained with West Wind for the next seven years, ending his time with them as captain on an ATR42, flying to various mines in northern Saskatchewan. He felt that he was ready for Air Canada. "I now had the experience to fulfill my goal that I had set out for." Wherever he flew, he kept a close eye on that company's fortunes. Hardly had it dealt with the effects of 9/11 when the war in Iraq and the outbreak of sudden acute respiratory syndrome (SARS) in China devastated its Asian routes. As the carrier lost more than $1.6 billion between April 2001 and April 2003, CEO Robert Milton took drastic action. On April 1, 2003, as United Airlines, Continental, and Delta had done before it, Air Canada filed for bankruptcy protection, buying time to restructure.[1] To emerge from bankruptcy protection within a year, Air Canada

Celebrating Air Canada's return from bankruptcy in October 2004, outgoing CEO Robert Milton stands before the latest colour scheme for its fleet: the red Maple Leaf on the aircraft's tail complemented by the graphic dot pattern "Frosted Leaf."

looked for $700 million, negotiating between U.S. buyout specialist Cerberus Capital Management LP and Canadian businessman Victor T.K. Li. Mainly because of the foreign ownership laws, the board accepted Li's bid for a $650-million equity stake as part of a restructuring package. But when he demanded concessions from the airline's unions, negotiations stalled and the offer was withdrawn. Flying on a wing and a prayer by then, the airline was saved when Deutsche Bank AG agreed to underwrite an $850 million rights offering to its creditors.

Air Canada celebrated its return from bankruptcy on October 21, 2004, with a lavish nationwide party to demonstrate what the restructured, revitalized national carrier held in store for employees and the travelling public. An updated design and colour scheme for its fleet was unveiled: the red Maple Leaf on the tail of its aircraft would now be complemented by the "Frosted Leaf," a graphic dot pattern representation in a light shade of green. Front line staff was to get new uniforms created by Canadian fashion designer Debbie Shuchat, and the airline's first class customers would soon luxuriate on lie-flat seats. That year, Montie R. Brewer, formerly with United Airlines, succeeded Robert Milton as CEO, with the latter remaining with Air Canada as CEO of ACE, the airline's holding company.

Formerly with United Airlines, Montie Brewer succeeded Robert Milton as CEO in 2004.

routings to Asia would typically take us straight north out of Toronto. We would fly over the North Pole, down through Russia, Mongolia, and into China. Air traffic control in Russia and Mongolia took some getting used to, but as long as you stayed on course, everything seemed to be fine."

Later he transitioned to a first officer position on the Embraer 190, typically flying across Canada, the U.S., and the Caribbean. One of his favourite things about flying the Embraer was turning off all the automation and flying the Expressway visual approach into LaGuardia Airport. "There are airplanes everywhere," he says, "and you need to keep your speed up to stay in line, follow the Expressway, get slowed down, crank the airplane around Citi Field ballpark, land, and get off the runway as fast as you can because another plane is close behind! It is way easier to do this with the autopilot off, and it is a blast! It truly is a great job."

Mike Hillier received an email in 2007 from Air Canada inviting him to an interview. "I just about jumped through the roof," he recalled. "But my joy was short-lived, because I knew I had to get to work preparing for the interview." His hard work paid off and he was offered a job as a pilot. "You couldn't get the smile off my face."

Hillier's career at Air Canada began as a Relief Pilot on the Boeing 777. "We were typically a four-man crew flying long-haul flights to Hong Kong, Shanghai, Tokyo, and Sydney. The airplane was amazing and the destinations were equally as good. Our

ACKNOWLEDGEMENTS

My hometown of Ottawa is rich in time machines better known as museums. My favourite is the Canada Aviation and Space Museum. It is a hangar that H.G. Wells would have loved, so full of memories brought to life by aircraft, exhibits, memorabilia — and its curators. Besides the helmets and goggles, uniformed mannequins, and machines that bush pilot and air ace flew, is the Webster Trophy, Robert Tait MacKenzie's bronze figure of the god Icarus. Presented annually since 1932 to the best amateur pilot in Canada, it was won a record three times by one Gordon R. McGregor, then a Bell Telephone manager and future president of Air Canada.

The museum also has several aircraft that McGregor and the airline have known: among them "CF-TCA," the Lockheed 10A Electra the first aircraft that Trans-Canada Air Lines bought brand new, its first DC-3, a Vickers 757 Viscount donated by Air Canada in 1969, and the McDonnell Douglas DC-9-32 "CF-TLL" that I watched land at Rockcliffe Airport on September 26, 2002. McGregor would also have been familiar with the Museum's North Star, the Spitfire, the Kittyhawk, the Tiger Moth — and the Messerschmitt. After D-Day, he made a captured German fighter his personal aircraft, one that he was quite proud to add to his logbook.

The museum's library and archives are the most comprehensive source of primary information on Canadian aviation in the country, holding among them the log books, photo collections, and correspondence of Stuart Graham, Canada's first bush pilot, the collection of the museum's first curator, Kenneth M. Molson, and the archives of Canadair, Canadian Pacific Air Lines, Trans-Canada

Air Lines, and Air Canada. I am first and foremost indebted to all at the museum, especially its librarians, for allowing me access to the airline's archives.

My boundless gratitude goes to Brian Losito, who is much more than Air Canada's photographer, for providing, as he did with my *National Treasure: The History of Trans-Canada Airlines*, this book's imagery. It was the fear that he would retire before I completed the book that kept me on schedule writing it.

I would be remiss in not remembering Air Canada's first archivist, "Beth" Buchanan. Joining Canadian Airways on July 5 1934, and TCA in 1944, Beth became the executive assistant to President Gordon McGregor, and when he retired, the research assistant in Historical Records. Often, poring over McGregor's correspondence, I would feel Beth's presence over me. Responsible for the preservation of much of the TCA/Air Canada collection, when Beth Buchanan retired on January 22, 1981, much of the airline's corporate memory left with her.

I am equally grateful to those who work in Air Canada today for allowing me to help promote the airline's seventy-fifth anniversary, particularly Johanne Dumont, Louise McKenven, and Peter Fitzpatrick of the Media Centre. Wayne d'Entremont was the safety and regulatory auditor at Halifax Airport on the fateful day of 9/11 and generously shared his memories with me. Paul Howard of the Air Canada Pilots Association located retired captain Bruce Olson of Hudson, Quebec, who was able to provide the pilot's insights of past and present aircraft that the airline had operated. My thanks also to Kelly Smith for his father's experience with TCA, from the Lancastrian to the DC-8.

I met Mike Hillier at the WINTER Ops Conference in Montreal in 2011. On reading his aviation career featured in the epilogue, one of the airline's earliest employees came to mind. Stan Knight joined TCA in 1937, having begun his career on the Ontario Provincial Air Service flying boats in 1926. He would write: "The aviation business is a disease — once contaminated, there is little desire to recover." Equally passionate about his chosen profession, as a guest speaker Mike Hillier has inspired students in the Aviation Program at Algonquin College, Ottawa.

Finally, my thanks to two women, Donna Hudson, my fiancée, who although she had never flown in an aircraft until I met her took up the chores of collating the pages and photographs of this book with forbearance and enthusiasm. *Air Canada: The History* is dedicated to my late aunt Agnes Selwyn, who loved me dearly, countless times sitting patiently at Santacruz airport while a six-year-old ran madly about it. I like to think those women would have gotten along.

— Peter Pigott, 2013

NOTES

CHAPTER ONE

1. Although called "Trans-Canada Air Lines," it was always abbreviated to "TCA."

2. Howe's love for Lockheeds continued all through his career. When TCA sold off its Lockheed Lodestars in 1947, CF-TCY was slated to be used by the Department of Transport for ice patrols. Instead, it was refitted as a VIP transport for Howe's use, but not exclusively. When Prime Ministers Louis St. Laurent and Lester Pearson flew in it, it became Canada's first prime ministerial aircraft.

3. Unfortunately, CF-CMS, which ranks in Canadian aviation history slightly below the "Silver Dart" and Punch Dickins' Fokker "C-CASK," met an ignominious end. On June 1, 1945, on approach to Dorval Airport, its number three engine burst into flames and it crashed into a farm on the runway edge, ending up in a dung heap. No one thought to photograph or retrieve any part of TCA's (and Canada's) first transatlantic aircraft.

4. Mackenzie King took great delight in ensuring that his sworn enemy, Ontario premier George Drew, never got a seat on a CGTAS flight. When Drew wanted to go over to England to visit Ontario regiments, he had to take an RAF Dakota with multiple stopovers. At one, when Drew got out to stretch his legs, he fell into a stream and (to King's glee) arrived in England pantless.

5. Howe was determined to unload his North Stars and sold them to BOAC for $670,000 each, $100,000 less than he had charged Canadian Pacific Air Lines. Rumours have persisted that the British gave Canada their colony of Newfoundland as part of the deal.

CHAPTER TWO

1. Symington would be one of the founders of the International Civil Aviation (ICAO) and became the first president of the International Air Transport Association (IATA) that Howe had spoken of in 1945.

2. TCA had been given permission to purchase the Avro C-102 in April 1946 with its two Rolls-Royce Avon engines, but when the British made the Avon engine top secret to use on their Canberra and Valiant bombers, it was replaced by four Derwents and the aircraft's range was so reduced that McGregor cancelled the purchase.

3. This was at a time when Britain's state airline was British Overseas Airways Corporation (BOAC).

4. One of the first passengers on TCA's first DC-8 was J.A.D. McCurdy, the first man to fly an aircraft in the British Empire on February 23, 1909.

5. The company erected a Memorial Park (Exit 15 on the Laurentian Autoroute) four miles south of where the accident occurred.

CHAPTER THREE

1. Menard would resurface in 1979 as president of Ottawa-based TIW Industries, a conglomerate related to A.F. Lizotte Holdings, owned by Nordair president Andre Lizotte.

CHAPTER FOUR

1. A popular television program of the day.

2. PWA forced its flight attendants to take maternity leave in their fourth month in 1974, using safety as the excuse, although studies had proven otherwise. CALFAA fought this, pointing out to the airlines that it violated the Canada Labour Code.

3. Shirley Render, *No Place for A Lady: The Story of Canadian Women Pilots: 1928–1992* (Winnipeg: Portage and Main Press, 1992), 305.

4. Keith McArthur, *Air Monopoly: How Robert Milton's Air Canada Won — and Lost — Control of Canada's Skies* (Toronto: McClelland and Stewart, 2004), 17.

5. Service on BOAC was said to have been so bad that on a flight from Miami, The Beatles composed "Back in the U.S.S.R." Before the privatization of British Airways, the Brits said that the initials "B.A." stood for "Bloody Awful."

6. Anne Shortell, "A Wing and a Prayer." *Financial Times*, August 15, 1988.

7. Philip Smith, *It Seems Like Only Yesterday: Air Canada, The First Fifty Years* (Toronto: McClelland and Stewart, 1986), 330.

8. The type of aircraft that was chartered for an election campaign has always had symbolic connotations. During the 1980 referendum campaign, Liberal leader, federalist Claude Ryan, used an Air Canada DC-9 with its maple leaf logo. The Parti Québécois had originally considered a BAC 1-11 from Quebecair for Premier René Lévesque before realizing that it was British-made. It settled for a Quebecair Fokker F-27, the "Q"

emblazoned on its tail. One can only surmise how many votes Lévesque's prop-driven aircraft cost him.

9. Mackasey would be re-elected and serve in the House from 1979–84, when Prime Minister John Turner would appoint him ambassador to Portugal. The announcement prompted Brian Mulroney, on the campaign Air Canada DC-9, to make the famous (and what he thought was an off the record) remark: "There's no whore like an old whore." Mulroney cancelled the appointment when he was elected.

10. When Habyarimana's aircraft was shot down in 1994 as it was landing at Kigali, it precipitated the Rwandan massacre.

11. On January 15, 2009, when Captain Chesley "Sully" Sullenberger skillfully glided US Airways Flight 1549 onto the surface of the Hudson River, saving the lives of all 155 aboard, many were reminded of Pearson and Quintal's professionalism more than a quarter century before. Like Pearson, "Sully" was also a glider pilot.

12. I am indebted to Captain James Mason for his research into the fate and subsequent use of CF-TCC. Since the 1986 anniversary flights, TCC has continued "flying the corporate image" during summer (sometimes flown by Mason himself), returning to her winter home at the Western Canada Aviation Museum each fall. Few pilots exemplify the dedication to his profession better than Captain Mason.

CHAPTER FIVE

1. Craig Chouinard, *From 'Dedicated Amateurs To Dynamic Advocates': The Transformation of an Airline Union, 1946-1996* (Mississauga, ON: CAW Local 2213, 1996), 159–73.

2. Air Canada would pioneer several Fifth Freedom routes over the years: London–Düsseldorf, Paris–Geneva, Paris–Munich, Paris–Berlin, Frankfurt–Zürich, Zürich–Zagreb, Zürich–Vienna, Zürich–Delhi, Honolulu–Sydney, Lisbon–Madrid, and Brussels–Prague. In 2012, it only operated Santiago–Buenos Aires.

3. While in RCAF service, CF-TCB caught fire and was cannibalized for spare parts.

4. One stewardess who did not participate in the Sentimental Journey was Rose Lothian, née Crispin, who died on May 6. Rose was TCA's third stewardess, joining the airline on November 16, 1938.

5. Shortell, "A Wing and a Prayer," 12.

6. The 25 percent foreign ownership limit for Canadian airlines was included in the National Transportation Act because this was the U.S. limit.

7. King's famous obfuscation was "Conscription if necessary but not necessarily conscription."

8. Harvey Cashore, *The Truth Shows Up: A Reporter's Fifteen-Year Odyssey Tracking Down the Truth About Mulroney, Schreiber and the Airbus Scandal* (Toronto: Key Porter, 2010), 510.

9. At this, the French government suddenly discovered that it could give

Wardair landing rights at Charles de Gaulle Airport rather than the inconvenient Orly.

10. In connection with the Airbus affair, Lalonde would appear before the House of Commons Ethics Committee in 2008 with Karlheinz Schreiber.

11. Jonathon Gatehouse, "Secret Airbus Files Revealed." *Maclean's*, January 28, 2008.

12. J.C. Crosbie, *No Holds Barred: My Life In Politics* (Toronto: McClelland and Stewart, 1997), 426.

13. William Kaplan, *Presumed Guilty: Brian Mulroney, the Airbus Affair, and the Government of Canada* (Toronto: McClelland and Stewart, 1998), 25.

14. American hands were none too clean themselves since in the 1970s bribery by Lockheed had led to Interpol investigations, with the Dutch royal family and a Japanese prime minister being disgraced. When Boeing sold Dash 8s to Bahamasair, allegations of bribery were rampant. Since then, passage of the Foreign Corrupt Practices Act by the U.S. government forbids American companies and their officers (but not their consultants) from bribing.

15. Cashore, *The Truth Shows Up.*

16. In 1993 Pierre Jeanniot became president of IATA, following Symington, the airline's second president.

CHAPTER SIX

1. McArthur, *Air Monopoly: How Robert Milton's Air Canada Won — and Lost — Control of Canada's Skies.*

2. Robert Milton, *Straight From the Top: The Truth About Air Canada* (Vancouver/ Toronto: Greystone Books, 2004), 30.

3. *Air Transport World*, June 1996, 43.

4. Buffett's Berkshire Hathaway Inc. had bought 8.5 percent of US Airways in 1989. Due to a merger with Piedmont Airlines, by 1994 US Airways had lost a total of $2.4 billion (U.S.), wiping out its entire book value. Berkshire was forced to write off most of its investment in the airline.

5. Evidence before the Standing Committee on Transport, House of Commons, October 28, 1999.

6. Von Finckenstein could not know then that Ansett would go bankrupt in 2001. Learning from what happened in Canada, QANTAS decided not to lumber itself with its competitor, and the Australian government tolerated the massive layoffs in the industry. Domestic competition would be maintained by allowing start-up airlines (like Richard Branson's Virgin Blue) to be 100 percent foreign-owned.

7. Jean W. Rosenthal, Francesco Bova, and Jacob Thomas, "Air Canada: Selling the Company Slice by Slice." Yale School of Management, Yale Case 07-038, Oct. 15, 2007.

8. The House of Commons Standing Committee of Transport Minutes, October 27, 1999.

9. *Ibid.*

10. Hugh Winsor, "Collenette tries to keep Canadian in the sky," *Globe and Mail*, August 16, 1999.

CHAPTER SEVEN

1. Rosenthal, Bova, and Thomas, "Air Canada: Selling the Company by the Slice."
2. Bruce Wallace, "Capital Solution." *Maclean's*, September 13, 1999, 6.
3. Giles Gherson and Rod McQueen, "Offer has nod of political approval." *National Post*, August 25, 1999.
4. Milton, *Straight From the Top: The Truth About Air Canada*, 74.
5. This was not the first time that the Caisse had done this. In 1998, when Loblaw Co. Ltd tried to take over Quebec's Provigo chain of supermarkets, the Caisse used its 35.7 percent stake in Provigo to make sure that the Ontario company would continue to buy from Quebec agricultural producers.
6. Onex AirCo letter accompanying pink proxy form dated October 13, 1999, "Dear Air Canada Shareholder," signed by Gerald W. Schwartz.
7. *Vancouver Sun*, September 29, 1999, A1.
8. Milton, *Straight From the Top: The Truth About Air Canada*, 100–1.
9. Matthew Ingram, "Why does Milton still have a job?" *Globe and Mail*, November 10, 2003.
10. Initially encouraging Richard Branson to consider setting up an equivalent to Virgin Blue, his discount airline in Australia, Collenette got cold feet after Branson arrived in Toronto on November 29, 2000, to announce that he would enter the domestic market with Virgin Canada, also promising to "keep an eye" on Air Canada with its

"80 percent monopoly" [sic].

11. Paul Waldie, "Air Canada Kicks Granny, 88, Off Plane." *National Post*, July 20, 2000.
12. Lisa Wright, "Canadian on final course." *Toronto Star*, July 24, 2000, 3.
13. Perry Flint, "The World Has Changed Forever." *Air Transport World*, March 2003, 22–26.
14. Standing Committee on Industry, Science and Technology, November 7, 2001, House of Commons Library.
15. Keith MacArthur, "Air Canada changes tune, plans to merge Canadian." *Globe and Mail Report on Business*, October 6, 2000, B1.
16. Canadian Airlines' employees with twenty-five or thirty years of service meant they had joined when their employer was CP Air, Wardair, Transair, or PWA. Poignantly, from March 31, 2001 onward, they would receive an Air Canada long service recognition pin, plaque, or letter from the president.
17. In 2008, because of the Aeroman connection in San Salvador, ACTS would be rebranded as AVEOS — "AV" for aviation and "EOS" for new beginnings.
18. Milton, *Straight From the Top: The Truth About Air Canada*, 145.
19. The closest that an Air Canada aircraft came to a "terrorist" incident immediately after 9/11 was on September 27 when an Iranian immigrant travelling with his wife from Los Angeles to Toronto was caught smoking in the toilet. Javid Naghani, thirty-seven, a legal

U.S. resident, ran an office business unfortunately called "The Cleaning of America." He reportedly told the crew: "If you give me to the authorities, then my people will be mad," and "I am going to kill Americans." The aircraft returned to Los Angeles, where he was handed over to the authorities.

20. In a candid moment, Milton told students at Wilfrid Laurier University in January 2002, "I feel like I'm Dr. Evil in an Austin Powers movie."

EPILOGUE

1. Called Chapter 11 in the United States, filing for protection under the Companies' Creditors Arrangement Act (CCAA) gives companies time to reorganize their operations and negotiate with their major stakeholders — creditors, bond-holders, unions, and suppliers. While CCAA protection is in place, creditors are prevented from taking any action against the airline.

FURTHER READING

AVIATION BOOKS BY PETER PIGOTT

Flying Canucks: Famous Canadian Aviators. Toronto: Hounslow Press, 1994.

Flying Canucks II: Pioneers of Canadian Aviation. Toronto: Hounslow Press, 1997.

Flying Canucks III: Famous Canadian Aviators. Madeira Park, BC: Harbour Publishing, 2000.

Flying Colours: A History of Commercial Aviation in Canada. Vancouver: Douglas & McIntyre, 1997.

Gateways: Airports of Canada. Lawrencetown, NS: Pottersfield Press, 1996.

National Treasure: The History of Trans-Canada Airlines. Madeira Park, BC: Harbour Publishing, 2001.

On Canadian Wings: A Century of Flight. Toronto: Dundurn Press, 2005.

Taming The Skies: A Celebration of Canadian Flight. Toronto: Dundurn Press, 2003.

Wings Across Canada: An Illustrated History of Canadian Aviation. Toronto: Dundurn Press, 2002.

Wingwalkers: The History of Canada's Other Airline. Madeira Park, BC: Harbour Publishing, 1998.

TWO BOOKS WELL WORTH READING

McArthur, Keith. *Air Monopoly: How Robert Milton's Air Canada Won — and Lost — Control of Canada's Skies.* Toronto: McClelland and Stewart, 2004.

Milton, Robert, with John Lawrence Reynolds. *Straight From the Top: The Truth About Air Canada.* Vancouver and Toronto: Greystone Books, 2004.

All other material was sourced from Air Canada's archives held at the Canada Aviation and Space Museum, Ottawa.

INDEX